SOCIAL PROTECTION PROGRAMMES IN INDIA

ABOUT THE AUTHOR

Pinaki Das is an Associate Professor of Economics and Head of the Department of Economcis, Vidyasagar University, West Bengal. He got his M.Sc. and Ph.D. degrees in Economics from Vidyasagar University. He awarded the Gold Medal and Research Fellowship. His book entitled "*Rural Non-Farm Employment in India: Pattern of Growth and Determinants*" is higly acknoledged in the reserch and academic community. He published more than 50 articles in national and international peer-reviewed Journals and edited books. His published articles include: *Food Security in Relation to Entitlement of the Poor: Evidence from India; Impact of Social Protection on Multidimensional Poverty of the Rural Poor; Entitlement Failure and Food Insecurity; Growth Trajectory and its Implications for Employment in India; Productivity Nexus between Growth and Employment: Indian Experience during Pre and Post Economic Crisis; and Trends of Rural Employment in India: Reflections from Recent NSS Data.* He also conducted Major Research Projects funded by ICSSR and UGC and guided eight Ph. D. Research Scholars. His research interest includes rural non-farm employment, informal sector and social protection, food security, multidimensional poverty.

SOCIAL PROTECTION PROGRAMMES IN INDIA

Impact on Rural Poverty and Deprivation

Pinaki Das

CONCEPT PUBLISHING COMPANY PVT. LTD.
NEW DELHI-110059

ISBN-13: 978-93-88937-66-5

First Published 2020

Published and Printed by:

Concept Since 1974

Concept Publishing Company Pvt. Ltd.
A/15-16, Commercial Block, Mohan Garden,
New Delhi-110059 (INDIA)
T : +91 11 25351460, +91 11 25351794
E : publishing@conceptpub.com, *W* : www.conceptpub.com

Cataloging in Publication Data--Courtesy: D.K. Agencies (P) Ltd. <docinfo@dkagencies.com>

Das, Pinaki, author.
Social protection programmes in India : impact on rural poverty and deprivation / Pinaki Das.
pages cm
Includes bibliographical references and index.
ISBN 9789388937665

1. Human services—India—West Bengal. 2. Social integration—India—West Bengal. 3. Rural poor—Government policy—India—West Bengal. I. Title.

LCC HV394.W47D37 2020 | DDC 361.95414 23

My humble effort I dedicate to my

Father & Mother

Whose affection, love, encouragement make me able to complete such work

Foreword

Even though many of the emerging countries have been growing very rapidly, in many countries such growth has been uneven. As a result, a large section of the population in such countries have been missing out on many of the basic amenities of life which are taken for granted in the developed countries. Many societies across the globe have informal social security systems where the poor people help themselves in a cooperative fashion. However, these are not enough, and formal social protection of vulnerable population in the emerging countries is urgently needed. Many countries, and India in particular, have introduced a plethora of specific social protection programmes especially for this purpose.

The present book, written by an eminent academic economist – Dr. Pinaki Das – takes a very close look at the important social protection programmes in India. In particular, Dr. Das carries out an in-depth analysis of the programmes in three of the backward districts of his native state of West Bengal, namely Purulia, Bankura and Paschim Medinipur. The programmes vary widely in terms of their purpose and coverage, and include areas such as food security, healthcare, elementary education, housing, employment and income generation, and social assistance. Most of these programmes are initiatives by the federal government, although cooperation and partial funding from the state governments are required. Some of the programmes such as the Kanyashree Prakalpa are initiatives by the state government of West Bengal.

Since the implementation of the programmes require a large amount of scarce resources, a serious scrutiny is essential to make sure that the resources are efficiently used and the vulnerable groups are properly targeted. From this point of view, the present study is a very welcome initiative. Dr. Pinaki Das has through painstaking and scientific manner examined the working of the programmes in the aforementioned regions and come up with several important suggestions for the policymakers for improving the efficiency of the programmes.

Because of the importance of the topic, extent of the coverage, and the lucidity of the presentation, this book should be an essential part of undergraduate and graduate courses in development studies. I also hope that policymakers take a serious look at the book and benefit from the policy recommendations.

Sajal Lahiri
Vandeveer Chair Professor of Economics
and Distinguished Scholar, Southern Illinois University
Carbondale, U.S.A.

Preface

Inclusive growth and the Sustainable Development Goals cannot be achieved purely through the promotion of economic growth and the development of physical and social infrastructure. Interventions are necessary to directly address the needs of the poorest section and to prevent the members of vulnerable groups from falling into poverty through community-wide or household-specific shocks. Social protections have acquired relevance in the context of shocks and systematic risks which are being faced by the working poor in the context of globalization. Keeping this in mind, the present monograph answers the following questions: What is the breadth and depth of social protection floor in rural India? What is the extent of benefits of social protection programmes (SPPs) in the less developed regions? Do the poor households obtain the social protection benefits (SPBs) as per statutory provision of the programmes? How does SPBs contribute to the overall entitlement of households in the backward region? Are the SPBs able to overcome food insecurity, poverty and vulnerability of the households in the backward regions?

The present monograph on Social Protections in India has two parts. Part I which includes Chapter 1 and 2 is an exclusive study of SPPs that forms the social protection floor in rural India. The background, objectives, targeted group, provision of benefits, fund allocation, coverage, and the impact of twenty-four important SPBs across states of India are analyzed there.

Part II has been divided into five chapters. Chapter 3 explores the SPBs in the context of backward regions of West Bengal. SPPs are found to be crucial for the development of the backward regions. At what extent the backward regions are benefited from SPPs to eliminate poverty and deprivations are discussed here.

Chapter 4 to Chapter 7 of the present monograph make a humble attempt aimed at collecting basic information of households on different aspects of SPPs and poverty situation to analyse the entitlements of the households relating to SPBs and to examine the impact of SPBs on food insecurity, monetary poverty, multidimensional poverty and deprivations of the households in the backward region.

We have discussed SPBs at the aggregate levels, i.e., state and district based on secondary data from different sources. To what extent the household especially poor households are benefited from SPPs is yet to be analyzed. The major problem of this analysis is that the benefits of households from different SPPs are not available from secondary sources. Therefore, for the sake of an analysis of SPBs at the household level there is a need for an evaluation of SPBs of the poor on the basis of the grass root reality. In order to fill this gap, Chapter 4 discusses the characteristics of the sample households in the backward region and explores the SPBs that are enjoyed by them. Chapter 5 analyses the SPBs in relation to entitlement of the households. It explores endowment set, exchange entitlement mapping and entitlement of the sample households. The failure of entitlements causes food insecurity and poverty of the households. On account of insufficient productive assets endowment, labour entitlement is much more important than production entitlement. They survive by selling their labour power. But the labour entitlement is also not sufficient for the poor households to cope with the food insecurity. The benefits from other SPPs lead to increase in the overall entitlement of the poor households and also consumption.

Chapter 6 presents the theoretical framework followed by empirical analysis to examine the impact of social protection along with other entitlements on the status of food security of the households. Poverty in India was traditionally measured in terms of consumption expenditure. But income poverty does not accurately proxy other deprivations. Therefore, we have taken up both uni-dimensional and multidimensional measures of poverty. Chapter 7 examines the impact of SPBs on both monetary poverty and multidimensional poverty of the households. The empirical analysis of the relationship between entitlements of the households including SPBs and the status of poverty is made on the basis of Heckman two-step model. This chapter also analyses the impact of SPBs on specific deprivations of the household viz. education, health and standard of living as well as of the overall status of multidimensional poverty of the households.

To conclude, the SPBs significantly help in the reduction of the incidence and depth of food insecurity as well as poverty. It also significantly reduces the deprivations of the households relating to malnourishment, schooling, drinking water, sanitation, housing and electricity. But the benefits of SPPs are limited in respect of overcoming the problems of food insecurity and poverty. Most of the SPPs are deficient in fulfilling their objectives with respect to statutory provisions. The supply of SPBs is also lagging behind the demand. That raises the question regarding the effectiveness of SPPs in improving the status of poor households. The leakages and inefficient delivery mechanisms are found to be the main reasons for the ineffectiveness of SPPs. The present monograph recommends some policies for the effectiveness of SPPs.

Pinaki Das

Acknowledgements

Author is gratefully acknowledged to Indian Council of Social Science Research (ICSSR), New Delhi for financial support of the Major Research Project entitled with *"Social Protection and Poverty Reduction: A Study with Special Reference to Backward Region of West Bengal"*.

I express my sincerest gratitude to Prof. Sachinandan Sau (Formerly Professor of Economics and Coordinator of DRS-SAP and Head of Department of Economics with Rural Development, Vidyasagar University) for valuable comments and suggestions on the preliminary version of the report.

I am very much fortunate to take some important insights and suggestions for the present study that came from the interaction with Professor Sugata Marjit, Centre for Studies in Social Science Calcutta (CSSSC), Kolkata; Professor Ravi S. Srivastava, Jawaharlal Nehru University (JNU), New Delhi; Professor Rajkumar Sen, Rabindra Bharati University (RBU), Kolkata; and Professor Biswajit Chatterjee, Jadavpur University (JU), Kolkata.

I express my indebtedness to the anonymous referees who reviewed the final report and made their valuable comments. I am also thankful to the participants of different National and International Conferences for their valuable comments.

Special thanks also deserve Jagabandhu Mandal, the Research Associate of this Project who took active part in the field of survey and handled the burden of large data sets.

I am thankful to my research scholars Asit Pandit, Sk. Md Abul Basar and Sama Firdaus for active participation in this project.

I am also thankful to my Colleagues of Department of Economics with Rural Development and other faculty and staff at Vidyasagar University who provided an academically lively environment.

A part of data for my research work was procured from the field survey of four districts, namely Paschim Medinipur, Bankura, and Purulia. I am indebted to the panchayat functionaries and households of these four districts who were kind enough to give me the required information.

However, the views and findings in this report are my own, and none of the above individuals or organizations hold any responsibility for them.

My whole family—parents, sister, brother, wife and son—provided me with all the support I needed.

May 1, 2019

Dr. Pinaki Das
Associate Professor and HoD
Department of Economics
Vidyasagar University
Medinipur, West Bengal

Contents

Abbreviations

AABY	Aam Admi Bima Yojana
AAY	Antyodaya Anna Yojana
ACR	Additional Class Room
ADB	Asian Development Bank
AGY	Income from Agriculture
AIE	Alternative and Innovative Education
APL	Above Poverty Line
ARWSP	Accelerated Rural Water Supply Programme
ASHA	Accredited Social Health Activist
AWC	Anganwadi Centre
AWH	Anganwadi Helper
AWW	Anganwadi Worker
AY	Annapurna Yojana
BPHC	Block Primary Health Centre
BPL	Below Poverty Line
CAG	Comptroller and Auditor General
CAST	Caste
CBO	Community-based Organisation
CHC	Community Health Centre
CIP	Central Issue Price
CPI-R	Consumer Price Index for Rural
CPRY	Income from Common Property Resources
CRSP	Central Rural Sanitation Programme
CSC	Community Sanitary Complexes
DDP	Desert Development Programme
DHA	Designated Hill Areas
DLHS	District Level Household and Facility Survey
DPAP	Drought Prone Area Programme
DPEP	District Primary Education Project
DRD	Department of Rural Development

DRDA	Department of Rural Development Agency
DWCRA	Development of Women and Children in Rural Areas
EAS	Employment Assurance Scheme
EGS	Education Guarantee Scheme
EPC	Empowered Programme Committee
FAO	Food and Agricultural Organisation
FCI	Food Corporation of India
FIG	Food Insecurity Gap
FISH	Food Insecure Households
FPS	Fair Price Shop
GCA	Gross Cropped Area
GDI	Group Dimension Index
GDP	Gross Domestic Product
GEN	General Castes
GER	Gross Enrolment Ratio
gm	Gram
GoI	Government of India
GP	Gram Panchayat
HCR	Head Count Ratio
HDI	Human Development Index
HMIS	Health Management Information System
HPS	High Performing States
IAP	Integrated Action Plan
IAY	Indira Awas Yojana
IFS	Incidence of Food Insecurity
IGMSY	Indira Gandhi Matritva Sahayog Yojana
IGNDPS	Indira Gandhi National Disability Pension Scheme
IGNOAPS	Indira Gandhi National Old Age Pension Scheme
IGNWPS	Indira Gandhi National Widow Pension Scheme
IHHL	Individual Household Latrines
ILO	International Labour Office
IMIS	Integrated Management Information System
IMR	Infant Mortality Rate
IRDP	Integrated Rural Development Programme
ITDP	Integrated Tribal Development Projects
JMAHAL	Jangal Mahal
JRC	Joint Research Council
JRY	Jawahar Rozgar Yojana
JSY	Janani Suraksha Yojana
KCC	Kisan Credit Card
Kg	Kilogram
LABY	Income from Labour Power
LPS	Low Performing States
LWE	Left Wing Extremist

MDAY	Average Mandays
MDG	Millennium Development Goal
MoDWS	Ministry of Drinking Water Supply
MFP	Minor Forest Products
MGNREGA	Mahatma Gandhi National Rural Employment Guarantee Act
MMR	Maternal Mortality Ratio
MNP	Minimum Needs Programme
MoHFW	Ministry of Health and Family Welfare
MoHRD	Ministry of Human Resource Development
MoUD	Ministry of Urban Development
MPAT	Multidimensional Poverty Assessment Tool
MPC	Marginal Propensity to Consume
MPI	Multidimensional Poverty Index
MSG	Mission Steering Group
MSK	Madhyamik Siksha Karmasuchi
NAMHHR	National Alliance for Maternal Health and Human Rights
NBA	Nirmal Bharat Abhiyan
NCUES	National Commission for Enterprises in the Unorganised Sector
NDPS	National Disability Pension Scheme
NDWM	National Drinking Water Mission
NE	North East
NER	North Eastern Region
NFBS	National Family Benefit Scheme
NFHS	National Family Health Survey
NFP	National Forest Policy
NFSA	National Food Security Act
NGO	Non-Governmental Organization
NGP	Nirmal Gram Puraskar
NHM	National Health Mission
NHSRC	National Health System Resource Centre
NMBS	National Maternity Benefit Scheme
NOAPS	National Old Age Pension Scheme
NP-NSPE	National Programme of Nutritional Support to Primary Education
NRDWP	National Rural Drinking Water Programme
NREGA	National Rural Employment Guarantee Act
NREP	National Rural Employment Programme
NRHM	National Rural Health Mission
NRLM	National Rural Livelihood Mission
NSS	National Sample Survey
NSSO	National Sample Survey Organisation
NWPS	National Widow Pension Scheme
OBC	Other Backward Castes
OECD	Organisation for Economic Co-operations and Development
OPHI	Oxford Poverty and Human Development Initiative

P&L	Pregnant and Lactating
PBSSM	Paschim Banga Sarva Shiksha Mission
PCPDE	Per Capita Per Day Expenditure
PCPDI	Per Capita Per Day Income
PDS	Public Distribution System
PDSF	Foodgrains received from Public Distribution System
PESA	Panchayats (Extension to Scheduled Areas) Act
PGP	Poverty Gap
PGP	Poverty Gap Ratio
PHC	Primary Health Centre
PIP	Project Implementation Plans
PMU	Programme Management Unit
PRI	Panchayati Raj Institution
PRD	Panchayat and Rural Development
PWSS	Piped Water Supply System
RCH	Reproductive and Child Health Programme
RGNDWM	Rajiv Gandhi National Drinking Water Mission
RH	Rural Hospitals
RKS	Rogi Kalyan Samiti
RLEGP	Rural Landless Employment Guarantee Programme
RPDS	Revamped Public Distribution System
RSBY	Rashtriya Swasthya Bima Yojana
RTE	Right to Education
SC	Scheduled Caste
SFEX	Share of Food Expenditure to Total Expenditure
SFIG	Square Food Insecurity Gap
SGRY	Sampurna Gramin Rojgar Yojana
SHG	Self Help Group
SLWM	Solid and Liquid Waste Management
SPB	Social Protection Benefit
SPF	Social Protection Floor
SPGP	Squared Poverty Gap
SRS	Sample Registration System
SSA	Sarva Shiksha Abhiyan
SSK	Shishu Shiksha Karmasuchi
ST	Scheduled Tribe
TFR	Total Fertility Rate
TLC	Total Literacy Campaign
TLE	Teaching Learning
TPDS	Targeted Public Distribution System
TRADY	Income from Trade
TRYSEM	Training of Rural Youth for Self-Employment
TSC	Total Sanitation Campaign
UN	United Nations

UNCEB	United Nations Chief Executives Board
UNESCO	United Nations Educational, Scientific and Cultural Organisation
UNICEF	United Nations International Children's Emergency Fund
UT	Union Territory
VWSC	Village Water and Sanitation Committee
WEF	World Economic Forum
WHO	World Health Organization
WPR	Work Participation Rate
WQMS	Water Quality Monitoring and Surveillance

List of Tables, Figures and Boxes

LIST OF TABLES

LIST OF FIGURES

LIST OF BOXES

PART I

1
Introduction

1.1 Introduction

Inclusive growth and the Sustainable Development Goals for poverty reduction cannot be achieved purely through the promotion of economic growth and the development of physical and social infrastructure. Interventions are essential to directly address the requirements of the poorest and to prevent the members of vulnerable groups from falling into poverty following community-wide or household-specific shocks. The recognition is growing in the world for the implementation and promotion of social protections to eliminate poverty, deprivation and vulnerability. Social protection has also acquired relevance in the context of shocks and systematic risks which are being faced by the working poor in the context of globalisaiton.

Indian economy experienced a growth of almost 225 per cent in real national income between 1991-92 and 2015-16, and the per capita real income increased by almost 170 per cent over the same period. Furthermore, annual gross domestic product (GDP) growth rates were laid between 6 and 9 per cent during the last seven years. Although the growth rate of the GDP has decelerated in the recent years, India remains the second-fastest growing economy in the world (Himanshu 2013). Aggregate poverty in India by official poverty estimates declined by 13 percentage points between 1993-94 and 2009-10, rural and urban poverty declined from 51 to 39 per cent and 32 to 23 per cent respectively. Even in 2011-12, an estimated 363 million people were considered poor in India by the current method of estimating the poor (Planning Commission 2014). The high growth rate in India in recent decades has gone hand in hand with a decline in poverty and infant mortality rate, and improvements in indicators such as life expectancy and educational attainments.[1] However, these promising achievements still continue to co-exist with persistently high levels of poverty and food insecurity; low levels of education, skills and productivity; and low nutritional status among socially disadvantaged groups. It was accompanied by a decline of 210 calories in per capita per day calorie intake during 1993-94 to 2009-10. There is also the evidence of rising inter-group and inter-class inequalities. Within Asia, India is home to the largest number of malnourished people in the world. While the high levels of malnutrition are worrying, the fact that there has not been any significant reduction in malnutrition in the recent past despite India being the second-fastest growing economy of the world is intriguing. There has been concern about the deterioration in the food security situation in recent years because of a continuous spell of inflation which has remained above 10 per cent for the last 3 years (Himanshu 2013).

The food insecurity and poverty co-exist not only because of poverty–nutrition traps in developing countries but also because poorer households tend to spend more on food as a portion of their total expenditure. Therefore, improvements in income do tend to improve nutritional outcomes, but this not always be the case, in particular, while the elasticity of total expenditure to nutritional intake such as calories and proteins remains high. But some studies still hold that there has been worsening of nutritional intake in India even though overall incomes and expenditures have increased. This has been a long-standing puzzle in the Indian context (Deaton and Dreze 2009; Patnaik 2010; Gaiha, Jha and Kulkarni 2010; and Gaiha *et al.* 2012).

For food security, access and utilization of food are as important as producing food itself. Social protection helps provide access to, and helps utilization of, food for groups of sub-population who would otherwise not be able to access and utilize food (Mukherjee *et al.,* 2010). The great tragedy of Bengal famine of the early 1940s having granaries full of food with people dying in starvation as they had no purchasing power to buy the food (Sen 1981). Therefore, the entitlements to food are very

1. (a) IMR declined from 74 per cent in 1993 to 44 per cent in 2013, (b) Life Expectancy has increased from 58.5 years in 1990 to 66.4 years in 2013, (c) The Gross Enrolment Ratio (GER) at the primary level increased from 83.8 in 1990-91 to 116.0 in 2010-11. For the middle/upper primary level, the GER increased from 66.7 to 85.5. (d) Literacy rate increased from 52.2 per cent in 1991 to 74.0 per cent in 2011.

important: 'The mere presence of food in the economy, or in the market, does not entitle a person to consume it' (Dreze and Sen 1989). People gain entitlements to food by: producing their own food; by exchanging money (that they have been earned through labour) for food; or through transfers from kin, community or state. Public policy instruments to strengthen food security must support these entitlements in terms of incentives, relationships and assets. An important distinction between food insecurity and other types of vulnerability is that households can be expected to meet some proportion of their needs from their own entitlements, particularly through production, selling produce and labour power, and, to a lesser extent, through social transfers. Safety nets form one part of the broad range of social protection instruments. They can be appropriate in providing short-term support to the transitory food insecure, or to the chronically food insecure who are unable to work. It is important to acknowledge that safety nets can do more harm than good.[1] To overcome these limitations, social protection instruments must embrace all aspects of entitlement: production, exchange, and employment as well as transfers.[2]

The most significant development in the last two decades in the developing world has been a widespread growth in home working and self-employment. The share of employment in regular, permanent and full time jobs with adequate social protection has declined. The logic behind this change in the labour market undergone flexibalization process, induced by globalization. The widespread growth in the use of flexible and often unprotected workforce directly or through subcontracting of work results in increased labour market insecurity for a large proportion of the workforce.

Traditional social security is based on the assumptions that most members of society have achieved a satisfactory standard of living and has access to regular work and social security to meet contingencies of old age, ill health, death and unemployment. According to Sen (1991), a large proportion of the population lives in conditions of persistent deprivation. That is, the basic insecurities that they face are severe and

1. See, for example, the emergency response in Southern Africa in 2002-03 to a misdiagnosed crisis that was chronic rather than acute (FFSSA 2004).
2. A move away from an agriculture-led response to reducing rural people's food insecurity, towards supporting improved conditions from employment and petty trade in urban areas has been cogently argued on the basis of field-based evidence from Africa and multi-country studies (Bush, 2003).

have been so over a long period of time. In addition, there is the issue of vulnerability as a result of which a certain proportion of the population experience or are threatened by severe and sudden dispossession. There are therefore two problems to be addressed by any programme of social protection: firstly, countering the effect of random shocks and secondly, increasing security for all so that people do not live in constant fear of a calamity.

When social security arrangements are institutionalized, they address the problems of deficiency and adversity in collective terms. By definition, addressing the problem of deficiency contributes to poverty reduction. The narrow definition of poverty in terms of minimum consumption expenditure or the one that emphasizes the income dimension alone may not provide a satisfactory link between extension of social security and poverty reduction. The notion of poverty that conceptually links extension of social security with poverty reduction is that of deprivation. Such deprivation should include the minimum consumption of food and other essentials, health status, minimum education, etc. This is closer to the notion of human poverty to indicate the various manifestations of deprivation. As such the notion of basic social security emphasizing food security, health security, educational security, etc. is an attempt to link the human deprivation with a security-oriented notion of meeting the basic needs. Such a security-orientation could liberate the poverty reduction attempts beyond their *ad hoc* and/or short-term consideration to one of the needs to create institutional mechanisms to address problems of deficiency as a foundational one to all development goals.

Comprehensive social protection programmes are required to address the problems to poverty, food insecurity and other forms of deprivations. The social protection measures are basically non-contributory targeted transfer programmes to the poor and vulnerable groups. The presence of social protection measures can maintain an acceptable minimum floor for social cohesion and can prevent irreversible losses of human capital in hard times. The State has a role in terms of helping the poor in times of insecurity and in terms of ensuring minimum levels of provision to those unable to gain from the growth process. Government interventions are required to blend elements of both redistribution and insurance (World Bank 1990) in this regard. India also has a large plethora of social protection schemes, both at the Central and State levels, which cater to different segments of the population. The ambit of these schemes is quite large, covering basic education and health, employment creation and promotion, workers' social security, food and nutrition security, and social pensions. Some of these programmes are now supported legally (Srivastva 2013).

1.2 Perception of Social Protection

Social Protection comprises those measures which aim at preventing, reducing and eliminating economic and social vulnerabilities to poverty and deprivation. The term social protection is used in institutions across the world with a wider variety of meanings than social security. It is often interpreted as having a broader character than social security. Social security has been used to denote public action to protect workers' status in formal labour markets from contingency related risks. Traditional social security is based on the assumptions that most members of society have achieved a satisfactory standard of living, have access to regular work and social security to meet contingencies of old age, ill health, death and unemployment. Dreze and Sen distinguish between the protective and promotional aspects of social security (Dreze and Sen 1991; 2002). The former is concerned with preventing decline in living standards in general and in the basic conditions of living in particular. The latter has the objective to enhancing normal living conditions and helping people to overcome regular and persistent (capability) deprivation. Kanan (2004) has distinguished between 'Basic Social Security' (BSS) and 'Contingent Social Security' (CSS). BSS refers to the social provision of a critical minimum to conditions of 'deficiency' in such basic wants as food, health, education and housing, whereas CSS refers to socially-supported institution arrangements to meet conditions of 'adversity' such as sickness, accidents and old age. In order to map the extent of social protection coverage for any population, Saith (2004) has suggested three elements. The first of these represents the *multiple dimensions of social protection*, which include food and nutritional security, health, employment or work-related insecurity, old age cover, education, access to legal aid, etc. The second element pertains to *different social constituencies* in the population such as children, women, the aged, workers, migrants, excluded minorities, low castes, spatially marginalized groups, the unemployed, etc. The third element lists the *alternative provisioning systems* (potentially) available for addressing the specific dimensions of social protection identified on the first axis.

The International Labour Office (ILO) and many other international organizations use the concept of 'social protection' to cover not only social security schemes that are statutory but also non-statutory schemes.

Asian Development Bank (ADB) has defined it as "*the set of policies and programmes designed to reduce poverty and vulnerability by promoting efficient labour markets, diminishing people's exposure to risks, and enhancing their capacity to protect themselves against hazards and the interruption/loss of income*"(Ortiz, 2000). Furthermore, social protection is defined as comprising five major kinds of activities: labour market policies and programmes, social insurance, social assistance, micro/area-based schemes and child protection (ADB 2001). 'Social Protection' is defined by the ILO as *'a set of public measures that a society provides for its members to protect them against economic and social distress caused by the absence or a substantial reduction of income from work as a result of various contingencies (sickness, maternity, employment injury, unemployment, invalidity, old age or death of the bread earner), the provision of healthcare and the provision of benefits for families with children'* (ILO 2004).

UNICEF (2012) describes *social protection as the set of public and private policies and programmes aimed at preventing, reducing and eliminating economic and social vulnerabilities to poverty and deprivation.* On the other hand, the term is also used in a narrower sense to refer to measures which relate to contingency related risks although more in an informal economy and non-statutory setting.

In the context of social protection, however, Standing (2007) noted that neither rights nor needs exist as objective facts that are determined scientifically outside society. They are social constructs, determined by a process of consciousness. They are always relative and subject to refinements of definition. In practice, social protection systems evolve, and in doing so modify what is covered by the notion of need.

In the present study, we view social protection as a set of public measures evolved by the central or state government that create direct benefits to the households or members of households to eliminate poverty and deprivation.

1.3 The Notion of Social Protection Floor

The concept of a socio-economic floor and its relationship to social protection was emphasized by the World Commission on the Social Dimension of Globalization (2004). It is a rights-based approach and its core idea is that no one should live below a certain income level and everyone should at least be able to have access to basic social services to enhance decent work opportunities.

The term Social Protection Floor (SPF) has been used to mean a set of basic social rights, services and facilities that the global citizen should enjoy. The term "social floor" can correspond to the existing notion of "core obligations", to ensure the realization of, at the very least, minimum essential levels of rights embodied in human rights treaties (ILO & WHO 2009).

Since 2009, there has been an attempt to find and refine a universal agreed definition of SPF. The United Nations (UN) (ILO 2009a) stated that a social protection floor could consist of two main elements that help to realize respective human rights:

- *Essential services:* geographical and financial access to essential services (such as water and sanitation, adequate nutrition, health and education).
- *Social Transfers:* a basic set of essential social transfers, in cash and in kind, paid to the poor and vulnerable to provide a minimum income security and access to essential health care.

The social protection floor, as defined by the United Nations Chief Executives Board (UNCEB), is an integrated set of social policies designed to guarantee income security and access to social services for all, paying particular attention to vulnerable groups, and protecting and empowering people across the life cycle. It includes guarantees of:

(a) *basic income security,* in the form of various social transfers (in cash or in kind), such as pensions for the elderly and persons with disabilities, child benefits, income support benefits and/or employment guarantees and services for the unemployed and working poor;

(b) *universal access to essential affordable social services* in the areas of health, water and sanitation, education, food security, housing, and others defined according to national priorities (ILO 2009a).

Further, the social protection floors should comprise at least the following *four basic social security guarantees:*

(a) access to a nationally defined set of goods and services, constituting essential health care, including maternity care, that meets the criteria of availability, accessibility, acceptability and quality;

(b) basic income security for children, at least at a nationally defined minimum level, providing access to nutrition, education, care and any other necessary goods and services;
(c) basic income security, at least at a nationally defined minimum level, for persons in active age who are unable to earn sufficient income, in particular in cases of sickness, unemployment, maternity and disability; and
(d) basic income security, at least at a nationally defined minimum level, for older persons (Srivastava 2012).

The ILO Global Jobs Pact specified as core components of the social protection floor access to health care, income security for the elderly and persons with develop fiscal and policy space (ILO 2009b). The concept is consistent with a two-dimensional strategy for extending social security, comprising a basic set of social guarantees for all (horizontal dimension) and the gradual implementation of higher standards (vertical dimension). The 2011 International Labour Conference demonstrated resounding support for the floor and has further fine-tuned the above definitions of the concept. This refinement unified the relationship between income security and access to essential goods and services in the form of basic social security guarantees. The Conference agreed upon the following definition:

> ... social protection floors, containing basic social security guarantees that ensure that over the life cycle all in need can afford and have access to essential health care and have income security at least at a nationally defined minimum level. Social protection floor policies should aim at facilitating effective access to essential goods and services, promote productive economic activity and be implemented in close coordination with other policies enhancing employability, reducing informality and precariousness, creating decent jobs and promoting entrepreneurship (ILO 2011).

SPF combines the traditional life cycle approach comprising human development integrated programmes for children and their families, the underemployed and working poor (including those with disabilities) and the elderly (Figure 1.1), with new developments in poverty and vulnerability analysis.

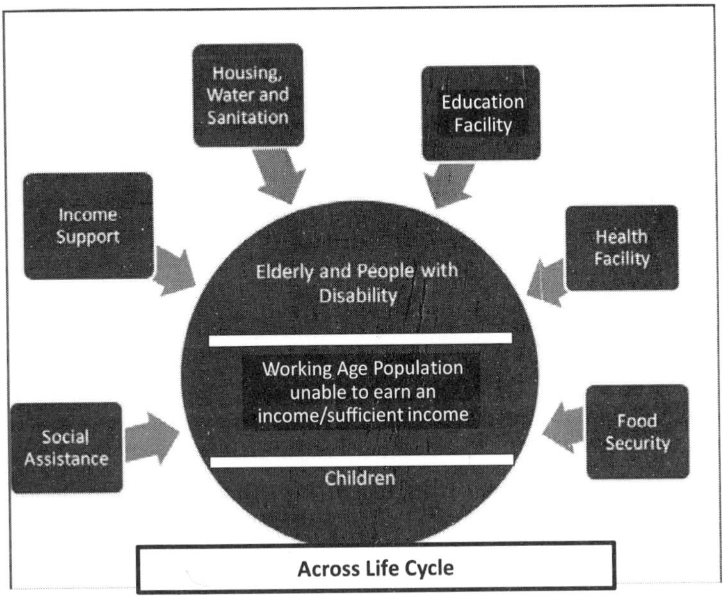

Fig. 1.1: The Social Protection Floor: Integrated Social Policies to Protect and Empower People across the Life Cycle.

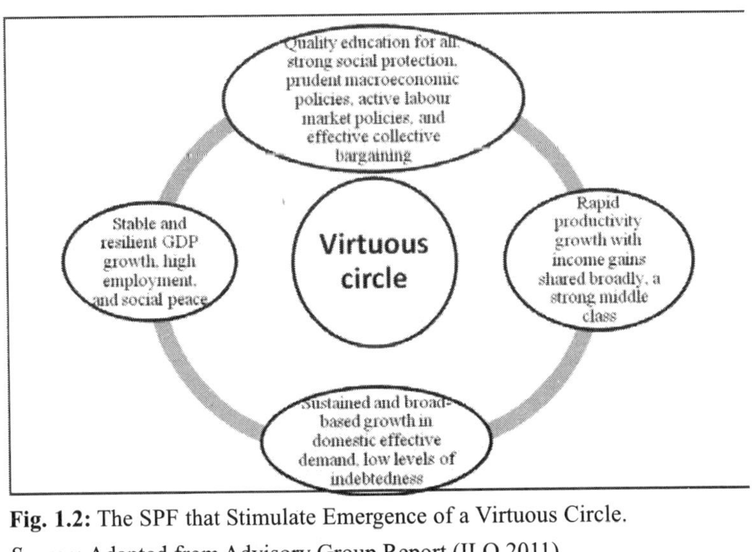

Fig. 1.2: The SPF that Stimulate Emergence of a Virtuous Circle.

Source: Adapted from Advisory Group Report (ILO 2011).

As shown in Figure 1.2, once a floor is in place it can also be understood to kick-start a virtuous circle of development that provides an exit route from poverty and inequality, and towards long-term economic resilience and inclusive growth. The virtuous circle created by social protection can become a self-propelling mechanism anchoring forms of human development progress that are sustainable, and which can be reproduced, leading to more and better development (ILO 2011).

Box 1.1: Why the Social Protection Floor?

- Realizing human rights and social justice
- An effective tool for combating poverty and inequality
- Accelerating progress towards achieving the MDGs and beyond
- Affordable even in low-income countries
- Ensuring adequate opportunities for decent work
- Helping to address the social and economic impact of crises and global economic imbalances
- A tool for gender empowerment
- Enhancing social cohesion

1.4 Importance of Social Protection Programmes

Social protection measures and social protection systems emanate from chronic as well as contingent insecurities that exist in human society, and the obligation of social systems to mitigate such insecurities within the limit of their competence and capabilities. Most generally, it is recognized that the social protection plays a crucial role in the process of development. The theoretical arguments in favour of social protection are set as follows:

First, since social protection covers various dimensions through the life cycle of the population its coverage extends to the entire population through the ***entire life span***, and not only to workers. Garcia and Gruat (2003) argue that social protection can be seen as a summation of statutory and non-statutory measures which are not taken to ensure not only decent work but also the extension of coverage of effective social protection measures for all.

Second, the sources of risks and vulnerability have increased with globalization, exposing the poor to new forms of risk, both due to systemic factors and shocks. The regional imbalance expedites the shocks and risks. Social Protection has acquired greater relevance in the context of ***shocks and systemic risks*** which are being faced by the working poor in the context of globalization and regional imbalance. This has brought the term "Social Protection" into increased current usage as a broad range of public measures deemed necessary to protect population against sources of risk (Srivastava 2013).

Third, social protection can help to stabilize aggregate demand during economic crisis, contributing to accelerated recovery and more inclusive and sustainable development paths. UNICEF (2012) argues that social protection is an important instrument for ***equity and social inclusion.***

Fourth, social protection represents a "win-win" investment that pays off both in the short term given its effects as ***macroeconomic stabilizer*** and in the long term, due to the impact on ***human development and productivity*** (ILO 2011).

Fifth, social protection can also act as an ***economic stabilizer during a crisis***. The stabilizing effects of social protection policies are generally accepted as important in maintaining purchasing power during a downturn, and, if governments allow deficits to rise as tax receipts fall, are important foundations on which a future recovery can be built (WEF 2012).

Sixth, social protections can kick-start demand as part of a stimulus package to speed up the exit from the crisis. Increased spending on social protection is a central element in the ***fiscal stimulus programmes*** implemented in the wake of the crisis. For example, in Brazil, the *Bolsa Familia* and unemployment insurance benefits were raised, injecting some US$ 30 billion into the Brazilian economy, saving or creating around 1.3 million jobs. In Indonesia, 7 per cent of the stimulus package was directed towards low-income households with an overall increase of 34 per cent on social protection spending in 2009. The results were impressive (Bachelet 2011).

Seventh, social protection can be used to boost domestic demand and reduce reliance on ***export-led growth in emerging economies***. Emerging market countries can use social protection to adapt their economic models and move towards a path that attaches importance to domestic markets and exports. Boosting domestic demand by expanding social protection is now at the heart of economic policy in China (WEF 2012).

Eighth, the establishment of a social protection floor can accelerate the ***pace of development in developing countries***. It is sometimes said that social protection is a luxury that developing countries cannot afford. But as the Bachelet (2011) report points out, relatively small investments can have big social effects: reducing poverty, encouraging entrepreneurship, boosting school attendance and improving nutrition. Creating a social protection floor is not just a consequence of development but is a part of the process of development.

Ninth, social protection ***promotes pro-poor growth*** (OECD 2009) enhancing the ability of the poor to participate in, contribute to, and benefit from growth. It does so by increasing access to social services (namely, heath and education), which reinforces the productivity and participation of the poor in the labour market, and by protecting the poor against shocks and reducing their vulnerability.

Tenth, social protection can have a direct ***positive impact on growth***. By raising the income of the poor, social security transfers increase domestic demand and, in turn, encourage growth by expanding domestic markets. Moreover, social protection makes growth equitable, builds social cohesion and hence makes growth more sustainable. The importance of equitable growth has been widely recognised. At the same time, the quality of growth can be enhanced through improved income distribution (Cichon 2006).

Overall, Social protection directly reduces poverty and helps make growth more pro-poor. It stimulates the involvement of poor women and men in economic growth, protects the poorest and most vulnerable in a downturn and contributes to social cohesion and stability. It helps to build human capital, manage risks, promote investment and entrepreneurship and improve participation in labour markets. Social protection programmes can be affordable for the poorest countries and represent good value for money.

1.5 The Backward Region

Regional imbalances in a country may be natural due to unequal distribution of natural resources and/or man-made factors in the sense of neglect of some regions and preference for others for investment and infrastructural facilities. In India, apart from uneven distribution of geographical advantages, historical factors have contributed to regional inequities. India's successive Five Year Plans have stressed the need to develop backward regions of the country. In promoting regional balanced development, public sector enterprises were located in backward areas of the country during the early phase of economic planning. In spite of pro-backward areas policies and programmes, considerable economic and social inequalities exist among different States of India as well as among the regions within a state (Bagchi 2011). During the era of liberalization the opening up of Indian economy appears to be correlated with rising spatial inequality. Global integration leads to a sharper expression of comparative advantage and regions well placed in terms of location, education, governance and other initial conditions tend to surge ahead as global opportunities are accessed while others lag behind. This is the case for China and for India, where sharply rising regional disparities have coincided with the period of external liberalization (Gajwani, Kanbur and Zhang 2007; Kanbur and Venables 2007). In India, the absolute inequality across households has increased in almost all states in the era of economic liberalization (Mondal 2014). High and rising inequality in general dissipates the favourable impact of growth on poverty reduction. Spatial disparities in India align with other cleavages which threaten national unity and peace, whether it is the extreme of the "Maoist corridor" that matches the corridor of deprivation. The south-west part of West Bengal was also affected by extreme Maoist movement during 2009 and 2011. That generated shocks and risk on livelihood.

Characteristics of the Backward Region in West Bengal

The Planning Commission (1981) on the development of backward areas recommended that the following types of problem area be treated as backward for the purpose of planning: (i) Chronically drought prone area. (ii) Desert areas, (iii) Tribal areas, (iv) Hill areas, (v) Chronically flood affected areas, and (vi) Coastal areas affected by salinity. These six categories can be viewed as six types of fundamental backwardness. In this sense an area may suffer from the handicap of more than one type of fundamental backwardness. According to the Task Force Report (2003), the index of backwardness is based on the three parameters, e.g. (a) value of output per agricultural worker, (b) agricultural wage rate and (c) percentage of SC/ST population. Under Rastriya Sam Vikas Yojana (now Backward Region Grant Fund) eight districts of West Bengal are listed as backward districts, namely Paschim Medinipur, Bankura, and Purulia, Birbhum, 24-Parganas (South), Dakshin Dinajpur, Uttar Dinajpur and Jalpaiguri. Out of them the three districts—Paschim Medinipur, Bankura and Purulia which are in the south-western region of West Bengal and boarding with Orissa, Jharkhand and Bihar is our proposed study area. This region is backward in respect of two categories of backwardness, namely drought prone and tribal areas. Nearly 38 per cent of tribal population of West Bengal is living in these four districts (Census of India 2011). Among 19 districts of West Bengal these three districts are also treated as drought prone districts (Entire Purulia district, 27 per cent of Paschim Medinipur and 32 per cent of Bankura are drought prone area). Not only that a significant area of these districts is forest land—

22 per cent Bankura, 18 per cent in Paschim Medinipur and 12 per cent in Purulia (State Forest Report 2010-11). These three districts are described as Jangal Mahal of West Bengal meaning forest regions largely inhabited by tribal population. The region also exhibits the following socio-economic backwardness: (a) agriculture is the main occupation; according to latest Census (2011) 63 per cent of the population are predominately dependent on agriculture for their livelihood), (b) low agricultural productivity and low agricultural wage (Das 2010), (c) excessive dependence on forest for livelihood and the problem of deforestation, (d) cattle breeding, cottage industries, artisan products and collection of forest products are subsidiary occupations (Das 2010), (e) lack of infrastructure and modern industries, (f) lack of education, healthcare and other civic amenities, (g) low level of education; estimated literacy rate in this region is 61 per cent as per Census 2011 which is much lower than state average, and (h) social backwardness with high unemployment and high incidence of poverty.

Maoist Movement in the Backward Region of West Bengal

The western part of South Bengal including a major part of West Medinipur, Bankura and Purulia district is now literally marked as *Jangal Mahal*. The name says that the major part of this region is covered by forest or jungle. Maoist Movement (terrorism according to the state government of West Bengal) strongly affected the Jangal Mahal region of West Bengal. Apparently, the reason behind this is the backwardness and historical deprivation of an ethnical group. But it is not the only reason. The various reasons lying behind this also include their demand for cultural identity (Iqbal 2014).

In fact, West Bengal has witnessed a dramatic spurt in Maoist-related fatalities in 2010. According to available data, 425 people including 328 civilians, 36 security forces personnel and 61 Maoists including cadre of the Maoist-backed People's Committee against Police Atrocities, were killed in West Bengal in 2010 till December 26, as against 158 people including 134 civilians, 15 security forces personnel and nine Maoists killed in the State in 2009. With this, West Bengal has now earned the dubious distinction of recording the highest Maoist-related fatalities in 2010 dislodging Chhattisgarh which had topped the list since 2006. The intervening years have seen an extraordinary rise in Maoist-related fatalities in West Bengal from just six in 2005, through 24 in 2008, and up to 158 and 418 people, respectively in 2009 and 2010 (Iqbal 2014). The incidents of terrorist activities and deaths are depicted in Figure 1.3.

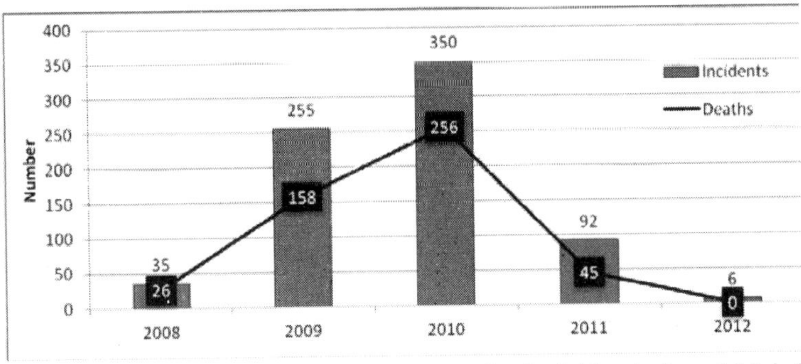

Fig. 1.3: The Incidents and Deaths by Maoist Activities in Jangal Mahal Region of West Bengal, 2008 to 2012.

The Maoist affected region is relatively backward. According to the Human Development Report HDI of West Bengal is 0.625 where in Bankura and Purulia it is 0.52 and 0.45 respectively which possess 11th and 16th rank among the nineteen districts of West Bengal. But in extremely Maoist influenced almost forty blocks in Bankura, Purulia and West Medinipur district the scenario is really miserable. Earlier, it has been touched upon that the Maoist dominated blocks are situated in remote areas. There is lack of fertile agricultural land and most of the poor local tribes are landless. Most of them suffer from acute poverty. The situation worsened during 2009 to 2011 and the livelihood of the people in Maoist affected area was deteriorating. After that the West Bengal State Government has attempted to execute and extend the social protection measure especially in the Maoist affected region.

1.6 Objectives of the Present Study

A few questions that arise against this brief backdrop are: What is the breadth and depth of SPF in India? What is the extent of benefits of social protection programmes (SPP) in the backward region? Do the poor households obtain the social protection benefits (SPB) as per statutory provision of SPP? How does SPB contribute to the overall entitlement of households? Is the SPB able to overcome food insecurity, poverty and vulnerability of the households in the backward region?

The brief review of the existing literature on the present theme (as given in Annexure A) reveals that there is hardly any study on impact of social protection programme on poverty and deprivations at the household level. There are needs for household surveys, particularly in Maoist affected backward region which would look deeply into the situations of those covered by social protection schemes and the resultant outcome on poverty alleviation or deprivation. To ameliorate this situation, the present study would make a humble attempt aimed at collecting basic information on different aspects of social protection scheme and poverty situation to analyse the impact of social protection benefits on food insecurity, poverty and deprivations of the households in the backward region. The study sets the following specific objectives for itself:

(1) To explore the social protection programmes that are evident in India.
(2) To analyse social protection programmes and their benefits in the context of Backward Region of West Bengal.
(3) To analyse the social protection benefits that are enjoyed by the households in the Backward Region of West Bengal.
(4) To evaluate the social protection benefits in relation to entitlement of the sample households.
(5) To examine the impact of social protection programmes on the status of food security, poverty and deprivations of the sample households.

1.7 Data Base of the Study

While the overall objective of the present study is to analyze the social protection benefits for the poor and examine the impact of social protection on poverty in the context of the backward region of West Bengal we try to explore the social protection programmes and status of poverty and for this purpose we take resort to the secondary data. However, on account of the limitations of the secondary data and for the sake of an in-depth and detailed study we have tried to collect and use primary data to realise our research objectives. This section deals with the sources of the secondary data, methodology of collection of primary data and that of analysis of secondary and primary data.

1.7.1 Secondary Data and their Sources

Data relating socio-economic criteria of four selected districts and their blocks as well as the information regarding different schemes of social protection have been collected from the secondary sources. The important secondary sources are: (1) *Census of India*, (2) *National Sample Survey Organisation (NSSO)*, (3) *Statistical Abstract*, Government of West Bengal, (4) *Economic Survey*, Government of West

Bengal, (5) *District Census Handbook*, Government of West Bengal, (6) *Annual Administrative Report*, Government of West Bengal and (7) *District Statistical Handbook*, Government of West Bengal. Detailed information of the different government schemes are also collected from official websites of different Ministries and Departments of Government of India, namely (a) Ministry of Consumer Affairs, Dept. of Food and Public Distribution, (b) Ministry of Health and Family Welfare, (c) Ministry of Drinking Water & Sanitation, (d) Ministry of Women and Child Development, (e) Ministry of Human Resource Development, (f) Ministry of Rural Development etc. and also from official websites of the Government of West Bengal, namely (a) Directorate of School Education, (b) Directorate of Rationing, (c) Department of Panchayats & Rural Development, (d) Department of Health and Family Welfare, (e) Bureau of Applied Economics and Statistics, (f) Backward Class Welfare Department, (g) Department of Food and Food Supplies, (h) Department of Forest, and (i) Department of Health and Family Welfare, etc.

NSSO Unit Level data relating to the Level and Pattern of Consumption Expenditure for the years 2004-05, 2009-10 and 2011-12 have also been used to estimate the status of poverty and food insecurity in the backward region of West Bengal.

1.7.2 Primary Data and Sample Design

Preparation of Schedules

We have prepared two separate questionnaires—one for village survey which is general in nature and other for household survey. The questionnaire for household survey is specially designed to address the issues of social protection, status of livelihood and multidimensional framework of poverty.

Pilot Survey

A pilot survey has been conducted to test the correctness of the instructions to be measured by whether all the respondents in the pilot sample are able to follow the directions as indicated. The respondents are asked what they can say about the questionnaire, specifically their reactions, comments and suggestions. For instance, we asked them about how clear the instructions are or which questions are hard to answer.

Internal and participatory pilot survey methods have been used. Therefore, the respondents in the pilot survey are the first participants in the main survey.

After obtaining and analyzing the results of the pilot survey logistical, technical and other issues or problems have been addressed. The questionnaire or interview format has been revised. After the revision of the questionnaire, we have conducted a second pilot survey to determine whether the errors and issues are effectively solved. After the confirmation that the problems are minor we have processed the large-scale survey. The final questionnaire is appended in Appendix 2.

Selection of Sample Frame

Three districts of West Bengal, namely Paschim Midnapore, Bankura, and Purulia are purposely chosen for the present study. On the basis of 12 indicators relating to agricultural development, urbanisation, infrastructure, per capita income, employment, and poverty ratio etc. we have judged that these three districts are relatively less developed. The relevant information of these indicators for 2011 is shown in Appendix Table A1. In Figure 1.4 Districts of West Bengal are arranged by the value of Group Dimension Index (GDI) where Paschim Midnapore, Bankura, and Purulia districts having lower value of GDI. The region formed with these three districts is treated as backward region and a part of the region is Jangal Mahal which is affected by extreme Maoist movement.

Multistage stratified random sampling is used to construct the sample frame. These three districts constitute the 1st stage unit. Four blocks were randomly selected from each district with distinct socio-economic characteristics and these 12 blocks constitute the 2nd stage unit. On the basis of the information available in Census of India 2011, we have prepared a village list of each of the sample blocks. Two villages were selected randomly from the village list of each block. That is, in the 3rd stage we have selected 24 villages. For each village we have prepared a list of BPL households and 25 households were randomly selected from this list of BPL households for survey. The sample frame is shown in Appendix Table A2. From the above sample design 600 households were selected for detailed survey. Reference period for the study is the financial year 2012-13.

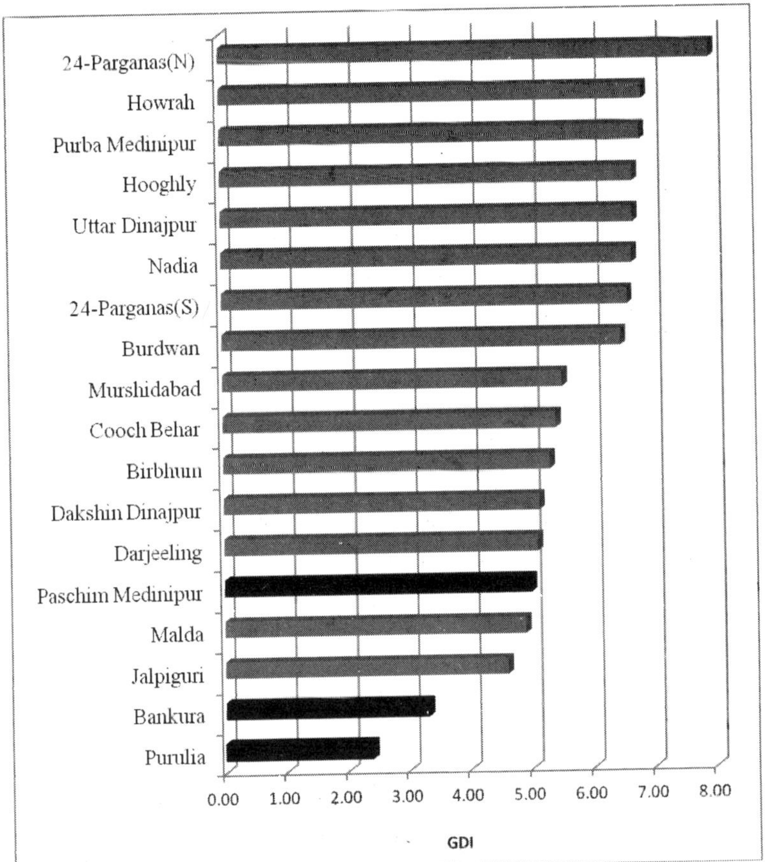

Fig. 1.4: Group Dimension Index (GDI) by Districts of West Bengal.

Data Collection

The necessary information has collected from the sample households on the following socio-economic heads:

(a) *General Information of Households:* General information of households includes caste, sub-castes, BPL status, housing condition, assets etc. and age, sex, income earner, education level, status of the ration card, etc. of the members of household.

(b) *Occupation and Earnings of the Households:* It includes (i) own labour entitlement: employeemnt pattern of the household members includes main, marginal or non-workers; working time, wage rate, status of employment either casual labour, regular employment or self-employed and earnings; (ii) production-based entitlement: pattern of agricultural land, Goss cropped area, agricultural production, estimates cost of production, net income from agriculture, agri-allied production, non-farm production and production process of sample households etc.; (iii) trade-based entitlement: investment, labour use and net income, (iv) asset-based entitlement: value of livestock, machinery and other assets and net earnings, and (v) use of common property resources: nature of use, earnings etc.

(c) *Coverage of Social Protection Schemes of Government:* Nature of scheme, detailed information of the schemes, eligible and benefited households, benefits of social protection schemes, options for extension of their coverage, social protection expenditure, and the estimated cost of increasing the coverage.

(d) *Expenditure of the Households to Estimate Poverty:* Cost on basic consumption, expenditure on education, expenditure on health, expenditure on clothing, energy consumption, other miscellaneous expenditure, information of ICDS and mid-day meals taken by the households.

(e) *Multidimensional Poverty Indicators:* Status of the households in respect of food security, domestic water supply, health and health care, sanitation & hygiene, housing & energy, education, agricultural assets, non-agricultural assets, exposer & resilience to shocks and gender inequality.

About Generalisation of Data

With regard to generalization of survey results, there are at least three reasons why this is possible. *First,* the study area is relatively backward and having the population of all communities—relatively developed (e.g. general castes [GEN]), backward (e.g. other backward castes [OBC]), most backward (e.g., scheduled castes [SC] and Scheduled Tribes [STs]). Therefore, there is the scope of the execution of most of the social protection programmes. *Secondly,* our survey villages are in the state of West Bengal, which is widely acknowledged as one with widespread coverage of social protection programmes. *Thirdly,* India is also committed to advancing the agenda of a Social Protection Floor as is evident from its support to ILO Recommendation 202 and the Ministerial Declaration at the third Inter-Ministerial conference in Colombo in 2011 (UNESCO 2011). The basis of a rights-based approach to a social protection floor in India also overlaps with the ingredients of a SPF as envisaged by the United Nations (ILO 2012).

1.8 Plan of the Study

The rest of the present work is divided into seven chapters. Chapter 2 explores the social protection programmes those are evident in India. Chapter 3 analyses social protection benefits in the context of Backward Districts of West Bengal. Chapter 4 analyses the characteristics of the sample households in the backward region and explores the social protection benefits that are enjoyed by them. Chapter 5 evaluates the social protection benefits in relation to entitlement of the households. Chapter 6 analyses the theoretical framework and empirical evidence of the impact of social protection benefits on the status of food security of the households. Chapter 7 examines the impact of social protection benefits on poverty and deprivations of the households. Finally, Chapter 8 summarises the main findings and makes concluding observations including policy recommendation.

2
Social Protection Programmes in India

2.1 Evidence of Social Protection for Rural Households in India

Provision of social protection is enshrined in Articles 38 (securing a social order for the promotion of welfare of the people), 39 (certain principles of policy), 41 (within the limits of its economic capacity and development, make effective provision for securing the right to work, to education and to public assistance in cases of unemployment, old age, sickness and disablement, and in other cases of undeserved want), 42 (just and human conditions of work and maternity relief), 43 (living wage etc.) and 47 (regarding the raising level of nutrition and the standard of living of its people and the improvement of public health as among its primary duties) of the Constitution of India as a part of the Directive Principles of State Policy (Pillai 2011).

After liberalization, in the initial phase, social protection measures were neglected, but this began to change from the mid-1990s when there was an expansion in the budget for rural employment generation and social assistance programmes. While the ambit of social security schemes relating to workers and which are statutory in nature, has also grown, in the last few years, a major expansion has occurred in the expenditure on sectors where the courts or the constitution have created specific entitlements through legislative changes or legal oversight. The total expenditure by the Government of India on six of the major social protection related sectors (elementary education, health and family welfare, labour and labour welfare, social security and welfare and rural development) has increased from 1.06 per cent of GDP in 1995-96 to 1.35 per cent of GDP in 2005-06 and further to 1.75 per cent of GDP in 2010-11. The states of India spend almost twice as much as the Central Government on these sectors but their expenditure (as percentage of GDP) has not changed much in the last decade. The Central Government's expenditure on major social protection programmes (excluding those in health and education sectors including the scholarship schemes of the Ministry of Social Justice) have increased particularly significantly between 2005-06 and 2011-12—from 1.29 per cent of GDP to 1.73 per cent of GDP (Srivastava 2013).

The most significant development in the last two decades in India has been a widespread growth in home working and self-employment. The share of employment in regular, permanent and full-time jobs with adequate social protection has declined (Das 2012). The logic behind this change in the labour market has been the flexibility process, induced by globalization. The employment structure in India is such that only a small proportion of their workforce is engaged in formal employment with stable contracts and associated benefits (NCUES 2007, Das 2010). The social protection schemes in India is quite large, covering food and nutrition security, basic education, health, housing, employment generation and promotion, social assistance including social pensions. The schemes can be broadly categorized as promotional, protective or preventive, depending on the type of intervention (World Bank 2011) and are broadly defined as follows:

- ***Protective*** or 'social assistance' measures provide relief ex-post for the chronically poor or for those who fall into poverty as a result of shocks. By providing food, social pensions and assets such as housing, protective measures mitigate the need for households to run through their savings, sell off assets or take children out of school to deal with sharply reduced income. Protective measures such as the Public Distribution System (PDS) for food, 'protect' family's nutritional security during times of need, but unlike promotional measures which are not trying to incentivize certain behaviours in doing so.
- ***Preventive*** measures seek to stave off poverty or other hardships before they hit, by protecting household's ex-ante against shocks, and supporting them through failed risks, typically through social insurance programmes. MGNREGA, for example, by guaranteeing employment and providing an assured income, prevents families from falling into poverty.
- ***Promotional*** measures aim to improve incomes both in the short and long run often by encouraging a particular practice or behaviour. For instance, programmes such as mid-day meals

promote school attendance and proper nutrition which in turn improves livelihood prospects. Similarly, conditional cash transfers support investments in human capital, and programmes such as the newly formulated NRLM-Aajeevika (formerly known as Swarna Jayanti Gram Swarozgar Yojana) facilitate development of sustainable livelihoods.

While such categories are not mutually exclusive, they assist in understanding the direction and emphasis of the country's social protection system. Protective spending is the largest component of India's social protection system (IRDR 2012-13) (*see* Table 2.1 and Table 2.2).

The major social protection programmes in India are summarised in Table 2.1. The list of social protection programmes is not exhaustive. Here we have listed only those programmes which are witnessed in field survey and create direct benefit to households in the rural India. The listed programmes directly enhance the entitlement of the households which, *inter alia*, includes food, health, education, housing, employment and income and social assistance related programmes. Social protection programmes and their nature, i.e., whether they are protective, promotional or preventive are specified in Table 2.1. The Social Protection Floor (SPF) in India is formed by these programmes. The SPF in India includes the guarantees of (a) *basic income security*, in the form of income support benefits and/or employment guarantees by MGNREGA, SGSY and NTFP; along with pensions for the elderly and persons with disabilities by NOAPS, NFBS, NWPS, NDPS and IGMSY; and (b) *universal access to essential affordable social services* in the areas of food security (by TPDS), health (by rural primary health care, RSBY and JSY), water & sanitation (by NRDWP and TSC), education (by ICDS, SSK, MSK, MDM, etc.), and housing (by IAY).

Table 2.2 summarizes the major social protection programmes introduced and financed by both the Central and State governments of India. Each of these programmes is now briefly discussed.

2.2 Evolution of Public Distribution System in India

Introduction

The Public Distribution System (PDS) evolved as a system of management of scarcity and for distribution of food grains at affordable prices. Over the years, PDS has become an important part of Government's policy for

Table 2.1: Major Social Protection Programmes for Rural Households in India and their types

	Name and Specification of the Programme	*Type of the Programme*
Food		
(1a)	Targeted Public Distribution System (TPDS) for BPL Ration Card Holders	Protective
(1b)	TPDS under Antyodaya Anna Yojana (AAY)	Protective
(1c)	TPDS under Annapurna Yojana (AY)	Protective
(1d)	TPDS for APL Ration Card Holders	Protective
Health		
(2)	Rural Primary Health Care	Preventive
(3)	Janani Suraksha Yojana (JSY)	Promotional
(4)	Rashtriya Swasthya Bima Yojana (RSBY)	Preventive
Water and Sanitation		
(5)	National Rural Drinking Water Programme (NRDWP)	Promotional
(6)	Total Sanitation Campaign (TSC)	Promotional
Education		
(7)	The Integrated Child Development Services (ICDS)	Protective and Promotional
(8)	Sishu Siksha Karmasuchi (SSK)	Promotional
(9)	Madhyamik Siksha Karmasuchi (MSK)	Promotional
(10)	Kanyashree	Promotional
(11)	National Programme of Mid-Day Meal (MDM)	Promotional
(12)	Books and Book Grant	Promotional
(13)	Other Grants (Dress)	Promotional
(14)	Education for Minority Children	Promotional
Housing		
(15)	Indira Awas Yojana (IAY)	Protective
Employment and Income		
(16)	National Rural Employment Guarantee Programme (NREGP)	Protective and Preventative
(17)	Swarna Jayanti Gram Swarozgar Yojana (SGSY)	Promotional
(18)	Procurement of Non-timber Forest Produces (NTFP)	Protective and Preventative
Social Assistance		
(19)	Indira Gandhi National Old Age Pension Scheme (IGNOAPS)	Protective
(20)	National Family Benefit Scheme (NFBS)	Preventative
(21)	Indira Gandhi National Widow Pension Scheme (IGNWPS)	Protective
(22)	Indira Gandhi National Disability Pension Scheme (IGNDPS)	Protective
(23)	Indira Gandhi Matritva Sahayog Yojana (IGMSY)	Protective and Promotional
(24)	Bi-cycle for Students	Promotional

Table 2.2: Objectives, Target Group and Provision of Benefits of Social Protection Programmes

Name of SPP	*Objectives*	*Target Group*	*Statutory Provision*
Food			
(1a) TPDS for BPL Ration Card Holders	Provision of subsidized *food grains* to poor households and Stabilization of food prices	BPL card holders of BPL Households	35 kg *food grains* per month (Rice Rs. 5.65/kg, Wheat Rs. 4.15/kg)
(1b) TPDS under Antyodaya Anna Yojana (AAY)	-Do-	AAY Card holder of BPL Households	35 kg *food grains* per month (Rice: Rs. 3/kg, Wheat: Rs. 2/kg)
(1c) TPDS under Annapurna Yojana (AY)	Do-	Senior citizens (65 years age and above) who are eligible for old age pension but are not getting it	10 kg of *food grains* per person per month are supplied with free of cost
(1d) TPDS for APL Ration Card Holders	Stabilization of food prices	APL Households	15 to 35 kg *food grains* per month depends on the availability (Rice: Rs. 8.30/kg and Wheat: Rs. 6.10/kg)
Health			
(2) Rural Primary Health Care	Reduction of infant and maternal mortality rate, prevention of communicable and non-communicable diseases etc.	Especially to women, children and the poor residing in rural areas	Free Medical services and Medicines
(3) Janani Suraksha Yolana (JSY)	To reduce overall maternal mortality ratio and infant mortality rate, and to increase institutional deliveries	All BPL pregnant women who are 19 years or above, (up to two live birth)	Rs. 500.00 and an additional benefit of Rs. 100.00 will be given to these women, if her delivery takes place in any government health center
(4) Rashtriya Swasthya Bima Yojana (RSBY)	Subsidized health insurance	BPL Poor families and other families of informal workers	Cashless health Treatment
Water and Sanitation			
(5) National Rural Drinking Water Programme (NRDWP)	Provide solutions for safe drinking water	All rural households	Drinking Water

(Contd.)

Table 2.2: *(Contd.)*

Name of SPP	Objectives	Target Group	Statutory Provision
(6) Total Sanitation Campaign (TSC)	To accelerate sanitation coverage in rural areas & to develop community Managed environmental sanitation systems	All rural families with an incentive to Below Poverty Line families	Sanitation at subsidized price
Education			
(7) The Integrated Child Development Services (ICDS)	Improvement in the nutritional and health status of children	All children 0-6 years and pregnant and lactating mothers	Supplementary nutrition, immunization, health check-up, referral services, pre-school non-formal education and nutrition & health education
(8) Sishu Siksha Karmasuchi (SSK)	To support universal enrolment and retention of children in elementary schooling and to support the provision of quality education	6-14-year children in elementary schools	Education free of cost
(9) Madhyamik Siksha Karmasuchi (MSK)	To support universal enrolment and quality of education	Upper Primary Education (Class V-VIII)	Education free of cost
(10) Kanyashree	To improve the status and well-being of girl child	Unmarried Girls aged 13-18 years enrolled in classes VIII-XII	Annual Scholarship of Rs. 500/- and One-time grant Rs. 25,000/-
(11) National Programme of Mid-Day Meal	Mid-Day Meal for School children up to Class VIII	School going children in all recognized schools and educational centers	One Mid-Day Meal in the School
(12) Books and Book Grant	To support universal enrolment and quality education	Students of Upper Primary Class	Text Book Grant @ Rs. 400/- (maximum) per child
(13) Other Grants (Dress)	To improve Education support services	Students up to Class VIII (specially ST children)	Dress with free of cost
(14) Education for Minority Children	To undertake economic welfare of minorities	Minority Students	Educational support service and Scholarship

(Contd.)

Table 2.2: (*Contd.*)

Name of SPP	*Objectives*	*Target Group*	*Statutory Provision*
Housing			
(15) Indira Awas Yojana (IAY)	Construction of dwelling units and up-gradation of existing *kutcha* houses by providing grant-in-aid	Rural people below the poverty-line	Rs. 45,000/- in plains and Rs. 48,500/- in hilly area for dwelling units.
Employment and Income			
(16) MGNREGA	Provision of up to 100 days of granted employment	All rural households Demanding unskilled manual employment	Rs. 160.00 per day wage rate
(17) SGSY and SHG	To reduce poverty by enabling the poor households to access gainful self-employment	(Rural poor (specially women)	Available group loan and Cash benefits for production and business
(18) Procurement of Non-timber Forest Produces (NTFP)	Provides seasonal employment and income generation	Tribal people specially for women living in close proximity to forest	Employment and Income generation
Social Assistance			
(19) Indira Gandhi National Old Age Pension Scheme (IGNOAPS)	Provision of pensions	All old age persons (above the age of 65 years) in BPL households	Rs. 200/- per month from the Central Government. In addition, State Governments provide old age pension ranging from Rs. 200/- to Rs. 1000/- per month.
(20) National Family Benefit Scheme (NFBS)	One-time benefit on death of breadwinner	BPL families	Rs. 10,000/- at a time
(21) Indira Gandhi National Widow Pension Scheme (IGNWPS)	Provision of pensions	Widows aged between 45 and 64 years of age of BPL households.	Rs. 400/- per month per beneficiary
(22) Indira Gandhi National Disability Pension Scheme (IGNDPS)	Provision of pensions	BPL person aged between 18-64 years of age and suffering from severe or multiple disability	Rs. 400/- per month per beneficiary

(*Contd.*)

Table 2.2: *(Contd.)*

Name of SPP	Objectives	Target Group	Statutory Provision
(23) Indira Gandhi Matritva Sahayog Yojana (IGMSY)	A cash incentive is provided for first two live births subject to the woman fulfilling conditions relating to material & child health nutrition	Pregnant & lactating women of 19 years and above	Rs. 4000/-
(24) Bi-cycle for Tribal Girl's	To reduce school dropout and encouraging the girl's student	Tribal Girl students of class IX to XII	One bi-cycle for each girl

Note: The statutory provisions of benefits are applicable for 2012-13.

Sources: 1. Srivastav (2013).

2. Official websites of different Ministries and Departments of Government of India, namely (a) Ministry of Consumer Affairs, Dept. of Food and Public Distribution, (b) Ministry of Health and Family Welfare, (c) Ministry of Drinking Water & Sanitation, (d) Ministry of Women and Child Development, (e) Ministry of Human Resource Development, (f) Ministry of Rural Development etc.
3. Official websites of the Government of West Bengal, namely (a) Directorate of School Education, (b) Directorate of Rationing, (c) Department of Panchayats & Rural Development, (d) Department of Health and Family Welfare, (e) Bureau of Applied Economics and Statistics, (f) Backward Class Welfare Department, (g) Department of Food and Food Supplies, (h) Department of Forest, (i) Department of Health and Family Welfare, etc.

management of food economy in the country. Of all the safety net operations that exist in India, the most far-reaching in terms of coverage as well as public expenditure on subsidy is the PDS.

PDS is operated under the joint responsibility of the Central and the State Governments in India. The operational responsibility includes identification of eligible families, issue of Ration Cards, allocation of food and non-food items and supervision of the functioning of Fair Price Shops (FPSs) etc. and it is rested with the State Governments. Under the PDS, presently the commodities namely wheat, rice, sugar and kerosene are being allocated to the States/UTs for distribution. Some States/UTs also distribute additional items of mass consumption through the PDS outlets such as pulses, edible oils, iodized salt, spices, etc. PDS provides rationed amounts of basic food and non-food items at subsidized prices to consumers through a network of fair price shops.

Background

Public distribution was initially introduced in 1939 as a war-time rationing measure. The British Government introduced it in Bombay and later extended it to six other cities and a few other regions. The drought and food shortages of the mid-sixties highlighted the need for strengthening and continuing with a system of food distribution and the PDS was made a universal scheme in the 1970s. As the national agricultural production had grown in the aftermath of Green Revolution, the outreach of PDS was extended to tribal blocks and areas of high incidence of poverty in the 1970s and 1980s. PDS, till 1992, was a general entitlement scheme for all consumers without any specific target.

The Revamped Public Distribution System (RPDS) was launched in June 1992 in 1775 blocks throughout the country. The area specific programmes such as the Drought Prone Area Programme (DPAP), Integrated Tribal Development Project (ITDP), Desert Development Programme (DDP) and Designated Hill Areas (DHAs) were identified in consultation with State Governments for special focus to improve the PDS infrastructure. Food grains for distribution in RPDS areas were issued to the States at 50 paisa below the Central Issue Price. The scale of issue was up to 20 kg per card. In 1997, following the advice given in an influential World Bank document (World Bank, 1996), the Government of India introduced the TPDS in order to curtail the food subsidy (GoI, 1997). As a result, RPDS changed to TPDS.

The Targeted Public Distribution System (TPDS) was introduced with effect from June, 1997. The policy initiated targeting households on the basis of an income criterion, that is, the income poverty line was used to demarcate 'poor' and 'non-poor' households. The TPDS differs from earlier variants of the PDS in certain key respects. The TPDS was long lasting, i.e. for more than one and a half decade in India and didn't change till 2013.

In 2013, The National Food Security Act, 2013 (NFSA) was notified. The coverage, entitlements of food grains, etc. under the NFSA, 2013 have undergone changes as compared to those under the existing TPDS referred above. NFSA, 2013 *inter alia* provides for coverage of up to 75 per cent of the rural population and up to 50 per cent of the urban population in each state of India. Under the NFSA, 2013, the priority households are entitled to receive food grains at the rate of 5 kg per person per month at the issue prices of Rs. 3.00, Rs. 2.00 and Rs. 1.00 per kg for rice, wheat and coarse grains respectively. The existing AAY households, however, will continue to receive 35 kg of food grains per households per month (GoI 2014) (*see* Box 2.1).

Box 2.1: SALIENT FEATURES OF THE NATIONAL FOOD SECURITY ACT, 2013

- *Coverage and entitlement under TPDS:* Up to 75% of the rural population and 50% of the urban population will be covered under TPDS, with uniform entitlement of 5 kg per person per month. However, since AAY households constitute poorest of the poor, and are presently entitled to 35 kg per household per month, entitlement of existing AAY households will be protected at 35 kg per household per month.
- *State-wise coverage:* Corresponding to the all-India coverage of 75% and 50% in the rural and urban areas, State-wise coverage will be determined by the Central Government. Planning Commission has determined the State-wise coverage by using the NSS Household Consumption Survey data for 2011-12 and also provided the State-wise "inclusion ratios". In case, any State's allocation under the Act is lower than their current allocation, it will be protected up to the level of average offtake during last three years, at prices to be determined by the Central Government.
- *Subsidised prices under TPDS and their revision:* Foodgrains under TPDS will be made available at subsidised prices of Rs. 3/2/1 per kg for rice, wheat and coarse grains for a period of three years from the date of commencement of the Act. Thereafter prices will be suitably linked to Minimum Support Price (MSP).
- *Nutritional Support to women and children:* Pregnant women and lactating mothers and children in the age group of 6 months to 14 years will be entitled to meals as per prescribed nutritional norms under Integrated Child Development Services (ICDS) and Mid-Day Meal (MDM) schemes. Higher nutritional norms have been prescribed for malnourished children up to 6 years of age.
- *Maternity Benefit:* Pregnant women and lactating mothers will also be entitled to receive maternity benefit of not less than Rs. 6,000.
- *Women Empowerment:* Eldest woman of the household of age 18 years or above to be the head of the household for the purpose of issuing of ration cards.
- *Grievance Redressal Mechanism:* Grievance redressal mechanism at the District and State levels. States will have the flexibility to use the existing machinery or set up separate mechanism.
- *Cost of intra-State transportation & handling of foodgrains and FPS Dealers' margin:* Central Government will provide assistance to States in meeting the expenditure incurred by them on transportation of foodgrains within the State, its handling and FPS dealers' margin as per norms to be devised for this purpose.
- *Transparency and Accountability:* Provisions have been made for disclosure of records relating to PDS, social audits and setting up of Vigilance Committees in order to ensure transparency and accountability.
- *Food Security Allowance:* Provision for food security allowance to entitled beneficiaries in case of non-supply of entitled foodgrains or meals.
- *Penalty:* Provision for penalty on public servant or authority, to be imposed by the State Food Commission, in case of failure to comply with the relief recommended by the District Grievance Redressal Officer.

Source: GoI (2014).

The PDS in India since its inception is summed up in four phases (Swaminathan (2000). The *first phase* was from its origins to 1960, a period when the system was expanded to other cities. During the first phase, distribution through the PDS was generally dependent on imports of foodgrains. The *second phase*, from 1960 to 1978, was one which saw major organizational changes. Specifically, in response to the food crisis of the mid-1960s, the Government of India took a holistic approach to food security, and set up the Agricultural Prices Commission and the Food Corporation of India in order to strengthen domestic procurement and storage. The *third phase*, from 1978 to 1991, was marked by large-scale expansion of the PDS, supported by domestic procurement and stocks. The *fourth phase*, from 1991 to the present, is one in which the policy of universal PDS has been replaced by a targeted policy in line with the objectives of economic liberalization. Thus, over the entire period, the PDS grew from a rationing scheme in selected cities to a national universal programme of food distribution and then to a policy targeted at the income-poor (Swaminathan 2008). Along with these four phases, the new phase (*fifth phase*) of PDS was observed in India after the enactment of National Food Security Bill, 2013. The TPDS is now being transformed into a legal entitlement-based household and individual food security system.

Objectives

Historically, the objectives of the PDS have been:

- Maintaining price stability,
- Provisioning subsidized foodgrains to poor households,
- Increasing the welfare facilities for the poor (by providing access to basic foods at reasonable prices to the vulnerable population),
- Rationing during situations of scarcity, and
- Keeping a check on private trade of foodgrains.

These objectives are also important today as it was in the past. Maintaining price stability is crucial in the post-liberalization period when private traders have been given a freer hand and when international price fluctuations can more easily affect domestic prices. In the context of widespread malnutrition and inflation in food prices, access to basic foods at reasonable prices remains an important policy intervention.

Target Groups

The most distinctive feature of the TPDS in relation to previous policy in India is the introduction of targeting, specifically, the division of the entire population into below-poverty line (BPL) and above poverty line (APL) categories, based on the poverty line defined by the Planning Commission. In TPDS these two groups are treated differently in terms of quantities and prices. Government of India introduced the Antyodaya Anna Yojana (AAY) as a sub-scheme to benefit the poorest of the poor at very low cost who does not get two square meals a day. In addition to this, Annapurna is centrally sponsored scheme introduced to provide food security for the senior citizens of 65 years of age or above having no or little income.

Provision of Benefits

Dual (or manifold) price is the key distinguishing feature of TPDS. The TPDS now has dual central issue prices: prices for BPL consumers and prices for APL consumers. A third price, introduced in 2001, is for beneficiaries of the Antyodaya Scheme (a scheme for the 'poorest of the poor', in which foodgrains are distributed with an additional subsidy). In March 2000, a major policy change occurred when it was announced in the budget that central issue prices—i.e. prices at which the Food Corporation of India (FCI) sells grain for the PDS to State governments—will be set at half the 'economic cost' incurred by the FCI for BPL households and at the full 'economic cost' for APL households. In short, there was to be no subsidy for APL households. The provisional benefits can be provided in three sub-categories (Figure 2.1):

- *APL:* The above poverty level people purchased foodgrains from fair price shop (FPS) as per their entitlement at the subsidized rates of Rs. 6.10 per kg. and Rs. 8.30 per kg. for wheat and rice respectively. It involves subsidy of more than Rs. 9 per kg. on wheat and Rs. 12 per kg. on rice. But many APL families did not lift their PDS ration from FPS. This foodgrains were diverted into black market. So, Government of India abolished the subsidy of APL families with the introduction of TPDS in 1997.
- *BPL:* Beneficiary (BPL card holder) gets foodgrains at subsidized rate of Rs. 4.65 per kg. for wheat and Rs. 6.15 per kg for rice. The kerosene and sugar are also available for them at subsidized price. The scheme ensures 35 kg of food-grains per family per month since April 2002.

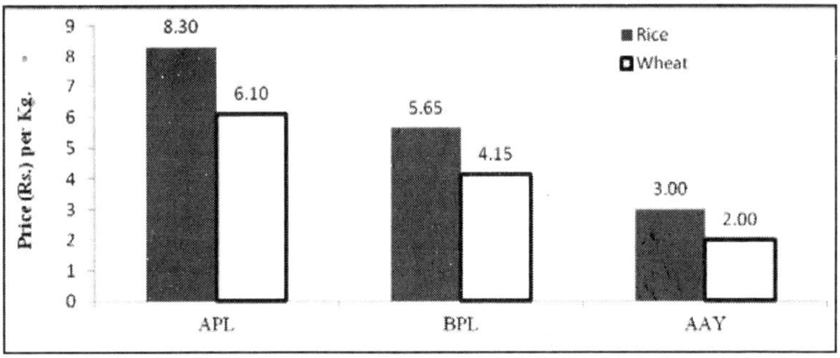

Fig. 2.1: The Central Issue Price (CIP) of Foodgrains being supplied under TPDS

- *AAY:* Beneficiary gets foodgrains at a highly subsidized rate of Rs. 2 per kg. for wheat and Rs. 3 per kg for rice. The kerosene and sugar are also available for them at subsidized cost. The scheme ensures 35 kg of food-grains per family per month since April 2002.
- *Annapurna Scheme:* This scheme aimed at providing food security to meet the requirement of those senior citizens who, though eligible, have remained uncovered under the NOAPS. Under the Annapurna Scheme 10 kgs of foodgrains per month were provided free of cost to the beneficiaries.

Fund Allocation

The important feature of the Targeted PDS is that it has changed center-state responsibilities with respect to entitlements and allocations to the PDS. PDS is designed and managed by State Governments, and they differ with respect to entitlements, the commodities offered, the retail price (state issue price) and so on. In the past, the State Governments demanded certain allocation from the Central pool, and based on certain factors, most importantly, past utilization and the requirements of statutory rationing, the Central Government allocated grain and other commodities to States for their public distribution systems. With the TPDS, the size of the BPL population and the entitlements for the BPL population are decided by the Central Government. And the allocations and additional allocations for BPL and APL populations are decided somewhat arbitrarily based on past utilization and demands from States (Swaminathan 2008).

Coverage

The programme is spread all over the country and entitled all section of the people but due to increasing pressure of budget deficit, government introduced the TPDS. Now all BPL households are covered under TPDS. Total numbers of BPL families (w.e.f. 1.12.2000) in the country come to 652.03 lakh as against 596.23 lakh families originally estimated when TPDS was introduced in June, 1997 (GoI 2014). The number of BPL families and the estimated number of AAY families across states in India are given in Table 2.3. Most of the states have identified the AAY families and issued the ration card. The only exception is West Bengal—out of 19.86 lakhs estimates AAY families only 14.8 lakh families have been identified and were issued the ration card till March 2013. There was a significant gap in West Bengal between identification and issue of AAY entitlement cards (Table 2.3).

The total offtake and allotment of Rice and Wheat under TPDS are shown in Table 2.4 and Table 2.5 respectively. The offtake of foodgrains and their allotment widely varied across states but for BPL and AAY, the allotment of foodgrains marginally lag behind the offtake of the state. In some states, the allotment is more than the offtake.

Impact Study

Dev and Suryanaryana (1991) made an evaluation of the performance of PDS on the basis of the NSSO data. Their findings showed that the relative dependence on the PDS was much higher in rural areas as compared to that of urban areas. It may be noted that although the objective of the PDS is to help vulnerable sections of the society, the rich are getting about 20 to 50 per cent of their purchases from the PDS particularly for commodities like rice, sugar and kerosene. Taking primary data, Khera (2008) showed that in Rajasthan only about one-third households have accessed to the PDS.

TPDS did improve targeting but not significantly. While the targeting halved the richest quintile's access to PDS, the poorest quintile's access did not improve much (Himanshu and Sen 2011). This may in part be due to exclusion and inclusion errors, i.e., many poor people are not covered and many covered are not poor. There is no definitive information on the extent of mis-targeting. According to World Bank (2011) estimates, almost half the poor are identified as non-poor and almost half the non-poor as poor. Another estimate (MSSRF 2008) indicates that about 18 per cent of BPL households do not have ration cards.

Table 2.3: Number of BPL and APL Households (in Lakhs) across States in India (as on 31.03.2013)

States	No. of BPL families	Estimated No. of AAY Families	Families Identified & Ration Card Issued	Gap of Ration card Issued
Andhra Pradesh	40.63	15.58	15.58	0.00
Arunachal Pradesh	0.99	0.38	0.38	0.00
Assam	18.36	7.04	7.04	0.00
Bihar	65.23	25.01	25.01	0.00
Chhattisgarh	18.75	7.19	7.19	0.00
Delhi	4.09	1.57	1.04	0.53
Goa	0.48	0.18	0.15	0.04
Gujarat	21.20	8.13	8.10	0.03
Haryana	7.89	3.03	2.68	0.35
Himachal Pradesh	5.14	1.97	1.97	0.00
Jammu & Kashmir	7.36	2.82	2.56	0.27
Jharkhand	23.94	9.18	9.18	0.00
Karnataka	31.29	12.00	11.38	0.62
Kerala	15.54	5.96	5.96	0.00
Madhya Pradesh	41.25	15.82	15.82	0.00
Maharashtra	65.34	25.05	24.85	0.20
Manipur	1.66	0.64	0.64	0.00
Meghalaya	1.83	0.70	0.70	0.00
Mizoram	0.68	0.26	0.26	0.00
Nagaland	1.24	0.48	0.48	0.00
Orissa	32.98	12.65	12.53	0.11
Punjab	4.68	1.79	1.79	0.00
Rajasthan	24.31	9.32	9.32	0.00
Sikkim	0.43	0.17	0.17	0.00
Tamil Nadu	48.63	18.65	18.65	0.00
Tripura	2.95	1.13	1.13	0.00
Uttar Pradesh	106.79	40.95	40.95	0.00
Uttarakhand	4.98	1.91	1.91	0.00
West Bengal	51.79	19.86	14.80	5.06
TOTAL	**649.75**	**249.39**	**242.18**	**7.20**

Sources: Government of India, Ministry of Consumer Affairs, Dept. of Food and Public Distribution, http://dfpd.nic.in/?q=node/101 dated 22.05.2014.

Leakages, the most important drawback of TPDS, over the period 1993-94 to 2004-05 almost doubled (Khera 2011a; Himanshu and Sen 2011). As much as 58 per cent of subsidized grains failed to reach the target group (Planning Commission 2005). This high leakage comprised an estimated 21 per cent diversion to APL households and 36 per cent siphoned off the supply chain (*ibid.*). Inefficiency, corruption and leakages

Table 2.4: Allocation and Offtake of Rice (in thousand tons) under TPDS across States in India, 2012-13

States	Allotment				% Offtake			
	BPL	AAY	APL	TOTAL	BPL	AAY	APL	TOTAL
(1)	(2)	(3)	(4)	(5)	(6)	(7)	(8)	(9)
Andhra Pradesh	1052.1	654.3	2073.0	3779.4	100.2	98.4	67.7	82.0
Arunachal Pradesh	22.5	16.0	53.7	92.1	99.3	99.2	96.8	97.8
Assam	475.2	295.7	721.9	1492.8	99.2	99.3	93.1	96.3
Bihar	1253.8	630.3	1.3	1885.4	82.6	95.6	12.5	86.9
Chhattisgarh	427.9	301.9	306.5	1036.4	100.5	100.0	96.7	99.2
Delhi	33.2	18.0	97.5	148.7	98.7	71.3	88.3	88.6
Goa	5.5	6.1	41.9	53.6	100.6	100.0	99.8	99.9
Gujarat	173.8	155.6	0.0	329.4	100.0	96.3	0.0	98.3
Haryana	0.0	0.0	0.0	0.0	0.0	0.0	0.0	0.0
Himachal Pradesh	57.1	35.4	102.8	195.3	98.1	99.7	99.2	99.0
Jammu & Kashmir	151.5	86.2	295.4	533.2	101.7	100.9	98.8	99.9
Jharkhand	620.0	385.5	176.6	1182.1	95.4	96.2	8.3	82.6
Karnataka	691.4	395.0	1337.9	2424.3	97.5	91.1	71.7	82.2
Kerala	318.8	250.3	618.2	1187.2	99.8	99.9	100.6	100.2
Madhya Pradesh	213.6	104.1	0.0	317.7	158.0	111.8	0.0	142.8
Maharashtra	824.1	510.2	553.4	1887.6	94.9	93.9	57.8	83.8
Manipur	41.7	26.7	69.4	137.9	101.0	99.9	103.7	102.2
Meghalaya	47.4	29.5	84.5	161.4	100.0	99.8	100.5	100.2
Mizoram	17.6	10.9	34.1	62.7	95.2	93.1	95.2	94.8
Nagaland	25.9	16.1	52.3	94.3	109.4	114.1	104.1	107.3
Orissa	1165.6	531.1	35.2	1731.9	100.5	97.6	45.6	98.5

(*Contd.*)

Table 2.4: *(Contd.)*

(1)	(2)	(3)	(4)	(5)	(6)	(7)	(8)	(9)
Punjab	0.0	0.0	0.0	0.0	0.0	0.0	0.0	0.0
Rajasthan	0.0	0.0	0.0	0.0	0.0	0.0	0.0	0.0
Sikkim	11.3	6.9	23.1	41.3	107.9	99.6	99.6	101.9
Tamil Nadu	1259.2	783.1	1515.1	3557.4	101.5	99.6	98.0	99.6
Tripura	76.4	47.5	152.7	276.6	97.5	100.7	91.5	94.7
Uttar Pradesh	1567.4	1153.6	0.0	2721.0	100.5	98.0	0.0	99.5
Uttarakhand	85.5	56.2	144.2	285.9	100.4	99.6	89.7	94.8
West Bengal	956.5	349.1	125.6	1431.1	103.0	98.6	84.3	100.3
TOTAL	11610.8	6874.2	8655.3	27140.3	99.0	97.6	81.2	93.0

Sources: As in Table 2.3.

Table 2.5: Allocation and Offtake of Wheat (in thousand tons) under TPDS across States in India, 2012-13

States/UT's	*Allotment*				*% Offtake*			
	BPL	AAY	APL	TOTAL	BPL	AAY	APL	TOTAL
Andhra Pradesh	0.0	0.0	43.5	43.5	0.0	0.0	67.9	68.0
Arunachal Pradesh	3.1	0.0	6.4	9.4	89.0	0.0	86.7	87.4
Assam	0.0	0.0	394.1	394.1	0.0	0.0	100.0	100.0
Bihar	435.6	420.2	962.7	1818.5	94.2	97.5	18.8	55.0
Chhattisgarh	57.8	0.0	150.0	207.8	89.3	0.0	65.6	72.2
Delhi	75.5	45.1	329.7	450.3	104.6	71.8	98.2	96.6
Goa	0.0	0.0	9.5	9.5	0.0	0.0	99.3	99.3
Gujarat	376.5	184.5	1194.7	1755.7	90.6	91.1	36.2	53.6
Haryana	208.6	122.8	424.6	756.0	104.1	98.9	29.9	61.6
Himachal Pradesh	76.1	47.3	209.3	332.6	96.3	100.9	100.6	99.7
Jammu & Kashmir	50.2	21.1	152.3	223.6	96.2	97.8	104.3	101.9
Jharkhand	0.0	0.0	176.6	176.6	0.0	0.0	0.4	0.4
Karnataka	145.1	82.9	154.7	382.6	99.9	89.6	59.6	81.4
Kerala	83.6	0.0	201.9	285.5	98.7	0.0	99.4	99.2
Madhya Pradesh	854.5	560.2	1004.0	2418.7	190.4	124.6	77.0	128.1
Maharashtra	885.3	524.7	1521.4	2931.4	93.6	89.6	55.5	73.1
Manipur	1.3	0.0	31.8	33.1	100.0	0.0	96.0	96.2
Meghalaya	0.0	0.0	27.2	27.2	0.0	0.0	102.5	102.5
Mizoram	0.0	0.0	7.5	7.5	0.0	0.0	95.0	95.0
Nagaland	6.2	3.9	22.5	32.6	108.3	108.3	106.2	106.9
Orissa	0.0	0.0	462.4	462.4	0.0	0.0	89.6	89.6
Punjab	121.2	75.4	631.4	828.0	87.1	67.7	72.4	74.2

(Contd.)

Table 2.5: (*Contd.*)

States/UT's	*Allotment*				*% Offtake*			
	BPL	AAY	APL	TOTAL	BPL	AAY	APL	TOTAL
Rajasthan	629.5	391.5	1158.5	2179.5	98.9	97.7	98.8	98.6
Sikkim	0.0	0.0	3.0	3.0	0.0	0.0	100.0	100.0
Tamil Nadu	0.0	0.0	165.4	165.4	0.0	0.0	55.7	55.7
Tripura	0.0	0.0	28.2	28.2	0.0	0.0	96.8	96.8
Uttar Pradesh	1198.3	565.9	2783.3	4547.6	101.5	100.2	74.6	84.9
Uttarakhand	43.5	24.0	264.6	332.1	99.6	98.8	97.6	98.0
West Bengal	597.1	272.6	1556.4	2426.1	95.2	86.3	88.5	89.9
TOTAL	**5850.5**	**3342.4**	**14135.4**	**23328.2**	**110.6**	**98.9**	**69.8**	**84.2**

Sources: As in Table 2.3.

became rampant, often resulting in uncertain and irregular availability of food. Poor northern and eastern states which performed badly under universal PDS continue to perform badly under TPDS with very low per capita PDS purchase and highest leakage due to dysfunctional delivery systems. The poor in these states clearly are not benefitting. In Bihar, for example, households in the bottom quintile purchased only 2 per cent of the per capita foodgrains consumption through PDS as compared to 68 per cent in Karnataka and 50 per cent in Tamil Nadu (Dev and Sharma 2010). By 2009-10, the diversion of foodgrains declined to an estimated 41 per cent at the national level, reflecting an improvement in almost all states, but particularly so in certain states, such as Andhra Pradesh, Jharkhand, and Orissa (Dreze and Khera 2011). A few states, such as Tamil Nadu and Chhattisgarh pioneered reforms to improve access and reduce leakages. TPDS did not address nutritional security as there was a continued emphasis on rice and wheat without diversification into coarse cereals, pulses and edible oils (IRDR 2013).

Himanshu (2013) found a reversal of the trend of worsening PDS access by the poor after the introduction of the TPDS. The TPDS performs poorly not only in terms of its stated objective of better access to subsidized food for poor households, but also in terms of programme implementation, which is marked by leakages and corruption. Precisely because of dissatisfaction with the TPDS, many state governments in India (initially implemented only in richer states such as Tamil Nadu and Andhra Pradesh, have been adopted by poorer states such as Chhattisgarh and Orissa) have undertaken state-specific measures of expanding coverage to universal or quasi-universal access, along with further subsidies to provide cheap foodgrains. During the recent years, West Bengal has also adopted state specific measures to extent the coverage of subsidized food grains. In backward regions of West Bengal, particularly in Jangal Mahal, the state government has extended the universal access of cheap foodgrains.

2.3 Programmes to Improve the Health Status

2.3.1 Rural Primary Health Care

Introduction

The health care system in India was a three-tier structure to provide health care services to her people. The first tire, known as primary tire, has been developed to provide health care services to the vast majority of rural people. The primary tire comprises three types of health care institutions: Sub Centre, Primary Health Centre (PHC) and Community Health Centre (CHC). The rural health care infrastructure has been developed to provide primary health care services through a network of integrated health and family welfare delivery system (Majumder *et al.* 2004).

Background

As early as 1928, Government of Mysore established the first health unit in India at Mandya. Establishment of health centres at Nazafgarh, Singur, Poonamallie, Trivandrum, Lucknow and at other places in collaboration with Rockefeller Foundation and Government of India between 1931 to 1939 was an important landmark in the history of health care delivery system.

In 1946, Bhore Committee recommended establishment of primary and secondary health units under short- and long-term programme. In 1948, the West Bengal Government started their scheme of having a 10 bedded health centre at the Union and a 50 bedded health centre at each Thana (an area covered by Police Station), to serve a population of 10,000 and 1,00,000 respectively. Later on, it was observed that the state of West Bengal was one of the earliest states to implement the recommendation by introducing Primary Health Centre units in a block with 3-5 subsidiary health centres for 60 to 80 thousand population to cover entire state based on the Bhore Committee recommendation. Late Chief Minister of West Bengal, Dr. B.C. Roy, initiated these ideas. This was considered later on by Government of India as CHC for 100,000 and PHC for 30,000 population. In 1952, the Planning Commission gave the standard health plan of 6 bedded health centre at each block and a 40 bedded health centre, at the head quarter of each Community Development Project Area, which was later on modified (Roy *et al.* 2011).

To provide the better-quality health services to rural people, Government of India introduced National Rural Health Mission (NRHM) on 12th April, 2005 for a period of seven years (2005-2012). In 2013, the programme was renamed as National Health Mission (NHM) and covers both rural and urban areas.

Objectives

The objectives of the programme are to provide accessible, affordable, effective, acccuntable and reliable health care to all citizens, and in particular, to the poorer and vulnerable sections of the population. In specific, it has targeted for reduction of infant and maternal mortality rate (along with other mortality rate), prevention of communicable and non-communicable diseases etc.

Target Groups

All rural people constitute the target group of the programme namely Rural Primary Health Centre, especially the women, children and the poor residing in rural areas. The programme was introduced mainly to facilitate the poor BPL families who are unable to entitle the medical benefit.

Provision of Benefits

The thrust of the rural health centres is on establishing a fully functional, community owned, decentralized health delivery system with inter-sectoral convergence at all levels. From the disease centric approach, the NRHM attempts to shift the focus to a functional health system. The key features to achieve the goals of the NRHM include making the public health delivery system fully functional and accountable to the community, human resources management, community involvement, decentralization, rigorous monitoring and evaluation against standards, convergence of health and related programmes form village level upwards, innovations and flexible financing and also interventions for improving the health indictors. The targets set to be achieved under the NRHM by the end of the Mission (2012) are as follows:

- IMR to be reduced to 30/1000 live births.
- Maternal Mortality to be reduced to 100/1,00,000 births.
- TFR to be reduced to 2.1.
- Malaria Mortality Reduction Rate—50 per cent up to 2010, additional 10 per cent by 2012.
- Kala Azar Mortality Reduction Rate—100 per cent by 2010 and sustaining elimination until 2012.
- Filaria/ Microfilaria Reduction Rate—70 per cent by 2010, 80 per cent by 2012 and elimination by 2015.
- Dengue mortality reduction rate—50 per cent by 2010 and sustaining at that level until 2012.

- Cataract operations increasing to 46 lakhs.
- Leprosy Prevalence Rate to reduce from 1.0 per 10,000 in 2005 to less than 1 per 10.000 thereafter.
- Tuberculosis DOTS series—maintain 85 per cent cure rate through entire Mission period and also sustain planned case detection rate.
- Upgrading all Community Health Centres to Indian Public Health Standards.
- Increase utilization of First Referral Units from bed occupancy by referred cases of less than 20 per cent to over 75 per cent.
- Engaging 4,00,000 female Accredited Social Health Activists (ASHAs).

Rural Primary Health Care System extends all sorts of benefits to achieve the goal of the Mission.

Fund Allocation

Annual allocation is communicated to each state by the Ministry of Health & Family Welfare, GoI for preparing plan for the year. There are three streams of funding; *one* for the Reproductive and Child Health (RCH) Programme related services, the *second* one is for meeting all critical gap through a flexible fund, which also have some specific components and the *third* one is for controlling diseases through various national programmes. For district level activities in every sector there should be a District Health Plan to be approved by the Zila Parishad and the District Plan should be based on the Block Plans so that needs felt at those levels are reflected in the District Plan. The specific components under the NRHM Flexible component includes untied fund for all health facilities—Rs. 10,000 per Sub Centre, Rs. 25,000 per PHC and Rs. 50,000 per PHC. For proper maintenance of the facilities, fund is allocated at fixed rates to each type of hospitals, which is Rs. 10,000 for Sub Centre, Rs. 50,000 for PHC and Rs. 1.0 lakh for PHC. The other important component is the fund for the Rogi Kalyan Samiti (RKS), which is formed for each hospital. Allocation under NRHM for West Bengal for the year 2011-12 was Rs. 1246.68 crore of which the GoI share of RCH component and the Flexible component were Rs. 399.37 crore and Rs. 358.93 crore respectively. State share of the total allocation mentioned above is 15 per cent and therefore, the state should make full use of the entire allocation. However, West Bengal has not been able to spend the entire allocation in any of the years. One immediate task is to ensure full absorption of fund available under NRHM.

The Centre was set to earmark a whopping Rs. 1,36,147 crore for the health sector in the Eleventh Five Year Plan out of which Rs. 89,478 crores were spent on the flagship NRHM scheme. This represents almost three times hike for the programmes covered under the NRHM scheme. The Centre had earmarked only Rs. 28,338.19 crore for these during the Tenth Five Year Plan. In view of the striking deficit in health infrastructure in the country, the Centre has decided to allocate Rs. 2,780 crores for the up-gradation of district hospitals, and Rs. 6,035.32 crore for the redevelopment of other mega hospitals between 2007 and 2012 (www.nrhm.nic.in).

The spending in the health sector has been continually increasing in all states of India. Over the last ten years, in West Bengal the health budget has doubled. The increase in budget (On-Budget funds) in 2010-11 over that in 2009-10 has been by Rs. 254 crores. If along with the On-Budget funds, Off-Budget funds are taken into account, then the allocation of total budget is found to have increased by 30 per cent in 2010-11 over than in 2009-10. The drug budget has also raised from Rs. 94 crores in 2002-06 to Rs. 151.24 crore in 2010-11, significantly an increase by 60 per cent. Under NRHM, the expenditure in West Bengal increased 68 per cent (549.57 crore in 2010-11 against 327.98 crore in 2009-10).

Coverage

Rural Health Centres cover the entire country. Under NRHM the 18 high focus States are Uttar Pradesh, Bihar, Rajasthan, Madhya Pradesh, Orissa, Uttaranchal, Jharkhand, Chhattisgarh, Assam, Sikkim, Arunachal Pradesh, Manipur, Meghalaya, Tripura, Nagaland, Mizoram, Himachal Pradesh and Jammu & Kashmir. Government of India would provide funding for key components in these 18 high focus States. Other States would fund interventions like ASHA, Programme Management Unit (PMU), and up-gradation of Sub Centre, PHC, CHC through Integrated Financial Envelope.

Impact Study

Both the allocation of budget and percentage of budget utilization increases over the years. The introduction of ASHA is a milestone in the arena of rural health service. The ASHA programme is an important instrument of community outreach under NRHM. ASHAs are accountable to panchayats and act as an interface between communities and the public health system. They are supposed to create awareness on obstetric and child rearing services through home visits and counselling. The health service has come to the door step of the rural people. The array of service increases year after year. Yet rural health system is not free from criticism. Roy *et al.* (2011) has shown that increase in user fees in health care in government sector make the poor face back to government health services. Their observation revealed that 25.89 per cent utilized government health facilities i.e., Sub Centre, PHC and CHC, followed by private practitioners (18.3%) and Quacks or unqualified practitioners (19.64%). As per their study, some people are reluctant to get government medical service due to dissatisfactory service (25.04%), high cost (38.6%), long waiting (30.77%), and non-availability of medicines (23.08%) among the respondent. Their study reveals that as education increases people are likely to avoid public health facilities for reproductive health related services. This was due to poor quality of services provided at the health centres. Increasing cost of medical care has emerged as the second biggest cause of rural indebtedness in India. A user fee at point of service delivery is now common even at the basic primary health care level (Roy *et al.* 2011).

The rural health service in West Bengal has developed over the years. Now a days, Rural Health Service has got the maturity than earlier. The admission of the indoor and outdoor patient in the Rural Hospitals (RH) have increased from 4,13,594 in 2004 to 5,33,709 and 5,95,643 respectively in 2009 and 2011. The proportion of institutional delivery has registered an increase from 56.3 per cent in 2004 to 60.2 per cent in 2009 and further to 71 per cent in 2010-11. The full immunization coverage for children between 12 and 13 months has also registered increase over the period. The coverage reported 75.8 per cent in DLHS-3 (2007-08) compared to 50.3 per cent reported in DLHS-2 (2002-04). Fully immunized children in 2010-11 were 70.45 per cent. There was a significant decrease in reported number of diarrheal and malarial deaths over years in West Bengal. The diarrheal death reported during 2009 was 541 and 247 in 2010-11. For malaria the death reported during 2010-11 was 47, compared to 74 in 2009. There was a significant reduction in maternal mortality from 266 (SSR 1996-97) to 145 (RGI report 2007-09). The infant mortality rate in West Bengal was 33 as against the country's average of 51 in 2010-11. The state was in fourth position after Kerala (12), Tamil Nadu (31) and Maharashtra (33). In 2010-11 about

38.26 lakh patients of those GPs where there were no health care facilities or no Allopathic doctors who were engaged in GPs were treated in 48,903 Gram Panchayat (GP) camps on fixed day basis. In 2010-11, 44,815 ASHA were engaged at village level (GoWB 2011).

Rural Health Statistics in India (2012) revealed that there was a lack of doctors and nurses in PHCs and CHCs. For example, in West Bengal, the deficit was 1,168 and 2,731 for doctors and nurses respectively. There is also lack of ASHA worker. Their performance on community level counselling on child rearing and care has reportedly been poor (Planning Commission 2011e). ASHAs lack the knowledge needed to fulfil their roles and training was not standardized across states (Bajpai and Dholakia 2011; Planning Commission 2013a). The existing workers need more training to cater better service. In most of the cases drug kits are not supplied to the ASHAs. The 24 hours delivery system cannot be introduced in all PHCs in the districts. Districts health units were not able to utilize fund. On the whole, the rural healthcare system is facing the problems of (a) poor accountability of healthcare providers, (b) inadequate infrastructure and human resources, (c) predominant unregulated private providers and (d) financial burden of healthcare on households (IRDR 2013).

2.3.2 Janani Suraksha Yojana (JSY)

Introduction

Janani Suraksha Yojana (JSY) is an ambitious scheme launched under the NRHM, the Government of India's flagship health programme, while States implemented it in urban as well as rural areas. The scheme is a safe motherhood intervention and seeks to reduce maternal and neo-natal mortality by promoting institutional delivery, i.e. by providing a cash incentive to mothers and get them to deliver their babies in a health facility. There is also the provision for cost reimbursement for transport and incentives to ASHAs for encouraging mothers to go for institutional delivery. The scheme is fully sponsored by the Central Government and is implemented in all States and Union Territories (UTs), with special focus on low-performing states. There is provision for roping in the private sector by giving accreditation to willing private hospitals/nursing homes for providing delivery services.

Background

The United Nations Millennium Summit adopted the Millennium

Development Goals (MDGs) as a response to the world's main development challenges. One of the MDGs aims at reducing Maternal Mortality Ratio (MMR) by three quarters between 1990 and 2015. The MMR, defined as number of maternal deaths per 1,00,000 live births, declined from 398 in 1997-98 to 301 in 2001-03 in India, as per the estimates provided by Sample Registration System (SRS).

In order to reduce the maternal and infant mortality, JSY replaces the National Maternity Benefit Scheme under the NRHM. The JSY, launched on 12th April, 2005, is being implemented in all states and UTs with special focus on low performing states. The programme is being implemented to promote institutional deliveries so that skilled attendance at birth is available and women and new born can be saved from pregnancy related deaths. The criterion and target group remain almost same as National Maternity Benefit Scheme (MoHFW 2006).

Objectives

The main objectives of JSY are:

- To reduce overall maternal mortality ratio.
- To reduce infant mortality rate.
- To increase institutional deliveries.
- To provide cash incentives for women to deliver in a government or accredited private medical facility.

Targeted Group

All BPL pregnant women who are 19 years or above in age are eligible for this scheme. This scheme is eligible up to two live births. Those women who hold a BPL card or enlisted under Antyodaya Yojana or Pavement dwellers will also be entitled for the scheme. Those certified as BPL by the concerned Commissioner/Councillor/MLA/MP/PRI elected member are also entitled for the scheme.

Initially, only BPL women over 19 were eligible for their first two live births. Because these criteria may deny benefits to the most vulnerable women, in 2006, the eligibility criteria were relaxed. Now any woman in low performing states is eligible regardless of poverty status, number of births and age, and monetary incentives have been enhanced. Women delivering at home with the assistance of skilled personnel are also entitled to cash incentive.

Provision of Benefits

The initiative entitles all pregnant women delivering in public health institutions to absolutely free and no-expense delivery, including caesarean section. The entitlements include free drugs and consumables, free diet up to 3 days during normal delivery and up to 7 days for caesarean section, free diagnostics, and free blood wherever required. This initiative also provides for free transport from home to institution, between facilities in case of a referral and drop back home. Similar entitlements have been put in place for all sick newborns accessing public health institutions for treatment till 30 days after birth. This has now been expanded to cover sick infants. It provides cash incentives for women to deliver in government or accredited private medical facility. The monetary assistance of this programme is shown in Table 2.6.

Table 2.6: Monetary Assistance in JSY by Region and Category of States

Category	*Rural Area*			*Urban Area*		
	Mother's Package	*ASHA's Package*	*Total*	*Mother's Package*	*ASHAs Package*	*Total*
Low Performing States (LPS)	1400	600	2000	1000	200	1200
High Performing States (HPS)	700	600	1300	600	200	800

Source: http://mohfw.nic.in.

Fund Allocation

The allocation increased over the years. The low performing states have got the higher share compared to the high performing states. The fund allocation of the Centre by divisions is shown in Table 2.7.

Coverage

The programme has been executed all over the country classifying the states into Low Performing States (LPS) and High Performing States (HPS) on the basis of institutional delivery rate, i.e. states having institutional delivery 25 per cent or less were termed as LPS and those which have institutional delivery rate more than 25 per cent were classified as HPS. Accordingly, eight states, namely Uttar Pradesh, Uttarakhand, Madhya Pradesh, Chhattisgarh, Bihar, Jharkhand, Rajasthan, Odisha and

Table 2.7: Centrally Allocated Fund (Rs. Crore) for JSY by the Categories of States in India, 2005-06 to 2013-14

Year	*India*	*High Focus-Non-NE*	*High Focus-NE*	*Non-High Focus-Large*	*Non-High Focus-Small & UT*
2005-06	4633.39	2285.89	405.35	1893.51	48.64
2006-07	6997.05	3362.45	801.81	2754.05	78.73
2007-08	9023.34	4390.43	1008.79	3517.24	106.89
2008-09	10192.24	4937.22	1022.68	4093.26	139.09
2009-10	11581.32	5515.75	1414.67	4481.77	169.12
2010-11	12923.28	6199.56	1445.39	5085.19	193.15
2011-12	14263.72	6930.43	1388.33	5735.27	209.69
2012-13	17030.68	8361.66	1727.46	6701.51	240.06
2013-14	18369.01	9410.35	1886.75	6830.89	241.02

Source: http://mohfw.nic.in/WriteReadData/l892s/file28-99526408.pdf.

the states of Assam as well as Jammu & Kashmir were classified as LPS. The remaining States were grouped into HPS.

The scheme is estimated to benefit more than 12 million pregnant women who access Government health facilities for their delivery. Moreover, it motivates those who still choose to deliver at their homes to opt for institutional deliveries.

The demand for institutional deliveries increases due to awareness of the people about the risk of maternal mortality. JSY beneficiaries increased very rapidly (Table 2.8).

Table 2.8: Number of Beneficiaries of JSY by the Categories of States in India, 2005-06 to 2013-14

Year	*India*	*High Focus-Non-NE*	*High Focus-NE*	*Non-High Focus-Large*	*Non-High Focus-Small & UT*
2005-06	738911	125140	23219	589599	953
2006-07	3158307	1448204	217311	1489534	3258
2007-08	7328501	4535824	361088	2417923	13666
2008-09	9036913	5874281	403543	2729344	29745
2009-10	10078275	6671656	469588	2908345	28686
2010-11	10696895	7319972	487451	2862867	26605
2011-12	10937383	7624954	513117	2771262	28050
2012-13	10657091	7406405	523802	2699407	27477
2013-14	10648487	7559299	544936	2524797	19455

Source: http://mohfw.nic.in/WriteReadData/l892s/file28-99526408.pdf

Impact Study

JSY has helped to increase institutional deliveries and improve child feeding practices (Iyengar *et al.*, 2009; Mazumdar *et al.*, 2011; Lim *et al.*, 2010). Inequities have declined as the effects have been greater among the less educated, poorer and social disadvantaged women and in low performing states (NHSRC 2011). The Maternal Mortality Rate (MMR) declined to 154 in 2008-09. A study in eight districts of low performing states found that most women received the monetary incentive at the facility itself, usually by cheque as recommended by guidelines, and only few had to pay bribes to receive the money (Dongre and Kapur 2013).

The maternal health conditions, especially in the high focus states (in NRHM) namely, Bihar, Madhya Pradesh, Orissa, Rajasthan and Uttar Pradesh continue to be unfavourable, resulting in higher MMR for the states, ranging from 303 in Orissa to 440 in Uttar Pradesh (Mode 2009). MoHFW and WHO (2009) also studied the performance of JSY in these five high focus states. The study revealed that percentage of JSY beneficiaries was higher in Madhya Pradesh and Orissa whereas in Uttar Pradesh it was low. Madhya Pradesh, Orissa and Rajasthan were able to provide maximum benefits to the SC/ST and OBC. One striking thing was that about 80 per cent of JSY beneficiaries did not get monetary benefit after delivery.

The view of JSY in respect of providing financial support for women in accessing institutions is also to be questioned. The National Health System Resource Centre (NHSRC) study documents an average out-of-pocket expenditure incurred of Rs. 1028 per delivery in an institution excluding transport costs. Assured referral transport systems like Janani Express Service were used only by 13 per cent of women to reach institutions. NGOs working in Jharkhand reported that the state has recently initiated the Mamta Vahan emergency transportation service, which is available only to bring women from their homes to the often ill-equipped PHC/CHC and not to the nearest appropriate health facility which may be a private hospital or in a neighbouring state. For women with complications, this leads to further delays, and has obvious life-threatening consequences. Reports from NGOs in different parts of India indicated that women have to visit the hospital many times before they can get the JSY money and they need to spend each time for travel, which discourages them further. In addition to incentivizing institutional deliveries, JSY attempts to disincentivize home deliveries. While the programme provides Rs. 500 as a financial package for women delivering at home, several states have stipulated additional conditions on eligibility: the woman should be over 19 years of age, only for the first two deliveries, possess a BPL card. It is well known that the poor, lower caste women, young women, and multiparous women are at higher risk for maternal mortality. It is also well known that in view of their social marginalization, and lack of decision-making power, these women are more likely to have difficulties in accessing institutions and to have a home delivery.

Narayanan *et al.*, (2008) pointed out that only around 8.4 per cent and 20.7 per cent of all eligible BPL women in Chhattisgarh and Maharashtra respectively got the JSY benefit in 2006-07. The NHSRC (2011) study documents that many of these women are not even counted. By excluding them from the programme, JSY loses a valuable opportunity to bring them into contact with the health system. The state also thus fails in its role to provide social security in terms of maternal health care to these marginalized groups. The conditionality of age is blind to the Indian reality that 44 per cent of the women in the age group 20 to 24 years were married before 18 years of age.

Vikram *et al.* (2013) conducted the study from December 2009 to November 2010 in the urban slums and resettlement colonies of the East and North East districts of Delhi (trans-Yamuna area) where the ASHAs were posted under NRHM. The awareness regarding JSY scheme was 62.3 per cent, of whom 72 per cent were not aware as they were eligible for monetary benefits under the scheme. Some of the beneficiaries were able to provide either BPL card or caste certificate of SC/ST, while some restricted to SC or ST women while majority of the eligible women did not have any proof of their belonging to SC, ST or BPL status. The constraint of age limits and certificate of BPL or SC/ST makes the programme non-universal.

2.3.3 Rashtriya Swasthya Bima Yojana (RSBY)

Introduction

Majority of the workers in India are unorganized workers and one of the major insecurities for workers in the unorganized sector is absence of health cover for them and their family members. Thus, with a view to provide health insurance cover to BPL workers in the unorganized sector and their families, the Central Government of India announced the Rashtriya Swasthya Bima Yojana (RSBY). Government of India introduced the Rashtriya Swasthya Bima Yojana or National Health

Insurance Programme in 2008 (GoI 2008). RSBY is uniquely mandated to cover the entire territory of India and all occupational groups. Eligibility for RSBY coverage, applies to all the BPL population, entails full premium subsidy, and the Government of India extended the same terms to certain APL groups.

Background

From the time of its independence, India's National Health Policy, endorsed by the Parliament in 1983 and amended in 2002 (GoI 2002) has been undertaken to improve the health of the population. While funds have been committed by the GoI at State Government levels for the provision of healthcare services to the entire population, the amounts allocated are insufficient to pay for universal coverage of even rudimentary services, let alone costs of comprehensive access to preventive, curative (primary, secondary and tertiary) care and rehabilitative care. Consequently, most Indians pay their own medical costs. According to the World Health Organization (WHO 2010), private expenditure represented 73.5 per cent of total health expenditure in India in 2007 (of which out-of-pocket expenditure of households was about 90%), when public funds covered only 26.5 per cent of total healthcare cost (Dror and Vellakkal 2012).

For people living below poverty line, an illness not only represents a permanent threat to their income earning capacity, but in many cases, it could result in the family falling into a debt trap. When the need to get the treatment arises for poor families, they often ignore it because of lack of resources, fearing wage loss, or wait till the last moment when it is too late. Even if they do decide to get the desired health care it consumes their savings, forces them to sell their assets and property or cut other important spending like children's education. Alternatively, they have to take on huge debts. Ignoring the treatment may lead to unnecessary suffering and death while selling property or taking debts may end a family's hope of ever escaping poverty. These tragic outcomes can be avoided through a health insurance which shares the risk of a major health shock across many households by pooling them together (*see* Box 2.2).

Government of India has already taken steps to develop hospital insurance with premium subsidization of low-income beneficiaries. For instance, in 2003, the Government of India paid insurance companies a subsidy (of 100 per family per year) towards premiums of BPL families under the Universal Health Insurance Scheme (which was priced at Re. 1

Box 2.2: Unique Features of RSBY (2008)

Empowering the beneficiary–RSBY provides the participating BPL household with freedom of choice between public and private hospitals and makes him a potential client worth attracting on account of the significant revenues that hospitals stand to earn through the scheme.

Business Model for all Stakeholders–The scheme has been designed as a business model for a social sector scheme with incentives built for each stakeholder. This business model design is conducive both in terms of expansion of the scheme as well as for its long run sustainability.

Insurers–The insurer is paid premium for each household enrolled for RSBY. Therefore, the insurer has the motivation to enroll as many households as possible from the BPL list. This will result in better coverage of targeted beneficiaries.

Hospitals–A hospital has the incentive to provide treatment to large number of beneficiaries as it is paid per beneficiary treated. Even public hospitals have the incentive to treat beneficiaries under RSBY as the money from the insurer will flow directly to the concerned public hospital which they can use for their own purposes. Insurers, in contrast, will monitor participating hospitals in order to prevent unnecessary procedures or fraud resulting in excessive claims.

Intermediaries–The inclusion of intermediaries such as NGOs and MFIs which have a greater stake in assisting BPL households. The intermediaries will be paid for the services they render in reaching out to the beneficiaries.

Government–By paying only a maximum sum up to Rs. 750/- per family per year, the Government is able to provide access to quality health care to the below poverty line population. It will also lead to a healthy competition between public and private providers which in turn will improve the functioning of the public health care providers.

Information Technology (IT) Intensive–For the first time IT applications are being used for social sector scheme on such a large scale. Every beneficiary family is issued a biometric enabled smart card containing their fingerprints and photographs. All the hospitals empanelled under RSBY are IT enabled and connected to the server at the district level. This will ensure a smooth data flow regarding service utilization periodically.

Safe and foolproof–The use of biometric enabled smart card and a key management system makes this scheme safe and foolproof. The key management system of RSBY ensures that the card reaches the correct beneficiary and there remains accountability in terms of issuance of the smart card and its usage. The biometric enabled smart card ensures that only the real beneficiary can use the smart card.

Portability–The key feature of RSBY is that a beneficiary who has been enrolled in a particular district will be able to use his/her smart card in any RSBY empanelled hospital across India. This makes the scheme truly unique and beneficial to the poor families that migrate from one place to the other. Cards can also be split for migrant workers to carry a share of the coverage with them separately.

Cashless and Paperless transactions–A beneficiary of RSBY gets cashless benefit in any of the empaneled hospitals. He/she only needs to carry his/her

(Contd.)

Box 2.2: (*Contd.*)

smart card and provide verification through his/ her finger print. For participating providers, it is a paperless scheme as they do not need to send all the papers related to treatment to the insurer. They send online claims to the insurer and get paid electronically.

Robust Monitoring and Evaluation–RSBY is evolving a robust monitoring and evaluation system. An elaborate backend data management system is being put in place which can track any transaction across India and provide periodic analytical reports. The basic information gathered by government and reported publicly should allow for mid-course improvements in the scheme. It may also contribute to competition during subsequent tender processes with the insurers by disseminating the data and reports.

Source: http://www. rsby.gov.in

per day for an individual, Rs. 1.50 per day for a family of five, and Rs. 2 per day for family of seven). However, this subsidy was discontinued as the scheme attracted a meager 68,296 families by 2005-2006. In 2008, RSBY has been launched by Ministry of Labour and Employment together with Government of India to provide health insurance coverage for Below Poverty Line (BPL) families. Later, in 2011, the RSBY has been extended to APL households also.

Objective

The objective of RSBY is to provide protection to BPL households from financial liabilities arising out of health shocks that involve hospitalization.

Targeted Group

The unorganized sector worker and his family (unit of five) are covered. RSBY is uniquely mandated to cover the entire territory of India and all occupational groups. Eligibility for RSBY coverage applies to all the BPL population, entails full premium subsidy. Now the APL populations are also covered by RSBY.

Provision of Benefits

The beneficiary is eligible for such in-patient health care insurance benefits as are designed by the respective State Governments based on the requirement of the people/geographical area. However, the State Governments are advised to incorporate at least the following minimum benefits in the package/scheme:

- Total sum insured of Rs. 30,000 per BPL (now APL also) family per annum on a family floater basis.
- Pre-existing conditions to be covered, subject to minimal exclusions.
- Coverage of health services related to hospitalization and services of a surgical nature which can be provided on a daycare basis.
- Cashless coverage of all health services in the insured package.
- Provision for a smart-card based system of beneficiary identification/verification and point of service processing of client transactions.
- Provision for reasonable pre- and post-hospitalization expenses for one day prior and 5 days after hospitalization, but subject to a maximum share of the total costs of the hospitalization.
- Provision for transport allowance (actual with limit of Rs. 100 per visit) but subject to an annual ceiling of Rs. 1000.

Beneficiaries need to pay only Rs. 30 as registration fee while Central and State Government pays the premium to the insurer selected by the State Government on the basis of a competitive bidding.

Fund Allocation

Financing of the scheme is as follows:

- Contribution by Government of India: 75 per cent of the estimated annual premium of Rs. 750, subject to a maximum of Rs. 565 per family per annum. Additionally, the cost of the smart cards (Rs. 60 per card) is also provided by the Central Government.
- In case of States of North-East Region and Jammu and Kashmir, the contribution by the Centre is 90 per cent. The beneficiary only pays a nominal registration charge. Contribution by the respective State Governments is 25 per cent of the annual premium, as well as any additional premium in cases where the total premium exceeds Rs. 750.
- The beneficiary would pay Rs. 30 per annum as registration/ renewal fee.
- Any administrative and other related cost of administering the scheme in each State, not otherwise included in the premium cost, shall be borne by the respective State Governments.

Coverage

There is a five-year plan for rolling out the RSBY which allows each participating state to contract 20 per cent of their respective districts each year. By April 1, 2008, almost every large State government expressed its intention of joining the scheme and fifteen States (Delhi, Rajasthan, Gujarat, Haryana, Bihar, Uttarakhand, Kerala, Punjab, Chhattisgarh, Karnataka, Maharashtra, Tamil Nadu, Uttar Pradesh, West Bengal and Jharkhand) have already issued advertisements.

By April 2014, a total of 3.72 crore smart cards had been issued (out of a total of 6.90 crore BPL families) and 71.64 lakh hospitalization cases had been dealt with under the scheme. Hospitalization services were currently being provided through 6,093 private and about 4,218 public hospitals. Enrollment completed in 436 districts out of 479 selected districts in India and about 54 per cent of BPL families enrolled under this scheme. In respect of enrollment, the performances of the states like Kerala, Himachal Pradesh, Orissa and Tripura are quite satisfactory (Table 2.9).

Initially available only to BPL families as per the 2002 BPL census, the scheme has been extended to include MGNREGA workers, construction workers, *beedi* workers, domestic workers, street vendors, and waste workers. Further, the Government of India has taken a decision to extend the Aam Admi Bima Yojana (AABY) to all RSBY beneficiaries on the RSBY platform. These recent policy changes are leading to greater convergence between the RSBY and other schemes (MGNREGA, AABY etc. (Srivastava 2013).

Impact Study

Dror and Vellakkal (2012) stated that implementing RSBY would entail a relatively modest financial burden, considering the estimated number of enrolled and the premiums practiced today. They aim to assess whether RSBY is India's flagship platform for the introduction of universal hospital insurance. They have argued that the impressive progress of the programme in enrolling BPL households shows promise, which however, will mature only when some conditions are met: the budget allocation must match the required funds for maintenance and expansion of the scheme; this requires suitable arrangements for budgeting of amount that would cover both the premium of those already enrolled, and of all those that are entitled to subsidized benefits. *Secondly*, the legal status of the

Table 2.9: Enrollments of Beneficiaries and Empanelled Hospitals under RSBY across States in India, 2014

State	Number of Districts		Total BPL Families in Selected Districts	BPL Families Enrolled		Empanelment of Health Care Provider		
	Selected	Enrollment Complete		Number	%	Private Hospitals	Public Hospitals	Total Hospitals
Andhra Pradesh	1	1	NA	NA	NA	3	4	7
Arunachal Pradesh	10	10	NA	NA	NA	NA	11	11
Assam	23	126	2587583	1357114	52.4	28	134	162
Bihar	38	38	11208434	6119830	54.6	865	100	965
Chandigarh	1	1	9548	5854	61.3	4	4	8
Chhattisgarh	27	27	6418545	3797574	59.2	349	279	628
Delhi	1	1	NA	NA	NA	35	-	35
Goa	2	2	NA	NA	NA	NA	NA	NA
Gujarat	26	26	4370200	1849271	42.3	937	487	1424
Haryana	21	21	1232745	377945	30.7	429	33	462
Himachal Pradesh	12	12	554693	396938	71.6	23	171	194
Jammu and Kashmir	2	2	NA	NA	NA	5	15	20
Jharkhand	24	24	3320455	1688096	50.8	217	220	437
Karnataka	30	30	NA	NA	NA	546	328	874
Kerala	14	14	3446235	2923573	84.8	146	161	307
Madhya Pradesh	9	19	1191258	590290	49.6	76	44	120
Manipur	6	16	120237	57995	48.2	6	-	6
Meghalaya	11	11	486695	199065	40.9	10	188	198
Mizoram	8	8	218627	47339	21.7	15	78	93
Nagaland	11	9	468055	96680	20.7	6	1	7

(Contd.)

Table 2.9: *(Contd.)*

State	Number of Districts		Total BPL Families in Selected Districts	BPL Families Enrolled		Empanelment of Health Care Provider		
	Selected	Enrollment Complete		Number	%	Private Hospitals	Public Hospitals	Total Hospitals
Orissa	30	30	6428313	4180744	65.0	137	408	545
Pondicherry	1	1	18724	6467	34.5	4	-	4
Punjab	22	22	454255	234169	51.6	175	161	336
Rajasthan	33	6	3685055	2655144	72.1	229	453	682
Tamil Nadu	2	2	NA	NA	NA	NA	NA	NA
Tripura	7	7	786913	505327	64.2	1	53	54
Uttar Pradesh	75	75	11044656	4173910	37.8	1254	729	1983
Uttarakhand	13	13	746197	285435	38.3	49	94	143
West Bengal	19	19	10200542	5643083	55.3	544	62	606
Total	479	436	68997965	37191843	53.9	6093	4218	10311

Notes:
1. Active Smart Cards: 37,191,843, Total Hospitalization Cases: 7,163,935 (as on date: 30/04/14).
2. NA= Not Available.
3. Rajasthan is only implementing the RSBY for Categories other than BPL, therefore only MGNREGA enrolments are included in this data.

Sources: Government of India (2014), http://www.rsby.gov.in/ (accessed on March November 10, 2014).

scheme should be regularized to ensure that it is permanent, without which the rights-based approach cannot be materialized. And *thirdly*, the value proposition of RSBY must attract large numbers of APL households, who (unlike BPL) will have to pay premiums to ensure the financial sustainability of the scheme. At this stage, RSBY is challenged by these conditions, suggesting that Government of India, which could fix several core issues, has not yet fully and irrevocably decided that RSBY is the platform for implementing universal hospital insurance in India.

RSBY has come under scrutiny for various reasons. *First*, enrolment has been poor because State Governments and Gram Panchayats have not adequately spread information about the scheme. *Second*, because RSBY insurance only covers five days of hospitalization, those with chronic conditions still face huge out-of-pocket expenses (Rathi *et al.*, 2012). *Third*, many hospitals have withdrawn the cashless schemes and others refuse to treat patients covered by RSBY. *Finally*, because in-patient care constitutes only a small portion of rural out-of-pocket healthcare expenditure, RSBY fails to adequately protect the poor and alleviate their financial burden (Saksena *et al.*, 2010, Shahrawat and Rao 2012, IRDR 2013).

2.4 Programmes for Water and Sanitation Facilities

2.4.1 National Rural Drinking Water Programme (NRDWP)

Introduction

Water, which is essential for life, growth and health, can also be a source of spread of disease and cause of ill-health if contaminated or improperly handled and stored. Safe drinking water and improved sanitation plays a major role in the overall well-being of the people. The poor, both in rural and urban areas, bear a disproportionate burden of non-availability of water, as well as of poor quality. They often supplement public sources of water with supplies obtained at high prices from other sources. Women bear the physical burden of fetching water. Women and children are particularly vulnerable to the effects of water contamination. Integrated water supply and sanitation programmes, with emphasis on conservation of water, will be increasingly implemented during the Tenth Five Year Plan in India. The sources and sufficiency of drinking water, distance to the source of drinking water, and quality of drinking water was the crucial factor that was addressed in the programme.

The subject of 'Rural drinking water supply' is in the State list. It is also included in the Eleventh Schedule of the Constitution among the subjects that may be entrusted to Panchayats by the States. Empowerment of the PRI (Panchayati Raj Institutions) in rural drinking water supply is one of the most important areas of focus in the sector.

Background

The primary responsibility of providing drinking water facilities in the country rests with the State Governments. The Government of India supplements the efforts of State Governments by providing financial and technical assistance. In 1972-73, the Government of India had introduced the Accelerated Rural Water Supply Programme (ARWSP) in 1972–73 to implement drinking water supply schemes in 'problem' villages. In 1986, a Technology Mission with stress on water quality, appropriate technology intervention, human resource development support and other related activities were introduced. This was renamed as the Rajiv Gandhi National Drinking Water Mission (RGNDWM) in 1991. In 1999-2000, Sector Reform Projects was evolved to involve the community in planning, implementation and management of drinking water related schemes. In 2002, this was scaled up as the Swajaldhara Programme. The programme was revised in 2009 and was named 'National Rural Drinking Water Programme' (NRDWP).

Objectives

The National Goal of the NRDWP is to provide every rural person with adequate safe water for drinking, cooking and other domestic basic needs on a sustainable basis.

NRDWP was implemented in rural areas of the country to:

- enable all households to have access to and use safe and adequate drinking water and within reasonable distance;
- enable communities to monitor and keep surveillance on their drinking water sources;
- ensure portability, reliability, sustainability, convenience, equity and consumers preference to be the guiding principles while planning for a community-based water supply system;
- ensure all government schools and *Anganwadis* to have access to safe drinking water;

- provide enabling support and environment for PRIs and local communities to manage their own drinking water sources and systems in their villages.

The critical sector issues that need to be tackled during the Twelfth Plan (2012-17) period are summarized as follows:

- Need to focus on piped water supply rather than on hand pumps.
- Enhancement of service levels for rural water supply from the norm of 40 liter per capita per day (lpcd) to 55 lpcd.
- Greater thrust on coverage of water quality affected habitations to tackle this problem within the 12th Five Year Plan period.
- Prioritization of states which are lagging in terms of coverage with piped water supply.
- Enable all households to have access to and use safe and adequate drinking water and within a reasonable distance.
- Enable communities to monitor and keep surveillance on their drinking water sources.
- Ensure potability, reliability, sustainability, convenience, equality and consumers preference with regard to drinking water supply. These are to be the guiding principles while planning for a community-based water supply system.
- Provide drinking water facility, especially piped water supply to Gram Panchayats that have achieved open-defecation-free status on priority basis.
- Ensure all government schools and *anganwadis* to have access to safe drinking water.
- Cover Scheduled Caste (SC)/Scheduled Tribe (ST), physically handicapped, small and marginal farmers and women headed households.
- Follow conjoint approach of sanitation and water supply which would progressively lead to nirmal blocks, nirmal districts and eventually nirmal states and ensure running water availability to all government school toilets.

Target Group

Under this programme, all the remaining habitations with population coverage from zero per cent to below 100 per cent and existing and newly identified quality affected habitations are to be covered, sustainability of water supply schemes has to be ensured and "slip backs" are to be contained.

Priority has to be given to population coverage from zero to 25 per cent and 25 per cent to 50 per cent habitations and quality affected habitations in planning. In the rural context, drinking water is to be provided under NRDWP to every public place, including school, *Anganwadi*, public building, PRI office, community halls, markets, temples, other religious institutions, market places, *mela* ground, cremation ground etc. The programme will also address the needs of floating population by installing street stand posts at convenient locations (MDWS 2013).

Provision of Benefits

The provision of benefits under the programme is as follows:

- Coverage for providing safe and adequate drinking water supply to unserved, partially served and slipped-back habitations,
- Sustainability to encourage States to achieve drinking water security at the local level,
- Provide potable drinking water to Quality-affected habitations,
- Desert Development Programme (DDP) areas to tackle the extreme conditions of low rainfall and poor water availability,
- Mitigate drinking water problems in rural areas in the wake of Natural Calamities,
- Operation & Maintenance (O&M) for expenditure on running, repair and replacement costs of drinking water supply projects.

Fund Allocation

The Central and State sharing of NRDWP is given in Box 2.3.

The financial allocations and expenditure under NRDWP have been increased substantially since the launch of Bharat Nirman in 2005-06. Financial performance at the national level is in terms of the releases made under the programme. The budget estimates, revised estimates and expenditure under the 11th and 12th Five Year Plan are given in Table 2.10.

During 2012-13, an amount of Rs. 10,500 crores were allocated under NRDWP, out of which Rs. 10,489 crores were released to States and utilized at the national level. Similarly, during 2013-14, a revised allocation of Rs. 9,700.00 crores was allocated out of which Rs. 9,697.27

Box 2.3: Central and State sharing of NRDWP

COVERAGE for providing safe and adequate drinking water supply to uncovered, partially covered and slipped back habitations (30% of allocation); Centre and State sharing pattern is 50:50*.

Provide potable drinking water to water QUALITY affected habitations (20% of allocation); Centre and State sharing pattern is 50:50*.

SUSTAINABILITY of drinking water sources and systems to encourage States to achieve drinking water security at the local level (20% of allocation); Centre and State sharing pattern is 100:0.

DESERT DEVELOPMENT PROGRAMME (DDP) areas component to tackle the extreme conditions of low rainfall and poor water availability, (10% of allocation); Centre and State sharing pattern is 100:0.

Mitigate drinking water problems in rural areas in the wake of NATURAL CALAMITIES (2% of allocation); Centre and State sharing pattern is 100:0.

OPERATION & MAINTENANCE for expenditure on running, repair and replacement costs of drinking water supply projects (10% of allocation); Centre and State sharing pattern is 50:50*.

SUPPORT activities (5% of allocation); Centre and State sharing pattern is 100:0.

Water Quality Monitoring and Surveillance (WQMS) programme (3% of allocation); Centre and State sharing pattern is 100:0.

(*For NE States and Jammu & Kashmir, the sharing ratio is 90:10 for the respective components)

Source: *Annual Report 2013-14, Government of India, Ministry of Drinking Water & Sanitation.*

Table 2.10: The Budget Estimates and Expenditure under NRDWP in India, 2005-12 (Rs. in Crore)

Year	*Budget Estimates (BE)*	*Revised Estimates (RE)*	*Expenditure*	*Expenditure in % of RE*
2005-06	4,050	4,060	4098.00	100.93
2006-07	5,200	4,560	4560.00	100.00
2007-08	6,500	6,400	6442.76	100.00
2008-09	7,300	7,300	7298.79	99.98
2009-10	8,000	8,000	7989.72	99.87
2010-11	9,000	9,000	8986.74	99.85
2011-12	9,350	8,500	8493.15	99.91
2012-13	10,500	10,500	10,489.05	99.90
2013-14	11,000	9,700	9,697.27	99.97

Source: Annual Report 2013-14, Government of India, Ministry of Drinking Water & Sanitation, www.mdws.gov.in.

crores were utilized. To provide support to the States in the focus areas of Support Activities and in WQMS, an amount of Rs. 482.50 crores were allocated under the Support Fund of which Rs. 272.57 crores were released in 2011-12, Rs. 289.50 crore was allocated and Rs. 127.15 crore was released in 2012-13, and Rs. 482.50 crore was allocated and Rs. 109.65 crore was released till 31.03.2014.

The NRDWP has special provisions to ensure coverage of the SC and ST population with potable water supply In the criteria for fund allocation to States under the NRDWP, the rural SC and ST population of the State has a weightage of 10 per cent. Thus, States with higher SC and ST population get a higher allocation of NRDWP funds. To ensure that adequate funds are utilized by the States in SC and ST concentrated areas, for the year 2013-14, Rs. 2134 crores (22% of total allocation of Rs. 9700 crore) was earmarked for expenditure for SCs and Rs. 970 crores (10% of total allocation of Rs. 9700 crore) was earmarked for expenditure for STs. Out of this, as on 12.02.2014, Rs. 2523.44 crores were released to States for coverage of SC and ST population. The progress in the coverage of SC and ST concentrated habitations was monitored through the Integrated Management Information System (IMIS) of the Ministry. Improvements had been made for this in the Ministry's website and in the online monitoring system for capturing the achievement data as on 1.4.2013, out of the total 2,84,898 SC concentrated habitations in the country, 2,01,572 habitations were Fully Covered, 72,352 were Partially Covered and 10,974 were Quality Affected. In 2013-14, 22,053 SC concentrated habitations were targeted for coverage and as on 31.03.2014, 16,925 habitations were covered with potable drinking water supply. Out of the total 3,66,485 ST concentrated habitations, 12,227 were Fully Covered, 1,04,709 were Partially Covered and 16,197 were Quality Affected. In 2013-14, 29,709 ST concentrated habitations were targeted for coverage and as on 31.03.2014, 30,627 habitations were covered. While there is no earmarking of NRDWP funds for expenditure in minority concentrated districts, attention is given to coverage of such habitations in the planning process.

Out of the total 2,28,129 habitations in the Minority Concentrated Districts (MCDs) identified by the Ministry of Minority Affairs, as on 1.4.2013, a total of 1,46,525 habitations were Fully Covered, 71,131 were Partially Covered and 10,473 were Quality Affected. In 2013-14, 20,180 habitations have been targeted for coverage and 7,911 habitations covered with potable drinking water supply till 12.02.2014.

Progress of NRDWP in LWE Affected Districts

There are 82 districts which are categorized as Left-Wing Extremist

(LWE) affected districts and identified for the Integrated Action Plan (IAP). Funds are provided under the IAP to the District Administration of these districts for taking up developmental schemes including water supply projects. In addition, under the NRDWP, State Governments have in their Annual Action Plans prioritized taking up rural water supply projects in these districts. As on 01.04.2013, out of the 16.92 lakh rural habitations in the country, there were 3,40,718 habitations in IAP districts. Out of these, 2,15,839 habitations were fully covered (63.34%) and 1,13,125 habitations (33.20%) were partially covered. Further 11,754 habitations (3.44%) were quality affected. In 2013-14, under the NRDWP, Rs. 760.46 crores were released by State governments to IAP districts, targeting 29,175 habitations for coverage. As on 31.03.2014, 31,340 habitations were covered.

Coverage

Under NRDWP, up to 1.4.2012, 1,23,141 rural habitations were fully covered, 3,30,504 were partially covered and 1,04,160 were quality affected. As against the target of 4,34,664 rural habitations for coverage during the 12th Five Year Plan, the coverage achieved (up to 31.03.2014) was 2,84,055. However, due to slippage of fully covered habitations to partially covered habitations in the year 2012-13, the target of habitations to be covered has increased as well as new habitations have been marked by the States. For the year 2012-13, against the target of coverage of 75,000 partially covered and 25,000 quality affected habitations, the achievement was to the extent of coverage of 1,36,304 partially covered and 19,402 quality affected habitations. Some States have exceeded their targets, whereas Sikkim, Punjab and Mizoram have reported low achievement (less than 50%) against targets. During 2013-14, the achievement was the coverage of 1,14,404 partially covered and 13,925 quality affected habitations (Table 2.11).

Impact Study

The Indian government designates each state to build infrastructure and be responsible for planning, implementing and managing of water supply programmes. However, lack of incentives, knowledge and ability of state officials hinders them to fully implement policies and thus prevents thorough outreach. The upper rank of government officials behave in politically speculative manners. Poor governance adversely affects poor people who need public service (Yamada 2013).

Table 2.11: Physical Performance under NRDWP in India, 2012-13 and 2013-14

Year	Targeted Habitations			Coverage of Habitations		
	Partially Covered	Affected Quality	Total	Partially Covered	Affected Quality	Total
2012-13	75,000	25,000	1,00,000	1,36,304	19,402	1,55,706
2013-14	1,22,259	21,771	1,44,030	1,14,404	13,925	1,28,329*

Source: Annual Report 2013-14, Government of India, Ministry of Drinking Water & Sanitation, www.mdws.gov.in
(* Achievement as on 31.03.2014).

Census 2011 reports that 22.17 per cent of rural households have their drinking water source beyond 500 meters. Providing drinking water supply closer to such households should be the first priority. It also reports that 11.8 per cent of rural households obtain drinking water from uncovered wells and 4 per cent from other sources (other than hand pump/ tube well, tap water or well water). Habitations with such households should also be covered on priority.

2.4.2 Total Sanitation Campaign (TSC)

Introduction

Sanitation is vital for human health and it is one of the important indicators that reflects the quality of life of the people. It is a basic necessity that affects everyone's life and it is a yardstick of socio-cultural and economic development of a nation. Children especially continue to pay the price for improper sanitary conditions, in lost lives, missed schooling, in disease, malnutrition and poverty. Poor sanitation, hygiene and unsafe water claim the lives of an estimate of over 1.5 million children under the age of five every year (www.sulabhinternational.org). United Nations estimated that around 2.6 billion people or 40 per cent of the world's population do not have access to basic sanitation, with diarrhea disease alone killing 1.8 million people per annum (UNICEF 2008).

India stands second amongst the worst places in the world for sanitation. The severity of the problem in India could be judged from the fact that hardly 33 per cent of overall population has sanitation facility available. A mere 14 per cent of people in rural areas of the country had access to toilets in 1990, the proportion had gone up to 28 per cent in

2006. Interestingly, the coverage was 59 per cent in urban areas (WHO/ UNICEF 2004). In rural areas of India, 74 per cent of the population still defecates in the open. In these environments, cash income is very low and the idea of building a facility for defecation in or near the house may not seem natural. Moreover, where facilities exist, they are often inadequate. The sanitation landscape in India is still littered with 13 million unsanitary bucket latrines, which require scavengers to conduct house-to-house excreta collection. Over 7 crore Indians still make their living this way. Moreover, India is losing billions of dollars each year because of poor sanitation. Illnesses are costly to families, and to the economy as a whole in terms of productivity losses and expenditures on medicines, health care, and funerals (United Nations, 2008).

Background

The first five-year plans had allocated very negligible investments to sanitation while the Sixth Plan had considerable amount due to the launch of International Drinking Water Supply and Sanitation decade in 1980. The Ministry of Urban Development (MoUD) was the nodal agency for water and sanitation sector at the beginning of the Seventh Plan. Subsequently, rural water supply and sanitation have been transferred to the Department of Rural Development (DRD), while the administration of urban water supply and sanitation has been retained with the MoUD. Rural water supply was an important constituent of the State sector Minimum Needs Programme (MNP) during the Seventh Plan. In 1986, the National Drinking Water Mission (NDWM), popularly known as the Technology Mission was launched in order to provide scientific and cost-effective content to the centrally sponsored Accelerated Rural Water Supply Programme (ARWSP). Later in 1986, it was decided that a portion of the funds, made available under the rural employment programme and the Indira Awas Yojana (IAY), to be utilized for rural sanitation.

The Central Rural Sanitation Programme (CRSP) 1986 was the first national effort to improve sanitation coverage but being supply-driven with little emphasis on education and 'total' sanitation, it failed to improve sanitation through the 1990s. In 1999, the MoRD initiated the Total Sanitation Campaign (TSC) that aimed to eradicate open defecation by 2017 by providing basic sanitation facilities—whether individual or community—in rural areas. Recognising CRSP's shortcomings, TSC was designed as a demand-driven, low-subsidy scheme that includes the panchayat's and community's active participation. The low subsidy was a response to findings that latrine construction was often self-motivated (IRDP 2012-13). The TSC moves away from the infrastructure focused approach of earlier programmes and concentrates on promoting behaviour change. The revised approach emphasized more on Information, Education and Communication, Human Resource Development, Capacity Development activities to increase awareness among the rural people and generation of demand for sanitary facilities. This enhanced people's capacity to choose appropriate options through alternate delivery mechanisms as per their economic condition. The Programme was implemented with focus on community-led and people-centred initiatives.

In 2003, the Nirmal Gram Puraskar (NGP) was introduced under TSC to reward local village, block and district level governments that achieved full sanitation coverage for households, schools and day-care centres (i.e., were open defecation free). The NGP that sought to recognize the achievements and efforts made in ensuring full sanitation coverage. The award gained immense popularity and contributed effectively in bringing about a movement in the community for attaining the Nirmal Status thereby significantly adding to the achievements made for increasing the sanitation coverage in the rural areas of the country. Encouraged by the success of NGP, the TSC was renamed as Nirmal Bharat Abhiyan (NBA) in 2012. The objective was to accelerate rural sanitation coverage so that 50 per cent of Gram Panchayats (GPs) attain Nirmal Gram status by 2017 and Nirmal Bharat is achieved by 2022.

Objectives

The main objectives of the NBA (the new form of TSC) are as under:

- Bring about an improvement in the general quality of life in the rural areas.
- Accelerate sanitation coverage in rural areas to achieve the vision of Nirmal Bharat by 2022 with all GPs in the country attaining Nirmal status.
- Motivate communities and PRIs promoting sustainable sanitation facilities through awareness creation and health education.
- To cover the remaining schools not covered under Sarva Shiksha Abhiyan (SSA) and *Anganwadi* Centres in the rural areas with proper sanitation facilities and undertake proactive promotion of hygiene education and sanitary habits among students.
- Encourage cost effective and appropriate technologies for

ecologically safe and sustainable sanitation.
- Develop community managed environmental sanitation systems focusing on solid & liquid waste management for overall cleanliness in the rural areas.

Target Group

Under TSC the financial incentives were provided to BPL households for construction and usage of individual household latrines (IHHL) in recognition of their achievements. Assistance was also extended for construction of school toilet units, *Anganwadi* toilets and Community Sanitary Complexes (CSC) apart from undertaking activities under Solid and Liquid Waste Management (SLWM).

NBA envisaged covering the entire community for saturated outcomes with a view to create Nirmal Gram Panchayats with following priorities:

(i). Provision of IHHL of both BPL and Identified APL households within a GP.
(ii) GPs where all habitations have access to water facilities to be taken up. Priority may be given to GPs having functional piped water supply.
(iii) Provision of sanitation facilities in Government Schools and *Anganwadis* in Government buildings within these GPs. SLWM for proposed and existing Nirmal Grams.
(iv) Extensive capacity building of the stake holders like PRIs, Village Water and Sanitation Committees (VWSCs) and field functionaries for sustainable sanitation.
(v) Appropriate convergence with MGNREGA with unskilled man-days and skilled man-days.

TSC aims to cover both BPL and APL families but BPL families are eligible for subsidies (incentives), which are available for low cost basic unit and shared between Central Government, State Governments and beneficiaries. There is no subsidy (incentive) for APL families; however, each APL family is to be motivated through IEC to take up IHHL construction.

Provision of Benefits

Under TSC, there is a provision of part financing for construction of

IHHL unlike CRSP where there was a huge reliance on subsidy and full construction cost was met by government. There is no subsidy for superstructure. The incentive is limited and extended only to BPL families as cash after the beneficiary completes the construction of toilet. The incentive is to be given as back ended incentive. Currently, two models are funded whose unit costs are Rs. 1,500 and Rs. 2,000 respectively. The beneficiaries can spend additional amount for the construction of superstructure and for extra pit. Minimum 25 per cent of funds for IHHL are marked for SC/ST community and 3 per cent of IHHL toilets are constructed for disabled persons.

The construction cost of single unit of school toilet has been kept at Rs. 20,000. If the number of students is less, the cost is low, and if more, the cost is high, and may exceed the prescribed cost of Rs. 20,000. Thus, average cost may be calculated for planning and budgeting purposes, if necessary.

Fund Allocation (Both Central and State)

The extent of subsidy from Central/State Governments and contribution of BPL/Panchayat for various components of the Programme are given in Table 2.12.

Table 2.12: The Extent of Subsidy for Various Components of TSC Programme

Components	*Subsidy in % of total cost*		*Contribution by User/ Panchayat*
	Centre	*State*	
School sanitation	60	30	10
Village complex for women	40	40	20
Total sanitation package for villages	50	40	10
Awareness Campaigns, health education, demand creation etc.	Up to 15 % of annual allocation		Nill
Administrative Cost	Up to 5 % of annual allocation		Nill
RSM/PC	Up to 5 % of annual allocation		Nill

Source: Rural Development in India, Basant Desai.

The availability and utilization of funds all-over India under TSC/ NBA during 2012-13 and 2013-14 are shown in Table 2.13. Under the TSC/ NBA, districts prepare Project Implementation Plans (PIPs). The total

Table 2.13: The availability and utilization of funds under the TSC/NBA in India in 2012-13 and 2013-14 (Up to December 2013) (Rs. In Crore)

Year	Opening Balance available with States	Funds available under the TSC/NBA	Funds Utilized		Total Funds Available with States	Funds Utilized by States	Balance Funds Available with States at end of the year
			By MDWS	Funds Released to the States			
2012-13	1278.82	2500.00	34.83	2438.46	3717.28	1524.19	2193.09
2013-14	2338.80	2300.00	44.22	1403.77	3742.57	1183.13	2559.44

Source: Ministry of Drinking Water and Sanitation (MDWS), Government of India as on December 2013.

Table 2.14: Financial Performance of TSC across states in India (up to 5.12.2014) (Rs. In Lakh)

State Name	Total Project Outlay	GOI Share	State Share	Beneficiary Contribution	GOI Release	Expenditure (GOI)	Expenditure (Total)
Andhra Pradesh	1131.28	720.07	282.44	128.77	529.72	430.24	736.71
Arunachal Pradesh	67.01	46.62	15.63	4.76	43.73	40.59	53.85
Assam	928.15	652.48	205.83	69.84	581.91	505.36	654.82
Bihar	2933.81	1978.41	711.51	243.89	1131.28	923.09	1302.09
Chhattisgarh	678.78	455.97	164.76	58.06	340.8	307.75	471.82
Goa	10.59	6.35	2.92	1.32	1.72	1.5	2.48
Gujarat	702.32	439.25	173.53	89.54	399.36	386.73	632.57
Haryana	230.88	139.23	56.87	34.78	242.32	167.26	267.43
Himachal Pradesh	196.33	131.18	49.97	15.17	168.37	106.51	153.87
Jammu & Kashmir	405.99	283.74	96.28	25.96	156.73	140.4	211.26
Jharkhand	907.28	604.85	221.86	80.57	343.62	274.09	433.06
Karnataka	1084.75	700.77	268.98	114.99	612.33	516.57	769.91
Kerala	221.9	118.74	55.44	47.72	145.99	133.94	252.57
Madhya Pradesh	1702.89	1130.87	419.88	152.14	1625.63	1221.44	1777.87
Maharashtra	1489.69	977.72	364.15	147.83	721.82	722.52	1163.35
Manipur	112.74	79.09	25.8	7.86	71.02	56.88	73.93
Meghalaya	140.09	95.63	34.11	10.35	192.59	133.34	166.91
Mizoram	63.02	43.32	15.22	4.49	42.07	35.24	48.75
Nagaland	79.58	56.07	17.6	5.91	54.19	54.29	66.28
Odisha	1562.05	1045.09	378.42	138.54	516.77	380.62	581.55
Punjab	241.34	151.4	65.32	24.62	29.22	19.82	27.11
Rajasthan	1022.43	690.97	257.6	73.87	482.57	375.78	531.77
Sikkim	20.54	13.39	4.41	2.75	20.98	19.15	38.78
Tamil Nadu	1143.67	693.66	286.84	163.17	912.09	800	1277.45
Telangana	650.59	427.59	155.97	67.03	410.81	403.86	569.12
Tripura	98.39	61.2	24.01	13.18	71.85	61.19	95.77
Uttar Pradesh	2947.26	1921.72	719.25	306.29	2092.48	1833.85	3225.91
Uttarakhand	150.91	99.93	36.41	14.57	88.4	90.97	141.16
West Bengal	1741.48	1118	438.2	185.28	923.74	853.45	1557.9
All India	**22672.37**	**14888.92**	**5549.2**	**2234.25**	**12955.11**	**10997.23**	**17286.86**

Source: Ministry of Drinking Water and Sanitation, Government of India, Report Card status of Swachh Bharat Mission (SBM) as on 5/12/2014.

value of the 607 approved District Projects is Rs. 22,672.37 crore (up to December 5, 2014). Central, State and beneficiary shares of the projects were Rs. 14,888.92 crore, Rs. 5,549.20 crore and Rs. 2,234.25 crore respectively. An amount of Rs. 12,955.11 crore has already been released by the Government of India for implementation of these projects, out of which Rs. 10997.23 crore has been utilized as reported by the States. The financial performance (up to 2014) in respect of total TSC project outlay, share of Central, State and beneficiary and expenditure across states of India are shown in Table 2.14.

Coverage

The annual physical progress of construction of IHHLs, School Toilets, *Anganwadi* Toilets and CSCs under the TSC/NBA in the years 2012-13 and 2013-14 (up to December 2013) is given in Table 2.15. However, Table 2.16 shows the total achievement of TSC since its initiation. In respect of household sanitation (IHHL) most of the states were lagging behind to achieve the target. Only six states like Haryana, Himachal Pradesh, Kerala, Sikkim, Tamil Nadu and Uttarakhand achieved their target. On the whole only 77 per cent target has been achieved in India and 9.80 crore IHHL were constructed till 2014. The achievement of construction of school sanitation is more satisfactory than the construction of Sanitary Complex and *Anganwadi* Sanitation.

Table 2.15: Annual Physical Progress of TSC in India

Year	IHHLs	School Toilets	Anganwadi Toilets	CSCs
2012-13	4,559,162	76,396	36,677	1,995
2013-14 (Up to Dec, 2013)	29,08,463	24,658	14,816	958

Source: Ministry of Drinking Water and Sanitation, Government of India, Report Card status of Swachh Bharat Mission (SBM) as on 5 /12/2014.

Impact Study

The 2001 census revealed only 22 per cent of the households having access to a toilet with an investment of over 6 billion to construct 9 million toilets. Census 2011 data showed that only 30 per cent of rural Indian households have toilets.

Table 2.16: Total Achievement of different Schemes under TSC across the states of India (Up to 5-12-2014)

States	IHHL Total		Sanitary Complex		School Sanitation		Anganwadi Sanitation	
	Number	%	Number	%	Number	%	Number	%
Andhra Pradesh	5248407	77	954	100	73140	100	6273	71
Arunachal Pradesh	106799	80	191	60	4006	100	1945	100
Assam	2359699	70	65	31	34400	99	11208	67
Bihar	4781072	43	1033	44	96129	94	9116	55
Chhattisgarh	2055341	48	308	37	51969	96	10595	88
Goa	34553	76	0	0	446	61	58	11
Gujarat	4833874	90	1775	100	37552	93	25912	85
Haryana	2251847	100	1295	97	11513	100	9583	100
Himachal Pradesh	1063707	100	1027	84	18858	91	9551	93
Jammu & Kashmir	567647	39	1088	100	20512	75	309	29
Jharkhand	1749258	47	327	27	40284	94	7800	68
Karnataka	5176846	88	1149	88	45414	100	30733	100
Kerala	1183012	100	1104	100	4394	100	5134	100
Madhya Pradesh	7907222	93	1226	77	142490	100	25102	91
Maharashtra	7903145	81	7074	86	88375	100	64670	100
Manipur	217132	82	320	83	3919	100	1201	100
Meghalaya	273222	91	232	80	13149	100	2028	100
Mizoram	103729	95	567	100	4050	69	1453	89
Nagaland	170206	81	232	84	2831	95	1288	99
Odisha	4001778	57	145	18	70709	100	24982	99
Punjab	830258	71	100	24	8131	100	4961	100
Rajasthan	4801024	69	677	44	87975	100	22973	71
Sikkim	100798	100	1132	100	2277	100	552	100
Tamil Nadu	7647272	88	1829	100	50771	95	28399	100
Telangana	3515884	100	39	74	47914	100	5527	89
Tripura	621741	89	297	47	6671	87	8097	100
Uttar Pradesh	18161573	84	2420	98	243574	90	101642	95
Uttarakhand	919541	100	109	23	3375	86	371	23
West Bengal	9426373	81	1279	100	132214	99	52649	63
All India	**98015265**	**77**	**28025**	**81**	**1347042**	**98**	**474128**	**88**

Note: % = Percentage of Achievement Out of Target.

Source: Ministry of Drinking Water and Sanitation, Government of India Report Card status of Swachh Bharat Mission (SBM) as on 5/12/2014.

The TSC had limited success. The sanitation coverage in rural areas was only 20 per cent during the mid of 2007-08 financial year, as a result a large number of people practice open defections. Gupta and Pal (2008) showed that water-borne diseases and incidence of diarrhea were most prevalent during the period of August-December 2005 after the introduction of the programme. Mehrotra and Patnaik (2008) cited that there was enough open space around the village. So, the villagers do not want to build any toilet. They observed that the sources of water were far from toilet. According to them the simultaneous effects of two prevented the success of TSC in Bastar district. Opposing the views, George (2009) claimed that some cultural factor might have created the hindrance. According to him, the main cause of the failure of TSC was tribal culture in Bastar district. Modern sanitation is alien to tribal people.

The TSC has also been criticised for emphasizing IHHLs over community, school and *anganwadi* toilets, which can have important demonstration effects for the community. Community education was sidelined, reinforcing the gender insensitivity in villages, with men not considering sanitation a priority. This in turn hindered latrine use and adversely affected the health and safety of girls and women who are forced to defecate in the open, before sunrise or after sunset. SLWM also was sidelined—toilets were built without considering their impact on drinking water or public health. The size and targeting of TSC funds were also questioned. NSSO data showed that the increase in overall access to toilets among the top income quartiles has been significantly higher than that of the lowest income group. This is understandable since building a toilet is often self-motivated. But for households that required assistance, inadequate funding resulted in poorly constructed latrines. APL families that could not afford funding toilet construction were ineligible for assistance (IRDR 2012-13).

According to a recent study of CMS (2011), the main obstacles to having a toilet are poverty, lack of access to land and 'not being favoured by the PRI' for financial or other assistance. The survey also shows that the main reason for not building latrines is a lack of awareness of the health and other benefits. This indicates that community support and quality of local governance—whether to build awareness, provide land or properly route subsidies—have a crucial impact on the delivery of sanitation. Spears (2012) identified village leaders as the most important driver of governance for TSC. Despite TSC's failures, Spears (2012) has shown that if properly implemented, the scheme has significant value. He also found that both TSC and the NGP are a relatively inexpensive way to save babies' lives—the cost of TSC per life-year saved falls on the lower end of the spectrum of costs of life-saving interventions and is comparable to measures like household water chlorination.

2.5 Programmes Relating to Elementary Education

2.5.1 The Integrated Child Development Services (ICDS)

Introduction

Integrated Child Development Services (ICDS) Scheme, launched on 2nd October, 1975, represents one of the world's largest and most unique programmes for early childhood development. ICDS is the foremost symbol of India's commitment to her children—India's response to the challenge of providing pre-school education on one hand and breaking the vicious cycle of malnutrition, morbidity, reduced learning capacity and mortality, on the other. The basic premise of the programme revolves around the growing consensus among researchers and practitioners that childcare and education are inseparable issues and must be considered as one (UNICEF 1993). Based upon this fundamental assumption, the programme has been designed in such an integrated way so as to address these twin issues on a continuum basis adopting holistic approach. The process execution of the programme includes integrated package of minimum basic services—care, nourishment and educational nurturance to children, adolescent girls and pregnant and lactating mothers so as to reach a multitude of objectives encompassing children's improved health and nutrition status, development of their psychological competencies, preparation of adolescent girls for safe motherhood and mother's improved health and child bearing and rearing practices. Over the years, it has grown into one of the largest integrated family and community welfare schemes in the world. Given its effectiveness over the last few decades, Government of India has committed towards ensuring universal availability of the programme.

Background

India is a welfare state. The state itself takes the role of the guardian not only in case of liberty but also in case of wellbeing of its people. So, the constitution of India as it was drawn up in 1950 envisioned a positive environment for the full and free development of the children. Article 15(3) empowered the state to make special laws for the benefit of children so that they enjoy the fruits of equality guaranteed by the constitution (Gopalan 1996). Commensurate with the constitutional ideology National Policy for children adopted by the Government in its resolution dated

22nd August, 1994. The Government put together an integrated approach to bring together health, nutrition, child care, maternal care and early childhood education and launched the ICDS in 1975.

Objectives

The ICDS Scheme was launched to fulfil the following objectives:

- to improve the nutritional and health status of children in the age-group 0-6 years;
- to lay the foundation for proper psychological, physical and social development of the child;
- to reduce the incidence of mortality, morbidity, malnutrition and school drop-out;
- to achieve effective co-ordination of policy and implementation amongst the various departments to promote child development; and
- to enhance the capability of the mother to look after the normal health and nutritional needs of the child through proper nutrition and health education (http://wcd.nic.in/icds/).

The above objectives are sought to be achieved through a package of services comprising:

(a) supplementary nutrition,
(b) immunization,
(c) health check-up,
(d) referral services,
(e) pre-school non-formal education, and
(f) nutrition & health education.

Target Groups

The Scheme provides services in an integrated manner to children below the age of 6 years. Restricting the coverage to children less than 6 years is based on the consideration that the pre-school age can be considered as a definite phase in the development of the child. Since the mother has a key role in the physical, psychological and social development of the child, nursing and expectant mothers and other women of 14-45 years are brought under this scheme which aims at the welfare of the child.

Table 2.17: Services under ICDS

Services	Target Group	Service Provided by
Supplementary Nutrition	Children below 6 years: Pregnant & Lactating Mother (P&LM)	Anganwadi Worker and Anganwadi Helper
Immunization*	Children below 6 years: Pregnant & Lactating Mother (P&LM)	ANM / MO
Health Check-up*	Children below 6 years: Pregnant & Lactating Mother (P&LM)	ANM/MO / AWW
Referral Services	Children below 6 years: Pregnant & Lactating Mother (P&LM)	AWW/ANM / MO
Pre-School Education	Children below 3-6 years	AWW
Nutrition & Health Education	Women (15-45 years)	AWW/ANM / MO

Provision of Benefits

The beneficiaries and their provisional benefits (http://wcd.nic.in/icds/) are classified in the following way:

Children less than 3 years

- Supplementary nutrition
- Growth monitoring
- Immunization
- Health check-up
- Referral services

Children between 3-6 years

- Non-formal pre-school education
- Supplementary nutrition
- Growth monitoring
- Immunization
- Health check-up
- Referral services

Expectant and Nursing mother

- Health check-up
- Tetanus Toxoid Immunization to pregnant women

- Supplementary nutrition
- Nutrition and health education

Other Women 15-45 years

- Nutrition and health education
- IFA supplementation and de-worming intervention
- Non-formal education
- Home-based skill training and vocational training
- Supplementary nutrition

The concept of providing a package of services is based primarily on the consideration that the overall impact will be much larger if the different services develop in an integrated manner as the efficacy of a particular service depends upon the support it receives from related services. For nutritional purposes ICDS provides 300 calories (with 8-10 grams of protein) every day to every child below 6 years of age. For adolescent girls it is up to 500 calories with up to 25 grams of protein every day.

Fund Allocation

ICDS is a Centrally-sponsored Scheme implemented through the State Governments/UT Administrations. Prior to 2005-06, 100 per cent financial assistance for inputs other than supplementary nutrition, which the States were to provide out of their own resources, was being provided by the Government of India. Since many States were not providing adequately for supplementary nutrition in view of resource constraints, it was decided in 2005-06 to support the States up to 50 per cent of the financial norms or to support 50 per cent of expenditure incurred by them on supplementary nutrition, whichever is less.

From the financial year 2009-10, Government of India has modified the funding pattern of ICDS between Centre and States. The sharing pattern of supplementary nutrition in respect of North-Eastern States between Centre and States has been changed from 50:50 to 90:10 ratio. So far as other States and UTs, the existing sharing pattern of 50:50 continues. However, for all other components of ICDS, the ratio has been modified to 90:10 (100% Central Assistance earlier).

Table 2.18: Budget Allocation and Expenditure under ICDS Scheme during 2009-10 to 2013-14 (Rs. crore)

Year	Budget Amount	Released Amount	Utilized Expenditure	Percentage of Utilization
2009-10	6705.00	8162.00	8157.76	99.9
2010-11	8700.00	9280.00	9763.11	105.2
2011-12	10,000.00	14048.40	14272.21	101.6
2012-13	15,850.00	15,850.00	15701.50	99.1
2013-14 (as on 30.11.2013)	17,700.00	17694.89	13235.78	74.8

Source: http://wcd.nic.in/icds/.

The allocation and utilization funds under ICDS Scheme increased over time. The utilization fund increased from 8151.74 crores in 2009-10 to 15701.5 crores in 2012-13. The scheme utilized the allocated fund. In some of the years actual expenditure exceeded the allocated amount (Table 2.18).

The pattern of funding was shared between the Centre and State Government was 90:10 for 11th Plan and the share remained the same so far. The Central and State share was Rs. 225422 lakh and Rs. 13174.01 lakh respectively during the 11th Plan. In the financial year 2012-13, Rs. 37330.40 lakh and Rs. 57722.70 lakh were disbursed by the Centre and State Government as administration and training purposes. Anticipated expenditure was above 100 per cent in 2012-13 as against 100 per cent during 11th Plan. The proposed outlay was Rs. 115310.25 lakh and Rs. 2012 lakh for administrative and training purposes showing the increasing trend of outlay for ICDS programme (GoWB 2014)

Coverage

ICDS started in 33 blocks of the country and was extended to the entire country in 2005 with the objective of reducing child mortality by two-third between 1995 and 2015 (HNP, 2005). It was delivered through a network of over one million *Anganwadi* Centres (AWCs) and reaches more than 70 million children and 15 million pregnant and lactating mothers in 2008. However, the third round of the National Family Health Survey (NFHS) conducted in 2005-06 found that only 80 per cent of children in the 0-6-year age range were in areas covered by AWCs and that only 28 per cent had received any services from AWCs during pregnancy or lactation period.

Table 2.19: Physical Progress of ICDS Scheme in India, 2009 to 2013

Year ending	No. of operational projects	No. of operational AWCs	No. of Supplementary nutrition beneficiaries	No. of pre-school education beneficiaries
31.03.2009	6120	1044269	873.43 lakh	340.60 lakh
31.03.2010	6509	1142029	884.34 lakh	354.93 lakh
31.03.2011	6722	1262267	959.47 lakh	366.23 lakh
31.03.2012	6908	1304611	972.49 lakh	358.22 lakh
31.03.2013	7025	1331076	927.66 lakh	346.66 lakh
30.09.2013	7066	1340001	1032.31 lakh	349.21 lakh

Source: http://wcd.nic.in/icds/.

The ICDS currently (as on 30.9.2013) operates through a network of 7,066 fully operational projects and 13.4 lakh AWCs. The services are currently availed by 1032.31 lakh beneficiaries which include 841.49 lakh children (6 months to 6 years) and 190.82 lakh pregnant and lactating mothers. Number of Children beneficiaries within age group 3-6 years for pre-school education increased to 349.21 lakh.

Impact Study

Delivery of services under ICDS scheme is managed in an integrated manner through AWCs, its workers and helpers. The services of Immunization, Health Check-up and Referral Services delivered through Public Health Infrastructure under the MoHFW. UNICEF has provided essential supplies for the ICDS scheme since 1975. World Bank has also assisted with the financial and technical support for the programme. The cost of ICDS programme averages $10–$22 per child a year. The scheme is centrally sponsored with the state governments contributing up to ₹1.00 per day per child.

A general conception is that ICDS is women specific due to inclusion of pregnant women and nursing mothers along with the children up to six years. This is not justifiable because of consideration of child from both boys and girls. ICDS is a universal programme. But the implementation of programme is not full proof. The process of monitoring and evaluating of ICDS suffers from serious drawbacks. Notably, there is lack of timely and effective feedback from higher to lower levels (Das & Mishra 2006; Das & Pradhan 2007). Agnihotri (1999) studied the district of Orissa to find out the reason of malnutrition in a disaggregated manner. He had shown that ICDS worker and supervision were mainly responsible for the failure of the programme. They went to the centre once or two in a month. On the basis of NSSO data (1999-2000) Viswanathan (2006) analyzed the performance of nutritional programmes of children in India. He found that a large majority of children in India from poorer households did not have access to the meal schemes operational in the country.

Saxena and Srivastava (2009) using NFHS III data found that: *First*, AWCs were found to make a difference. Results show that children who are in areas not covered by an AWC are significantly more undernourished than those in areas covered by an AWC that had been in existence for more than five years. *Second*, children seen by an *Anganwadi* Worker (AWW) in the past three months are likely to be significantly less undernourished than those who were not seen, suggesting that mothers have faith in AWWs and take their children to her when there is a problem. *Third*, the only variable that is highly significant and has a positive impact on nutritional status is if the child received early child care at the AWC. Maharashtra (50%), West Bengal (39%) and Chhattisgarh (37%) reported the highest percentage of children receiving early childcare/pre-school. These states are among the top five performers in reducing undernutrition. This strengthens the argument for better focus on these services.

Srivastava and Bhaskar (2011) further use state-wise data on coverage and changes in undernutrition rates between NFHS II (1998-99) and NFHS III (2005-06) and concluded that: (a) even in areas that have the worst chronic poverty, there is hope. Wherever AWCs have done well, under-nutrition has gone down dramatically. (b) AWCs which have been in existence for over five years have a highly significant positive impact on children's weight for age score. This impact is highest for children at the lowest quintiles. (c) AWCs which were in existence for less than five years also had a positive impact on the nutritional status of children at the lowest quintiles. However, the magnitudes as well as significance levels of these coefficients were much lower.

Although the Supreme Court directed that ICDS be universalised, it has not reached all children, girls and pregnant women that need it. Even now, about a quarter of the intended beneficiaries received no benefits (PEO 2011) and between 33 and 45 per cent of the beneficiaries receive no supplementary nutrition (CAG 2013). Many AWCs also lack the equipment needed to provide supplementary nutrition and medical kits to prevent the outbreak of seasonal diseases. 40 to 65 per cent of AWCs, for instance, lack separate spaces for cooking and storing food and for indoor and outdoor activities, half lack toilets, and a third have no drinking water facilities (*ibid.*). This exposes children to unhygienic conditions, risking their health and compromising nutritional security (IRDR 2012-13).

There is also a great variation of performance of ICDS across states in India. ICDS seems to be working well in Tamil Nadu, Himachal Pradesh and Maharashtra, whereas Chhattisgarh, Bihar, Haryana, Rajasthan and Uttar Pradesh showed poor coverage (PEO 2011). Tamil Nadu's ICDS and its broader noon meal programme present valuable learning experiences for other states. Tamil Nadu's success is arguably a result of pressure from below (public expectations and participation) and from above (in the form of political will) (IRDR 2012-13).

2.5.2 Sishu Siksha Karmasuchi (SSK)

Introduction

Since the 1990s, the government focused on the universalization of education among children in the age group 6 to 14 years, initially through centrally sponsored programmes such as Operation Blackboard and state-based programmes such as the District Primary Education Project (DPEP) (Srivastava 2013). A flagship government programme, Sarva Shiksha Abhiyan (SSA) has operated since 2001 to ensure free and compulsory education to children in the 6 to 14 years age group. SSA primarily aims to strengthen the existing school infrastructure and bridge gender and social gaps in elementary education.

Between 2002 and 2009, primary school education improved substantially in terms of infrastructure, access, and enrolment (IRDP 2012-13). The programme guidelines have subsequently been revised to support the Right to Education (RTE) Act, 2009, which came into effect in 2010 (MoHRD, 2011a). This has been done on the basis of the recommendations of a committee on the Implementation of RTE Act and the Resultant Revamp of SSA (MoHRD 2010) and the road map prepared for the implementation of the RTE Act.

In West Bengal, SSA implemented by Paschim Banga Rajay Sarva Shiksha Mission (PBSSM) with two programmes namely, Shishu Shiksha Karmasuchi (SSK) (schooling up to class IV) and Madhyamic Siksha Karmasuchi (MSK) (schooling for the class V to VIII).

Background

The SSK launched in the year 1997-1998 was an endeavour towards supplementing the initiative of the school education department in the field of universalization of elementary education. Such an initiative came into emergence as it became increasingly clear that the existing network of formal primary schooling will be unable to meet the rising demand for education at the grassroots level. It was evident that this will fall short in achieving the goal of universalisation of elementary education as envisaged in the Constitution of India. This is an initiative which attempts to strengthen the mission of achieving 'Education for All' by involving the common people into the process of decision making such that the management, supervision and monitoring of the SSK rests on Panchayats and Rural Development (PRD) Department.

The PRD Department, with a view to opening 1000 Child Education Centre (later known as Shishu Shiksha Kendra) in the state of West Bengal, issued an order, dated 04/08/1997. After about two years, the Paschim Banga Rajya Shishu Shiksha Mission, under the PRD Department, Government of West Bengal, was formed on 24/11/1999, as a registered Society under the Society Registration Act, 1961, to look after the Child Education Centres by implementing the SSK. The Mission acts, as the apex body for implementation of the SSK under the direct administrative control of the PRD Department, Government of West Bengal. The Paschim Banga Rajya Shishu Shiksha Mission functions to assist the efforts of the School Education Department for bringing about the fundamental changes in the field of elementary education and through it overall improvement of socio-economic and cultural atmosphere of the society (Source: http://pbrssm.org/main).

Objectives

- Access to primary education through Shishu Shiksha Kendra for the learners who don't have access to school till then.
- Retention of every child till the age appropriate, so that they can complete the elementary education, i.e. up to standard IV.
- Ensuring quality education for the learners enrolled.
- Provision of reduction of disparity, if any, in enrolment, retention and learning achievement amongst gender and social categories, and
- Improvement of Quality of Education by in-depth capacity building and other action research activities.

For various reasons not all the children of the state get opportunity to go to the primary schools or many of them drop-out after having registered there. The situation had to be rectified in order to achieve the cherished goal of universalization of primary education. Demand for education also went up after Total Literacy Campaign (TLC) was successfully launched in the State in the early nineties. But the demand for the situation could not be fully and effectively met with formal primary education systems. At the same time, it was almost impossible to open primary schools at every nook and corner of the State wherever there were some children not having access to the school. Therefore, the Government of West Bengal decided to introduce an alternative elementary education system in West Bengal, which could reach any corner of the state, cater to the special needs of the children, less costly, but qualitatively comparable with the formal education system.

Box 2.4: Features of Shishu Shiksha Kendras

They are opened at the initiative of the community and are owned and managed by them.

Funds are provided by the State Government and Panchayats act as facilitators only.

It is a demand driven programme; Shishu Shiksha Kendras can be opened in school-less villages/village with schools which have inadequate infrastructures (in terms of space and/or teachers etc.)

Curriculum and syllabus as prescribed by the West Bengal Board of Primary Education Textbooks as prescribed for the formal primary schools.

Classroom transaction on the principles of Joyful Learning.

Target Groups

PRD Department took up the programme as SSK, and decided to set up the Shishu Shiksha Kendras, wherever there were at least twenty children not having access to any existing primary school or require some special dispensation, which are not available in the formal primary schools.

Coverage

The programme was launched in 1997-98 in West Bengal. In 2002-03, total number of SSKs was 14,699. Though the absolute number of enrollments decreased, 5,499 new SSKs were sanctioned till 2011-12 out of which 984 were completed. In the financial year 2012-13, the total number of Shishu Shiksha Kendras were 16,100. 5408 new class room, were created in financial year 2012-13 as against 8934 in 2011-12. So far about 33000 *Sahayikas* and 529 Academic Supervisors have been appointed.

Fund Allocation (Both Central and State)

The funding pattern of the SSA has also been revised and provides for 65:35 share for Centre and States for the period 2010-11 to 2015-16. An amount of Rs. 20,841 crores was spent by the Central Government on the programme in 2011-12 (Srivastava 2013).

The PRD Department assigned the responsibility of implementing the programme to a Mission created in December 1999 in the name and style of PBSSM. The task of the Mission is the supervision and monitoring of the programme, customization of training of the Para-teachers, Supervisors, Managers of the Shishu Shiksha Kendras, development of Management Information System, experimentation in the field of community mobilization, experimentation with and development of TLM, generation of demand for education where demand is still low.

In its turn, the PBSSM is supposed to operate with the help of the Zilla Parishads. At the Zilla Parishad level a cell under the Shiksha-Sanskriti-Tathya-O-Krira Sthayee Samiti of the Zilla Parishad renders necessary help in implementing the programme. At Panchayat Samiti level also there is one cell to assist the Sthayee Samiti of the Panchayat Samiti. Once a community fulfils the conditions and decides to set up a Shishu Shiksha Kendra, it will form a managing committee and apply for approval of the Zilla Parishad (through the Panchayat Samiti) and also for release of fund. The managing committee of the Kendra will appoint the Sahayikas (teachers) in accordance with the guidelines. For supervising the functioning of the Kendras, Academic Supervisors are appointed by the Zilla Parishads.

Impact Study

The main objective of SSA as well as SSK is to fulfil the mission of elementary education for all. Education must be free and reachable to the child of common people. The other objective is to bring back the education to the doorstep of the child. From this conception, it is said that within 1 km. there must be an SSK. Sau (2012) observes that the Sarva Siksha Mission (SSM) initiatives and interventions have made considerable utilization of SSM grants for development of primary and upper primary schools and also of the cluster level and circle level resource centres. This constitutes a major success of the SSM. Other success stories are observed in respect of enrolment of different categories of children, which ensures equity in access to education. While the objective of access to education is fulfilled through educational institutions, particularly new set up schools, Shishu Shiksha Kendra appear to be oversupplied in some cases. In his study he also observed that quality education for 100 per cent children is, however, yet to be achieved. In respect of learning, achievement of children there is insignificant record. A considerable percentage of children at the primary and upper primary level is seen to fare unsatisfactory learning outcome while they took learning achievement tests. Actually, the children learn so little that the whole education system has come under scanner. The issue of quality of education remains a great concern for SSM and the society.

2.5.3 Madhyamik Siksha Karmasuchi (MSK)

Background

Since a huge number of children passing out from class IV either from primary schools or from Shishu Shiksha Kendras do not get chance to get admission in High Schools due to distance factors and infrastructural problem, it was decided to execute and continue the MSK until the target is reached. The MSK was launched in the year 2003. The PBSSM also executes MSK along with SSK. Mission acts as the apex body for the implementation of MSK under the direct administrative control of the PRD Department, Government of West Bengal. Under MSK, Madhyamik Shiksha Kendras are the permanent nature of upper primary educational centres established for ensuring universal access and enrolment of all the children between the age of 9 to 14 years of the catchment area of Madhyamik Shiksha Kendras. (Source: http://pbrssm.org/main).

Objectives

Keeping in view the objectives as envisaged in SSA framework, the Mission has decided to ensure enrolment of all the children of every locality between the age, 9-14 years who pass out from primary schools, Shishu Shiksha Kendras, private schools etc. and also drop-outs from High Schools as well as ensure 100 per cent retention of the children by introducing a Community Audit System. The specific objectives of this programme are:

- Access to upper-primary education through Madhyamik Shiksha Kendras, for the learners who do not have access to school till then,
- Retention of every child till the age appropriate, so that they can complete the elementary education, i.e. up to standard VIII,
- Ensuring quality education for the learners enrolled,
- Provision of reduction of disparity, if any, in enrolment, retention and learning achievement amongst gender and social categories, and
- Improvement of Quality of Education by in-depth capacity building and other action research activities.

Target Group

Madhyamik Shiksha Kendras enroll (in class V to VIII) all the children of every locality between the age 9-14 years who pass out from primary schools, Shisu Shiksha Kendras, private schools etc. and also dropouts from High Schools. All Madhyamik Shiksha Kendras are co-educational.

Coverage

Almost all Madhyamik Shiksha Kendras have their own *pucca* building. Sometimes Kendra is also run in Primary school in morning in case of no own building. The programme MSK covers all districts including Siliguri MP area as educational districts except Kolkata. Total number of Madhyamik Shiksha Kendras was 1593 in 2005-06. It was proposed to extend the number 2093 in 2006-07. But the target cannot be fulfilled at all even in 2011-12. In 2010-11, the figure was 1915. In MSKs out of total learners 50.01 per cent were girls, 39.90 per cent were minority, 30.24 per cent were SC and 11.54 per cent were ST learners respectively. The number of Samprasaraks/Samprasarikas (the teaching personalities) working in the Madhyamik Shiksha Kendras during 2012-13 were 9715 (GoWB 2014).

Impact Study

Elementary School education under SSM is based on two alternative educational systems—SSK and MSK. The amount of disbursement has increased over the year and so on for West Bengal. SSM in West Bengal has witnessed a sea change in the globalization era in terms of development of capita-intensive physical infrastructures including school building, kitchen sheds, teaching learning materials and distributions of books and uniforms. But this phenomenal quantitative achievement has not translated itself into the improvement of quality education of children (Sau, 2014). Under SSA, it is said that the SSK and MSK will be formed in such a way for primary and upper primary, students do enjoy going to school to play and to learn. But on an average only 14 per cent of the student attended school regularly. The reason that has come out from the study of Jalan and Panda (2010) in West Bengal and Jharkhand was the non-regularity in teacher attendance and non-trained teacher in rural area (Jalan *et al.,* 2010). For these loopholes of RTE Act 2009, directed to MSKs and SSKs teacher to be as qualified as per NCTE norms within 31st March 2015 (GoWB 2014). Though there are many criticisms against MSKs, yet the study by Pratichi Trust (2009) revealed that MSK was better than conventional education system in West Bengal. The sympathetic attitude of the Samprasaraks/Samprasarikas has not only raised the attendance of the children generally, but has also, most importantly, drawn more girls into the upper primary schooling system. While in the high schools, the percentage of enrolled girls is less than that of boys, it is just the opposite in the MSKs. There are many factors that contribute to this high female enrolment, including the timing, which is generally scheduled in consultation with the village communities. Perhaps the most important factor, however, is the teachers' dedication to bringing the children into the schooling system, something that seems to be often lacking among the High school teachers. In the second phase of the study by Pratichi Trust, it was found that when a child is absent from school, Samprasaraks/ Samprasarikas seek an explanation from the child's parents in 95 per cent of cases, while the comparative figure for High school teachers is just 55 per cent (Pratich Trust 2009).

Accepting the importance of MSK, emphasis was laid on the expansion of Madhyamik Shiksha Kendras within 2 km. of habitation in MSK guideline. But there are 14,165 habitations in West Bengal having neither Upper Primary schools nor Madhyamik Shiksha Kendras within 2 km (DISE 2011-12). The number of habitations having no schools/MSKs is relatively high in three backward districts of Bankura, Purulia and Paschim Midnapore (Table 2.20).

Table 2.20: Number of Habitations having Schools/MSKs across Districts of West Bengal, 2010-11

District	*No. of habitations having no Upper Primary schools MSK within 2 km.*	*District*	*No. of habitations having no Upper Primary schools MSK within 2 km.*
Bankura	2337	Maldah	919
Bardhaman	903	Murshidabad	543
Birbhum	665	Nadia	0
Dakshin Dinajpur	672	North 24 Parganas	253
Darjiling	0	Paschim Medinipur	2432
Haora	49	Purba Medinipur	286
Hugli	244	Puruliya	1451
Jalpaiguri	944	South 24 Parganas	667
Koch Bihar	571	Uttar Dinajpur	1229
Kolkata	0	**Total**	**14165**

Source: Provisional DISE data 2010-11.

2.5.4 *Kanyashree Prakalpa*

Kanyashree Prakalpa 2013, a conditional cash transfer scheme for improving the status and well-being of the girl child in the state has been formulated by the Department of Women Development and Social Welfare, Government of West Bengal. The scheme also aims at improving the status and well-being of the girl child in West Bengal by incentivizing schooling of all teenage girls and delaying their marriage until the age of 18, the legal age of marriage. Protecting and empowering all adolescent girls and supporting their healthy development by creating an enabling environment for their participation and meaningful contribution to society. The details of the scheme are given in Box 2.5.

Box 2.5: Kanyashree Prakalpa

Objectives

The scheme aims at improving the status and well-being of girl child by:

- Discouraging early marriage of girls to ensure compliance with the legal provisions pertaining to the minimum age at marriage.
- Incentivize through scholarships, the continuation of education of the girl child in Secondary and Higher Secondary classes and those undergoing vocational training or sports training.
- Improving IMR and MMR by delaying the age of marriage and consequently increasing the median age of first birth.
- Reducing the incidence of dropouts, especially amongst girls from poor families.

Box 2.5: (*Contd.*)

- Eradicating undernutrition and malnutrition of girl child.
- Preventing trafficking and exploitation of the girl child.

Components of the Scheme

The scheme has two components:

- Annual Scholarship of Rs. 500/-(Rupees Five hundred only)
- One-time Grant of Rs. 25,000/-(Rupees Twenty-five thousand only)

Eligibility

The Annual Scholarship is for unmarried girls aged 13-18 years enrolled in classes VIII-XII in government recognized regular or equivalent open school or equivalent vocational/technical training course. The One-time Grant is for girls turned 18 at the time of application, enrolled in government recognized regular or open school/college or pursuing vocational/technical training or sports activity or is an inmate of Home registered under J.J. Act, 2000. Both the benefits under the scheme will be granted to girls who belong to families with annual family income not more than Rs. 1,20,000/-(Rupees One Lakh and twenty thousand only.

Complete Applications Received for 2013-14
Annual Scholarships: 18,86,688; One Time Grant: 1,36,730
Scholarships Awarded in 2013-14
Annual Scholarships: 17,95,421; One Time Grant: 1,25,247
Complete Applications Received for 2014-15
Annual Scholarships: 2,76,115; One Time Grant: 41,708
Scholarships Awarded in 2014-15
Annual Scholarships: 11,474; One Time Grant: 1,064

Source: Govt. of West Bengal, wbkanyashree.gov.in/kp_home_php

2.5.5 National Programme of Mid-Day Meal (MDM)

Introduction

Every child is the wealth of the nation. So, development of child is co-related to the progress of the country. But the children are highly neglected in our society. Due to abject poverty, they suffer from hunger, malnutrition, underweight, disease etc, they fail to go to the school. To overcome poverty situation, the parents are compelled to engage their children in various labour-oriented work which makes them child labour. As per rough estimate, at least 20 per cent of Indian children (in the 6-14 age group) are out of school. This too, impairs their future in many ways.

This situation is a gross violation of the fundamental rights of children. Under Article 21 of the Constitution, all Indian children have a fundamental right to life. And as the Supreme Court has made clear on several occasions, the right to life is a right to live with dignity, which includes the right to food and related necessities. Under Article 21A of the Constitution, Indian children are entitled to free and compulsory education from the age of 6 to 14. Moreover, Article 47 of the constitution says that "the state shall regard the raising of level of nutrition and the standard of living of its people and the improvement of public health ...." It means that every child has right to get education and to be protected from hunger (Mid-day Meals: Primer, October 2005).

However, in view of deteriorating primary education scenario and rise in number of non-going school children due to abject poverty, the Govt. of India took a policy decision in 1995 to provide food to the children in primary schools in the country. In this direction, a National Programme of Nutritional Support to Primary Education (NP-NSPE) was launched which is commonly known as Mid-Day Meal Scheme. Under this programme, provision was made to provide a free cooked meal to every child in Classes I-V of government, government aided and local body schools, and also children studying in centres run under the Education Guarantee Scheme (EGS) and Alternative and Innovative Education (AIE) Scheme. On 28 November, 2001, the Supreme Court directed State Governments to introduce cooked mid-day meals in all government and government-assisted primary schools within six months. This landmark order was one of the first achievements of the right to food campaign. The order was followed by organized public pressure for the introduction of cooked mid-day meals in primary schools, e.g. in the form of a country-wide 'day of action on mid-day meals' in April 2002 (Midday Meals: Primer, October 2005).

Background

NP-NSPE was launched as a Centrally Sponsored Scheme on 15th August, 1995, initially in 2408 blocks in the country. By the year 1997-98, the NP-NSPE was introduced in all blocks of the country. It was further extended in 2002 to cover not only children in Classes I-V of government, government aided and local body schools, but also children studying in EGS and AIE centres. Central Assistance under the scheme consisted of free supply of food grains @ 100 grams per child per school day, and subsidy for transportation of food grains up to a maximum of Rs. 50 per quintal.

In September 2004, the scheme was revised to provide cooked mid-day meal with 300 calories and 8-12 grams of protein to all children studying in classes I-V in Government and Government aided schools and EGS/AIE centres. In addition to free supply of food grains, the revised scheme provided Central Assistance for (a) Cooking cost (Rs. 1 per child per school day), (b) Transport subsidy was raised from the earlier maximum of Rs. 50 per quintal to Rs. 100 per quintal for special category states, and Rs. 75 per quintal for other states, (c) Management, monitoring and evaluation costs (2% of the cost of food grains, transport subsidy and cooking assistance), (d) Provision of mid-day meal during summer vacation in drought affected areas.

In July 2006, the scheme was further revised to provide assistance for cooking cost at the rate of (a) Rs. 1.80 per child/school day for States in the North Eastern Region (NER), provided the NER states contribute Rs. 0.20 per child/school day, and (b) Rs. 1.50 per child/school day for other States and UTs, provided that these States and UTs contribute Rs. 0.50 per child/school day (Source: mdm.nic.in/PAB.htm). In 2007, the scheme extended to all Upper Primary Classes (Class VI to VIII).

Objectives

- Improving the nutritional status of children in classes I-V in Government, Local Body and Government aided schools, and EGS and AIE centres.
- Encouraging poor children, belonging to disadvantaged sections, to attend school more regularly and help them concentrate on classroom activities.
- Providing nutritional support to children of primary stage in drought affected areas during summer vacation.

Target Groups

All School leaving children from class I to class VIII.

Provision of Benefits

In 2001, following orders of the Supreme Court, the MDM became a cooked MDM Scheme under which every child in every Government and Government aided Primary School was to be served a prepared MDM with a minimum of 300 calories and 8-12 grams protein per day for a minimum of 200 days. The nutritional norm for Upper Primary Classes was fixed at 700 calories and 20 grams of protein (James, 2013).

Fund Allocation

The Central Government bears the major cost of the project. Central

Government provides Rs. 2.21 per child per school day in primary school in 2004. The breaking is given in Table 2.21. But assistance is higher for upper primary and high school.

Table 2.21: Central Assistance for Mid-Day Meals (December 2004)

Item	*Central Assistance (Rs./child per school day*
Average "economic" cost of food grain (100 gms per child)	1.11
Average transport subsidy (FCI godown to school)	0.08
Assistance for cooking costs	1.00
Assistance for "management, monitoring and evaluation"	0.02
Total	2.21

Source: MoHRD Guidelines, December 2004.

The programme had a budget of Rs. 6,678 crores in 2007-08, which increased to Rs. 10,380 crores in 2011-12 and covers about 12 crore children in 12 lakh schools in India. For management, monitoring and evaluation of the scheme at two per cent of the cost of food grains, transport subsidy and cooking assistance. The Central Government also assist to facilitate construction of kitchen cum store room (Rs. 60,000 per unit) and procurement of kitchen devices in schools (Rs. 5,000 per school) in a phased manner was provided. The achievements of MDM scheme are given in Table 2.22.

Table 2.22: Achievements of MDM Scheme in Primary and Upper Primary Schools during 2005-06 to 2011-12

Components	*2005-06*	*2006-07*	*2007-08*	*2008-09*	*2009-10*	*2010-11*	*2011-12*
Children covered (in Cr.)	11.94	10.68	11.37	11.19	11.36	10.46	10.35
Food grain allocated (in lakh MTs)	22.51	21.6	24.79	29.3	27.71	29.4	29.09
Budget allocation (in Cr.)	3345.26	5348	6678	8000	7359.15	9440	10380
Total Exp. (in Cr.)	3186.33	5233.47	5835.44	6688.02	6937.79	9128.44	7697.24

Source: Annual Report 2011-12, MHRD, Government of India.

Box 2.6: Fact File of MDM Scheme in India

- 10.45 crore children benefit from hot cooked nutritious food in 11.58 lakh schools during 20013-14.
- 5.70 lakh cook-cum-helper mainly from SC/ST/OBC communities have been engaged to provide mid-day meal to the school children.
- 6.70 lakh kitchen-cum-stores have been constructed to endure safety of food grain and ensure hygienic meals to the children.

Source: http://mdm.nic.in

The MDM programme has a good ideological view from Indian perspective and circumstances. Along with India West Bengal too achieved a significant success in MDM programme. During 2010-11 to 2012-13, West Bengal covered more than 90 per cent of the approved institutions under MDMs with increasing coverage of children against enrolment in primary and upper primary. The percentage utilization of foodgrains against allocation in primary and upper primary had also improved over the period. The utilization of food grains was increased from 64 per cent in 2010-11 to 70 per cent in 2012-13.

Table 2.23: Fund Allocation from Centre to State West Bengal (Rs. in Lakh)

Year	*Recurring Fund (Received & Release)*			*Non-Recurring Fund (Received & Release)*			*Grand Total*
	Central	*State*	*Total*	*Central*	*State*	*Total*	
2010-11	71459.77	21015.68	92475.45	0	0	0	92475.45
2011-12	70069.94	21413.72	91483.66	16269.23	7423.08	23692.31	115176
2012-13	88686.27	26026.14	114712.4	5299.04	1089.06	6388.1	121100.5

Source: *Joint Review Mission on MDM: West Bengal, 28th November, 2013.*

Coverage

The Scheme was introduced with Government and Government-aided Primary Schools only. The scheme was further extended in 2002 to cover not only children studying in Government aided and local body schools, but also children studying in EGS and AIE centres. In October 2007, the scheme was extended to cover children of Upper Primary Classes (Class VI to VIII) studying in 3,479 educationally backwards blocks and the name of the scheme was changed from National Programme of Nutritional Support to Primary Education to National Programme of Mid-Day Meal in schools. The scheme was extended to all Upper Primary Classes in all areas across the country from April, 2008 with the introduction of the scheme in recognized as well as unrecognized Madarasas/Maqtabs supported under SSA. Since 2009, the scheme also, covers National Child Labour Project (NCLP) schools.

The government of West Bengal took some time to overcome the initial hiccups and has finally come up to meet the terms of the Supreme Court directives to implement the programme in every primary schooling institution (including the Sishu Siksha Kendras–SSKs). The beginning was made with some 1,100 primary schools in five districts (Murshidabad, Birbhum, Bankura, Paschim Midnapore, and Jalpaiguri) and extended to some other districts. A total of 5,200 primary schools were brought into the fold of the programme till March 31, 2004. Further, a decision has been taken to bring all the primary schools and SSKs into the fold of the programme. Thereafter, coverage of schools increased gradually. As on 30th June 2009, the number of primary schools and students eligible were 78571 and 9639348 respectively. Against this eligibility, 73678 and 9012435 schools and students were respectively covered. So, the coverage of schools and coverage of enrolment was 94 per cent respectively for the state. But the coverage for Upper Primary School was 75 per cent and 77 per cent. The coverage of students was increased by 10 per cent during 2009 to 2012-13. Along with the increase in coverage of students, there was a significant increase in coverage of the schools for both Primary and Upper Primary (99% and 98% respectively) (Economic Review 2013-14).

Impact Study

Garg *et al.* (2013) found that MDM as policy intervention benefits the disadvantaged groups through increasing enrolments, attendance and improved nutrition. Evaluations of MDM by various agencies also showed that the scheme has been successful in improving rural school enrolment and attendance (Jayaraman *et al.*, 2010; ASER 2011; De *et al.*, 2011).

Many studies reported about prevalence of caste discrimination in MDM (Macwan 2010, Menon 2003, Nambissam 2009, Thorat and Lee 2005). Students from SC and ST groups were made to sit away from upper castes; in some cases, they were not given food or they were served leftover food (Garg *et al.*, 2013). They also found that MDM programme has benefited children from marginalized sections by bringing them to the school and in terms of nutritional intake (evenly in modestly), but in terms of the most substantial goal of benefiting the educationally marginalized, the achievements of MDM are marginal. But Khera (2013) observed that MDM has also helped in breaking caste barriers as children from different communities eat together.

The programme failed to have any significant positive effect on learning outcomes (Jayaraman *et al.*, 2010). One possible reason may be the diversion of teacher time toward managing and overseeing the MDM, as teachers in many states spend between one and two hours a day on activities related to the programme, which compromises on teaching time and contributes to poor test scores (Muralidharan 2012). One concern that remains is that infrastructure constraints persist; apart from Tamil Nadu and Kerala, schools in most states lack a clean source of water, kitchen sheds and storerooms, making it difficult to ensure that the food served is hygienic (PEO 2010). In addition, there are concerns relating to pilferage and adulteration of the food, and most states do not follow PDS guidelines, which sometimes compromises the quality of food and threatens the health and safety of children.

But due to lack of infrastructure created by school authority and indifferent attitude of MDM worker, the programme is turned to a tragedy after 22 children lost their lives by consuming a government provided school meal containing organophosphate pesticides in Chhapra, Bihar (Khera, 2013). Not only that, there are other major criticisms levelled against the MDM programme. The first observation is that it will lead to fiscal disaster. The second criticism is of colossal waste since it is based on the PDS which has been shown to be ineffective and wasteful (Editorial, EPW July 2013).

2.5.6 Books and Other Grants

Different educational development schemes for SC, ST and OBC students both at pre- and post-matric stages in operation in the State West Bengal are summarized below:

Book Grants and Examination Fees: The purpose of this scheme is to provide financial assistance to purchase books for the students studying in classes V to X and also for the payment of examination fees of Madhyamik Examination in government aided schools. Approximately 24 lakh and 27 lakh SC/ST students were benefited under this scheme during the years 2010-2011 and 2011-12 respectively.

The financial assistance is given to the students reading in classes V to X in Government /Govt. aided schools to purchase the books. Children whose family income is up to Rs. 36,000 per annum are entitled to this grant. The amounts of book grants of different classes are given in Table 2.24.

Table 2.24: The Rate of Book Grants in West Bengal, 2012-13

Class	*V*	*VI*	*VII*	*VIII*	*IX*	*X*
Rs. Per annum	20	150	200	280	300	275*

Note: Along with Examination Fee (As charged by the Board).
Source: www.anagrasarkalyan.gov.in/pdf/edu-schms.pdf

Eligible students are to apply in the prescribed form through their Head of the Institution just after admission/promotion into new class. The achievement of the state West Bengal in this respect is given in Table 2.25. In 2012-13 about 13.79 lakh SC students and 4.90 lakh ST students obtained book grants.

Table 2.25: Beneficiaries and Amount Spent on Book Grants for SC and ST Students (Class V to VIII) in West Bengal

Year	*Scheduled Caste*		*Scheduled Tribe*	
	Amount utilized (Rs.)	*No. of Beneficiaries (V to VIII)*	*Amount utilized (Rs.)*	*No. of Beneficiaries (V to VIII)*
2007-08	30,04,56,995	15,08,735	5,09,32,905	2,72,817
2008-09	21,44,02,040	10,91,616	6,06,04,850	3,05,098
2009-10	49,52,70,222	23,28,861	6,13,02,839	3,11,474
2010-11	43,37,11,363	20,60,712	7,23,30,824	3,65,844
2011-12	41,48,50,700	19,93,544	8,01,54,643	3,80,391
2012-13	23,25,55,459	13,79,474	90,770,840	4,90,515

Source: www.anagrasarkalyan.gov.in/pdf/edu-schms.pdf

However, with the introduction of Pre-Matric Scholarship for students of classes IX & X both for SC & ST, Book Grants to these students will be discontinued.

Other Compulsory Charges for Students Belonging to ST Communities

This scheme is meant exclusively for ST students. Under the scheme each ST student gets Rs. 35 per annum to enable them to pay various compulsory charges to the School on account of development fee, library fee etc. Family income limit has been fixed at Rs. 36,000 per annum as a condition of eligibility. Number of beneficiaries and amount spent on them for the period 2007-2013 are given in Table 2.26. In 2012-13 about 2.5 lakh ST students received benefits.

Table 2.26: Benefits of Other Compulsory Charges received by the School for Scheduled Tribe Students in West Bengal

Year	2007-08	2008-09	2009-10	2010-11	2011-12	2012-13
Amount Utilized (Rs.)	69,58,615	77,09,378	85,02,140	89,73,935	98,63,095	88,43,005
No. of Benefi-ciaries	1,89,161	2,20,519	2,43,013	2,56,271	2,77,204	2,53,168

Source: www.anagrasarkalyan.gov.in/pdf/edu-schms.pdf

Hostel Charges

Hostel charges are provided to SC/ST students residing in the school-attached Hostels and Ashram Hostels attached to the Junior or Secondary School. These hostels are attached to the Junior High or Secondary Schools, run and managed by the respective school authorities. This scheme provides opportunity to SC/ST students to grow up in an academic environment free from the hazards of undertaking long journeys for attending their schools. There are at present more than 1522 school attached hostels all over the State. The students are advised to communicate with the Hostel Advisory Committee through their respective Head of the Institution for admission into Hostel just after admission into new class. In April 2010, the Hostel charges have been enhanced from Rs. 600 to Rs. 750 per month. Each student residing in the Hostel gets hostel grant for 10 months only (Rs. 750 per month). Thus, the total amount of grant for each student is Rs. 750 × 10 = Rs. 7,500 per year. Children whose family income is up to Rs. 36,000 per annum are entitled to this grant. The quota of school-attached boarders increased from 36,000 to 50,000 for SC beneficiaries and from 32,000 to 45,000 for ST beneficiaries. During 2010-11 total number of beneficiaries covered under this scheme was 83,808. In 2012-13, the SC/ST beneficiaries increased to 94,400 (Table 2.27).

Ashram Hostels for SC and ST Students

In West Bengal, Ashram hostels were constructed for providing residential facilities to SC and ST students reading in primary, junior high and high

Table 2.27: Hostel Grants and Beneficiaries in West Bengal, 2007-08 to 2012-13

Year	Scheduled Caste		Scheduled Tribe	
	Amount utilized (Rs.)	No. of Beneficiaries	Amount utilized (Rs.)	No. of Beneficiaries
2007-08	20,22,47,040	34,485	18,67,84,200	31,462
2008-09	23,54,59,620	42,940	21,34,60,080	39,291
2009-10	22,38,09,542	46,102	21,31,10,631	43,606
2010-11	28,51,66,700	44,609	25,98,40,258	39,199
2011-12	31,89,99,731	47,481	27,66,56,900	43,976
2012-13	28,83,27,063	48,009	33,50,91,197	46,391

Source: www.anagrasarkalyan.gov.in/pdf/edu-schms.pdf.

school so that they may continue their studies in congenial atmosphere. Such ashram hostels are normally attached to Junior Basic, Junior High and High Schools. Presently in total 260 Ashram, Hostels are running with 7635 SC and ST Ashramites. Besides boarding and lodging, all other essential facilities are also provided at Government cost. The Ashramites are provided with residential facilities, meal charges (Rs. 300 per month per student) for 12 months, garments charges (Rs. 80 per student per annum) and other essential charges, sports & games (Rs. 50 per annum), medical allowances, bedding (Rs. 100 for every two years) and kerosene oil (Rs. 300 per annum). Enhancement of meal charge from Rs. 300 per month to Rs. 400 per month is under active consideration of Government.

Maintenance Charges

Under this scheme each eligible SC/ST day scholar of secondary stage (from class V to X) belonging to the families having annual income within Rs. 18,000 is paid Rs. 40 per month as maintenance grant to meet their conveyance and other sundry expenses. From April, 2010, quota of SC students was enhanced to 3 lakhs from 1,63,750. Nearly 5 lakh and 6 lakh SC/ST students were benefited under this scheme during the years 2010-11 and 2011-12 respectively.

Post-Matric Scholarship: The objective of this scheme is to provide financial assistance to the SC, ST and OBC students studying at post-secondary stages to enable them to complete their education. For SC/ST students the scholarship is grouped into four categories was enhanced to 600 per month in 2010-11. Total number of beneficiaries under this scheme was 2.98 lakh which increased to about 5.80 lakh in 2011-12.

Up-gradation for Merit of SC/ST Students Reading in Classes IX to XII

This scheme has been introduced with a view to remove deficiencies in school subjects and specially for preparing SC/ST students for competitive examinations required for entry into professional courses like Engineering and Medicine. The emphasis of remedial coaching is to remove educational deficiencies from which these students suffer and to promote study habits. Quota for SC is 368 and quota for ST is 72. A package grant is given with the break-up as shown in Table 2.28. In 2012-13, 254 SC students and 38 ST students obtained benefits under up-gradation of merit (Table 2.29).

Table 2.28: Break-up of Grants (Rs.) for Up-gradation of Merit for SC/ST Students reading Classes IX to XII in West Bengal

Grants	*S.C.*	*S.T.*
Boarding & lodging charge for 10 months	5,000	7,000
Pocket money for 10 months	1,000	2,000
Books & Stationery	2,000	2,500
Honorarium to Principal, expert & other incidental charges	7,000	8,000
Total	15,000	19,500

Source: www.anagrasarkalyan.gov.in/pdf/edu-schms.pdf.

Table 2.29: Beneficiaries and Grants for SC/ST Students reading Classes IX to XII in West Bengal, 2007-08 to 2012-13

Year	*Scheduled Caste*		*Scheduled Tribe*	
	Amount utilized (Rs.)	*Beneficiaries*	*Amount utilized (Rs.)*	*Beneficiaries*
2007-08	10,48,125	100	5,62,725	58
2008-09	6,70,750	65	2,58,375	20
2009-10	Not fund	-	Not fund	-
2010-11	8,09,000	145	4,64,575	35
2011-12	16,74,800	149	4,96,000	35
2012-13	33,05,200	254	6,65,000	38

Source: www.anagrasarkalyan.gov.in/pdf/edu-schms.pdf.

Scholarships/Grants for Students of Minority

Merit-cum-Means Scholarship: Scholarship up to Rs. 30,000 (i.e., Actual course fee or Rs. 20,000 per annum whichever is less plus Maintenance Allowance up to Rs. 10,000/- for Hosteller/Rs. 5000 for Day

Scholar) per year per student is given for pursuing professional/ technical courses at graduate and post-graduate level.

Post-matric Scholarship: Scholarship is given to students for pursuing studies from class XI to Ph.D. Scholarship amount ranges from Rs. 2700 to Rs. 10,800 comprising course fee and maintenance charge per year. The students should obtain minimum 50 per cent marks in the last final examination.

Post Matric Stipend (Under Talent Support Programme): This stipend is awarded to the students who are the resident of West Bengal and have passed their last final examination and obtained below 50 per cent marks. He/she must also be continuing his/her studies.

- Scholarship is given to students for pursuing studies from Class XI and onwards up to Ph.D.
- Annual Family Income up to Rs. 2 lakh.
- 30 per cent of scholarship is earmarked for girl students.
- Scholarship is provided subject to availability of Fund.
- Yearly Scholarship (including maintenance charge and course fee) for Class XI & XII is Rs. 2,550 for Graduation Rs. 4,800, and for Post-Graduate Rs. 4900.

Pre-Matric Scholarship: Scholarship is given to students for pursuing studies from class 1 to Class X. Yearly scholarship for Class I to V is Rs. 1000, Class VI to X is Rs. 1240 for Day Scholar and Rs. 6240 per year for the Hosteller.

2.6 Programme for Housing

2.6.1 Indira Awas Yojana (IAY)

Introduction

Housing is a fundamental human need; it is a basic requirement for human survival as well as for a decent life. Housing is not just for individual families alone; it is for the community. Basically, houses afford shelter from the elements of nature, privacy and protection from the hustle and bustle of the external world. As a dwelling place, it provides security and enables access to different facilities based on its location. Going beyond mere shelter, dwelling and house, ultimately everyone desires a home which gives a sense of ownership and identity, affords psychological satisfaction and promotes self-esteem and confidence. A home contributes significantly to well-being and is essential for a person's social and economic development. It supports livelihoods and promotes social integration. It is a form of cultural expression and symbolizes social position.

Background

Indira Awas Yojana (IAY) was launched in June 1985 as a sub-scheme of Rural Landless Employment Guarantee Programme (RLEGP) by earmarking a part of the fund for construction of houses for SCs/STs and freed bonded labourers. When Jawahar Rozgar Yojana (JRY) was launched in April, 1985, 6 per cent of the funds was allocated for housing for the SCs/STs and freed bonded labourers. In 1993-94, the coverage was extended to Non-SC/ST families by increasing the earmarked fund for housing under JRY to 10 per cent and allowing the use of the additional 4 per cent for this category of beneficiaries. IAY was made an independent scheme with effect from 1st January, 1996. It is now a flagship programme of the Ministry of Rural Development, Government of India, as a part of the larger strategy of rural poverty eradication, in order to reduce the rigours of poverty and to provide the dignity of an address to the poor households to enable them to access different rural development programmes. Initially, the unit cost was fixed at Rs. 10,000 which was enhanced to plain area from Rs. 12,700 in 1990, to Rs. 14,000 in 1994 and further to Rs. 20,000 in 1996, Rs. 25,000 in 2004, Rs. 35,000 in 2008 and Rs. 45,000 in 2010. In hilly area, the unit cost increased from Rs. 14,500 in 1990 to Rs. 15,800 in 1994 and further to Rs. 22,000 in 1996, Rs. 27,500 in 2004, Rs. 38,500 in 2008 and Rs. 48,500 in 2010 (IAY, Briefing Book, August 2013).

Objectives

Aim of IAY is to provide financial assistance to the rural houseless poor families and those living in dilapidated and *kutcha* houses for construction of house and also to provide house sites to the landless poor as well.

Target Groups

BPL rural households of Scheduled Caste, Scheduled Tribe as well as non-Scheduled Caste and non-Scheduled Tribe are the target groups of the programme. Priority should be given to families of manual scavengers, including those rehabilitated and rehabilitated bonded labourers. Thereafter the priority to be adhered to is as follows:

- Women in difficult circumstances, including widows, those divorced or deserted, women victims of atrocities and those whose husbands are missing for at least three years and women headed families.
- Mentally challenged persons (with at least 40% disability).
- Physically challenged persons (with at least 40% disability).
- Transgender persons.
- Widows and next-of-kin of members of defense/paramilitary/police forces killed in action (even if not BPL).
- Other houseless BPL families (IAY guide line, http://iay.nic.in/netiay/home.aspx).

Provision of Benefits

The financial assistance provided under IAY is as under:

(i) Financial assistance for construction of a new house is Rs. 70,000 in plain areas and Rs. 75,000 in hilly/difficult/IAP areas.
(ii) Financial assistance for upgradation of *Kutcha* or dilapidated house is Rs. 15,000.
(iii) Financial assistance for acquiring house site is Rs. 20,000 (http://iay.nic.in/netiay/home.aspx).

Fund Allocation

The cost of the scheme except the component for provision of house sites would be shared between Government of India and State Governments in the ratio 75:25. In the case of North Eastern States, the ratio is 90:10. The cost of providing house sites would be shared 50:50 between Government of India and State Governments. Government of India would provide the full cost in respect of Union Territories (UTs). At the national level, 60 per cent of the funds would be earmarked for SCs and STs with the proportion between SCs and STs being decided from time to time by the Ministry of Rural Development and reflected in the targets. Further, 15 per cent of the funds would be set apart for beneficiaries from among the minorities. The State should ensure that at least 3 per cent of beneficiaries are from among persons with disabilities. Ninety-five per cent of the total budget would be utilized for the components relating to new houses, upgradation of houses and provision of house sites and administrative expenses. The remaining 5 per cent would be reserved for special projects.

The financial and physical performance of IAY during 11th Plan is given in Table 2.30. During this plan about 127 lakh houses were constructed/renovated under IAY. But the utilization of available fund for IAY was not satisfactory. On the whole during the 11th Plan 72.33 per cent of available fund are utilized.

The budget proposed for Rural Housing to Planning Commission for the Twelfth Five Year Plan was Rs. 1,50,000 crore. Planning Commission has approved Rs. 80,085 crore. The budget allocation for the year 2012-13 i.e. the first year of 12th Five Year Plan was 11,075.00 crore. Budget provided for 2013-14 is Rs. 15,184 crore (IAY, Briefing Book August, 2013). The financial and physical performance of IAY during first two years of 12th Five Years Plan is summarized in Table 2.31.

For the 11th financial plan (2007-12) total release for West Bengal was Rs. 3,56,270 lakh which consisted of Rs. 2,69,342 lakh and Rs. 86,928 lakh with the contribution of Centre and State Government respectively. For the financial year 2012-13, Rs. 1,20,000 lakh and Rs. 40,000 lakhs were disbursed by the Government of India and West Bengal Government. The total anticipated expenditure was 100 per cent for this year. The outlay has increased by 1.05 per cent in the annual plan 2013-14 (GoWB).

IAY in the Context of Bharat Nirman

Bharat Nirman Programme is a plan comprising six different components addressing the rural sector and housing is one of them. Rural Housing was one of the six components of Bharat Nirman Programme. Under Bharat Nirman, 60 lakh houses were envisaged to be constructed under the Scheme of IAY in four years from 2005-06 to 2008-09. Against this target, 71.76 lakh houses were constructed thereby exceeding the target of Bharat Nirman.

The Target under Phase-II of Bharat Nirman is for construction of 120 lakh houses for a period of five years starting from 2009-10. During the first four years (up to 31.7.2013) about 107.58 lakh houses have been constructed. The physical target and expenditure under Bharat Nirman in India are given in Table 2.32. Further, for the current financial year of 2013-14, the total budgetary outlay for rural housing was Rs. 15,184 crore with a physical target for construction of 24.80 lakh houses.

Table 2.30: Financial and Physical Performances of IAY in the 11th Five Year Plan in India

Years	*Total allocation (C+S) (in crore*	*Total Releases (C+S) (in crore)*	*Total Available Funds (in crore)*	*Utilization (in crore)*	*% Utilization*	*Physical target (in lakh)*	*Physical Achievement (in lakh)*	*% Achievement*
2007-08	5374.19	5175.10	6527.17	5464.54	83.72	21.27	19.92	93.65
2008-09	7523.85	11727.04	14460.35	8348.34	57.73	21.27	21.34	100.32
2009-10	11131.59	11316.90	15852.34	13292.46	83.85	40.52	33.86	83.55
2010-11	13181.32	13295.22	17956.54	13465.73	74.99	29.09	27.15	93.36
2011-12	12436.47	12920.36	19159.30	12926.33	67.47	27.27	24.71	90.64
Total	49647.42	54434.62	73955.7	53497.4	72.33	139.42	126.98	91.08

Note: C = Central, S = State

Source: IAY, Briefing Book August, 2013.

Table 2.31: Financial and Physical Performances of IAY in the 12th Five Year Plan in India (as on 31.07.2013)

Year	*Total allocation (C+S) (in crore*	*Total Releases (C+S) (in crore)*	*Total Available Funds (in crore)*	*Utilization (in crore)*	*% Utilization*	*Physical target (in lakh)*	*Physical Achievement (in lakh)*	*% achievement*
2012-13	13776.21	7208.49	13531.38	9386.22	75.48	30.10	21.86	72.62
2013-14	13894.90	5915.87	7037.23	1134.55	16.12	24.80	0.25	1.00

Note: C= Central, S = State

Source: IAY, Briefing Book August, 2013.

Table 2.32: The Physical Target and Expenditure under Bharat Nirman in India

Year	2009-10	2010-11	2011-12	2012-13	Total
Target (in lakh)	40.52	29.09	27.27	30.1	126.98
Expenditure (Rs. in crore)	13292.46	13406.51	12926.33	9386.22	49011.52

Source: IAY, Briefing Book August, 2013.

Coverage

IAY beneficiaries are chosen from BPL list which is constructed by BPL census. The list was formulated by Gram Sabha every year. However, it was recognized that irregularities/ biased approached was rampant in the selection of beneficiaries. To make the selection process transparent, it was decided that permanent IAY waitlists will be prepared based on the BPL list 2002. In Phase II of IAY for the financial year 2012-13; 270 districts, 793 blocks and 2569 villages were covered under IAY. A Scheme to provide homestead sites to those rural BPL households, who neither have agricultural land nor a house site, has been launched, as part of IAY, w.e.f. 24th August, 2009. Out of 2565 villages visited by National Level Monitors (NLMs) homestead sites were provided only in 501 villages. Sixty six per cent of these villages had a maximum of 5 beneficiaries, 11 per cent villages had up to 10 and 24 per cent villages had more than 10 beneficiaries (MoRD 2013). During 2009-10 to 2012-13 about one crore houses were constructed for rural BPL households in India (Table 2.33).

Table 2.33: Number of Houses Constructed under IAY in India, 2009 to 2013

Year	2009-10	2010-11	2011-12	2012-13	Total (2009-13)
Houses constructed (in lakh)	33.86	27.15	24.71	21.86	107.58

Source: IAY, Briefing Book August, 2013.

Impact Evaluation

In the present form, IAY is one of the popular schemes of the Ministry of Rural Development. The popularity can be attributed to the fact that the scheme enables beneficiaries to participate and involve themselves in construction of their houses. The role of the State Government is limited to release and facilitating the use of appropriate technology. In spite of criticism from certain quarters about IAY being a full subsidy scheme, experience reveals that houses get completed more or less on time. Not surprisingly, evaluation studies revealed high levels of occupancy and satisfaction. Providing houses to the poorest also has a positive impact on people's physical and mental health. Once the basic need of housing is fulfilled, citizens develop a sense of opportunity for livelihood, for improving living conditions and for continuing children's education. Undoubtedly, there is a direct link between a safe and secure housing and improved standards of living and reduction in vulnerability (IAY, Briefing Book August, 2013).

Kapur *et al.,* (2008) argued that direct cash transfer was the best articulation. They said that IAY supported the poor people providing the basic needs of shelter. Shah (2008) claimed that IAY was not the magic bullet to eradicate poverty.

Most deserved category in the age group of above 60 years had been given top priority for the allotment of houses with 30 per cent under IAY in Rajasthan followed by Chhattisgarh with 17.5 per cent, Maharashtra with 16.3 per cent and Himachal Pradesh with 12.5 per cent. SC population had been given top priority while sanctioning the houses under IAY especially in Himachal Pradesh with 24.7 per cent among the states studied followed by Tamil Nadu with 19 per cent, Rajasthan with 17.2 per cent, Orissa with 16.5 per cent and Andhra Pradesh & Karnataka with 16.2 per cent each. Highest percentage of ST population had been given top priority while sanctioning the houses under IAY especially in the states of Chhattisgarh with 31.8 per cent followed by Orissa with 22.1 per cent and Jharkhand with 26.3 per cent. Widows were given highest priority in allocating the houses under IAY in the states like Himachal Pradesh with 22.5 per cent, Kerala (26.3%), Rajasthan (21.25%), Orissa (15%) and Chhattisgarh (13.8%). As per different social categories fund was allotted by different amount. Except Kerala no other state was providing the unit cost according to the priority, wise categories, for examples Rs. 1,25,000 has been provided to the STs followed by SC category with an amount of Rs. 1,00,000 and for General category it was only Rs. 75,000 out of the total construction cost for the house sanctioned under IAY, only 50 per cent of the percentage of amount had been provided by the government as a unit cost under IAY. Most of the beneficiaries compelled to take loan at usurious interest rate from non-institutional financial sources. Majority of about 74.27 per cent of the housing walls constructed under IAY were made with burnt bricks, among these less quality (third quality) of bricks had been used.

2.7 Programmes for Employment and Income Generation

2.7.1 Mahatma Gandhi National Rural Employment Guarantee Act (MGNREGA)

Introduction

National Rural Employment Guarantee Act (NREGA) is considered as a Silver Bullet for eradicating rural poverty and unemployment by way of generating demand for productive labour force in villages. Rural poverty and unemployment in India have grown in an unprecedented manner during the last few decades. There is a growing incidence of illiteracy, blind faith, hungry people, malnourished children, anaemic pregnant women, farmer suicides, starvation deaths, migration resulting from inadequate employment, poverty, and the failure of subsistence production during droughts. In 2005, the Government of India introduced a National Employment Guarantee Act to provide a legal guarantee for at least 100 days of employment to begin with on asset creation public works programme every year at minimum wages for at least one able-bodied person in every rural and urban poor and lower middle-class household. The Act came into force with effect from February, 2006 in 200 districts initially and later on extended to all the rural districts of India from the financial year 2008-09. The Act is an important step towards realization of the right to work and aims at arresting out-migration of rural households in search of employment simultaneously enhancing people's livelihood on a sustained basis by developing the economic and social infrastructure in rural areas.

Background

The Government of India has implementing a series of wage employment programmes since the late 1960s, when the rural public works programme was introduced. This programme was followed by National Rural Employment Programme (NREP), Rural Landless Employment Guarantee Programme (RLEGP), Jawahar Rozgar Yojana (JRY), Employment Assurance Scheme (EAS), Sampurna Gramin Rojgar Yojana (SGRY) among others. Though one observes some improvement in the performance of these programmes over the years, the basic weaknesses of the programmes have always been there: (a) the programmes have had a limited impact in terms of generation of man days of employment per worker, (b) they had limited impact in terms of production of durable and good quality assets, (c) the planning component of the programme has been weak in terms of selection and sequencing of assets and in terms of ensuring productive use of the assets of generating sustainable employment in the mainstream. These programmes have neither reduced poverty levels in a sustainable manner, nor have they expanded the labour absorption capacity of the mainstream economy on any significant scale. Consequently, these programmes have remained a long-term financial drain on the economy. Today, labourers cannot count on employment being provided to them during the lean season. An employment guarantee gives labourers more confidence in the prospect of local employment, and discourages seasonal migration. The NREGP with a legal guarantee of work seeks to remove many of these weaknesses of earlier wage employment programmes.

So, the NREGA is an Indian job guarantee scheme, enacted by legislation on August 25, 2005. The law was initially called the National Rural Employment Guarantee Act but was renamed as Mahatma Gandhi National Rural Employment Guarantee Act (MGNREGA) on 2nd October, 2009. The MGNREGA covers the entire country with the exception of districts that have a hundred per cent urban population.

Objectives

MGNREGA is a powerful instrument for ensuring inclusive growth in rural India through its impact on social protection, livelihood security and democratic empowerment:

(a) Social protection for the most vulnerable people living in rural India through providing employment opportunities;
(b) Livelihood security for the poor through creation of durable assets, improved water security, soil conservation and higher land productivity;
(c) Drought-proofing and flood management in rural India;
(d) Empowerment of the socially disadvantaged, especially women, SCs and STs, through the processes of a rights-based legislation;
(e) Strengthening decentralized, participatory planning through convergence of various anti-poverty and livelihoods initiatives;
(f) Deepening democracy at the grass-roots by strengthening PRIs;
(g) Effecting greater transparency and accountability in governance.

Target Groups

Rural unskilled workers are the target group of the programme. There is no categorization barrier under social strata. The people who are willing to work unskilled manual work are entitled for MGNREGA:

(a) Scheme is open to all rural households who are in need of wage employment and desire to do manual and unskilled work.
(b) Period of employment should ordinarily be at least fourteen days continuously with not more than six days in a week.
(c) Priority to works where at least one third of wage seekers are women.
(d) Person desiring to work may submit their applications to the Gram Panchayat (GP).

GP registers the household. After verification, job card is to be issued to the applicant household. GP shall provide unskilled manual work to the applicant within 15 days of receipt of application preferably within a radius of 5 kilometers of the village, where the applicant resides. In case the employment is provided outside such radius, it must be provided within block and the labourers shall be paid 10 per cent of the wage rate as extra wages to meet additional transportation and living expenses (*see* Box 2.7).

Provision of Benefits

The provisions of benefits under MGNREGA are as follows:

First, every household in rural India has right to *at least 100 days of guaranteed employment* every year. Any number of persons of a family can participate in the scheme, provided they share among themselves the maximum annual cap of 100 mandays.

Second, the employment will be in the form of casual manual labour at the *statutory minimum wage*, and the wages shall be paid within 7 days during which work was done.

Third, work should be provided within *15 days of demanding* it, and the work should be located within 5-kilometer distance.

Fourth, if *work is not provided* to anybody within the given time, he/she will be paid a daily *unemployment allowance*, which will be at least one-third of the minimum wages.

Fifth, workers (employment on public works) will be entitled to *medical treatment* and hospitalization in case of injury at work, *along*

Box 2.7: Features of MGNREGA

- Adult members of a rural household may apply for employment if they are willing to do unskilled manual work.
- Employment will be given within 15 days of application for work by an employment seeker.
- If employment is not provided within 15 days, daily unemployment allowance in cash has to be paid. Liability of payment of unemployment allowance is of the States.
- At least one-third of the total persons to whom work is allotted will have to be women.
- Disbursement of wages has to be done on weekly basis and not beyond a fortnight.
- Panchayati Raj Institutions (PRIs) have a principal role in planning and implementation.
- Each district has to prepare a shelf of projects. The works to provide employment are to be selected from the list of permissible works.
- Work should ordinarily be provided within 5 km. radius of the village or else extra wages of 10 per cent are payable.
- Work site facilities such as crèche, drinking water, shade, first-aid box will have to be provided.
- Social Audit has to be done by the Gram Sabha at least once in every six months.
- Grievance redressal mechanisms have to be put in place for ensuring a responsive implementation process.
- All accounts and records relating to the Scheme are to be made available for public scrutiny and to any person who desires to obtain a copy of such records, on demand and after paying a specified fee.

Source: (www.MGNREGA.nic)

with a daily allowance of not less than half of the statutory minimum wages.

Sixth, for transparency and accountability, all accounts and records of the programme will be made available for *public scrutiny.*

Seventh, the district collector/Chief Execute Office will be responsible for the programme at the district level. The *gram sabha will monitor* the work of the gram panchayat by way of social audit.

Eighth, the scheme has been *universalized to all persons* living in the rural areas instead of its being available only to the families 'below poverty line'.

Ninth, facilities to be provided at work sites will be (a) safe *drinking water*, (b) shade for small children and workers for rest, (c) *first aid* box with adequate material for emergency treatment of minor injuries, body ache and other health hazards, and (d) *crèche* for baby.

Tenth, strict *penalties* have been laid down in the Bill for non-compliance with rules relating to employment guarantee, terms of employment and entitlement of works.

Last but not the least, one third preference to be given for women in areas where the number of applicants are very large.

Each state prepares its own employment guarantee programme and formulates rules for the purpose. Each person wanting employment must be registered with the gram panchayat and get a *job card* from the panchayat along with his/her photograph. Work is to be provided to all registered persons as per the rules laid down in the state. The programme officer at the block level is responsible for matching the demand for employment with employment opportunities available in the area. At the village level, gram panchayat is responsible for planning projects as per recommendation of Gram Sabha.

By providing job in lean agricultural season, MGNREGA gives a supplementary income to maintain a minimum standard of living. MGNREGA workers have been identified as a category for Jana Shree Bima Yojana for insurance cover. MGNREGA has aided in enhancement of agricultural productivity (through water harvesting, check dams, ground water recharging, improved moisture content, check in soil erosion and micro-irrigation) increased access to markets and services through rural connectivity works.

Fund Allocation

The Central Government bears the cost on the following items:

- The entire cost of wages of unskilled manual workers.
- Seventy-five per cent of the cost of material and wages of skilled and semi-skilled workers.
- Administrative expenses as may be determined by the Central Government, which will include the salary and allowances of the Programme Officer and his supporting staff and work-site facilities.
- Expenses of the National Employment Guarantee Council.

The State Government bears the cost on the following items:

- Twenty-five per cent of the cost of material and wages of skilled and semi-skilled workers.
- Unemployment allowance if state fails to provide job within 15

days of application for job.

- Expenses of the State Employment Guarantee Council (MGNREGA.nic.in).

Coverage

The national level Ministry and associated State Department of Rural Development are responsible for implementing MGNREGA across the entire country. Following its launch in 2006, the programme expanded rapidly, covering the country's entire rural segment. The performance of MGNREGA is presented in Table 2.34. It has provided employment to

Table 2.34: Performance of MGNREGA in India 2006-07 to 2012-13

Parameters	2006-07	2007-08	2008-09	2009-10	2010-11	2011-12	2012-13	Growth rate*
1. Spread of programme (as number of districts)	200	330	615	619	626	626	632	-
2. Cumulative number of job cards issued (crore)	3.8	6.5	10	11.3	12	12.3	12.6	18.1
3. Household employed (crore)	2.1	3.4	4.5	5.3	5.5	5	4.8	12.3
4. Total Person days (crore)	91	144	216	284	257	211	210.8	12.4
5. Person days: SC and ST (% of total person days)	62	57	55	51	51	40	38.2	-8
6. Person days: women (% of total person days)	40.6	42.5	47.8	48.1	47.3	48.1	52.1	3.5
7. Person days per household	43	42	48	54	47	42	45	0.4
8. At least 100 days person days per household (lakhs)	21.6	36	65.2	70.8	55.6	39	48.2	8.6
9. Total expenditure (Rs. crore)	8823.4	15856.9	27250.1	37905.2	39377.3	38034.7	29422.2	20
10. Utilization of Fund (%)	73	82	73	76	73	78	69	-1
11. Work completed against total work taken up (%)	47.2	46.1	43.8	48.9	50.8	20.3	15.8	-
12. MGNREGS expenditure as % of GDP	0.2	0.3	0.5	0.6	0.5	0.4	0.3	6.4

Note: * Trend growth is estimated.

Source: Report to the people (MGNREGS), www.MGNREGA.nic.in.

48 million households—the equivalent of 28 per cent of all rural households and average of 40-50-person days of employment per household. The geographical coverage as well as coverage in various sections of rural disadvantaged increased over the year. In the first five year the main beneficiaries were rural SC and ST, received 50 per cent of the employment generated. Women, many of them also SC and ST, received 48 per cent of total person days of employment, a significant benefit. Although the programme expanded rapidly after 2009-10 there is a deceleration.

Table 2.35: Total Funds (Rs. Lakh) available (including Opening Balance) across states in India, 2008-09 to 2012-13

States	2008–09	2009–10	2010–11	2011–12	2012-13
Andhra Pradesh	370,670	538,355	909,450	175,552	365,674
Arunachal Pradesh	4,338	4,290	5,679	6,999	9,238
Assam	136,558	142,473	126,928	83,880	70,223
Bihar	218,786	235,820	315,634	240,501	193,398
Chhattisgarh	200,591	162,933	218,676	250,819	275,267
Goa	951	1,222	1,610	933	497
Gujarat	28,127	98,181	127,159	83,779	87,326
Haryana	16,416	19,455	23,209	27,466	32,044
Himachal Pradesh	50,125	62,309	133,946	53,940	52,686
Jammu & Kashmir	15,279	25,461	41,741	98,042	96,765
Jharkhand	236,337	192,451	163,811	169,547	1,21,891
Karnataka	62,007	335,205	215,277	131,266	1,63,961
Kerala	27,468	56,079	84,333	104,587	1,39,257
Madhya Pradesh	507,517	567,823	515,236	491,965	3,09,078
Maharashtra	61,829	63,532	60,698	144,771	2,36,893
Manipur	38,596	51,120	42,163	72,809	71,560
Meghalaya	10,976	25,229	33,901	34,119	25,301
Mizoram	17,426	29,705	28,392	39,043	29,312
Nagaland	28,921	62,865	52,912	67,483	48,283
Odisha	105,129	97,673	179,187	137,182	128,585
Punjab	11,493	21,128	23,052	19,007	16,152
Rajasthan	724,535	820,273	587,878	412,431	3,81,433
Sikkim	4,969	10,256	8,348	11,019	9,356
Tamil Nadu	180,285	241,132	277,068	366,488	4,45,718
Tripura	47,135	92,405	63,802	100,873	98,976
Uttar Pradesh	470,693	713,268	722,148	643,494	3,11,998
Uttarakhand	15,566	35,911	40,407	44,595	32,532
West Bengal	133,255	240,854	273,106	309,244	3,99,479
All-India	**3,729,029**	**4,950,772**	**5,280,710**	**4,326,738**	**17,656,041**

Note: All-India includes figures for UTs.

Source: As in Table 2.36.

The allocation of fund increases over the year though there is a variation of distribution of fund among the states (Table 2.35). The performances of the scheme across states in respect of (a) percentage of household get job with issued job card (see Table 2.36), (b) average person days of employment per household (see Table 2.37), (c) percentage of household receiving at least 100 days of employment (see Table 2.38), (d) percentage of SC & ST participation in total MGNREGA job (see Table 2.39) and (e) percentage of women participation in to total person days generated under MGNREGA (see Table 2.40) also widely varied.

Table 2.36: Percentage share of Household who got Job with Issued Job Card across States in India, 2006-07 to 2012-13

States	*2006-07*	*2007-08*	*2008-09*	*2009-10*	*2010-11*	*2011-12*	*2012-13*	*Average*
Andhra Pradesh	42.7	54.3	50.2	52.5	51.7	41.2	45.5	48.3
Assam	86.4	89.6	63.2	59.2	41.2	34.4	30.7	57.8
Bihar	47.4	48.3	37.2	33.3	36.3	13.7	14.9	33.0
Chhattisgarh	68.0	79.5	67.7	56.7	63.6	62.2	59.8	65.3
Gujarat	35.8	33.6	29.6	44.7	27.7	20.1	17.7	29.9
Haryana	47.5	43.9	43.2	34.0	40.4	41.3	39.3	41.4
Himachal Pradesh	63.9	68.9	52.4	50.0	42.3	45.2	43.2	52.3
Jammu & Kashmir	67.7	54.6	40.1	50.6	49.9	50.8	53.9	52.5
Jharkhand	60.5	56.8	46.7	46.0	50.7	38.8	34.4	47.7
Karnataka	68.5	36.1	26.2	67.7	42.0	29.6	24.8	42.1
Kerala	46.3	38.7	36.5	36.8	40.3	76.3	60.7	47.9
Madhya Pradesh	64.5	60.1	46.4	41.8	38.7	31.5	25.5	44.1
Maharashtra	14.0	15.2	18.8	9.4	7.7	20.9	22.1	15.5
Orissa	53.8	26.8	22.8	24.1	33.3	22.4	25.4	29.8
Punjab	84.8	50.8	28.6	38.5	33.9	28.3	25.9	41.5
Rajasthan	77.9	75.6	75.3	73.9	63.2	46.5	42.2	64.9
Tamil Nadu	59.0	56.1	60.7	66.9	67.6	77.5	78.8	66.7
Uttar Pradesh	64.3	56.0	40.7	46.9	49.3	50.2	32.8	48.6
Uttarakhand	67.4	52.8	36.5	58.5	55.7	44.8	38.5	50.6
West Bengal	59.9	44.8	31.7	33.6	46.6	48.7	50.2	45.1
India	**55.5**	**52.4**	**45.0**	**46.7**	**45.9**	**40.6**	**37.9**	**46.3**

Source: As in Table 2.36.

Impact Study

MGNREGA provided around Rs. 141,030 from 2006-07 to 2012-13 and 210.8 crore person-days were created in 2012-13. Evidence suggests that MGNREGA is succeeding as a self-targeting programme with high participation from marginalized groups including the SCs and STs. At the national level, the share of SCs and STs in the work provided under

Table 2.37: Average Person days of Employment Per Household across states in India, 2006-07 to 2012-13

States	2006-07	2007-08	2008 09	2009-10	2010-11	2011-12	2012-13	Average
Andhra Pradesh	31	42	48	66	54	56	50	50
Assam	72	35	40	34	26	26	25	37
Bihar	35	22	26	28	34	38	43	32
Chhattisgarh	56	58	55	51	45	44	45	51
Gujarat	44	31	25	37	45	38	41	37
Haryana	48	50	42	38	36	39	44	42
Himachal Pradesh	47	36	46	57	49	52	49	48
Jammu & Kashmir	27	24	40	38	42	45	49	38
Jharkhand	37	45	48	49	42	39	39	43
Karnataka	41	36	32	57	49	42	46	43
Kerala	21	33	22	36	41	45	55	36
Madhya Pradesh	69	63	57	56	50	42	36	53
Maharashtra	41	39	46	51	44	47	53	46
Odisha	57	37	36	40	49	33	34	41
Punjab	49	39	27	28	27	26	27	32
Rajasthan	85	77	76	69	52	47	52	65
Tamil Nadu	27	52	36	55	54	48	58	47
Uttar Pradesh	32	33	52	65	52	36	28	43
Uttarakhand	30	42	35	35	42	42	40	38
West Bengal	14	25	26	45	31	26	34	29
India	**43**	**42**	**47**	**53**	**46**	**42**	**44**	**45**

Source: As in Table 2.36.

MGNREGA has been high at 40-50 per cent across each of the years of the programme implementation. In the financial year 2012-13, 39.6 per cent of the total person-days of employment were provided to SCs and STs. In financial year 2011-12, around 12 per cent of the total MGNREGA works taken up have been on private lands. Since 2006-07, around 20 lakh individuals have benefited under this category of works. The increasing work opportunity and durable assets which facilitate agricultural productivity boost the real daily agricultural wage rates by 5.3 per cent. The wage effect is equal for both men and women and is in favour of unskilled labour (Berg *et al.*, 2012). For the positive impacts of MGNREGA such as reduction in distress migration, increase in the local wage rate, improvement in local agriculture and allied activities, women's empowerment and empowerment of the poor etc. most of the people are in favour of MGNREGA.

This is not to say that the scheme does not have any problems. The report of Comptroller and Auditor General (CAG) as well as large number of studies have brought out many weaknesses of the scheme ranging from

Table 2.38: Percentage share of Households who Received at Least 100 Days of Employment under MGNREGA, 2006-07 to 2012-13

States	2006-07	2007-08	2008-09	2009-10	2010-11	2011-12	2012-13	Average
Andhra Pradesh	2.68	9.00	8.48	22.66	15.56	17.76	17.11	13.32
Assam	23.37	17.07	9.42	6.10	2.53	1.26	0.82	8.65
Bihar	3.57	1.37	2.68	6.85	5.99	9.22	7.87	5.37
Chhattisgarh	10.37	11.21	11.08	7.94	7.42	7.90	9.10	9.29
Gujarat	5.40	3.93	5.78	6.50	6.17	5.05	7.70	5.79
Haryana	11.08	10.44	6.05	5.65	3.86	4.89	6.72	6.96
Himachal Pradesh	26.47	5.11	11.26	9.71	4.96	8.87	6.66	10.43
Jammu & Kashmir	9.69	3.02	3.84	6.36	12.06	6.57	6.61	6.88
Jharkhand	3.66	2.97	6.06	7.83	6.60	3.67	5.87	5.24
Karnataka	12.80	4.20	3.01	12.61	5.91	2.73	8.16	7.06
Kerala	0.54	32.06	2.07	4.56	5.78	8.78	22.28	10.87
Madhya Pradesh	18.54	21.21	18.80	14.40	10.60	6.96	3.90	13.49
Maharashtra	1.39	1.76	3.59	4.22	6.26	11.27	13.72	6.03
Odisha	11.05	3.52	4.38	5.92	10.19	3.46	4.77	6.18
Punjab	16.83	5.32	2.65	2.83	1.89	1.54	1.56	4.66
Rajasthan	54.39	41.98	41.30	23.22	8.46	7.22	9.73	26.61
Tamil Nadu	0.27	6.24	15.19	17.39	22.18	9.48	19.17	12.85
Uttar Pradesh	6.02	10.64	14.93	14.53	9.34	4.15	1.33	8.71
Uttarakhand	2.77	8.27	4.23	3.96	4.69	4.47	3.14	4.51
West Bengal	0.61	0.82	0.76	2.07	2.10	2.01	3.98	1.76
India	**10.28**	**10.67**	**14.45**	**13.48`**	**10.12**	**7.81**	**9.94**	**10.97**

non-delivery of the basic entitlements to people (work on demand, payment of minimum wages, timely payment of wages, payment of unemployment allowances and worksite facilities), to poor performance in self-targeting, weak planning and *ad hoc* selection of works, top-down implementation rather than participatory, low transparency, poor accountability, corruption etc. A serious problem with MGNREGA, however, is that its role of generating productive assets in the economy and in promoting labour-intensive and pro-poor growth (Hirway *et al.* 2010). In his study Palanichamy (2011) showed that backward class, Hindu, agricultural labours are the most respondent of MGNREGA. The persons with annual income of less Rs. 5000 decreased to 7 per cent from 18 per cent after the introduction of MGNREGA. Sankaran (2011) cited that MGNREGA wages ensured a minimum wage rate allowing sufficient flexibility to account for regional or geographical variation. There can be no dispute that ensuring a basic minimum for a decent life is a first charge upon any government. MGNREGA wage rate bring about true need-based minimum wage. So MGNREGA ensures a decent work. Jacob (2008) surveyed in Villupuram district, Tamil Nadu to see the impact of MGNREGA on Rural-Urban migration. He chose Kalrayan Hill block, Kallkurichi block as the region

Table 2.39: SC & ST Participation in total MGNREGA Jobs, 2006-07 to 2012-13 (per cent)

State	2006-07	2007-08	2008-09	2009-10	2010-11	2011-12	2012-13	Average
Andhra Pradesh	42.83	40.51	39.09	39.39	40.34	45.35	38.85	40.9
Assam	54.91	46.72	44.86	43.17	38.25	28.37	26.56	40.4
Bihar	50.28	48.12	52.72	47.46	47.54	26.34	25.98	42.6
Chhattisgarh	57.56	56.3	57.73	53.52	51.08	47.19	47.24	52.9
Gujarat	71.3	71.84	63.23	54.33	55.72	48.11	47.03	58.8
Haryana	60.03	53.81	53.03	53.6	48.93	49.7	50.77	52.8
Himachal Pradesh	52.81	43.35	41.3	42.06	40.77	36.19	35.39	41.7
Jammu & Kashmir	28.64	34.19	35.89	34.52	32.28	22.34	21.89	30.0
Jharkhand	63.77	62.39	58.07	59.03	55.52	51.85	53.14	57.7
Karnataka	53.4	49.41	41.64	25.27	25.52	24	25.81	35.0
Kerala	32.52	33.77	28.73	22.1	19.32	16.69	17.83	24.4
Madhya Pradesh	64.51	66.63	64.63	63.82	62.79	48.58	46.82	59.7
Maharashtra	57.07	56.94	60.68	58.77	47.57	22.91	21.58	46.5
Odisha	72.92	63.98	56.05	55.42	53.68	55.67	55.23	59.0
Punjab	69.36	76.3	74.22	78.92	78.33	77.44	78.69	76.2
Rajasthan	80.33	65.63	52.03	49.03	48.78	41.3	42.33	54.2
Tamil Nadu	58.44	59.99	62.01	61.57	59.9	30.16	29.27	51.6
Uttar Pradesh	59.96	55.6	55.52	57.89	56.06	32.8	34.55	50.3
Uttarakhand	28.11	31.65	32.3	30.08	30.61	21.23	20.7	27.8
West Bengal	54.69	50.08	52.26	51.24	50.32	43.98	42.46	49.3
India	**61.81**	**56.71**	**54.72**	**51.19**	**51.48**	**40.25**	**38.23**	**50.6**

Source: As in Table 2.36.

Table 2.40: Women Participation in MGNREGA, 2006-07 to 2012-13 (per cent)

State	2006-07	2007-08	2008-09	2009-10	2010-11	2011-12	2012-13	Average
Andhra Pradesh	54.79	57.75	58.2	58.1	57.05	57.79	58.32	57
Assam	31.67	30.85	27.2	27.7	26.51	24.92	26.01	28
Bihar	17.38	26.62	30.0	30.04	28.5	28.64	30.46	27
Chhattisgarh	39.32	42.05	47.4	49.21	48.63	45.25	46.93	46
Gujarat	50.19	46.54	42.8	47.55	44.23	45.23	42.8	46
Haryana	30.59	34.44	30.6	34.81	35.62	36.43	39.88	35
Himachal Pradesh	12.24	30.11	39.0	46.09	48.25	59.51	60.63	42
Jammu & Kashmir	4.45	1.08	5.8	6.67	7.47	17.72	20.5	9
Jharkhand	39.48	27.17	28.5	34.25	33.47	31.28	32.64	32
Karnataka	50.56	50.27	50.4	36.79	46.01	45.93	46.25	47
Kerala	65.62	71.39	85.0	88.19	90.39	92.85	92.99	84
Madhya Pradesh	43.24	41.67	43.3	44.23	44.4	42.65	42.47	43
Maharashtra	37.07	39.99	46.2	39.65	45.88	45.98	44.48	43
Odisha	35.6	36.39	37.6	36.25	39.4	38.65	35.96	37
Punjab	37.76	16.29	24.6	26.28	33.83	43.24	46.67	33
Rajasthan	67.14	69	67.1	66.89	68.34	69.17	68.99	68
Tamil Nadu	81.11	82.01	79.7	82.91	82.59	74.02	74.17	79
Uttar Pradesh	16.55	14.53	18.1	21.67	21.42	17.13	19.67	18
Uttarakhand	30.46	42.77	36.9	40.28	40.3	44.59	45.99	40
West Bengal	18.28	16.99	26.5	33.42	33.69	32.44	33.61	28
India	**40.65**	**42.52**	**47.9**	**48.1**	**47.73**	**48.17**	**52.13**	**47**

Source: As in Table 2.36.

for survey. In his survey he collected data from the State Government and the concerned field. The survey result is contradictory. Some men like to migrate because the wage is much more than MGNREGA wage. But some of them want to stop migrating.

Kelkar (2009) has mentioned the close link between gender equality and economic growth. He has shown that domestic violence against women can push the economically fragile households into economic crisis. According to him, women are likely to have a greater prestige in the households and community. So, they want to direct more of the household income towards improvement of their own economic agency as well as education and nutrition of children. Hence his policy prescription is to facilitate women for MGNREGA work to asset and achieve a position in her family. Sudarshan *et al.,* (2011) examined the impact of women's participation in MGNREGA in selected areas in three states—Kerala, Himachal Pradesh and Rajasthan. Field work was carried out in areas selected from the first 200 most backward districts where MGNREGA was implemented in 2006. The participation of women in Kerala and Gujrat was more than that in Himachal Pradesh.

IIM Lucknow (2009) assessed that the participation of women in MGNREGA work enhanced women to move around the places like GP Office, banks, schools, block office without anybody to accompany them. It was also shown that women involvement in MGNREGA work reduced wage gaps prevalent in the labour market due to gender discrimination. Bhatty (2006) examined about the child rights in Dungarpur district in Rajasthan due to introduction of MGNREGA. The study showed that mother leaves the child to home alone. They feed their child at the time of leaving for and return from work. Infant children come to work site with their mother. But there is no crèche facility where most of the workers are women due to migration capability of men. Narayanan (2008) found that MGNREGA had created a problem of child care though the Act has brought about major important changes in the lives of women. The survey covered eleven villages and fifteen MGNREGA work site located in two blocks of Viluppuram district. In most of the work sites, there was no child care facility. So, a child comes with their mother and wandered in harsh weather. 85 per cent of women say if there are crèches, they will bring their child. But though there had a provision of crèches at MGNREGA work site, it was not seen in most of the cases. Dev (2011) examined the role of MGNREGA on child well-being in Chaksu block near Jaipur of Rajasthan in India. His analysis showed that child labour had been reduced and nutritional level had been increased. There seemed to be a positive correlation between programme participation of parents' development of health and mental of child although did not robust across all the specifications. Shah (2008) investigated the structures of power in Indian society.

Indians Adivasi pockets have suffered exploitation and discrimination qua region and community. *Adivasi* and marginalized people are controlled by the ruling classes. But after the introduction of MGNREGA and abolition of contractor raj, marginal people are able to construct democracy, equality and development at the grass roots through empowering local bodies of self-government. Banerjee *et al.* (2010) investigated the MGNREGA and Maoists. Maoists are flourished in backward and less developed area. The main support of Maoists comes from the groups which identify large scale displacement, forest issue, usury, land alienation, insecure tenancy contracts. Maoists counter developmental activity due to rise of anger against government. But their study showed that MGNREGA was implemented successfully. The purchasing power, wage rate were raised. The Maoist blocked the road construction but not the other permissible work under MGNREGA-land development on SC/ST land, small irrigation facilities, afforestation.

Das and Pradhan (2007) examined the reality of MGNREGA. They have shown that there is a difference between cost and fund sanctioned under MGNREGA. The negligence and corruption of government official make this difference. They have pointed the major discrepancies in several villages in Koraput, Rayagada and Nabrangpur districts in Orissa. The tribal members in the villages refused to work because most of them did not receive payment in the first phase. Complete and correct job card entries were not completed. So, most of the people had been given up hope about MGNREGA. Saho (2007) evaluated and assessed the performance of the MGNREGA in 100 villages in six most backward districts of Orissa-Bolangir, Nuapada, Kalahandi, Koraput, Nabrangpur and Rayagada. The preliminary findings of his survey were shocking, scandalous and outrageous. The MGNREGA was hijacked by officials responsible for implementing this scheme. Job cards remained with the Pradhan and he makes misuse of it. Dreze (2007) also looked into the corruption in rural employment programmes in Orissa. Chakraborty (2007) examined the effectiveness of MGNREGA through the ratios—Employment Guarantee (EG) enrolment as percentage of total number of rural households, EG enrolment as a percentage of rural BPL households, EG enrolment as a percentage of application for enrolment. The first two ratios reflect the preference of the households (non-BPL and BPL) for MGNREGA employment. The third indicates supply side performance. MGNREGA enrolment as a percentage of the number of applicants is abysmally low in Maharashtra, followed by Karnataka, Bihar and Jharkhand. The higher per-capita income states used the fund more appropriately.

Ambasta *et al.,* (2008) examined how far MGNREGA is successful on question of performing prospect in livelihoods of the poorest and heralding a revolution in rural governance in India. According to them, there is lack of professionals and staff. The main project implementers like DM, BDO and Panchayat staffs work on additional charge basis. Delays in administration and lack of project planning make this project faulty. Inappropriate wage rate restrains the worker from MGNREGA work. Mockery of social audit drains the resources in the pocket of implementer. But they think that information technology will help the transparency of MGNREGA. Different civil organization will make it more effective in future. Siddhartha and Vanik (2008) analyzed the CAG Report on MGNREGA to synthesize the employment programme. According to them analyzing the CAG Report MGNREGA, the last word on the MGNREGA, it can be said that MGNREGA as the last resort of employment must be avoided. Each registered household received 18 days of employment on average and only 3.2 per cent of registered households worked for the full 100 days. Worksite facilities were not provided in 202 GPs in Andhra Pradesh, Assam, Chhattisgarh, Gujarat, Haryana, Himachal Pradesh, Jammu & Kashmir, Jharkhand, Karnataka, Manipur, Orissa, Rajasthan, Uttar Pradesh, Uttarakhand and West Bengal.

In Bihar, Rs. 8.99 lakh was paid as a wage to fictitious labourers in respect of 7 works in 2007. Tempering of muster roll by using white fluid and marking absent as present and also over-writing the number of days worked were noticed in general during examination of muster rolls pertaining to the work selected in certain selected GPs.

Sharif (2009) assessed the outreach and benefits of MGNREGA. For his study he took survey data from seven states and sixteen districts located in northern India. The empirical estimate shows a meager penetration, suggesting a marginal reach of the MGNREGA to the deprived households with some notable exceptions. It appeared that Rajasthan, Madhya Pradesh, Orissa and Chhattisgarh are doing well in reaching out to the deprived households in providing MGNREGA employment though there is a wide variation between the selected districts. On the other hand, Bihar, Uttar Pradesh and Jharkhand have reached only a small fraction of the deprived and eligible households. Dey *et al.* (2010) studied the functioning of MGNREGA during February 2006 and July 2009 in Birbhum district, West Bengal. Their study reveals that in order to serve as an effective employer of last resort, the programme should provide more job-days during lean season and wages should be paid in a timely manner. This study shows that in Birbhum, there is a universal awareness about the MGNREGA. But there is a long delay in wage payments during the first year of the programme. Since then, the payment lag has declined and it is now in the range of 20 days.

Raabe *et al.* (2010) investigated the challenges of MGNREGA—the challenge of avoiding elite capture and actually reaching the poor and the deprived, the challenge of managing the funds allocated to the programme effectively and avoiding leakages and corruption. They use process-Influence Mapping tool to evaluate the functioning, transparency and accountability of MGNREGA. For their analysis they selected two districts in Bihar—one is developed and other is the lowest developed in the light of parameters like poverty, social vulnerability, livelihood potential and social capital criteria. Their study reveals that the actor of MGNREGA does not work properly. Though MGNREGA is a demand-based work without mobilization of fund there is no job. The case study evidence also points irregularities in the job card issue procedure. The panchayat president wants bribe for applying job cards. The job cards are issued to those who had voted for the president of Panchayat. The President of Panchayat also issues job cards to them who belong to the same caste as his. MGNREGA works will be successful with co-ordination of all implementing agencies. But there is a lack of co-ordination between Panchayat and Block. The shortage of staff augments the problem. Block officer and programme engineer are most corrupted. Since all funds are transferred by block officer and all measurement and estimation of project is done by engineer, they can negotiate among themselves and reap the benefits of difference between actual cost and estimated cost of the project.

Zanker *et al.* (2011) examined the comparative effectiveness on employment guarantee schemes and Cash Transfers on the poor. In order to increase the likelihood of being able to make meaningful comparisons between the studies in line with the systematic review methodology, the number of studies included on the basis of full text (222) was reduced to only those examining money-metric poverty outcome measures (poverty indices, expenditure and income). Finally, they include 37 studies for their analysis. The analysis revealed that while 28 studies found positive impacts from either Conditional Transfer (CT) or EGS participation, there were 9 instances of negative impacts, indicating that the evidence relating to the impact of cash transfers and EGS on money-metric poverty indicators is not exclusively positive. The ratio of positive to negative impacts identified varied by intervention and indicator. It was consistently higher for cash transfers than EGS across all indicators.

Vanaik *et al.* (2008) showed that the payment of MGNREGA work through bank would reduce corruption in MGNREGA. They considered Mayurbhanj district (Odisha) for field study. It ensured that money sanctioned for wage payment can be received only by the labour listed on the muster roll. So, the possibilities of middle man, bribe of government official would be reduced. But bank accounts in Mayurbhanj had been opened in the name of male household member. This was against the gender equality as well as transparency. Afridi (2008) studied the accountability system of MGNREGA in Rajasthan and Andhra Pradesh. His study revealed that civil society and NGOs constituted the main monitor of MGNREGA whereas state resource person, district resource person and villagers social auditor trained by state government in AP were the auditor of MGNREGA. Political parties and Sarpanch did not give official document of MGNREGA to NGOs on the ground of outsider. They wanted to give accounts to the villagers. But villagers were greatly influenced by powerful elite. In Yendabetla Panchayat almost 36 per cent expenditure was unaccounted. Gopal (2009) examined the social audit of MGNREGA in Ananthapur district in Andhra Pradesh. His study revealed that in most of the cases social audit system was fraud. He had shown that a huge number of frauds were detected in Ananthapur district in public meeting. But the amount recovered was very insignificant.

Adhikari *et al.* (2010) examined the wage payment through Banks and Post office as the last solution of corruption in MGNREGA wage distribution. They surveyed two blocks, each in Allahabad district (Uttar Pradesh) and Ranchi district (Jharkhand). They interviewed a total of 259 workers of which 201 (78%) were men and 58 (22%) were women. Their survey revealed that 87 per cent of the surveyed worker preferred Bank to Post office due to a charge levied by Post offices for transfer of MGNREGA funds. In 77 per cent case pass books were not updated. In most of the cases workers did not get wage from bank directly. So, there was a provision for corruption with collusion between bank and MGNREGA authority. Because panchayat secretary sends muster roll to the bank directly without publishing to the public domain. So, there is a possibility of manipulation to muster roll. In Kakram Gram Panchayat of Allahabad district, many upper caste men were included in payment though they had never worked on MGNREGA work.

Vij (2011) analysed the social audit framework from a policy design perspective in the light of field reports and recent changes in rules aims, to unravel why despite the merits, it was not yet the magic silver bullet for poverty alleviation. With Centre, State Government, in village level, different local government like Sarpanch, Panchayat conduct the social audit. Different NGOs and organizations also helped the work of social audit. Social audit from ground level would ensure transparency. But studies had noted that the problem of elite capture and control of the programme had failed the social audit system. They suggested that if we can change the traditional bureaucracy towards civil society organizations, there will be a sustainable development through MGNREGA.

2.7.2 Swarna Jayanti Gram Swarozgar Yojana (SGSY)

Introduction

Poverty reduction has been one of the major goals of development planning since Independence and the planning process has been sensitive to the needs of the poor. Accordingly, the development efforts have been directed in creating adequate livelihoods and provision of services for a better quality of life for the poor. Swarnajayanti Gram Swarojgar Yojana (SGSY) is an employment generation programme that provides income generating assets through a mix of bank credit and government subsidy. It is designed to stimulate self-employment activities and ensure every assisted BPL family. Formation of organizations of the poor at the grassroots level through a process of social mobilization for poverty reduction is central to the programme. The approach of SGSY is based on Self Help Groups (SHGs) that have to act as a financial intermediary and in many cases, there are women SHGs which are also expected to serve as vehicle for their empowerment. NGOs are expected to facilitate the formation of these groups. The community involvement as emphasized in SGSY, in contrast to Integrated Rural Development Programme (IRDP), is reflected in the mobilization for the formation of SHG groups (MoRD 2009).

Background

The SGSY was launched with effect from 01.04.1999 as the new self-employment programme. With the coming into effect of the SGSY, the earlier programmes of IRDP, Training of Rural Youth for self-Employment (TRYSEM), Development of Women and Children in Rural Areas (DWCRA), Supply of Toolkits in Rural Areas (SITRA), the Ganga Kalyan Yojana (GKY) as well as Million Wells Scheme (MWS) are no longer in operation.

Objectives

The objective of SGSY is to bring the assisted families (*swarozgaris*) above the poverty line by ensuring appreciable sustained level of income over a period of time. This objective is to be achieved by *inter alia* organizing the rural poor into SHGs through the process of social mobilization, training and capacity-building and provision of income generating assets. The SHG approach helps the poor to build their self-confidence through community action. This process would ultimately lead to the sterngthening and socio-economic empowerment of rural poor as well as improving their collective bargaining power. The specific objectives of SGSY are as follows:

- SGSY is a holistic programme covering all aspects of self-employment.
- It aims at establishing a large number of micro enterprises in rural area.
- The assisted families may be individuals or SHGs. However, emphasis would be given to group approach.
- In establishing the micro enterprises, the emphasis is on the cluster approach. However, emphasis would be on 4-5 key activities identified for micro enterprises in clusters.
- It envisages greater involvement of banks in project planning and infrustructre planning for the successful implementation of the programme.
- It promotes multiple credit rather than one-time credit injection.

Target Group

Members of BPL families especially women under SHGs constitute the main target group under SGSY.

Provision of Benefits

The provisions of benefits under SGSY (MoRD 2009) are as follows:

- NGOs, CBOs and Self-Help Promoting Institutions (SHPIs) are assisted up to Rs. 10,000 per group by government for the formation and development of SHGs.
- DRDA may incur a maximum amount of 10 per cent of allocation towards training and capacity building.

- SGSY Infrastructure Fund comprises up to 20 per cent of the allocation to States and 25 per cent in the case of North Eastern States.
- DRDA provides Rs. 10,000 to each SHG as Revolving Fund, banks provide cash credit of Rs. 15,000 for Grade-I SHGs.
- Banks provide loans to Grade-II SHGs with minimum repayment period of three to five years depending on the nature of scheme.
- Subsidy under SGSY is uniform at 30 per cent of the project cost, subject to a maximum of Rs. 7,500 per *swarojgari* (Rs. 10,000 for SC/ST/disabled *swarojgari*).
- *Swarojgaris* are not entitled for benefit of subsidy if the loan is fully repaid before the lock-in period.
- The programme envisages establishing a large number of microenterprises by the poor in rural areas with an emphasis on four to five key activities identified at the block level based on resources, occupational skills of the people and availability of markets.

Fund Allocation

The financing of the programme is shared between Central and State Government in the ratio of 75:25. For the special category states, including North-Eastern states Jammu & Kashmir, funding is shared by the Centre and State in the ratio 90:10.

The funds are released directly to DRDAs. Each DRDA is required to incur expenditure on training, infrustructure, revolving fund assistance to SHGs and subsidy for economic ativities to a maximum of ten per cent of total fund allocation. Of the total assistance, 50 per cent is reserved for SCs and STs, 40 per cent for women, 15 per cent for minorites and 3 per cent for disabled persons. SCs, STs and disabled are entitled to a subsidy of 50 per cent of project cost or Rs. 7,500 per *swarojgari* and 30 per cent for the other beneficiaries up to a maximum of Rs. 10,000 per *swarojgari*. The subsidy is disbursed along with the loan but is placed as a separate term deposit in the name of *swarojgari* and is available subject to proper utilisation and repayment of the loan (Table 2.41).

Credit target under the SGSY is fixed every year by a committee having representative from the Ministry of Finance, NABARD, Reserve Bank of India, State Bank of India and Ministry of Rural Development. Mobilizing and disbursing credit and subsidy were particularly low in the first four years of the programme, owing largely to the time required

Table 2.41: Credit Mobilized under SGSY during 2009-10

State	Credit Target	Credit Disbursed to SHGs	Credit Disbursed to Swarojgaris	Credit	Credit Disbursed (%)
Andhra Pradesh	23997.60	25119.25	3707.43	28826.68	120.12
Arunachal Pradesh	1041.15	45.82	109.50	155.32	14.92
Assam	27041.85	22831.05	10808.82	33639.87	124.40
Bihar	57085.05	21582.42	4889.74	26472.16	46.37
Chhattisgarh	12678.60	9983.97	3971.79	13955.75	110.07
Goa	330.00	223.63	25.26	248.89	75.42
Gujarat	9033.75	5290.41	4392.54	9682.95	107.19
Haryana	5314.65	6471.75	911.34	7383.09	138.92
Himachal Pradesh	2237.40	3249.90	1031.82	4281.73	191.37
Jammu & Kashmir	2770.35	281.24	1115.05	1396.30	50.40
Jharkhand	21524.25	10398.14	3252.02	13650.16	63.42
Karnataka	18118.65	20227.01	466.90	20693.91	114.21
Kerala	8131.20	8516.94	2292.28	10809.22	132.94
Madhya Pradesh	27165.60	18418.94	11840.23	30259.17	111.39
Maharashtra	35819.85	23987.05	5875.01	29862.06	83.37
Manipur	1813.35	500.40	0.00	500.40	27.60
Meghalaya	2031.15	211.10	15.05	226.15	11.13
Mizoram	470.25	121.45	28.40	149.85	31.87
Nagaland	1392.60	116.81	45.68	162.49	11.67
Orissa	27447.75	23936.66	4950.57	28887.23	105.24
Punjab	2582.25	1517.66	2760.57	4278.23	165.68
Rajasthan	13759.35	16783.36	3819.30	20602.66	149.74
Sikkim	519.75	210.45	37.97	248.42	47.80
Tamil Nadu	21219.00	29259.63	1736.55	30996.18	146.08
Tripura	3273.60	4387.56	0.00	4387.56	134.03
Uttar Pradesh	82183.20	66549.72	27897.45	94447.18	114.92
Uttarakhand	4327.95	4353.36	1182.71	5536.06	127.91
West Bengal	30503.55	22566.41	13.40	22579.81	74.02
All India	444391.20	347520.83	97181.81	444702.64	100.07

Note: N.R. = Not Reported.

Source: http://rural.nic.in/sites/downloads/programmes-schemes/Credit_Mobilisation_09-10.pdf

to create and nurture SHGs. In the next ten years, *Swarojgaris* received Rs. 10,000 crores as credit and Rs. 5,400 crores as subsidy. While individual *Swarojgaris* received Rs. 7,700 crore and Rs. 3,600 crores respectively.

West Bengal received a good amount of fund. The total fund available was Rs. 12458.08 lakh during the financial year 2012-13 (up to December). But there is a utilization gap between fund availability and expenditure. The utilization rate is 71.47 per cent for that point of time (Table 2.42).

Table 2.42: Financial Performance of SGSY in West Bengal during 2012-13 (up to December 2012) (Rs. in lakh)

Allocation under SGSY	*Central Share received*	*State Share received*	*Balance in hand as on 1st April*	*Total Fund available*	*Expenditure up to Dec. 2012*
19697.33	6999.45	2444.40	2496.94	12458.08	8903.41

Source: Annual Plan 2013-14, Government of West Bengal http://wbplan.gov.in/htm/ImportantLinks.htm.

Coverage

SGSY is an improvement over earlier livelihood support schemes such as IRDP and DWCRA, which gave loans to BPL without any training. For the three years of the scheme, individual *swarojgari* outnumbered the SHG *swarojgari*, the trend was reversed from 2002-2009. Over the decade 1999-2009, 34 lakh SHGs were formed but only 21 lakh passed grade I and 10 lakh passed grade II. During 2011-12, a total of 16.77 lakh *swarojgaris* were assisted out of which 11.03 lakh (68.63%) were women *swarojgaris*. In 2012-13, till December, 4.38 lakh *swarojgaris* have been assisted out of which 3.49 lakh (79.68%) are women (MoRD 2013).

The state of West Bengal has achieved a good position on the question of performance of SGSY in India among the states. Table 2.43 shows the evidence against our statement.

Impact Study

From 2006 to 2009 Andhra Pradesh was the leading state in respect of the number of *swarojgaris* assisted over, followed by Uttar Pradesh. They were followed by Maharashtra, Bihar, Tamil Nadu, Assam, Orissa, Karnataka, Jharkhand and Madhya Pradesh. Examination of the performance of states grouped as regions reveals that the central region (Chhattisgarh, Madhya Pradesh, Uttar Pradesh and Uttaranchal) accounts for 34 per cent of the country's poor, but only 30 per cent of the *swarojgaris* assisted were in this region. In comparison, the southern region (Andhra Pradesh, Karnataka, Kerala, Tamil Nadu, Lakshadweep and Pondicherry), accounted for 21 per cent of the *swarojgaris* assisted while having 11 per cent of the poor in the country. In 2008, credit disbursed as a proportion of credit targeted was only 40 per cent in the

Table 2.43: Progress under SGSY in West Bengal, 2012-13 (up to December 2012)

1. SHG formation	
No. of women groups (since inception)	334078
No. of Grade-I passed SHGs (since inception)	330377
No. of Grade-II passed SHGs (since inception)	133426
2. Group savings (since inception)	65484 lakh
3. No. of groups received Revolving fund after passing Grade I (since inception)	309792
4. No. of groups linked with Cash Credit (since inception)	277394
5. Total amount of Revolving fund released in favour of Grade I passed (since inception)	37668.65 lakh
6. Total amount of Cash Credit released (this is one-time disbursement and does not include CC fund revolving regularly) (since inception)	131688.67 lakh
7. Cash Credit limit per group	47381.27
8. Formation of SHG based Institutions	
(i) No. of Sub clusters at Gram Sansad level (total no. of gram sansad—37398)	24987
(ii) No. of Clusters at Gram Panchayat level (total number of Gram Panchayat—3349)	2474
(iii) No. of SHG Federations at Block level (Total number of blocks—341	24

Source: Annual Plan 2013-14, Government of West Bengal http://wbplan.gov.in/htm/ImportantLinks.htm

North-Eastern states, compared to 73 per cent for all India. Credit disbursed as a percentage of the target for the northern region was 119 per cent that for the southern region it was 109 per cent. In 2009, credit disbursed as a proportion of credit targeted decreased by 15.83 per cent whereas it was increased by 27.07 per cent for all India that is there is a divergence between objectives and design of SGSY. The aims to achieve sustained income through the formation of assets failed due to selection bias of the gram panchayats. Since SGSY is primarily targeted at BPL families, there are several instances where non-BPL families are selected, thus crowding out intended beneficiaries. Along with it, there is a lack of coordination between banks and government agencies. Not only that from the experience of non-recovery of loan for government schemes such as IRDP and DWRCA, bank is reluctant to give credit to the poor.

Performance of SGSY was assessed through concurrent evaluation, studies and reports including those conducted by NIRD, Hyderabad; BIRD, Lucknow; Centre for Management Development, Thiruvananthapuram; Reports of the Steering Committee constituted by the Planning Commission for the 11th Plan and the Prof. Radhakrishna

Committee on Credit Related issues related to SGSY, set up by the Ministry of Rural Development in April, 2008. Accordingly based largely on the recommendations of the Prof. Radhkrishna Committee, SGSY has been restructured as National Rural Livelihood Mission (NRLM), subsequently renamed as "Aajeevika" to implement it in a mission mode across the country. The programme was formally launched on 3rd July, 2011.

2.7.3 Procurement of Non-timber Forest Produces (NTFP)

Non-Timber Forest Products (NTFPs) are any product or service other than timber that is produced in forests. They include plant tissue used for fiber, building material, medicine, edible leaves, roots, flower, fruit, seed, nuts, honey, resin, glue, lac etc. and has both consumptive and exchange value. Actually, it refers to all biological materials other than timber extracted from natural forests for human and animal use. They have income potentials and provide employment opportunities. NTFPs are used and managed in complex socio-economic and ecological environments. In traditional forest communities, many NTFPs may be used for subsistence while others are the main or only source of income. Some NTFPs have significant cultural value, as totems, incense, and other ritual items. Others have important medicinal value and contribute to the community's health and well-being (CIFOR 2014).

The NTFP sector has however and unfortunately been neglected since the pre-independence period. Over the past two decades, governments, conservation and development agencies and non-governmental organizations have encouraged the marketing and sale of NTFPs as a way of boosting income for poor people in the tropics and encouraging forest conservation. Prior to National Forest Policy (NFP), 1988, NTFPs were popularly known as Minor Forest Products (MFP). In absence of a comprehensive national/central policy/approach, contradictory legal provisions still prevail while differential state regimes create some of the biggest limitations which constrain a healthy growth of the NTFP sector. Bamboo, for instance, is defined as a 'minor forest produce' in the Forest Rights Act, 2006 whereas the Indian Forest Act, 1927 treats it at par with timber. Panchayats (Extension to Scheduled Areas) Act (PESA), 1996 gives ownership rights to local communities over MFPs whereas the regime created under Wildlife Protection Act does not. NTFPs are a part of the socio-cultural life of tribal people who mainly maintain a symbolic relationship with the forest and forest-based products. More particularly, the reliance of tribal on NTFP becomes very high during uncertain agricultural yields for both food securities during seasonal shortages as well as for household medicine and income needs (CIFOR 2014, OFDC 2014, Hegde 2014).

To emphasize how people use forest resources, and on helping to improve the contribution these resources make to the livelihoods of the rural poor. The NTFP of economic importance in India can be grouped into the following categories:

(a) *NTFP for Food Security:* Honey, mushroom, edible fruits and nuts, foliage and rhizomes
(b) *NTFP for Wood and Biomass:* Useful for fuel, furniture, thatching, forage and manure
(c) *NTFP for Medicines and Plant Protection:* For human beings, animals and for control of pests and diseases in agricultural crops
(d) *NTFP for Aromatics, Dyes and Oilseeds:* For medicinal and industrial uses
(e) Collection, Processing and trade of Honey and few Non-timber Forest Product (NTFP) items.

For developing the NTFP sector in the country and recommended the following strategies to be adopted for this purpose with a total budgeted amount of Rs. 6590 crores for the 12th Plan.

2.8 Social Assistance Programmes

2.8.1 Indira Gandhi National Old Age Pension Scheme (IGNOAPS)

Introduction

The problem of the old age gets compounded due to lack of any proper social security system. Social security or social assistance is both a concept as well as a system. It represents a basic system of protection of individuals who are in need of such protection by the state as an agent of the society. Such protection is relevant in contingencies such as retirement, sickness, death, old age, unemployment, disability, etc. to enable them to live and maintain a standard of life in consistence with the prevailing social and economic norms. Many old people receive pension from the government on retirement known as social security or welfare payment. Some receive it from their previous employer. But for many elderly persons, who do not have any source of income have to face the hardships because no social security is available to them. Even though the Constitution of India is yet to recognize social security or social assistance as a Fundamental Right it does require that state should strive to promote the welfare of the people by securing and protecting, as effectively as it may, a social order in which justice, social, economic and political shall inform all institutions of national life. Article 41 of the Constitution requires that the state should, within the limits of its economic activity and capacity make effective provisions for securing right to work, providing education and extending public assistance in case of unemployment, old age, sickness and disability. Article 42 of the Constitution requires that the State should make provision for securing just and human conditions of work and for maternity relief. Article 47 requires that the State should raise the level of nutrition and the standard of living and improvement of public health among its primary obligations. The obligations cast on the State in the above Articles of the Constitution of India constitute the total spectrum of social security which is generally understood as protection provided by the society to its members through a series of public measures aimed at relieving economic and social distress which otherwise is caused by the stoppage or substantial reduction of earnings resulting from sickness, maternity, employment injury, occupational diseases, unemployment, invalidity, old age and death.

Background

In this perspective the governments at the Centre and State have taken several measures to provide social assistance or social security to various needy sections of the society. Indira Gandhi National Old Age Pension (IGNOAPS) is one of the Centrally Sponsored Scheme, which has been launched by the Government of India to mitigate the hardships faced by the destitute old population. The scheme announced by the Prime Minister of the country in his broadcast to the nation on July 28, 1995 was implemented with effect from August 15, 1995 throughout the country. The details of the scheme have been worked out by a committee under the Chairmanship of Secretary (Rural Development) in consultation with the representatives of state governments. Central assistance under the IGNOAPS is available for old age pensions provided (a) the age of the applicant (male or female) is 65 years or higher, and (b) the applicant must be a destitute in the sense of having little or no regular means of subsistence from his/her own sources of income or through financial support from family members or other sources. In order to determine destitution, the criteria, if any, currently in force in the

States/UT Governments was to be followed. Under the scheme an amount of Rs. 75 per month is paid to the beneficiaries. However, recently the government of Jammu & Kashmir has enhanced the amount of pension from Rs. 75 to Rs. 200 thereby brought this scheme at par with a parallel scheme of Integrated Social Security Scheme (ISSS) being implemented by the state government.

Objectives

In response to the growing changes in age composition and faster ageing, the Central Government in India has initiated IGNOAPS to help the older persons. Constitutionally, the poor—especially the destitute—are the responsibility of the state. To be more precise, the Constitution of India, entry 24 in list III of Schedule VII, deals with some of these issues including the welfare of labour, provident fund, maternity benefit, disability and old age pension (Alam 2004).

Target Groups

The age of the applicant (male or female) should be 60 years or above. The applicant should belong to a household living below the poverty line according to the criteria prescribed by the Government of India

Provision of Benefits

It has been provided to applicants over 65 years of age who are below the poverty line. As of mid-2009, the central transfer was Rs. 200 per month. From June 2011, the age of eligibility of the IGNOAPS has been brought down to 60 years, and a higher pension of Rs. 500 has been introduced for eligible old age persons above the age of 80 (Revised guidelines accessed from *http://nsap.nic.in/Guidelines/english_oaps.pdf on March 15, 2013).*

Since 2000-01, the Annapurna Scheme is supplementing IGNOAPS which covers the destitute elderly who are eligible for elderly social pensions but are not receiving them. These households receive 10 kg of foodgrains per month free through the Fair Price Shop.

Fund Allocation

IGNOAPS is a national sponsored scheme with budget share of 50:50

between Centre and State. In 11th Plan (2007-2012), the Central Government has released Rs. 153297.82 lakh and the same amount was also released by the State Government. The utilization of budget was 100 per cent. The Central Government released Rs. 49082 lakhs against the State share of Rs. 43504.50 lakh for the financial assistance during 2012-13. The proposed outlay for 2013-14 was Rs. 67097.98 and Rs. 95787.60 from Central Government and State Government respectively (GoWB 2014).

Beneficiaries and Coverage

The Government of India on 13.9.2007 modified the eligibility criteria for grant of old age pension to persons aged 65 years or higher and belonging to a household below the poverty line according to the criteria prescribed by the Government of India. With this modification National Old Age Pension Scheme (NOAPS) was renamed as IGNOAPS. Under NOAPS, 87.09 lakh beneficiaries were covered during 2006-07. However, with the modification of eligibility criteria to cover all persons of 65 years or higher and living below the poverty line, the number of beneficiaries under IGNOAPS increased to 171 lakhs. In view of the modification in age limit, 278 lakh beneficiaries are estimated to be covered under IGNOAPS against 171 lakh beneficiaries covered during the year 2010-11 (IRDR 2013). The status of IGNOAPS across states of India is shown in 2013-14 (Table 2.44).

West Bengal plays a significant role to provide National Social Assistance Programme. IGNOAPS beneficiaries under the age group of 60-79 were 904882 and 196421 in rural and urban areas respectively in 2012-13. On the other hand, the number of beneficiaries was 163382 and 45595 under the age group of above 80 years. So, the total beneficiaries were 1310280 for the financial year 2012-13 considering those in rural and urban area together (GoWB 2014).

Impact Study

Planning Commission (2009) asked all the beneficiaries whether the scheme has benefited them and if yes, in what way the scheme has benefited them and multiple responses were recorded. All the beneficiaries mentioned that the NOAPS is a very useful scheme and each one of them has benefited from the scheme in one way or the other. 72 per cent of respondents expressed that the scheme has made them self-dependent. Similarly, 46 per cent of the respondents mentioned that the scheme has helped them

Table 2.44: Pensioners under IGNOAPS across States of India, 2012-13

State	*Sanctioned Pensioners*					*New Applicants*	*Total*
	Sanctioned	*Female*	*Male*	*Below 80*	*80 and Above*		
Andhra Pradesh	806263	504206	302057	716605	89658	0	806263
Arunachal Pradesh	7793	5122	2671	5001	2792	0	7793
Assam	762857	400231	362626	641149	121708	16296	779153
Bihar	1572793	860112	712681	1357793	215000	5500	1578293
Delhi	374672	216570	158102	348087	26585	0	374672
Goa	1705	1056	649	1129	576	4	1709
Gujarat	333923	201224	132699	315854	18069	80781	414704
Haryana	118515	45223	73292	88522	29993	27197	145712
Himachal Pradesh	79493	43198	36295	49885	29608	0	79493
Jammu & Kashmir	54662	24859	29803	46486	8176	779	55441
Karnataka	980644	514886	454720	867467	113177	0	980644
Kerala	315165	169761	145404	250631	64534	0	315165
Madhya Pradesh	823022	471641	351381	705699	117323	51422	874444
Maharashtra	968186	608805	359381	908735	59451	54401	1022587
Manipur	60982	35586	25396	54641	6341	0	60982
Meghalaya	47764	28954	18810	40896	6868	1824	49588
Mizoram	23760	13040	10720	16302	7458	2	23762
Nagaland	42597	25224	17373	26598	15999	311	42908
Odisha	1498358	696461	801897	1295642	202716	74085	1572443

(Contd.)

Table 2.44: (*Contd.*)

State	Sanctioned Pensioners					New Applicants	Total
	Sanctioned	Female	Male	Below 80	80 and Above		
Punjab	242418	150717	91648	217016	25402	2445	244863
Rajasthan	926301	523033	403268	811383	114918	12014	938315
Sikkim	8638	3967	4671	7704	934	0	8638
Tamil Nadu	1239148	785501	453647	1113796	125005	100193	1339341
Tripura	141249	67025	74224	125692	15557	0	141249
Uttar Pradesh	3687759	1450152	2237607	3286953	400806	17	3687776
West Bengal	263004	140098	122906	224573	38431	0	263004
Chhattisgarh	526254	286058	240196	454807	71447	62344	588598
Jharkhand	561406	302243	259163	513877	47529	531	561937
Uttarakhand	169756	89286	80470	141954	27802	11	169767
Telangana	329953	214192	115761	299913	30040	0	329953
All India	17037917	8916955	8109871	14999756	2037814	490520	17528437

Source: http://nsap.nic.in/ReportBenfAbstract.do?method=showReportResult

to obtain the necessary health care services, due to which their health condition has improved. Besides, 16 per cent mentioned that the monetary assistance received by them under NOAPS has provided them the subsistence. One beneficiary reported that the scheme has helped him to gain some respect in the family and another 3 per cent of respondents were of the view that it has saved them from begging.

2.8.2 National Family Benefit Scheme (NFBS)

Background

National Family Benefit Scheme (NFBS) was issued in 1998 to provide a lump sum family benefit of Rs. 10,000 to the bereaved household in case of death of the primary bread winner irrespective of the cause of death.

Target Group

For purposes of determining Central assistance, the following criteria are required—

(a) The 'primary bread winner' is the member of the household—male/female whose earnings contribute substantially to the total household income.
(b) The death of such a primary bread winner should have occurred while he or she is in the age group of 18 to 64 years i.e. more than 18 years of age and less than 65 years of age.
(c) The bereaved household qualifies as one below the poverty line according to the criterion prescribed by the Government of India.

Government of India has revised the age limit from 18-64 years to 18-59 years under the ongoing NFBS w.e.f. 18.10.2012 (GoI 2012).

Provision of Benefits

The beneficiaries of the scheme got Rs. 10,000 with the introduction of the scheme. After revision of the guideline, the lump sum grant increased to Rs. 20,000 from Rs. 10,000 under NFBS w.e.f.18.10.2012. But it was directed that State Government will provide at least same amount of assistance as provided by the Central Government. West Bengal Government provided a sum of Rs. 40,000 at a time to each beneficiary.

Coverage

In the earlier years benefit of the scheme did not reach all the eligible families. With closer monitoring and taking up special drives in increasing awareness about the scheme, the coverage was relatively high during last five years. But, during 2008-09 to 2012-13, there was a declining trend of the number of beneficiaries in India (Table 2.45).

Table 2.45: Total Number of Beneficiaries under NFBS in India, 2002-2013

Year	Person	Year	Person
2002-03	85209	2008-09	423292
2003-04	209456	2009-10	382809
2004-05	261981	2010-11	334924
2005-06	272828	2011-12	330240
2006-07	204952	2012-13	291010
2007-08	117446	–	–

Source: Annual Report, 2008-09 & 2012-13, Ministry of Rural Development, GoI.

2.8.3 Indira Gandhi National Widow Pension Scheme (IGNWPS)

Background

The national widow pension scheme is a component of National Social Assistance Programme. The scheme is known as 'Indira Gandhi National Widow Pension Scheme' (IGNWPS). It came into existence from September 2009 for BPL persons with severe or multiple disabilities (GoI 2013).

Target Group

The eligibility criteria mentioned in the guidelines for the purpose of claiming central assistance was that the age of widow shall be in the age group of 40-64 years and must belong to a household living below the poverty line according to the criteria prescribed by the Government of India. After the revision of the scheme, the age of the widow was between 40-59 years w.e.f. 01.04.2011. At present the age limit has been increased up to 79 years.

Provisional Benefit

The central assistance under IGNWPS will be provided at the rate of Rs. 200 per month per beneficiary. The pension is to be credited into a post office or public sector bank account of the beneficiary (MoRD 2009). The amount of pension has been increased to Rs. 300 per month.

Coverage

The number of eligible beneficiaries to be assisted under IGNWPS will be determined as per the field report of all the beneficiaries who satisfy the eligibility criteria. It was estimated that 45 lakh beneficiaries were to be covered under the scheme at the time of introduction of the scheme. During 2009-10, till December 2009, 23 lakh beneficiaries have been covered under the scheme. So, there was a wide gap between target and actual achievement. Hence in the next FY 2011-12, it was estimated that 29 lakh beneficiaries would be covered. But as per report, till December 2012, only 41 lakh beneficiaries have been covered under the scheme. The widow pensioners across states of India are shown in Table 2.46.

The scheme has been launched in West Bengal in 2009. After that 211785 and 739932 beneficiaries have been benefited from the scheme in the Financial Year 2013-14 in urban and rural area respectively (GoWB 2014).

2.8.4 Indira Gandhi National Disability Pension Scheme (IGNDPS)

Background

Indira Gandhi National Disability Pension Scheme (IGNDPS) came into existence from February 2009 for BPL persons with severe or multiple disabilities (MoRD 2009).

Target Group

For the purpose of claiming central assistance under IGNDPS, the following criteria are required to be fulfilled:

(a) The age of disabled should lie between 18 and 64 years.
(b) The applicant must belong to a household below the poverty line according to the criteria prescribed by the Government of India.

Table 2.46: Pensioners under IGNWPS across States of India, 2012-13

State	*Sanctioned Pensioners*					*New Applicants*	*Total*
	Sanc-tioned	*Female*	*Male*	*Below 80*	*80 and Above*		
Andhra Pradesh	277208	277208	0	277208	0	0	277208
Assam	109973	109973	0	109963	10	9433	119406
Bihar	20267	20266	1	20267	0	322	20589
Delhi	112626	112626	0	112626	0	0	112626
Goa	315	315	0	310	5	68	383
Gujarat	2322	2321	1	2322	0	1983	4305
Haryana	16947	16947	0	16905	42	19126	36073
Himachal Pradesh	11453	11453	0	11268	185	0	11453
Karnataka	194319	190264	4055	175955	18364	0	194319
Kerala	739875	739821	54	712755	27119	0	739875
Madhya Pradesh	126070	126062	8	126009	61	20100	146170
Maharashtra	17158	17083	75	17157	1	3068	20226
Meghalaya	6796	6796	0	6795	1	530	7326
Mizoram	1192	1192	0	1192	0	0	1192
Nagaland	574	574	0	574	0	0	574
Odisha	198566	198550	16	198417	149	16020	214586
Punjab	15585	15577	8	15585	0	1423	17008
Rajasthan	115912	115912	0	115868	44	3356	119268
Sikkim	103	103	0	102	1	0	103
Tamil Nadu	484608	484457	151	450670	33938	75496	560104
Tripura	18527	18338	189	18526	1	0	18527
Uttar Pradesh	2	1	1	2	0	0	2
West Bengal	205631	205630	1	205392	239	0	205631
Chhattisgarh	63815	63815	0	63802	13	20766	84581
Jharkhand	216783	214383	2400	215023	1760	245	217028
Telangana	143929	143929	0	143929	0	0	143929
All India	3106881	3099921	6960	3024907	81973	172249	3279130

Source: http://nsap.nic.in/ReportBenfAbstract.do?method=showReportResult

(c) The applicant should be suffering from severe or multiple disabilities as defined in 'Person with Disabilities Act, 1995' (PWD Act 1995) and the 'National Trust for the welfare of persons with Autism, Cerebral Palsy, Mental Retardation and Multiple Disabilities Act, 1999 (National Trust Act 1999).

(d) The State/UTs are required to furnish a certificate that all eligible disabled have been covered under IGNDPS (MoRD 2009).

As a result of decision of the Government of India, it has been decided to modify the eligibility criteria for IGNDPS only in age limit from 64 years to 59 years (MoRD 2009). The programme has further revised in

2012. The eligibility age (w.e.f. 1.10.2012) lies between 18 and 79 years (MoRD 2009).

Provision of Benefit

The central assistance under IGNDPS will be provided at the rate of Rs. 200 per month per beneficiary. The rate of assistance has been also increased to Rs. 300 from Rs. 200. The state government is urged to contribute at least equally towards the pension amount. The pension is to be credited into a post office or public sector bank account of the beneficiary (MoRD 2009).

Coverage

The number of eligible beneficiaries to be assisted under IGNDPS will be determined as per the field report of all the beneficiaries who satisfy the eligibility criteria. It was estimated that 15 lakh beneficiaries were to be covered under the scheme at the time of introduction of the scheme. During 2009-10, till December 2009, 5 lakh beneficiaries have been covered under the scheme. So, there was a wide gap between target and actual achievement. Hence in the next financial year 2011-12, it was estimated that 14 lakh beneficiaries would be covered. But as per report, till December 2012, only 8 lakh beneficiaries have been covered under the scheme (*see* Table 2.47).

The scheme has been launched in West Bengal in 2009. After that 9698 and 37842 beneficiaries have been benefited from the scheme in FY 2013-14 in urban and rural area respectively (GoWB 2014).

2.8.5 Indira Gandhi Matritva Sahayog Yojana (IGMSY)

Introduction

In India, high levels of undernutrition and anemia in adolescent girls and women are compounded by early marriage, early child bearing and inadequate spacing between births. Girls and women often face an inter-generational cycle of undernutrition compounded by multiple deprivations—gender discrimination, poverty and exclusion. Owing to economic and social distress many women continue to work to earn a living for their family right up to the last days of their pregnancy. Furthermore, they resume working soon after childbirth, even though

Table 2.47: Pensioners under IGNDPS across States of India, 2012-13

State	*Sanctioned Pensioners*					*New Applicants*	*Total*
	Sanctioned	*Female*	*Male*	*Below 80*	*80 and Above*		
Andhra Pradesh	35832	14471	21361	34645	1187	0	35832
Assam	34454	10303	24151	34448	6	1480	35934
Bihar	1542	459	1083	1542	0	79	1621
Delhi	47329	14765	31073	47329	0	0	47329
Goa	41	14	27	40	1	21	62
Gujarat	5049	1509	3540	5048	1	444	5493
Haryana	2246	564	1682	2244	2	4256	6502
Himachal Pradesh	359	123	236	358	1	0	359
Karnataka	83029	37822	45207	74945	8084	0	83029
Kerala	254691	106643	148048	251902	2789	0	254691
Madhya Pradesh	73236	30614	42622	73231	5	6625	79861
Maharashtra	2943	873	2070	2941	2	596	3539
Meghalaya	1431	621	810	1431	0	129	1560
Mizoram	589	260	329	589	0	0	589
Nagaland	363	52	311	363	0	0	363
Odisha	51056	15553	35503	51053	3	2987	54043
Punjab	3260	1480	1780	3260	0	311	3571
Rajasthan	22311	6787	15524	22308	3	823	23134
Sikkim	36	17	19	36	0	0	36
Tamil Nadu	51236	18479	32757	51065	171	9271	60507
Tripura	2503	1220	1283	2503	0	0	2503
Uttar Pradesh	39378	11281	28097	39378	0	1	39379
West Bengal	7508	2686	4822	7508	0	0	7508
Chhattisgarh	14749	5227	9522	14749	0	11105	25854
Jharkhand	15598	5340	10258	15581	17	17	15615
Uttarakhand	55	17	38	55	0	0	55
Telangana	6029	2505	3524	5771	258	0	6029
All India	757492	289906	466095	744962	12530	38211	795703

Source: http://nsap.nic.in/ReportBenfAbstract.do?method=showReportResult

their bodies might not permit it, thus preventing their bodies from fully recovering on one hand, and also impeding their ability to exclusively breastfeed their young infant in the first six months. In view of the above, the Ministry of Women and Child Development (MoWCD) formulated a new Scheme for pregnant and lactating mothers called Indira Gandhi Matritva Sahyog Yojana (IGMSY)—a Conditional Maternity Benefit Scheme, in 2005. It provides a differential one-time cash incentive to pregnant women for institutional/home births through skilled assistance. JSY, however, does not address the issues regarding a woman's socio-economic compulsions to work right up to the last stage of pregnancy and resuming work soon after child birth.

Background

Undernutrition continues to adversely affect majority of women in India. An undernourished mother almost inevitably gives birth to a low birth weight baby. In view of the above situations, there is an emergent need to address the nutritional deficits of the pregnant and lactating mother. Before implementing IGMSY there were also some schemes such as: Maternity Benefit Act, 1961, Employees' State Insurance Act, 1948, Central Civil Services (Leave) Rules, 1972, Infant Milk Substitute, Feeding Bottles and Infant Foods (Regulation of Production, Supply and Distribution) Act, 1992, National Maternity Benefit Scheme (NMBS), 2001 and Janani Suraksha Yojana (JSY), 2005. The above schemes do not holistically address the issues regarding the woman's compulsions to work right up to the last stage of pregnancy and resumption of work soon after child birth. A need therefore emerged for a new scheme which has been formulated with the aim to improve the health and nutrition status of pregnant and lactating women as well as to create opportunities for engagement of pregnant women with the AWCs so as to ensure Nutrition and Health Education, counselling and promotion of Infant and Young Child Feeding (IYCF) practices. So, the Scheme IGMSY—Conditional Maternity Benefit (CMB) Scheme would be implemented through the platform of ICDS Scheme. The focal point of implementation would be the *Anganwadi* Centres (AWCs) at the village.

Objectives

To improve the health and nutrition status of Pregnant and Lactating (P&L) women and their young infants by:

- Promoting appropriate practices, care and service utilization during pregnancy, safe delivery and lactation.
- Encouraging women to follow (optimal) IYCF practices including early and exclusive breastfeeding for the first six months.
- Contributing to better enabling environment by providing cash incentives for improved health and nutrition to pregnant and lactating women.

Beside this the Scheme aims to provide partial compensation for the wage loss so that the woman is not under compulsion to work till the last stage of pregnancy and can take adequate rest before and after delivery.

Target Groups

(a) P&L women of 19 years of age and above for their first 2 live births.
(b) All Government/Public Sector Undertakings (Centre and State) employees are excluded from the Scheme as they are entitled for paid maternity leave. The wives of such employees are also excluded from the Scheme.
(c) P&L *Anganwadi* workers (AWWs) and AWHs may also avail the benefit under the Scheme if they are not receiving paid maternity benefits from the Government.

Provision of Benefits

Under this Scheme, a cash incentive of Rs. 4000 is to be provided directly to women of 19 years and above for the first two live births subject to the woman fulfilling specific conditions relating to maternal child health and nutrition. Cash incentive is provided in three instalments, between the second trimesters of pregnancy till the infant completes 6 months of age. Women enrolled under IGMSY is encouraged to avail JSY package also for institutional delivery and *vice versa.* However, there is no cash incentive under IGMSY at the time of delivery since cash incentive for this is already provided under JSY.

Fund Allocation

IGMSY is a Centrally Sponsored Scheme under which full grant-in-aid would be provided to State Government/UTs. It is implemented using the platform of ICDS. The focal point of implementation is AWC.

Coverage

In order to ensure national coverage and diversity of implementation experiences, IGMSY would be piloted in 52 identified districts amongst all the States/UTs across the country. Out of these 52 districts, 11 each are selected from good and weak performing districts, 26 from medium performing districts and 4 are UTs. A mix of good performing, poor performing and medium performing districts have been selected to test check the success of implementation *viz-a-viz.* demand and supply. The districts have been selected from across the country based on six indicators which are available from DLHS-3. These were given equal weightings. The indicators are: (i) Literate female population (per cent) (Age 7+), (ii) Mothers registered in the first trimester when they were pregnant with last live birth/still birth (per cent), (iii) Mothers who had at least 3 Ante-Natal care visits during the last pregnancy (per cent), (iv) Institutional births (per cent), (v) Children (12-23 months) fully immunized (BCG, 3 doses each of DPT, and Polio and Measles) (per cent) and (vi) Children breastfed within one hour of birth (per cent).

In order to estimate the number of pregnant and lactating women that would be covered under the IGMSY, the surveyed population of P&L Women under ICDS (225 lakh) has been taken into consideration. 75 per cent of women in the 52 selected districts have been estimated to avail benefits initially under IGMSY, since it is a self-selecting scheme. Based on these calculations, the scheme would cover around 13.8 lakh pregnant and lactating women from these 52 selected districts.

Impact Study

The Ministry of Women & Child Welfare reasons that the designing of this scheme is such that it focuses on the roles and responsibilities of the beneficiaries with short-term objectives but in turn promotes long-term investments in human capital. The idea behind Conditional Cash Transfers is the linking of cash to certain desirable behaviours, whereby money is provided to poor families contingent upon certain verified actions. This approach is both an alternative to more traditional social assistance programmes and a demand-side complement to the supply of maternity health services. Conditional cash transfer programmes have almost always been subjected to rigorous evaluations of their effectiveness, unlike other development initiatives. The effectiveness of such programmes can only be evaluated, if accompanied by systematic efforts to measure their broader impact on household's behaviour. In understanding the effectiveness of IGMSY, the twin objectives of the scheme become important, because on the one hand it seeks to compensate for wage loss due to maternity, and on the other it tries to promote appropriate maternal and young infant feeding behaviours. Lingam & Yelamanchili (2011) point out that series of exclusionary clauses dampen the objectives of the scheme. The preconditions of the scheme not only permits those women who need s8uch benefits the most, but it also patronizes a certain acculturation, that puts those women who do not follow such behaviour at a risk of being termed as a bad example to society. It is difficult to determine which of the objectives is of greater significance, that is, whether compensation for wage loss due to maternity is the main objective of the scheme, and if so, the pre-conditions act as a rationing device, designed to keep out other entitled beneficiaries.

In a study conducted by the partners of National Alliance for Maternal Health and Human Rights (NAMHHR), on IGMSY (pilot phase) from an Equity and Accountability Perspective, Advocate Sashi Bindhani of SODA (Orissa), shared that the study examined in detail the situation of 57 women in four blocks (45 revenue villages) in four states of India. The study found that all of them had gone through three to seven pregnancies, where each episode of maternity exacerbates their vulnerability due to increased impoverishment and high expenses. With high pregnancy wastage and poor availability of health care, they are never sure whether their baby will survive, despite which the state has penalized them for having more than two living children.

In a leading newspaper article by Dhar (2012) cited Dr. Sebanti Ghosh of Association for Social & Health Advancement (West Bengal) who pointed out that despite their contribution to the economy of the country, and their productive and reproductive contributions to the community, women wage workers in the informal sector (148 million) remain deprived of full maternity benefits, forcing them to continue with physically strenuous wage work till the eighth month and shorten their post-partum rest. In the absence of food security, they are compelled to compromise on their own requirements, even in pregnancy. Therefore, it is clear that an ill-equipped health system compounds the problem. In the absence of the availability of this scheme (for even those who qualify), pregnancy and childbirth is seen as a period of financial crisis as it may mean increased expenses and also several weeks or months away from work.

Dr. Kalyani Meena of Prerana Bharti, an NGO in Jharkhand reiterated at the NAMHHR conference in 2012 that given the abysmal conditions of women workers in the informal sector, the IGMSY scheme in its very design defeats the purpose that it sought to address by imposing preconditions of parity. Partners of the NAMHHR strongly recommend unconditional maternity benefits, universal health coverage, and universal food security for all women, without any conditions, as a primary requirement for the improvement of maternal nutrition, reduction of maternal anemia and prevention of maternal mortality.

Jehan *et al.* (2012) state that, it has been reported that in India, increased use of maternal health services have increased since the schemes such as JSY began, though there has been no evidence to establish improvements in maternal health outcomes (due to lack of controlled studies). Their study points out certain areas for improvement in these schemes, such as the need for more efficient operational management, clear guidelines, financial transparency, plans sustainability, and above all, evidence and proven impact on quality of care and maternal mortality and morbidity.

2.8.6 Bi-Cycle for Tribal Girls

The West Bengal State Government has implanted a scheme of distribution of bi-cycles to the tribal girl students from Class IX to XII in the Left Wing Extremists (LWE) affected blocks in the districts of Paschim Medinipur, Bankura and Purulia from 2010-11. The scheme is aimed at reducing drop-out in the schools and to encourage the girl students to continue study. Besides, these bi-cycles help their families for multipurpose household activities. Though objective evaluation of the scheme is yet to be done, however, it appears that the scheme has a good impact on the girl students. There is huge demand from tribal areas and also from SC dominated backward areas. Under this Scheme 9418 bi-cycles were distributed in 2010-11. Hon'ble Chief Minister announced distribution of bi-cycles for all girl students studying in classes IX-XII in the 23 LWE Blocks of Jangal Mahal areas. Delivery of bi-cycles was completed in January, 2012. During 2011-12 financial year 32,092 bicycles were provided to Class IX to XII girl students of Jangal Mahal areas at a cost of Rs. 9.019 crore. Fund of Rs. 2.81 crore has also been provided to Backward Class Welfare Department for supply of 9728 more bicycles to such girl students. 88,000 bi-cycles have already been distributed and 60,000 bi-cycles are being distributed to all ST girl students of class IX to XII in all schools of West Bengal. In 2013-14, funds for 34265 bicycles have been provided to girls students of class IX to XII in Jangal Mahal (GoWB 2014). Now the programme is being executed for all boys and girls students of class IX to XII.

Note

1. The region constitutes with some parts of four Districts of West Bengal, Namely Purulia, Bankura, Paschim Midinipur and Birbhum.

PART II

3
Social Protection Benefits in the Backward Region of West Bengal

The Social Protection Programmes (SPP) are crucial for the development of the backward regions. They are indeed beneficial for the upliftment of the deprived people in those regions. The region consists of three districts namely, Purulia, Bankura and Paschim Medinipur which is one of the backward regions of West Bengal. The questions that naturally arise in this perspective are: Which social protection programmes are evident in the backward region? What is the extent of benefits of the SPPs in this region? The present chapter deals with these and allied issues in depath on the basis of secondary information.

The section that follows presents the brief profile of the sample blocks and villages based on data from Census of India. Section 3.2 deals with the trend of poverty and food security in the backward regions. Section 3.3, Section 3.4, Section 3.5, Section 3.6, Section 3.7, Section 3.8 discusses the social protection benefits for food, health, water & sanitation, education, housing, and employment & income respectively. Finally, Section 3.9 explains social security benefits in the backward regions.

3.1 Profile of the Backward Region

The ranking of the districts of West Bengal on the basis of socio-economic indicators substantiates that Purulia, Bankura and Paschim Medinipur occupied in bottom five ranks and they are relatively backward. These three districts are purposively chosen in the present study to analyse the evidence of SPB. This section deals with the profile of this backward region in comparison to West Bengal as a whole.

First, among three districts under our study Paschim Medinipur is the largest in terms of total population and density of population followed by Bankura and Purulia in 2001 as well as in 2011 (Table 3.1).

Table 3.1: Population in Selected Districts of West Bengal, 2001 and 2011 (in million)

District/ State	*2001*					*2011*				
	Male	*Female*	*Urban*	*Rural*	*Total*	*Male*	*Female*	*Urban*	*Rural*	*Total*
Paschim Medinipur	2.65	2.54	0.62	4.59	5.19	3.03	2.91	0.75	5.19	5.94
Bankura	1.64	1.56	0.24	2.96	3.20	1.84	1.76	0.30	3.30	3.60
Purulia	1.30	1.24	0.26	2.28	2.54	1.50	1.43	.37	2.56	2.93
West Bengal	41.47	38.71	22.43	57.75	80.18	46.93	44.42	29.1	62.2	91.3

Source: Census of India, 2001 and 2011.

The density of population is substantially low in these three districts as compared to the whole of West Bengal and it also increased at relatively low rate during 2001 to 2011 (Figure 3.1).

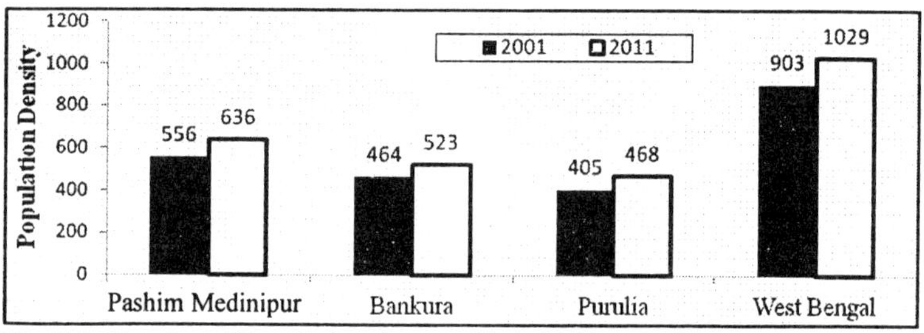

Fig. 3.1: Density of Population (per sq. Km), 2001 and 2011

Source: As in Table 3.1.

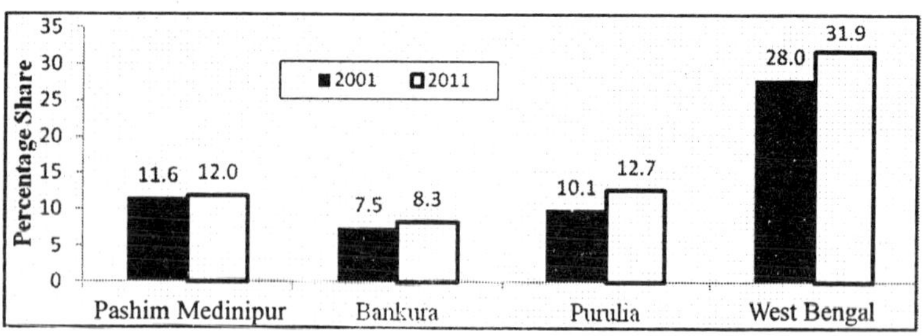

Fig. 3.2: Urbanization Rate in Sample Districts, 2001 and 2011

Source: As in Table 3.1.

Table 3.2: Percentage of SC and ST Population to Total Population in 2011

District/State	*T/R/U*	*SC*	*ST*	*SC+ST*
	Total	19.1	14.9	34.0
Paschim Medinipur	Rural	19.9	16.4	36.4
	Urban	13.0	3.7	16.8
	Total	32.7	10.3	42.9
Bankura	Rural	33.5	11.1	44.6
	Urban	22.9	1.1	24.1
	Total	19.4	18.5	37.8
Purulia	Rural	19.2	20.8	40.0
	Urban	20.7	2.4	23.1
	Total	23.5	5.8	29.3
West Bengal	Rural	27.5	7.8	35.3
	Urban	15.0	1.5	16.5

Source: As in Table 3.1.

Second, in terms of urbanisation all the three districts lagged behind compared to the level of urbanisation[1] in the whole of West Bengal. The spread (growth rate of Uttar Pradesh) of urbanisation was also relatively low in these three districts (Figure 3.2).

Third, the region is predominantly populated with Scheduled Castes (SC) and Scheduled Tribes (ST). Their share in total population is highest (among all districts of West Bengal) in Bankura, followed by Purulia and Paschim Medinipur (Table 3.2). The share of ST population to total population is also high in these three districts as compared with that in the whole of West Bengal.

Fourth, the literacy rates, both of rural and urban area, in two backward districts Bankura and Purulia was below than that of the State as a whole while Paschim Medinipur district recorded the higher literacy rate. There was the evidence of substantial increase of literacy rate, specifically rural literacy rate and the gap between rural and urban literacy rates declined from 2001 to 2011 (Table 3.3). The female literacy rate was abnormally low in Purulia and Bankura. During 2001 and 2011 these two districts, however witnessed a significant decline of the gender gap in literacy rate—10 per cent in Purulia and 17 per cent in Bankura (Table 3.4). The literacy rate in Paschim Medinipur district was higher (across sex and region) in comparison to whole of West Bengal (Figure 3.3).

Fifth, the female work participation rate (WPR) in three backward districts was relatively high. The high female WPR in the backward region is an indicator of distress. To maintain the livelihood of poor households, the female counterpart also highly participates in agricultural and other activities along with male workers of the households in the backward

Table 3.3: Rural and Urban Literacy Rates and their Gap, 2001 and 2011

District/State	2001		2011		Rural-Urban Literacy Gap	
	Rural	Urban	Rural	Urban	2001	2011
Paschim Midinipore	68.7	82.4	77.9	87.0	13.7	9.1
Bankura	62.0	80.2	69.6	85.2	18.2	15.6
Purulia	53.6	75.4	63.8	76.2	22.2	12.5
West Bengal	63.4	81.3	73.0	85.5	17.8	12.6

Source: As in Table 3.1.

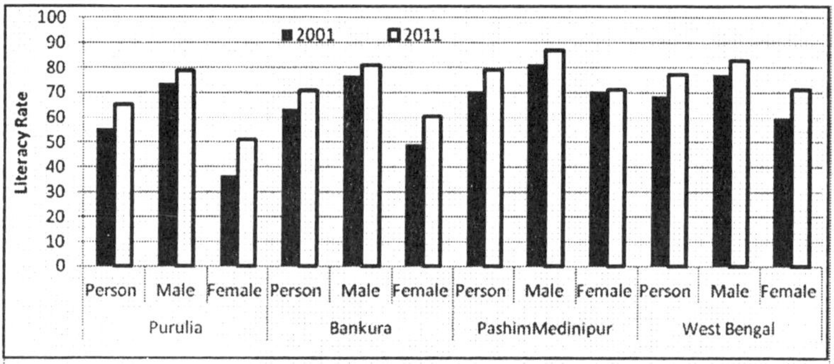

Fig. 3.3: Literacy Rate by Sex, 2001 and 2011

Source: As in Table 3.1.

Table 3.4: Gender Gap in Literacy Rate, 2001 and 2011

Region	Purulia		Bankura		Paschim Medinipur		West Bengal	
	2001	2011	2001	2011	2001	2011	2001	2011
Total	37.2	27.6	27.3	10.6	22.2	15.6	17.4	11.5
Rural	39.1	29.0	28.3	21.4	23.4	16.4	20.0	13.4
Urban	20.1	17.5	16.2	11.7	13.0	9.4	10.4	7.5

Source: As in Table 3.1.

districts. In Purulia, the female WPR was 36.11 per cent in 2001 and 31.29 per cent in 2011. Because of high female WPR, the difference between male WPR and female WPR was relatively low in the backward districts (Table 3.5).

Sixth, the share of marginal workers (who are working less than 180 days in a year) to total workers was much higher in case of females compared to males. In backward districts that share was substantially high in comparison with West Bengal as a whole. In 2011, the share of

Table 3.5: Work Participation Rate (WPR), 2001 and 2011

District/State	*WPR 2001*			*WPR 2011*		
	Male	*Female*	*Male-Female*	*Male*	*Female*	*Male-Female*
Paschim Medinipur	54.61	22.79	31.82	58.43	25.87	32.56
Bankura	56.89	31.96	24.93	57.17	23.62	33.55
Purulia	52.42	36.11	16.31	53.52	31.29	22.23
West Bengal	54.23	18.08	36.15	57.07	18.18	38.99

Source: As in Table 3.1.

marginal workers was 50 per cent in West Bengal, whereas that share was 73.2 per cent in Purulia, 62.9 per cent in Bankura and 65.6 per cent in Paschim Medinipur. Moreover, the share of marginal workers was much higher in the rural area of these districts than that in the urban area (Table 3.6).

Table 3.6: Percentage Share of Main and Marginal Workers to Total Workers by Sex and Region, 2011

District/State	*Region*	*% of main workers to total workers*			*% of marginal workers to total workers*		
		Persons	*Males*	*Female*	*Persons*	*Males*	*Female*
Paschim Medinipur	Total	60.2	71.3	34.4	39.8	28.7	65.6
	Rural	57.7	69.2	32.2	42.3	30.8	67.8
	Urban	82.5	87.3	64.2	17.5	12.7	35.8
Bankura	Total	62.5	72.5	37.1	37.5	27.5	62.9
	Rural	60.8	71.2	35.2	39.2	28.8	64.8
	Urban	83.6	88.0	68.2	16.4	12.0	31.8
Purulia	Total	49.1	61.6	26.8	50.9	38.4	73.2
	Rural	45.8	58.5	24.9	54.2	41.5	75.1
	Urban	79.9	84.0	62.7	20.1	16.0	37.3
West Bengal	Total	73.9	81.1	49.9	26.1	18.9	50.1
	Rural	68.5	77.0	42.1	31.5	23.0	57.9
	Urban	86.2	90.0	70.9	13.8	10.0	29.1

Source: As in Table 3.1.

Seventh, rural workers were predominantly engaged in agricultural sector in these backward districts of West Bengal. About 73.1 per cent of rural workers in Paschim Medinipur in 2011 were engaged in agricultural sector, this share was 70 per cent in Bankura and 66.6 per cent in Purulia. In the agriculture sector, the rural workers in these districts were predominantly engaged as agricultural labour (Table 3.7).

Table 3.7: Distribution of Rural Workers by Activity, 2011

District/ State	Cultiva-tors (CL)	Agricul-tural Labour (AL)	House-hold Industry (HHI)	Other Services	Total	CL +AL	HHI +OS
Paschim Medinipur	25.0	48.2	6.0	20.9	100	73.1	26.9
Bankura	22.7	47.4	4.0	25.9	100	70.1	29.9
Purulia	23.5	43.1	7.2	26.2	100	66.6	33.4
West Bengal	20.6	40.9	6.7	31.9	100	61.4	38.6

Source: As in Table 3.1.

Eighth, out of 36 drought prone blocks in West Bengal 34 are located in these three districts. Entire Purulia district is drought prone. In Paschim Medinipur and Bankura the drought prone areas are 27.7 per cent and 31.8 per cent respectively (Table 3.7).

Ninth, the Jangal Mahal region predominantly comprises with these three districts because of the significant area is covered by forest. Out of the total geographical area, share of forest area in Bankura, Paschim Medinipur and Purulia districts was 21.6, 18.5 and 12 per cent respectively. (Table 3.8).

Table 3.8: Drought Prone Area and Forest Area, 2011

District/State	Drought Prone Block	Drought Prone Area (sq. Km.)	Drought Prone Area (%)	Forest Area (%)
Paschim Medinipur	7	2707	27.7	18.5
Bankura	7	2185	31.8	21.6
Purulia	20	6305	100.0	12.0
West Bengal	36	11594	13.1	13.5

Source: Economic Review 2011-12, Govt. of West Bengal.

3.2 Trend of Poverty and Food Insecurity in the Backward Region

The status of poverty in general and food insecurity in particular are estimated from NSSO Unit Level data. At sub-state level, NSSO regional estimation is presentable. According to NSSO the three backward districts belong to the Western Plain of West Bengal. By following Tendulkar (2009) methodology we have estimated head count ratio (HCR), poverty gap ratio (PGP) and square poverty gap ratio (SPGP) in the selected backward region as well as in the state as a whole for the years 2004-05,

2009-10 and 2011-12. The trend of poverty in the backward region and West Bengal are depicted in Figure 3.4. In 2004-05, the HCR in the backward region (constituted by Medinipur, Bankura and Purulia) was 36.8 per cent in comparison to 38.2 per cent in the whole of West Bengal. In the years that follow, West Bengal witnessed significant reduction of poverty but not in the backward region. During 2009-10 to 2011-12, the HCR in the backward region stood near about 32 per cent whereas; in West Bengal the HCR fell from 28.8 per cent in 2009-10 to 22.5 per cent in 2011-12. The so-called Moist movement in the backward region adversely affected the livelihood of the people and hence the HCR was relatively high and the region failed to experience the reduction of poverty. The depth of poverty (PGP) and severity of poverty (SPGP) were also high in the backward region in comparison to West Bengal as a whole.

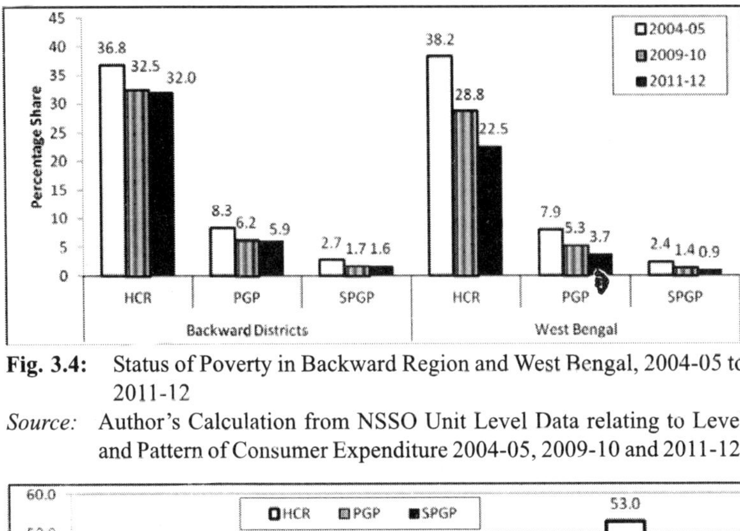

Fig. 3.4: Status of Poverty in Backward Region and West Bengal, 2004-05 to 2011-12

Source: Author's Calculation from NSSO Unit Level Data relating to Level and Pattern of Consumer Expenditure 2004-05, 2009-10 and 2011-12.

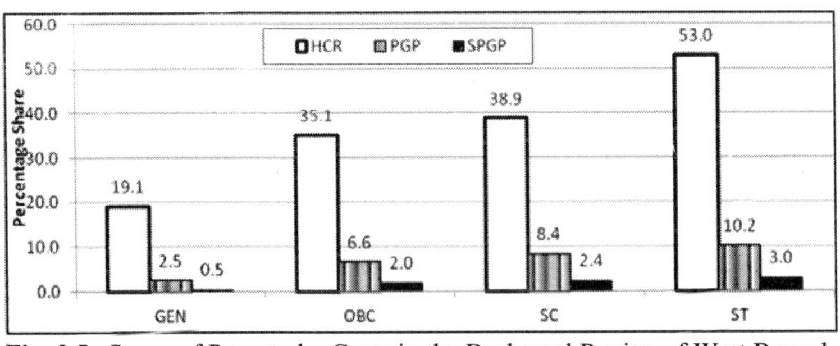

Fig. 3.5: Status of Poverty by Caste in the Backward Region of West Bengal, 2011-12.

Source: As in Figure 3.4.

The situation of tribal people was worst in the backward region in the aftermath of Maoist movement. The HCR of STs was as high as 53.0 per cent in 2011-12 in comparison with just 19.1 per cent of general caste (GEN) people. The poverty gap and square poverty gap were also substantially high for the STs (Figure 3.5).

The status of food insecurity in the backward region was also estimated on the basis of NSSO Unit Level data by following Tendulkar (2009) methodology. In the backward region 23.5 per cent households and 24 per cent people were food insecure in 2004-05. These shares successively declined in 2009-10 and 2011-12. In 2011-12 still 10.8 per cent households and 14.1 per cent people were food insecure. The incidence of food insecurity was substantially high for SC, ST and other backward castes. The food insecurity gap (FIG) and square food insecurity gap (SFIG) were low in the year 2011-12 (Figure 3.6 and Figure 3.7). Government measures (i.e., social protection programmes) that extended after Maoist activities was helpful in reducing food insecurity but was incapable to eliminate hunger in this region. In the recent past, the evidence of people's death due to hunger was detected.

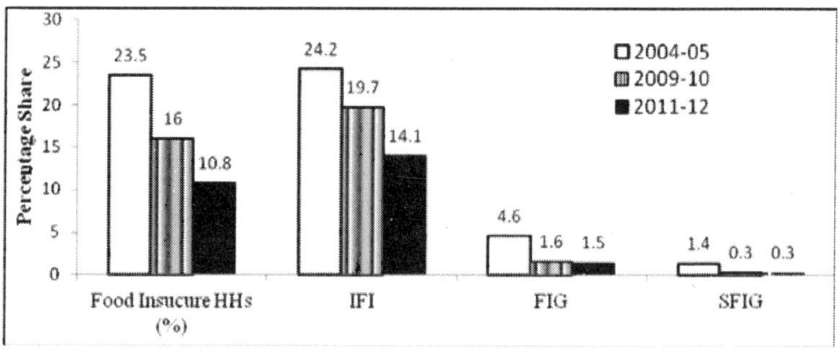

Fig. 3.6: Status of Food Insecurity in the Backward Region of West Bengal, 2004-05 to 2011-12

Source: As in Figure 3.4.

3.3 Social Protection Benefits for Food Security in the Backward Region

PDS facilitates the supply of foodgrains and this supply has been provided through the fare price shops and the status of ration cards. The benefits of this system differ for different types of ration cards, i.e., BPL, APL, AP, AAY and also differ in respect of the Jangal Mahal and Drought

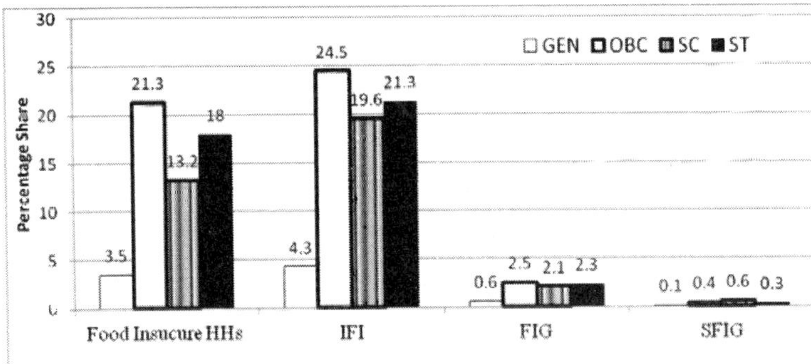

Fig 3.7: Status of Food Insecurity by Castes in the Backward Region of West Bengal, 2011-12

Source: As in Figure 3.4.

Prone region. Generally, the scale of distribution for BPL is 1Kg/head/week for rice and 1125 gm/head/week of wheat. In case of AAY, the scale of distribution of rice is 1250 gm /head/week and 750 gm /head/week for wheat. The number of ration cards and monthly allotment of foodgrains under TPDS for the month of April-May 2013 are given in Table 3.9 and Table 3.10 respectively. In these three districts namely Bankura, Paschim Medinipur and Purulia, most of the people have ration cards. Number of people without ration cards is only 0.3 per cent in Purulia, 1.0 per cent in Bankura and 1.4 per cent in Paschim Medinipur, which is relatively lower relating to the whole of West Bengal. But before 2011, nearly 15 per cent people of these three districts (24% in Purulia, 7% in Bankura and 15 per cent in Paschim Medinipur) did not hold any kind of ration card.

Table 3.9: Number of Ration Cards (for PDS) by Category in three Backward Districts of West Bengal

Districts/ State	*BPL*	*AAY*	*APL*	*AP*	*BPL-Jangal Mahal*	*BPL-ITDP*	*BPL-Other Program*	*Total Ration Cards*	*% of Population# without Ration Card*
Purulia	548198	445740	1108131	1559	709385	109600	0	2922613	0.3
Bankura	650904	587305	2024604	1934	260886	36651	0	3562284	1.0
Paschim Medinipur	1447894	382242	3024154	3282	895152	80334	0	5833058	1.4
West Bengal	16478800	6766208	55008435	49444	1964275	226585	2049211	82542958	9.6

Note: # — Population of the 2011.

Source: Department of Food and Food Supplies, Government of West Bengal.

Table 3.10: Monthly Allotment of Food Grains (in Metric Ton) under TPDS in three Backward Districts of West Bengal during April-May 2013

Districts/ State	*Allotment of Rice*				*Allotment of Wheat*			
	BPL	*AAY*	*APL*	*Total*	*BPL*	*AAY*	*APL*	*TOTAL*
Bankura	4692	2280	620	7592	1250	1780	2700	5730
Purulia	5200	2100	155	7455	400	1640	1310	3350
Paschim Medinipur	11487	1810	1152	14449	2265	1410	4110	7785
West Bengal	75677	28242	5606	109525	47242	22053	69495	138790

Source: As in Table 3.9.

The State Government has extended several measures to increase the livelihood in the Maoist affected Jangal Mahal. As a part of these measures the State Government has provided the quasi-universal PDS in Jangal Mahal by the means of Jangal Mahal BPL ration (and also in Drought Prone region by BPL-ITDP) since 2011. The provision of getting rice per head for specially identified BPL in Jangal Mahal area is 2 kg/ week and for wheat is 750 gm/week.

The monthly per capita allotment of rice and wheat under BPL, AAY and APL ration cards are shown in Table 3.11. In case of Purulia, Bankura and Paschim Medinipur, BPL categories are allotted more rice than other districts of West Bengal on account of higher allotment under the schemes of Jangal Mahal and drought prone area (BPL-ITDP). Since the BPL beneficiaries under special schemes are allotted more than AAY or APL, per capita allotment of foodgrains in these three districts are higher than that of West Bengal as a whole.

Table 3.11: Monthly Per capita Allotment of Rice and Wheat in three Backward Districts of West Bengal, 2013

Districts/State	*Rice (in Kg.)*			*Wheat (in Kg.)*		
	BPL	*AAY*	*APL*	*BPL*	*AAY*	*APL*
Purulia	9.5	4.7	0.1	0.7	3.7	1.2
Bankura	7.2	3.9	0.3	1.9	3.0	1.3
Paschim Medinipur	7.9	4.7	0.4	1.6	3.7	1.4
West Bengal	4.6	4.2	0.1	2.9	3.3	1.3

Source: As in Table 3.9.

3.4 Social Protection Benefits for Health

People have received the health-related facilities from different programmes of government. Among them are Rural Primary Health Care, JSY and RSBY which are of utmost importance. These programmes are explored one by one.

3.4.1 Rural Primary Health Care

The number of rural hospitals (RHs), block primary health centres (BPHCs), primary health centres (PHCs) and sub-centres in the three backward districts *vis-à-vis* the whole of West Bengal are shown in Table 3.12. Different types of health centres and health sub-centres (SC) extend the health facilities to the rural households. Their concentration in particular districts reflects the coverage of the people by government health facilities. One of the important indicators of health coverage is the population served per bed. Number of rural populations served per bed in the three backward districts was relatively lower than the state average (Table 3.13). The number of populations covered per health centres was also low in the backward districts. That is, the backward region is better covered by health centres but the quality of health service and the access to health service are not satisfactory. Recently, the Government of West Bengal has opened fair price medicine shops through the government hospitals and medical centres to save the out of pocket expenditure of the poor people with 48 to 72.6 per cent subsidized price.

Table 3.12: Health Facilities in the Rural Areas in three Backward Districts of West Bengal (as on 31.07.2013)

District/State	*RH*		*BPHC*		*PHC*		*Total*		*No. of SC*
	No.	*Beds*	*No.*	*Beds*	*No.*	*Beds*	*No.*	*Beds*	
Purulia	18	550	2	40	52	344	72	934	485
Bankura	18	640	4	70	69	512	91	1222	564
Paschim Medinipur	23	935	6	75	84	584	113	1594	858
West Bengal	268	9110	79	1160	909	6592	1256	16862	10356

Source: Health on the March 2012-13, Bureau of Health Intelligence Government of West Bengal.

3.4.2 Janani Suraksha Yojana (JSY)

The number of beneficiaries and institutional deliveries under JSY across districts of West Bengal are shown in Table 3.14. In Purulia, during the year 2010-11, 35737 beneficiaries are benefited at the rate of Rs. 500 and 3902 beneficiaries at the rate of Rs. 1400. The number of beneficiaries

Table 3.13: Hospital Bed and Population served per Bed in three Backward Districts of West Bengal, 2013

District/State	Population 2011	Total Number			Population Served Per		
		Beds	Health Centers (RH+BPHC +PHC)	SC	Bed	Health Centre	SC
Purulia	2556810	934	72	485	2737	35511	5272
Bankura	3296901	1222	91	564	2698	36230	5846
Paschim Medinipur	5190771	1594	113	858	3256	45936	6050
West Bengal	64183113	16862	1256	10356	3688	51101	6198

Source: Health on the March 2012-13, Bureau of Health Intelligence Government of West Bengal.

Table 3.14: Number of JSY Beneficiaries and Institution Delivery by Districts of West Bengal

Districts	JSY Beneficiaries			Institutional Delivery		
	2010-11	2011-12	2012-13	2010-11	2011-12	2012-13
Purulia	35737	32522	27803	29751	25291	23197
Bankura	33069	37364	21629	23368	26009	20939
Paschim Medinipur	51582	51684	44093	19675	36727	30809
Kooch Bihar	31201	35507	32545	19636	20837	22908
Jalpaiguri	42152	44653	41608	24438	27465	27863
Darjeeling	7318	7748	9279	8042	7853	8615
Malda	42989	32469	35709	21408	20838	19803
Uttar Dinajpur	36320	34758	37019	12871	14563	17346
Dakshin Dinajpur	15786	18906	13096	8982	11029	9120
Murshidabad	101379	82052	60056	32101	40727	35226
Nadia	41215	24754	22139	26780	22797	14362
North 24-Parganas	31400	32418	30889	15332	14127	18810
South 24-Parganas	75969	90140	81118	18574	31148	25462
Kolkata	NA	NA	6077	15058	9643	14979
Howrah	26553	28558	20322	18630	14485	12831
Hugli	31414	38494	33253	25619	20126	21607
Bardwan	52090	57128	37683	35971	26872	21840
Birbhum	40958	43590	32143	21809	32849	29356
Purba Medinipur	41498	43370	36315	3733	22501	20328
SUDA* Urban JSY	42538	51489	37220	6609	724	12839
Total	**781168**	**787604**	**659996**	**388387**	**426611**	**408240**

Notes: *Agency operating urban region, N.A. = Not Applicable

Source: http://nrhm.gov.in/nrhm-components/rmnch-a/maternal-health/janani-suraksha-yojana/background.html

in 2011-12 and 2012-13 were 32522 and 27803 respectively. In case of Paschim Medinipur district the number of beneficiaries remained 51500 during 2010-11 to 2011-12 but their number decreased thereafter. For the period 2010-11 and 2011-12 the numbers of beneficiaries were 33069 and 37364 respectively in Bankura district. Percentage change of beneficiaries substantially decreased in Bankura district during 2012-13 as compared to 2011-12.

JSY also promotes the institutional delivery to secure mother. Number of institutional deliveries had increased in 2011-12 over the period 2010-11 in Bankura and Paschim Medinipur. Thereafter, the institutional delivery decreased. But in case of Purulia the fact worsened during 2010-11 and 2012-13. The percentage share of institutional delivery to total JSY beneficiaries in these three districts gradually increased from 60 per cent in 2010-11 to 72 per cent in 2011-12 and further to 80 per cent in 2012-13. The target of full institutional delivery is yet to be achieved. Unfavourable distance from JSY beneficiary to health institution and lack of proper awareness about the safety of pregnant mother can be the explanation of low institutional delivery.

3.4.3 Rashtriya Swasthya Bima Yojana (RSBY)

Under RSBY there is the provision of health insurance at the extent of Rs. 30,000 per BPL (now APL also) family per annum on a family floater basis. Table 3.15 elucidates the duration of the programme implementation, premium of the facilities, targeted beneficiaries and hospital empanelled for RSBY. The duration period of the programme is 3 years in Bankura and Purulia. But the scheme is implemented for 4 years in Paschim Medinipur. The premium amount Rs. 460 is same for both Bankura and Purulia. The amount is Rs. 212 in Paschim Medinipur. Though the premium amount is quite low in Paschim Medinipur with respect to Bankura and Purulia, the percentage of enrolment to total target is significantly high in Bankura (84.71%). Paschim Medinipur managed to be near about the same level of state average (55.32%) followed by Purulia (50.15%). In the selected backward region (i.e., in three districts) 61 per cent of targeted families are enrolled under RSBY. Private and public hospitals are empanelld to get health facilities under RSBY. But actual benefits are significantly low. Table 3.16 depicts the actual scenario of beneficial outcomes from RSBY, i.e. the case of hospitalization and hospitalization utility provided to beneficiaries. Only 2.90 per cent enrolled families obtained the benefits of hospitalization in the backward region. Among the three districts under study, Bankura secured the first position in respect of both number of hospitalizations in absolute and relative sense. Only 5.82 per cent of hospitalization out of enrolled has been cited in Bankura district whereas the shares for Purulia and Paschim Medinipur were 3.80 per cent and 0.20 per cent respectively. Though Paschim Medinipur is more populous demographically, the actual benefit has gone to the people in terms of hospitalization and hospitalization value is quite low compared to the other two districts (Table 3.16).

Table 3.15: Coverage of RSBY by Districts of West Bengal, 2013

District	Year of Policy (e.g. First, Second)	Premium (With Service tax)	Target and Enrolled Families			Hospitals Empanelled	
			Targeted	Enrolled	Percentage Enrolled	Private	Public
Purulia	3	460	394035	197619	50.15	8	2
Bankura	3	460	418430	354436	84.71	30	2
Paschim Medinipur	4	212	813626	449362	55.23	26	2
Birbhum	3	460	424717	335541	79.00	24	2
Burdwan	5	232	972156	673953	69.33	70	5
Cooch Behar	3	460	472396	179391	37.97	3	5
Dakshin Dinajpur	2	460	234732	137000	58.36	3	4
Darjeeling	2	460	144484	33987	23.52	8	3
Hooghly	3	460	547375	347485	63.48	32	3
Howrah	3	460	238342	85626	35.93	29	1
Jalpaiguri	3	460	619180	228123	36.84	10	3
Kolkata	1	432	217846	112912	51.83	35	9
Malda	5	185	654264	366123	55.96	15	2
Murshidabad	4	205	1021376	558776	54.71	44	1
Nadia	4	262	690852	370858	53.68	52	1
North 24-Parganas	4	380	874840	444780	50.84	43	10
Purba Medinipur	4	380	461806	277280	60.04	63	1
South 24-Parganas	2	460	706669	343831	48.66	45	5
Uttar Dinajpur	3	460	293416	146000	49.76	4	1
Total	–	–	10200542	5643083	55.32	544	62

Source: www.rsby.nic.in

3.5 Social Protection Benefits for Water and Sanitation

National Rural Drinking Water Programme (NRDWP) provides drinking water facilities to the rural people by piped water supply system (PWSS), hand pump, bore wells etc. The expenditure of NRDWP for different schemes in three backward districts during 2011 and 2014 is shown in Table 3.17. The expenditure was high in Purulia district than other districts.

Table 3.16: Actual Benefits Provided under RSBY in three Backward Districts of West Bengal, 2013

District	Number of Hospitalization	Percentage of Hospitalization out of Enrolled	Hospitalization Value (Rs.)
Purulia	7500	3.80	42044750
Bankura	20633	5.82	119889443
Paschim Medinipur	899	0.20	5841475

Source: www.rsby.nic.in

Table 3.17: Financial and Physical Coverage of Safe Drinking Water Facility, 2011-14

Year	Districts	Expenditure (Rs. Crore)	Percentage of Utilization	Population Coverage		Total Schemes*
				Quality Affected	Partially Covered	
2011-12	Purulia	34.81	95.47	21615 (261.2)	49295 (100)	1
	Bankura	11.85	87.13	111109 (114.8)	82173 (100)	1
	Paschim Medinipur	11.97	89.86	29412 (138.9)	50778 (100)	0
2012-13	Purulia	39.93	64.62	31755 (166.5)	156527 (170.6)	0
	Bankura	23.98	74.13	22956 (41.2)	465979 (222.6)	459
	Paschim Medinipur	10.34	33.78	6422 (22.5)	147304 (126.1)	373
2013-14	Purulia	35.69	98.78	9126 (100)	63312 (51.1)	6
	Bankura	21.88	88.23	41332 (97.2)	184901 (123.8)	43
	Paschim Medinipur	27.26	93.01	17255 (73.6)	71569 (293.4)	3

Note: (1) * Total Scheme includes No. of schemes of PWSS, Hand pump, Bore wells and others.
(2) Figures in the parenthesis indicate the percentage share of Target.

Source: Ministry of Drinking Water and Sanitation, Government of India, Report Card status of Swachh Bharat Mission (SBM) as on 5.12.2014.

But the sanctioned amount is not fully utilized. On the whole, nearly 78 per cent of sanctioned fund was utilized in these three districts during 2011 to 2014. The scenario of population coverage in respect of both qualities affected and partially covered has been satisfactory—the facilities

Table 3.18: Report Card status of Swachh Bharat Mission (SBM) in three Backward Districts of West Bengal as on 5-12-2014

District/ State	IHHL BPL		IHHL APL.		IHHL TOTAL		Sanitation complex		School Sanitation		Anganwadi Sanitation	
	Achieve-ment	% of Target	Achiev-ement	% of Target	Achiev-ement	% of Target	Achiev-ement	% of Target	Achiev-ement	% of Target	Achiev-ement	% of Target
Purulia	119922	57	94052	31	213974	41	20	40	5808	77	1566	39
Bankura	113192	57	246526	74	359718	68	119	100	7991	100	1671	41
Paschim Medinipur	596731	100	329310	76	926041	89	73	100	15724	95	4938	85
West Bengal	6191748	94	3234625	65	9426373	81	1279	100	132214	99	52649	63

Note: IHHL = Individual Household Latrine.

Source: Ministry of Drinking Water and Sanitation, Government of India, Report Card status of Swachh Bharat Mission (SBM) as on 5-12-2014.

cross the targeted coverage of population. But lesser number of populations have been covered by quality affected drinking water facility.

Table 3.18 gives a clear picture about the physical achievement of TSC in Bankura, Paschim Medinipur and Purulia districts. Paschim Medinipur district was able to fulfil the target of individual household latrine (IHHL) for BPL households. In Purulia and Bankura districts only 52 per cent of targeted BPL households had IHHL. The percentage share of households having IHHL to total (both BPL and APL) targeted households was 41 per cent in Purulia and 68 per cent in Bankura which was much lower than the share of West Bengal as a whole (81%). That is, the backward region is lagging behind in respect of IHHL. School sanitation in West Bengal was 99 per cent of its target. In Bankura and Paschim Medinipur it was 100 per cent and 95 per cent respectively whereas in Purulia it was 77 per cent. Regarding sanitation complex, only 44 per cent of target was achieved in Purulia. In case of *Anganwadi* Sanitation, Paschim Medinipur had achieved 85 per cent of its target whereas Bankura and Purulia had achieved only 41 per cent and 39 per cent respectively.

The financial achievement of TSC in these three backward districts in comparison to West Bengal as a whole is represented in Table 3.19. The total expenditure on TSC is shared among the Government of India, State Government and beneficiary itself. But Government of India bears the lion share following the State Government and beneficiaries.

Table 3.19: Total Sanitation Campaign Expenditure (Rs. in lakh) in three Backward Districts of West Bengal (up to 5th December 2014)

District/ State	Total Project Outlay	GoI Share	State Share	Beneficiary Contribution	GoI Release	Expenditure (GoI)	Expenditure (Total)
Purulia	10065.74	6753.47	2583.02	729.25	4083.97	4374.62	8496.97
Bankura	7326.54	4901.8	1921.01	503.73	4280.42	3611.24	8457.71
Paschim Medinipur	8411.4	5367	2229.72	814.68	5268.92	4961.96	9570.67
West Bengal	174147.94	111799.51	43820.36	18528.07	92374.17	85344.52	155790.26

Note: GoI = Government of India.

Source: Ministry of Drinking Water and Sanitation, Government of India, Report Card status of Swachh Bharat Mission (SBM) as on 5.12.2014.

3.6 Social Protection Benefits of Education

3.6.1 Integrated Child Development Services (ICDS)

ICDS, launched on 2nd October 1975 in the country as well as in West Bengal, is the largest flagship programme to address nutrition and development needs of children below six years and reduce burden of undernutrition in the country. It also aims to improve nutrition status of pregnant and lactating women, thereby impacting on the nutritional outcomes among children and to break intergenerational cycle of undernutrition. To this end, a package of six services is provided by ICDS to the target groups. The status of ICDS in three districts is given in Table 3.20, Table 3.21 and Table 3.22. All sanctioned ICDS Projects are now operating in three backward districts. Most of the sanctioned AWCs are also operating in these districts. Percentage shares of operational AWCs to sanctioned centres are also high in Bankura (97.7%) and Purulia (96.2%) in comparison to whole of West Bengal (96.6%). But for supplementary nutritional programme (SNP), a programme under ICDS where AWC provides nutritional meals to the children and pregnant & lactating mother, these two districts are lagging behind the target. Percentage share of targeted AWCs providing SNP for 21 + days in a month is substantially low in Purulia (77.7%) and Bankura (83.1%) in comparison to West Bengal as a whole (92.8%).

Table 3.20: Status on ICDS and Anganwadi Centres in three Backward Districts of West Bengal (as on 31.03.2012)

District/State	*ICDS Projects*		*Anganwadi Centers*		
	Sanctioned	*Operational*	*Sanctioned*	*Operational*	*% of Sanctioned*
Purulia	23	23	4845	4734	97.7
Bankura	27	27	5541	5431	98.0
Paschim Medinipur	43	43	9009	8666	96.2
West Bengal	575	573	116390	112432	96.6

Note: % = Percentage share of operational centres to sanctioned centres.
Source: State Annual programme Implementation Plan, Government of West Bengal.

The outcomes of ICDS are assessed by the health situation relating to ICDS which is present in Table 3.22. Number of deaths per 100 live births was relatively high in Bankura and Purulia which was 2.5 and 3.2

Table 3.21: Detail of ICDS Beneficiaries in three Backward Districts of West Bengal (as on March, 2013)

District	*Percentage of targeted AWCs providing SNP for 21 + days in a month*	*Total beneficiaries within project*	*SNP beneficiaries*	*PSE beneficiaries (3-6) years*
Purulia	77.5	354842	313590	122258
Bankura	83.1	388591	356526	81360
Paschim Medinipur	97.5	622107	587574	242415
West Bengal	92.8	9119210	8134550	3396264

Note: AWC = Anganwadi Centre, SNP = Supplementary Nutritional Programme, PSE = Pre-School Education.

Source: As in Table 3.20.

respectively. Table 3.22 also presents the distribution of weighted children by their nutritional status which is classified as normal and malnourished (Grade I, Grade II, Grade III and Grade IV). The percentage share of children in normal grade are relatively low in all the three backward districts. That is, these districts have witnessed higher number of malnutrition children. The children with severe malnutrition (Grade III & IV) were also relatively high in these three districts—3.1 per cent in Bankura, 2.8 per cent in Purulia and 1.6 per cent in Paschim Medinipur.

Table 3.22: Health situation on Presence of ICDS in three Backward Districts of West Bengal (as on March, 2013)

District/ State	*Reported live births*	*No. of deaths (0-1) years*	*No. of deaths (1-5) years*	*Distribution of Children by nutritional status*				
				Normal	*Gr-I*	*Gr-II*	*Gr. III & Gr. IV*	*Total Children weighted*
Purulia	2941	95	16	70.2	27.0	0.0	2.8	247146 (100)
Bankura	2399	61	5	74.5	22.4	0.0	3.1	268456 (100)
Paschim Medinipur	4942	81	13	68.9	29.5	0.0	1.6	386509 (100)
West Bengal	70839	1459	344	75.4	23.3	0.0	1.3	5831423 (100)

Source: As in Table 3.20.

3.6.2 Shishu Shiksha Karmasuchi (SSK)

The Government of West Bengal had decided to introduce an alternative elementary education system in West Bengal, which could reach any corner of the state, to cater to the special needs of the children, less costly, but qualitatively comparable with the formal education system. The Panchayat and Rural Development Department took up the programme as SSK and decided to set up the Shishu Shiksha Kendras, wherever there were at least twenty children not having access to any existing primary school or require some special dispensation, which are not available in the formal primary schools. The benefits of SSK in the three backward *vis-à-vis* other districts of West Bengal are shown in Table 3.23 to Table 3.26. Following are the important features:

First, numbers of teachers per school are deficient in Bankura and Purulia, on average there are two teachers per school, whereas other districts as well as whole of the West Bengal have witnessed more than 3 teachers per school (Table 3.23).

Second, in West Bengal about 1557 number of habitations have neither any primary nor Shishu Shiksha Kendras within 1 km. Relatively a greater number of these types of habitation are in the three backward districts (nearly 40%). In Purulia, there were 141 habitations with no primary schools. These numbers were quiet high in Paschim Medinipur (289) and Bankura (225) (Table 3.23).

Third, both the number of Shishu Shiksha Kendras and teachers decreased in 2012-13 in comparison to that in 2010-11 in the three backward districts (Table 3.24).

Fourth, Shishu Shiksha Kendras are deficient in respect of physical infrastructure. There were no drinking water facilities in 4 per cent of the total Shishu Shiksha Kendras in Purulia (Table 3.25).

Fifth, the expenditures for Shishu Shiksha Kendras consists with construction grant, additional class room (ACR) grant, teaching learning (TLE) material grant, library grant, school grant and teacher grant (Table 3.26). Expenditure for teachers (Sahayika and Sahayak) was less than that in other heads of expenditure.

3.6.3 Madhyamik Siksha Karmasuchi (MSK)

MSK is a permanent nature of upper primary educational centres established for ensuring universal access and enrolment of all the children between the age of 9 to 14 years of the catchment area of

Table 3.23: Number of Schools & Teachers under SSK and Number of Habitations having no Primary School & SSK within 1 km across Districts of West Bengal, 2010-11

District	*Number of School (2010-11)*	*Number of Teacher (2010-11)*	*No. of habitation primary having & SSK no within 1 km.**
	(SSK) Pry.	*(SSK) Pry.*	
Purulia	416	791	141
Bankura	449	892	225
Paschim Medinipur	2458	6468	289
Burdwan	1063	3044	98
Birbhum	650	1549	26
Dakshin Dinajpur	531	1462	35
Darjeeling	541	1145	0
Howrah	307	859	7
Hugli	277	797	30
Jalpaiguri	1089	3234	157
Kooch Behar	695	1848	86
Kolkata	0	0	0
Malda	618	2217	95
Murshidabad	1580	5707	61
Nadia	555	1492	0
North 24-Parganas	955	3083	60
Purba Medinipur	1445	4008	38
Siliguri	281	818	0
South 24-Parganas	1213	4022	152
Uttar Dinajpur	971	3212	57
Total	16094	46648	1557

Source: 1. Provisional DISE (2010-11) Data.
2. * Riddhi Management Services Data.

Madhyamik Siksha Kendra. The objective is to bring all children under Secondary Education as the Constitution makes free and compulsory elementary education for the age group 6-14 years a Fundamental Right. In respect of benefits of MSK in the three backward *vis-à-vis* other districts of West Bengal (as shown in Table 3.27 to Table 3.30) the important features are:

First, numbers of teachers per school do not differed across districts of West Bengal. On average each Madhyamik Siksha Kendra has five teachers in Bankura, Purulia and Paschim Medinipur as well as other districts of West Bengal (Table 3.27).

Second, most of Madhyamik Siksha Kendras of Bankura, Purulia and Paschim Medinipur are Government aided and all the schools of

Table 3.24: Class-wise Shishu Shiksha Kendras (SSKs) Enrolment across Districts of West Bengal, 2012-13

District Name	*No. of SSKs*	*Teachers*	*Class-I*	*Class-II*	*Class-III*	*Class-IV*	*Total Learners*	*Student Teacher Ratio*
Purulia	416	788	8730	4683	3964	3493	20870	26
Bankura	448	888	6989	4769	4287	4313	20358	23
Paschim Medinipur	2459	6403	45906	29992	27922	28394	132214	21
Purba Medinipur	1444	3988	35105	19862	18794	19244	93005	23
Burdwan	1063	3015	27618	18658	16932	17030	80238	27
Birbhum	650	1528	14036	10859	10116	9774	44785	29
Dakshin Dinajpur	531	1450	13410	7614	6920	7284	35228	24
Darjeeling	539	1120	6717	4189	3749	3310	17965	16
Howrah	306	839	8411	6001	4975	5008	24395	29
Hugli	276	786	6031	4020	3772	3987	17810	23
Jalpaiguri	1089	3211	31548	19823	17739	18152	87262	27
Kooch Behar	698	1880	18447	13225	11901	12267	55840	30
Malda	618	2208	27602	19731	18503	17936	83772	38
Murshidabad	1584	5671	63152	46761	42533	41956	194402	34
Nadia	555	1481	14108	9739	9047	9352	42246	29
North 24-Parganas	955	3078	28915	20948	19801	19854	89518	29
Siliguri	282	822	8184	5324	4922	4854	23284	28
South 24-Parganas	1213	3979	46886	27973	24901	23932	123692	31
Uttar Dinajpur	979	3293	44645	26252	22446	21879	115222	35
Total	16105	46428	456440	300423	273224	272019	1302106	28

Source: Paschim Banga Rajya Sishu Siksha Mission.

these districts have drinking water and toilet facilities, though separate girls' toilet is not available in 32 per cent Madhyamik Siksha Kendras in Purulia, 9 per cent in Bankura and 8 per cent in Paschim Medinipur (Table 3.28).

Third, the expenditure pattern of Madhyamik Siksha Kendras is same as for Shishu Siksha Kendras and it consists of construction grant, ACR grant, TLE material grant, library grant, school grant and teacher grant (Table 3.29). The Expenditure for *Samprasaraks* and *Samprasarikas* (teachers in MSK) was less than that under other heads of expenditure.

3.6.4 Mid-Day Meal (MDM)

MDM programme was introduced in India including West Bengal to reduce drop-out from school and provide a nutritional benefit to the school-

Table 3.25: Infrastructures of Shishu Shiksha Kendras across Districts of West Bengal as per DISE, 2012-13

District	No. of SSKs	Building Status							No. of school having				
		Private	Rented	Govern-ment	Rent Free Building	No Building	Dilapi-dated	Under Construction	Boys Toilet	Common Toilet	Girl Toilet	No water	Water
Purulia	416	0	2	354	9	22	0	29	169	155	109	18	398
Bankura	448	2	1	444	1	0	0	0	301	442	282	0	448
Paschim Medinipur	2459	348	21	2034	24	10	1	21	1300	1795	1022	0	2459
Brahman	1063	143	5	907	6	0	0	2	880	769	406	18	1045
Birbhum	650	0	3	607	9	4	0	27	637	403	92	0	650
Dakshin Dinajpur	531	7	0	523	1	0	0	0	500	402	529	0	531
Darjeeling	539	203	47	221	45	1	22	0	133	53	102	236	303
Howrah	306	51	11	221	23	0	0	0	99	176	258	4	302
Hooghly	276	2	5	266	3	0	0	0	77	220	273	1	275
Jalpaiguri	1089	2	3	1018	10	53	0	3	318	602	804	69	1020
Cooch Behar	698	61	2	634	1	0	0	0	380	621	363	0	698
Malda	618	12	7	573	14	0	0	12	229	330	437	5	613
Murshidabad	1584	2	10	1024	266	282	0	0	1060	807	355	2	1582
Nadia	555	94	17	420	15	0	7	2	524	464	270	0	555
North 24-Parganas	955	50	11	838	40	11	0	5	922	888	343	17	938
Purba Medinipur	1444	74	2	1232	72	0	1	63	1279	1144	650	70	1374
Siliguri	282	70	3	203	0	5	0	1	40	224	273	14	268
South 24-Parganas	1213	3	2	1194	7	0	0	7	564	753	543	126	1087
Uttar Dinajpur	979	7	7	918	19	0	0	28	821	332	223	7	972
Total	**16105**	**1131**	**159**	**13631**	**565**	**388**	**31**	**200**	**10233**	**10580**	**7334**	**587**	**15518**

Source: Paschim Banga Rajya Sishu Siksha Mission.

Table 3.26: Approved Outlays (Rs. in Lakh) under SSK in three Backward Districts of West Bengal, 2012-13

District/ State	Construction	ACR	TLE	Libraries in School	School Grant	Teacher Grants
Purulia	1111.5	1387.7	61.44	24.96	20.8	3.965
Paschim Medinipur	NA	278.2	376.44	73.74	122.9	32.21
Bankura	170.43	15.5	68.47	26.94	22.45	4.465
West Bengal	26248.78	31244.9	2386.94	788.07	805	233.265

Note: ACR = Additional Class Room, TLE = Teaching Learning.
Source: Minutes of the 178th PAB meeting held on 12th March, 2012 for approval of the Annual Work Plan & Budget of West Bengal.

Table 3.27: District-wise Class-wise Madhyamik Siksha Kendra Enrolment for the Year 2012-13

District	No. of MSK	No. of Samprasaraks/ Samprasarikas	Class-V	Class-VI	Class-VII	Class-VIII	Total Learners	Student-teacher ratio
Purulia	139	686	4531	4645	4521	4190	17887	26
Bankura	73	379	3017	3222	3081	2812	12132	32
Paschim Medinipur	232	1200	9380	9524	9334	8985	37223	31
Burdwan	99	514	5597	5643	4838	4326	20404	40
Birbhum	101	495	5595	5374	4704	3886	19559	40
Dakshin Dinajpur	41	196	1867	1924	1874	1727	7392	38
Darjeeling	67	340	1730	1866	1880	1948	7424	22
Howrah	27	131	1514	1724	1388	1242	5868	45
Hugli	27	143	1322	1305	1237	1180	5044	35
Jalpaiguri	112	544	6298	6222	6109	6500	25129	46
Cooch Behar	119	605	4454	4996	5234	5002	19686	33
Malda	108	509	6446	6437	6096	5658	24637	48
Murshidabad	202	1041	14749	12468	11098	10250	48565	47
Nadia	106	556	7012	6980	6460	6236	26688	48
North 24-Parganas	116	611	7044	6772	6405	6105	26326	43
Purba Medinipur	153	787	5479	5631	5549	5000	21659	28
Siliguri	10	50	1065	1057	1070	893	4085	82
South 24-Parganas	80	384	5424	5084	4453	3759	18720	49
Uttar Dinajpur	107	532	9743	8901	7984	7096	33724	63
Total	1919	9703	102267	99775	93315	86795	382152	39

Source: http://www.wbpublibnet.gov.in (2012-13).

Table 3.28: Infrastructure of Madhyamik Siksha Kendra as per DISE across Districts of West Bengal, 2012-13

District	Number of MSKs	Building Status						No. of school having					
		Private	Rented	Government	Rent Free Building	No Building	Dilapidated	Under Construction	Boys Toilet	Common Toilet	Girl Toilet	No water	Water
Purulia	139	0	0	138	0	0	0	1	72	39	95	1	138
Bankura	73	1	0	70	2	0	0	0	57	62	67	0	73
Paschim Medinipur	232	65	1	161	3	1	0	1	221	48	211	0	232
Burdwan	99	5	0	93	1	0	0	0	93	21	88	0	99
Birbhum	101	0	0	97	2	1	0	1	100	28	53	0	101
Dakshin Dinajpur	41	3	0	36	2	0	0	0	41	24	41	0	41
Darjeeling	67	26	2	31	7	0	1	0	27	6	23	38	29
Howrah	27	1	0	26	0	0	0	0	23	7	26	0	27
Hugli	27	0	0	27	0	0	0	0	21	8	26	0	27
Jalpaiguri	112	0	0	106	4	1	0	1	82	45	106	2	110
Kooch Bihar	119	13	1	105	0	0	0	0	105	38	92	1	118
Malda	108	8	0	99	1	0	0	0	80	30	92	0	108
Murshidabad	202	0	0	136	46	20	0	0	161	68	145	0	202
Nadia	106	19	0	82	4	0	0	1	97	32	104	0	106
North 24-Parganas	116	13	0	98	5	0	0	0	112	60	109	1	115
Purba Medinipur	153	4	0	130	7	0	1	11	130	75	141	5	148
Siliguri	10	3	0	7	0	0	0	0	10	3	10	0	10
South 24-Parganas	80	0	0	80	0	0	0	0	68	19	73	5	75
Uttar Dinajpur	107	1	2	103	1	0	0	0	100	23	82	0	107
Total	1919	162	6	1625	85	23	2	16	1600	636	1584	53	1863

Source: http://www.wbpublibnet.gov.in

Table 3.29: Approved Outlay (Rs. in Lakh) under MSK in three Backward Districts of West Bengal, 2012-13

	Purulia	*Paschim Medinipur*	*Bankura*	*West Bengal*
Construction	96.74	104.366	55.28	4441.107
ACR	251.315	76.96	37.82	5508.29
Free Text Book	35.02	74.45	23.765	713.355
TLE	50.32	87.78	27.74	702.96
Libraries in School	27.8	46.1	14.6	338.3
School Grant	9.73	16.17	5.11	134.4
Teacher Grants	3.175	6	1.81	48.575

Note: ACR = Additional Class Room, TLE = Teaching Learning.
Source: Minutes of the 178th PAB meeting held on 12th March, 2012 for approval of the Annual Work Plan & Budget of West Bengal.

going children. The coverage of MDM programme in primary and upper primary schools across districts of West Bengal are given in Table 3.30 and Table 3.31 respectively. Programme Approval Board (PAB) is the prime agency to sanction the budget of school educational programme. The enrolments of the students in 2012-13 in both primary as well as upper primary level have been significantly higher than the PAB approval in 2011-12. The number of children who availed MDM was also higher than the number of approved (by PAB) children. All enrolled students did not avail the MDM. In Purulia district about 12 per cent did not obtain the MDM at Primary Level and 17 per cent in Upper Primary Level. In Paschim Medinipur district nearly 2 per cent students did not obtain MDM. Bankura is exceptional, where the number of MDM availed is higher than that enrolled at Primary Level.

3.6.5 *Scholarships/Grants for SC/ST Students*

Hostel Charges

SC and ST students of secondary stages (from class V to X) residing in hostels are given grants at the rate of Rs. 300/- per month for 10 months in a year on account of hostel charges. In the case of SC students, the hostellers coming from families belonging to below the poverty line are considered eligible for the grant.[2] In case of ST, there is no such income limit for the student. 55,000 SC students and 49,500 ST students have been brought within the fold of this scheme. Each student residing in the

Table 3.30: Coverage of MDM in Primary Section across Districts of West Bengal, 2012-13

District/State	*Enrolment in Primary Level*	*No. of children as per PAB Approval for 2011-12*	*Average number of children availed MDM*	*Difference between availed MDM and PAB Approval*	*Difference between enrollment and Availed MDM*
Purulia	355425	281395	318703	37308	36722
Bankura	378649	303081	379186	76105	-537
Paschim Medinipur	662197	581983	649632	67649	12565
Birbhum	386809	335207	368788	33581	18021
Burdwan	712538	514036	549320	35284	163218
Cooch Behar	351590	279904	298853	18949	52737
Dakshin Dinajpur	160718	152471	160718	8247	0
Uttar Dinajpur	343280	343280	343280	0	0
Hooghly	357168	383459	342771	-40688	14397
Howrah	393183	287412	388384	100972	4799
Jalpaiguri	451474	479975	383884	-96091	67590
Kolkata	224835	153907	145390	-8517	79445
Malda	475363	429999	473676	43677	1687
Murshidabad	934067	568472	519103	-49369	414964
Purba Medinipur	555054	422193	471797	49604	83257
Nadia	544440	401934	456059	54125	88381
North 24-Parganas	545383	539399	545033	5634	350
South 24-Parganas	924441	643533	877074	233541	47367
Siliguri	90582	83283	86712	3429	3870
West Bengal	8915479	7250300	7826646	576346	1088833

Source: mdm.nic.in/PAB.htm.

Hostel gets hostel grant for 10 months at the rate of Rs. 750 per month. Thus, the total amount of grant for each student is Rs. 7,500 in a year.

Number of running hostels and SC/ST student beneficiaries in three backward districts *vis-à-vis* other districts of West Bengal are given in Table 3.32. These hostels are attached to the Junior High or Secondary Schools run and managed by the respective school authorities. This scheme provides opportunity to SC/ST students to grow up in an academic environment free from the hazards of undertaking long journeys for attending their schools. There were 1522 school attached hostels in all over the State. Number of hostels and SC/ST students benefited in the three backward districts Purulia, Bankura and Paschim Medinipur are appreciably high compared to that in other districts. 51 per cent of total running hostels of the state were sanctioned in these three districts where 46 per cent of total SC students and 73 per cent of total ST students were benefited.

Table 3.31: Coverage of MDM in Upper Primary Section across Districts of West Bengal, 2012-13

District/State	*Enrolment Upper Primary*	*No. of Children as per PAB Approval for 2011-12*	*Average number of Children Availed MDM*	*Difference between Availed MDM and PAB Approval*	*Difference between Enrollment and Availed MDM*
Purulia	159578	116294	132152	15858	27426
Bankura	188783	140266	188003	47737	780
Paschim Medinipur	318031	269782	313420	43638	4611
Birbhum	181248	107882	171228	63346	10020
Burdwan	345635	103962	305211	201249	40424
Cooch Behar	187768	143672	159603	15931	28165
Dakshin Dinajpur	133659	121431	133659	12228	0
Uttar Dinajpur	140266	119427	140266	20839	0
Hooghly	345430	193609	278858	85249	66572
Howrah	213873	116795	208873	92078	5000
Jalpaiguri	203601	172942	172847	-95	30754
Kolkata	137142	100000	81095	-18905	56047
Malda	155411	105415	146031	40616	9380
Murshidabad	408576	234202	159412	-74790	249164
Purba Medinipur	281794	248872	239524	-9348	42270
Nadia	299515	100805	239561	138756	59954
North 24-Parganas	507427	223058	455735	232677	51692
South 24-Parganas	396614	198382	249276	50894	147338
Siliguri	69771	30826	39552	8726	30219
West Bengal	4705476	2890000	3845660	955660	859816

Source: mdm.nic.in/PAB.htm

Up-gradation of Merit for SC/ST Students for Classes IX to XII

This scheme has been introduced with a view to remove the deficiencies in school subjects and specially for preparing SC/ST students for competitive examinations required for entry into professional courses like Engineering and Medicine. The emphasis on remedial coaching thus removes the deficiencies in learning from which these students suffer and to promote study habits. The quota and SC/ST students benefited in Purulia, Bankura and Paschim Medinipur as well as in the whole of West Bengal are given in Table 3.33. A package grant of Rs. 15,000 per SC student and Rs. 19,500 per ST student are given for the beneficiaries (details in Table 2.30 in Chapter 2).

Table 3.32: Quota for School Attached Hostel at Pre-Matric Stage across Districs of West Bengal (as on 01-04-2013)

District	*Number of Running Hostel*	*No. of borders as per Quota for Hostel*	
		S.C.	*S.T.*
Purulia	188	4400	8400
Bankura	206	9020	13060
Paschim Medinipur	386	11870	14740
Howrah	8	380	20
S.24-Parganas	154	8250	660
N.24-Parganas	17	1100	290
Nadia	11	440	240
Murshidabad	19	770	1180
Burdwan	54	2420	2100
Hooghly	29	1020	600
Birbhum	68	1850	1560
Purba Medinipur	247	9080	550
Dakshin Dinajpur	50	1540	1720
Uttar Dinajpur	28	1100	790
Malda	23	650	730
Cooch Behar	11	380	70
Siliguri	03	40	360
Jalpaiguri	20	440	2040
Kolkata	–	60	10
Darjeeling (GTA)	–	190	380
Total	1522*	55,000	49,500

Note: *Except Kolkata and DGHC.
Source: www.anagrasarkalyan.gov.in/pdf/edu-schms.pdf

Table 3.33: Number of Quotas and Students Benefited for Up-gradation of Merit in three Backward Districts of West Bengal (as on 01.04.2012)

Students Category	*Purulia*		*Bankura*		*Paschim Medinipur*		*West Bengal*	
	Quota	*Bene-fited*	*Quota*	*Bene-fited*	*Quota*	*Bene-fited*	*Quota*	*Bene-fited*
SC	40	28	68	47	64	44	368	254
ST	16	8	12	6	28	15	72	38

Source: www.anagrasarkalyan.gov.in/pdf/edu-schms.pdf

3.7 Social Protection Benefits for Housing under IAY

The performance of IAY in the three backward districts is given in Table 3.34. The annual target of new house construction under IAY increased in Bankura and Purulia in 2013-14 over 2012-13. But the fact is reverse in case of Paschim Medinipur. West Bengal sanctioned 48.11 per cent of new construction of its Annual Target under IAY during 2012-13.

Table 3.34: Target and Sanction of IAY in three Backward Districts of West Bengal, 2012-13 and 2013-14

District/ State	2012-13			2013-14		
	Annual Target	House Sanctioned for New Construction	Percentage	Annual Target	House Sanctioned for New Construction	Percentage
Purulia	4785	109	2.3	10250	8408	82.0
Bankura	9823	2674	27.2	13193	12748	96.6
Paschim Medinipur	24637	3	0.0	19113	15437	80.8
West Bengal	219553	105631	48.1	224443	172273	76.8

Sources: http://iay.nic.in/netiay/Alloteetype_wise.aspx?lflag=eng&page1=d&state_name=West+Bengal&state_cod

The percentage share of sanctioned house for new construction out of annual target during 2012-13 was low in the three backward districts. Only 2.3 per cent target was achieved in Purulia and 27.2 per cent in Bankura. In case of Paschim Medinipur only 3 houses were sanctioned for construction out of 24,637. But the percentage covered as per target increased in 2013-14 compared to 2012-13. Among the three districts, Bankura had the first position securing 96.6 per cent of its target. Paschim Medinipur and Purulia are also above the state average (76.8%) with achievement to the tune of 80.7 per cent and 82 per cent of its target.

3.8 Employment and Income Benefits

3.8.1 Benefits under MGNREGS

Table 3.35 describes the employment opportunity created through MGNREGS in the three backward districts of West Bengal. Per household person days per year was 31 in Bankura followed by Purulia (29 days) and Paschim Medinipur (25 days) in 2011-12. It has increased after 2011-12 in all the three districts. But very few households obtained 100 days employment. During 2013-14, in the backward region MGNREGS has provided on an average 37-person days of employment per household

Table 3.35: Performance of MGNREGS in three Backward Districts of West Bengal, 2011-12 to 2013-14

District/ State	2011-12				2012-13				2013-14			
	DW	*W*	*PD*	*% 100W*	*D*	*W*	*PD*	*% 100W*	*DW*	*W*	*PD*	*% 100W*
Purulia	191159	190854	29	3.5	228364	233882	40	7.2	257997	243437	42	8
Bankura	327474	326841	31	3.9	354950	354231	39	7	372561	349959	36	4.3
Paschim Medinipur	522731	521596	25	1.2	553205	548981	30	2.3	611776	588768	36	3.4
West Bengal	5532363	5516968	27	2.2	5844592	5817331	35	4.4	6441376	6127324	37	4.6

Note: DW = Total households worked demanded, W = Total households worked, PD = Per HHs Person Days, % 100 W = Percentage of HHs reached 100 days limit.

Source: www.MGNREGA.nic.in

and only 5 per cent households obtained 100 days employment (8% in Purulia, 4.3% in Bankura and 3.4% in Paschim Medinipur districts). The unemployment, specifically seasonal unemployment is the serious problem in these three backward districts and it is expected that MGNREGS play an important role by creating sufficient mandays. But the performance of MGNREGS is not satisfactory which creates hopelessness of rural aspirants for employment.

3.8.2 Benefits under SGSY

Under SGSY the Self-Help Groups (SHGs) programme promotes the formation of organization of the poor at the grassroots level through a process of social mobilization for poverty reduction. Women are the main thrust under this programme. Table 3.36 shows the performance of SHGs across districts of West Bengal. Number of groups were relatively low in Purulia and Paschim Medinipur and not even one group has started economic activities up to 2009.

3.9 Social Security

3.9.1 Indira Gandhi National Old Age Pension Scheme (IGNOAPS)

The assistance of old age pension in the three backward districts namely Purulia, Bankura and Paschim Medinipur during 2004-05 to 2011-12 is shown in Table 3.37. The number of old age pensioners gradually increased during 2004-05 to 2011-12. The trend growth rate of the number of pensioners during this period was relatively high—20 per cent per annum in Bankura and 18 per cent per annum in Purulia and in Paschim Medinipur. The amount of pensions also increased during the period. The average pension (per capita per month) during 2004-05 to 2011-12 increased from Rs. 160 to Rs. 489 in Purulia, from Rs. 94 to Rs. 394 in Bankura and from Rs. 189 to Rs. 396 in Paschim Medinipur.

3.9.2 Indira Gandhi National Widow Pension Scheme (IGNWPS)

The assistance of widow pension in three backward districts Purulia, Bankura and Paschim Medinipur during 2004-05 to 2011-12 is shown in Table 3.38. The number of widow pensioners also gradually increased during 2004-05 to 2011-12. The trend growth rate was very high in all the three districts—60 per cent per annum in Purulia and 46 per cent per

Table 3.36: Performance of Self-Help Groups across Districts of West Bengal as on 31.03.2009 (Rs. in lakh)

Districts	Total SHG Formed	Total Member	Female Member	Total Deposit	Total Loan Disbursed	SHGs Obtained Credit Facility	Recovery (%)	SHGs Started Economic Activities
Purulia	2945	30768	29232	142.09	179.79	693	87	Nr
Bankura	12655	113459	109848	959.38	3379.18	9484	91	9434
Paschim Medinipur	4825	43644	33798	392.48	363.62	2982	83.16	Nr
Birbhum	1836	16150	13259	252.46	352	1101	96	
Burdwan-I	7770	56708	43168	398.86	186.35	4023	89	4651
Burdwan-II	7068	56110	43020	442.36	867.1	3958	92	3405
Burdwan-III	364	2646	1830	24.4	26.71	284	85	Nr
Cooch Behar	6992	62509	57000	357.08	489.81	6434	97	Nr
Dk Dinajpur	2584	23502	22542	242.36	671.55	1669	74	Nr
Darjeeling	618	5605	5006	56.97	45.08	328	78	Nr
Hooghly	29855	196262	195012	1875.74	7760.45	27215	99	Nr
Howrah	5364	29145	26321	437.34	861.52	2409	98.28	Nr
Jalpaiguri	2378	23374	22719	219.54	353.79	2124	33.69	Nr
Malda	12341	115487	101883	916.49	2130.17	9775	98.13	Nr
Murshidabad	12095	100301	90887	1529.93	4540.22	9388	92	Nr
North 24-Pgs	2302	22540	8702	185.97	97.04	852	40	Nr
Nadia	14156	127943	115384	1067.53	767.29	7703	97.28	Nr
Purba Medinipur-I	5670	44540	38621	420.65	864.92	3396	95.55	3396
Purba Medinipur-II	12549	98846	91724	954.03	582.78	6767	91	6767
South 24-Pgs	5123	40849	38558	278.99	723.66	4618	97.72	Nr
Uttar Dinajpur	8846	70126	63654	509.86	1354.18	6851	63	Nr
Total	158336	1280514	1152168	11664.5	26597.2	112054		27703

Source: http://rural.nic.in.

Table 3.37: Assistance to Old Age Persons (NOAPS) in three Backward Districts of West Bengal, 2004 to 2012

Year	Purulia		Bankura		Paschim Medinipur	
	Recipients	Amount (in '000 rupees)	Recipients	Amount (in '000 rupees)	Recipients	Amount (in '000 rupees)
2004-05	21239	40743	14037	15819	31852	72217
2005-06	53344	114694	43395	56637	36808	104766
2006-07	43745	128603	43872	204683	36199	198856
2007-08	49376	120954	71524	259108	41494	228087
2008-09	61014	255071	67852	285094	88445	347344
2009-10	83361	315684	68650	321290	118097	446243
2010-11	88444	411261	70533	255147	145945	631987
2011-12	92798	544952	98317	464385	162427	772356

Source: Govt. of West Bengal, District Statistical Hand Book Various round.

annum in Bankura and 48 per cent per annum in Paschim Medinipur. But the amount of pensions did not increase during the period. The average pensions (per capita per month) during 2004-05 to 2011-12 decreased from Rs. 525 to Rs. 436 in Purulia and from Rs. 709 to Rs. 691 in Paschim Medinipur, whereas, in Bankura it increased from Rs. 377 to Rs. 650.

Table 3.38: Assistance to Widow Persons (IGNWPS) in three Backward Districts of West Bengal, 2004 to 2012

Year	Purulia		Bankura		Paschim Medinipur	
	Recipients	Amount (in '000 rupees)	Recipients	Amount (in '000 rupees)	Recipients	Amount (in '000 rupees)
2004-05	523	3295	873	3948	1478	12579
2005-06	523	3295	808	3087	1135	9149
2006-07	1142	7021	577	3629	740	4664
2007-08	828	5216	872	5482	1106	6972
2008-09	1269	8566	1228	7930	1709	11666
2009-10	6030	23057	2261	18324	17839	81958
2010-11	8530	42728	12789	60901	43792	155027
2011-12	10557	55254	15239	118784	36507	302613

Source: District Statistical Hand Book, Govt. of West Bengal, Various issues.

3.9.3 Indira Gandhi National Disability Pension Scheme (IGNDPS)

The assistance of disability pension in three backward districts Purulia, Bankura and Paschim Medinipur during 2004-05 to 2011-12 is shown in

Table 3.39. The number of pensioners significantly increased during 2004-05 to 2011-12. In Purulia it increased from 1653 to 16287, in Bankura from 314 to 2407 and in Paschim Medinipur from 383 to 3625. The amount of pension also increased during the period. The average pension (per capita per month) during 2004-05 to 2011-12 increased from Rs. 525 to Rs. 672 in Purulia, Rs. 525 to Rs. 565 in Paschim Medinipur and Rs. 525 to Rs. 679 in Bankura.

Table 3.39: Assistance to Disability Persons (IGNDPS) in three Backward Districts of West Bengal, 2004-05 to 2011-12

Year	Purulia		Bankura		Paschim Medinipur	
	Recipients	Amount (in '000 rupees)	Recipients	Amount (in '000 rupees)	Recipients	Amount (in '000 rupees)
2004-05	262	1653	314	1978	383	2413
2005-06	262	1653	314	1978	383	2413
2006-07	307	1935	373	2324	459	2896
2007-08	445	2804	555	3497	685	4319
2008-09	969	6541	1152	7417	1549	10572
2009-10	1322	14981	1431	13463	2440	20271
2010-11	1436	15364	1877	15406	3553	30947
2011-12	2019	16287	2407	19519	3625	24593

Source: Govt. of West Bengal, District Statistical Hand Book Various round.

3.9.4 Bi-Cycle for Tribal Girls

The State Government is implementing a scheme of distribution of bi-cycles to the tribal girl students from Class IX to XII in the Left Wing Extremists affected (LWE) blocks in the districts of Paschim Medinipur, Bankura and Purulia. The scheme is aimed at reducing drop-out in the schools and to encourage the girl students to continue study. Besides, these bi-cycles help their families for multipurpose household activities. Though objective evaluation of the scheme is yet to be done, however, prima facie it appears that the scheme has a good impact on the girl students. There is huge demand from tribal areas and also from SC dominated backward areas. Under this Scheme 9418 bi-cycles have been distributed in 2010-11. In 2011-12, 39839 bicycles had been given. In 2013-14, funds for 34265 bicycles have been provided to girls students of class IX to XII in Jangal Mahal area (Table 3.40). This scheme is renamed as *Sabooj Sathi* since September 2015 and is for all the Students of class IX to XII studying in Government run and Government Aided Schools and Madrasas of the State.

Table 3.40: Bicycles provided in three Backward Districts of West Bengal, 2011-12

District	*SC*	*ST*	*OBC*	*GEN*	*Total*
Bankura	2046	1628	2664	3680	10018
Purulia	1077	1224	5166	4227	11694
Paschim Medinipur	3267	4895	3785	6180	18127
Grand Total	6390	7747	11615	14087	39839

Source: http://www.anagrasarkalyan.gov.in/htm/bi-cycle-schm.html.

Notes

1. Level of urbanization is measured by percentage of urban population to total population.
2. There is a ceiling of Parents/Guardians income of Rs. 36,000/- p.a.

4
Social Protection Benefits for Poor Households in the Backward Region

We have discussed social protection benefits at the aggregate levels of state and district based on secondary data from different sources. To what extent the households (specifically poor households) are benefited from social protection programmes is yet to be analyzed. The major problem of this analysis is that the benefits of households from different social protection programmes are not available from secondary sources. Therefore, for the sake of an analysis of social protection benefits at the household level, specifically for the poor households, there is a need for an evaluation of social protection benefits of the poor on the basis of grass root reality. This is what is done in this chapter based on primary data collected from 24 sample villages and 600 households of 12 sample blocks in the three backward districts of West Bengal.

The section that follows presents the brief profile of the sample blocks and villages based on data from Census of India. Section 4.2 discusses the features of sample households. Section 4.3 analyses social protection benefits enjoyed by the sample households. Estimated excess demand for social protection programmes is discussed in Section 4.4. Section 4.5 summarizes the main findings.

4.1 Profile of Sample Blocks and Villages in the Backward Region

Twenty-four sample villages from 12 sample blocks of the backward region in West Bengal vary in respect of socio-economic development. A number of socio-economic indicators based on Census 2011 present a brief profile of sample blocks and villages.

4.1.1 Demographic Features of Sample Blocks

Population including SC and ST, literacy rate, working status of people and distribution of workers of 12 sample blocks in 2011 are presented in the Table 4.1. Among 12 sample blocks the literacy rate was high in Datan-II (70%), Keshiary (68.0%) and Sankrail (65.0%) blocks of Paschim Medinipur districts. Joypur and Jhalda-II were two blocks of Purulia district where literacy rate was relatively low—48.1 per cent and 45.4 per cent respectively. This implies that the blocks are deficient in respect of education of the people.

Table 4.1: Demographic Features of Sample Blocks in three Backward Districts of West Bengal, 2011

Block	PP ('000)	SC (%)	ST (%)	LTR (%)	WPR (%)	Distribution of Population (=100%)			Distribution of Workers (=100%)			
						MW	MRW	NW	CL	AL	HHI	OW
Paschim Medinipur												
Keshiary	149.3	23.0	34.3	68.0	45.1	22.0	23.1	54.9	20.4	63.8	2.8	13.0
Dantan–II	155.0	8.9	7.0	72.9	36.1	23.7	12.4	63.9	30.1	46.3	2.4	21.2
Jamboni#	113.2	18.1	28.6	63.9	45.2	16.5	28.7	54.8	12.7	58.2	4.2	24.9
Sankrail#	115.4	18.2	25.0	65.0	45.4	26.4	19.0	54.6	30.7	56.6	2.2	10.5
Bankura												
Vishnupur	156.8	35.7	7.5	58.2	42.8	27.9	14.9	57.2	21.2	44.6	5.8	28.4
Taldangra	147.9	26.3	13.9	62.3	42.2	23.0	19.2	57.8	21.9	56.5	3.6	18.0
Khatra	104.6	26.5	24.0	62.0	39.5	20.7	18.8	60.5	18.2	58.2	1.8	21.8
Ranibundh#	119.1	11.5	47.1	60.5	48.3	23.0	25.2	51.7	22.8	58.5	5.2	13.6
Purulia												
Jaipur#	123.1	13.4	10.3	48.1	39.5	18.8	20.7	60.5	30.9	31.9	12.9	24.3
Kashipur	174.3	29.5	27.9	60.8	43.2	17.9	25.3	56.8	19.9	47.8	3.1	29.1
Hura	143.6	19.5	25.5	59.9	48.5	22.2	26.3	51.5	25.1	50.3	2.5	22.1
Jhalda–II#	135.8	9.1	13.8	45.4	45.5	28.7	16.8	54.5	16.9	16.0	47.8	19.3

Note: # marked blocks are Jangal Mahal blocks.
Source: Primary Census Abstract, Census of India 2011, Govt. of India.

The share of Scheduled Caste (SC) population was highest in Vishnupur (35.7%) in Bankura district, followed by Kashipur (29.5%) in Purulia district and Khatra (26.5%) in Bankura district. The share of

Scheduled Tribe (ST) population was highest in Ranibundh (47.1%), followed by Keshiary (34.3%), Jamboni (28.6%) and Kashipur (27.9 %).

Sample blocks also vary in terms of worker-population ratio (WPR). WPR was relatively high in two backward blocks, namely Hura (48.5%) in Purulia district and Ranibundh (48.3%) in Bankura district. WPR was relatively low in Dantan-II (36.1) and Jaipur (39.5). That is, most backward blocks have witnessed high WPR. Regarding working status of population there were six blocks with relatively higher share of the marginal workers as compared with main workers. These blocks are Keshiary and Jamboni in Paschim Medinipur district; Ranibundh in Bankura district; and Jaipur, Kashipur and Hura in Purulia district. That is, in these blocks major percentages of workers were not getting employment even 180 days in a year.

The nature of distribution of workers in these blocks also indicates their backwardness. In most of the blocks the share of agricultural workers to total workers is substantially high. The percentage share of cultivators was highest in Jaipur (30.9%), followed by Sankrail (30.7%) and Dantan-II (30.1%). This share was relatively low in Jamboni (12.7%) and Jhalda-II (16.9%). About 64 per cent of rural workers were agricultural labourers in Keshiary, followed by Ranibundh (58.5%). The share of agricultural labourers was relatively high in most of the blocks. The share of rural household industry workers was highest in Jhalda-II (47.8%) of Purulia districts followed by Jaipur (12.9) and lowest in Khatra (1.8%). Percentage share of 'other workers' was highest in Kashipur (29.1%), followed by Vishnupur (28.4%). This share was lowest in Sankrail (10.5%) led by Keshiary (13.0%) and Ranibundh (13.6%).

4.1.2 Demographic Features of Sample Villages

The size of the village in terms of population widely varies across villages (Table 4.2).

In Chekya village of Purulia district the number of persons were more than five thousand. Number of persons was also high in Panchmura (3719), Dakshin Arbana (3445) and Khairipihira (3161). The number of persons was relatively low in the tribal village Shampur (317). There were seven villages among 24, *viz.* Mitha-Am, Kulupukur, Phulbani, Murakata, Jarasol, Shampur and Chandania where the number of persons was less than one thousand. Number of households across the villages also vary a good deal ranging from 1166 in Chekya to 68 in Shampur.

Table 4.2: Demographic Features of Sample Villages in three Backward Districts of West Bengal, 2011

Village	*No. of HH*	*PP*	*SC %*	*ST %*	*LTR %*	*WPR %*	*Percentage in Total Population (=100)*			*Percentage in Total Worker (=100)*			
							MW	*MRW*	*NW*	*CL*	*AL*	*HHI*	*OW*
Paschim Medinipur													
Murakati#	136	577	10.7	8.3	30.7	58.6	2.9	55.6	41.4	4.1	74.9	9.2	11.8
Belia#	504	2268	25.2	10.6	34.0	36.5	20.6	15.9	63.5	14.7	21.6	10.9	52.8
Jarasol#	82	351	0.0	0.0	14.5	68.1	25.4	42.7	31.9	74.5	22.2	0.0	3.3
Phulbani#	155	750	0.7	71.5	34.4	53.1	51.9	1.2	46.9	2.8	92.0	3.5	1.8
Lenga Mara	587	2612	12.9	40.3	48.1	51.1	26.1	25.0	48.9	19.7	63.2	5.1	12.0
Murakata	231	1068	18.4	37.6	25.7	42.1	27.4	14.7	57.9	25.3	70.9	0.0	3.8
Kotpada	254	1100	42.8	24.3	32.7	33.3	21.1	12.2	66.7	16.1	73.2	0.0	10.7
Dakshin Arbana	725	3445	8.1	11.4	29.5	34.3	9.9	24.4	65.7	17.3	53.1	1.8	27.7
Bankura													
Bantilla	281	1194	20.0	8.4	37.0	48.3	16.7	31.7	51.7	21.8	62.9	2.1	13.2
Chandania	76	316	66.8	0.0	60.1	45.6	24.4	21.2	54.4	3.5	88.2	0.7	7.6
Panchmura	797	3719	35.0	0.6	32.1	35.7	30.0	5.7	64.3	5.2	29.6	12.5	52.7
Saldaha	247	1149	16.9	22.1	35.2	39.9	22.6	17.2	60.1	27.1	59.6	0.4	12.9
Mitha-Am#	226	986	9.8	83.4	43.0	45.2	15.1	30.1	54.8	14.8	79.6	0.0	5.6
Nachna#	240	1086	24.0	54.5	35.7	44.7	3.4	41.3	55.3	35.1	17.1	31.5	16.3
Baramara	443	2061	18.9	24.3	44.3	42.5	34.6	7.8	57.5	12.9	59.7	0.8	26.6
Kulupukur	175	878	0.0	15.1	29.6	33.0	18.6	14.5	67.0	36.9	26.2	14.1	22.8

(*Contd.*)

Table 4.2: *(Contd.)*

Village	No. of HH	PP	SC %	ST %	LTR %	WPR %	Percentage in Total Population (=100)			Percentage in Total Worker (=100)			
							MW	MRW	NW	CL	AL	HHI	OW
Purulia													
Mukundpur#	417	2076	27.4	1.6	60.0	33.5	1.9	31.6	66.5	5.6	62.1	3.3	29.0
Nutandi#	340	1886	69.0	0.5	65.3	41.1	15.2	25.9	58.9	6.2	36.1	38.3	19.5
Rudra	221	1085	19.4	0.6	39.8	27.5	20.8	6.6	72.5	39.3	15.1	2.0	43.6
Shampur	68	317	0.0	98.4	47.0	52.1	3.5	48.6	47.9	5.5	61.8	1.2	31.5
Chekya (CT) #	1166	5995	5.2	2.2	53.5	53.5	38.5	15.0	46.5	2.1	1.7	80.6	15.6
Dimu#	506	2471	1.3	24.0	63.8	44.0	29.4	14.6	56.0	12.7	16.5	33.0	37.8
Dholkata	247	1289	1.8	25.4	54.4	43.2	27.3	15.9	56.8	21.9	60.5	0.9	16.7
Khairipihira	629	3161	34.7	19.6	45.8	55.1	28.7	26.4	44.9	30.0	36.5	0.9	32.7
Total	8753	41840	19.5	17.7	43.9	43.7	24.1	19.6	56.3	15.4	39.2	21.4	24.1

Note: # marked villages are Jangal Mahal villages

Source: Primary Census Abstract, Census of India 2011, Govt. of India.

Shampur, Mitha-Am, Phulbani and Nachna are the villages where above fifty per cent of the inhabitants belonged to Scheduled Tribes (STs) whereas two villages, namely Jarasol in Paschim Medinipur, and Bankura and Chandania in Bankura had no ST population. The percentage share of Scheduled Caste (SC) was highest in Nutandi (69.0%) in Purulia district, followed by Chandania (66.0%) in Bankura district, Kotpada (42.8%) in Paschim Medinipur district. There was no SC population in Shampur, Kulupukur, and Jarasol. Literacy rate was relatively high in two sample villages of Purulia district, namely Nutandi (65.3%), and Dimu (63.8%). The literacy rate was relatively low in Jarasol (only 14.5%) of Paschim Medinipur district.

4.1.3 Employment Pattern of Sample Villages

As per Census of India 2011, the male WPR in the sample villages were about 55 per cent of male population. The percentage share of male workers to total male population varied from 47.9 per cent in Chandania to 69.5 per cent in Jarasol.

For the females, WPR varied largely. Female WPR was highest in Jarasol (66.7 %), followed by Murakati (58.2%), Chekya (55.8%) and Khairipihira (55.5%). The female WPR was high in sample villages in Purulia, the relatively backward district.

Among the eight sample villages in Purulia district, Dholkata, Mukundpur and Rudra registered high share of male and female agricultural workers. In Shampur all of the female workers were agricultural workers but in Rudra most of the workers were non-farm workers. The percentage share of workers was relatively low in Rudra, Mukundpur and Nutandi for male workers.

In Bankura, among the eight sample villages, percentage share of male agricultural workers was highest in Mitha-Am (92.7%) followed by Chandania (86.1%). For the females this share was significantly high in Chandania, where about 99 per cent of the female workers was engaged in agriculture. The share of household industry workers was relatively high in Kulupukur for males (12.3%) and in Nachna for females (81.4%). In Panchmura the 'Teracota' is a traditional craft household industry of repute and all the 'Kumbhakar' households by heredity are engaged in this activity. The share of male 'other workers' to total workers was 58.7 per cent in Panchmura and 31.7 per cent in Baramara.

In Paschim Medinipur district, 96.6 per cent of the rural male workers and 94.9 per cent of the rural female workers were engaged as 'agricultural worker' in Murakata. The percentage share of 'other workers' was also relatively high in Belia (for both males and females). The share of household industry workers was relatively high in Belia and this share was 6.7 per cent for males and 23.8 per cent for females (Table 4.3).

Table 4.3: Workers by Sector and Sex in Sample Villages, 2011

Name	*Male Workers*	*% of Male Workers (100)*			*Female Workers*	*% of Female Workers (100)*		
		AW	*HHI*	*OT*		*AW*	*HH I*	*OT*
Paschim Medinipur								
Murakati	175	80.6	3.4	16.0	163	77.3	15.3	7.4
Belia	626	31.0	6.7	62.3	202	53.0	23.8	23.3
Jarasol	123	95.1	0.0	4.9	116	98.3	0.0	1.7
Phulbani	225	94.7	2.7	2.7	173	94.8	4.6	0.6
Lenga Mara	828	80.3	3.0	16.7	508	87.2	8.5	4.3
Murakata	352	96.6	0.0	3.4	98	94.9	0.0	5.1
Kotpada	294	91.2	0.0	8.8	72	81.9	0.0	18.1
Dakshin Arbana	077	73.8	1.3	24.9	205	54.6	3.9	41.5
Bankura								
Bantilla	347	77.2	3.5	19.3	230	96.1	0.0	3.9
Chandania	79	86.1	1.3	12.7	65	98.5	0.0	1.5
Panchmura	1076	32.8	8.5	58.7	251	43.4	29.9	26.7
Saldaha	332	84.0	0.3	15.7	126	93.7	0.8	5.6
Mitha-Am	286	92.7	0.0	7.3	160	97.5	0.0	2.5
Nachna	324	71.6	6.8	21.6	161	13.0	81.4	5.6
Baramara	609	67.2	1.1	31.7	266	85.0	0.0	15.0
Kulupukur	228	65.8	12.3	21.9	62	53.2	21.0	25.8
Purulia								
Mukundpur	503	69.6	2.0	28.4	193	62.7	6.7	30.6
Nutandi	482	49.0	21.6	29.5	294	31.3	65.6	3.1
Rudra	282	54.3	1.8	44.0	16	56.3	6.3	37.5
Shampur	86	37.2	2.3	60.5	79	100.0	0.0	0.0
Chekya (CT)	1579	6.0	69.3	24.6	1631	1.5	91.5	6.9
Dimu	637	36.4	22.4	41.1	450	18.9	48.0	33.1
Dholkata	365	80.3	1.1	18.6	192	86.5	0.5	13.0
Khairipihira	885	52.3	0.3	47.3	857	81.1	1.4	17.5
Total	11700	55.9	13.8	30.3	6570	52.3	34.7	13.0

Source: Primary Census Abstract, Census of India 2011, Govt. of India.

4.2 Profile of Sample Households in the Backward Region

The characteristics of the sample households that have been observed in the information of the field survey are explained as follows:

First, the majority of the sample households were Hindu (90%) and only ten per cent were Muslim. Among 600 sample households, 118 households belong to General (GEN) caste, 122 to Other Backward Caste (OBC), 192 to Schedule Castes (SC) and remaining 168 to Scheduled Tribes (ST) category. The distribution of sample households across castes is shown in Figure 4.1.

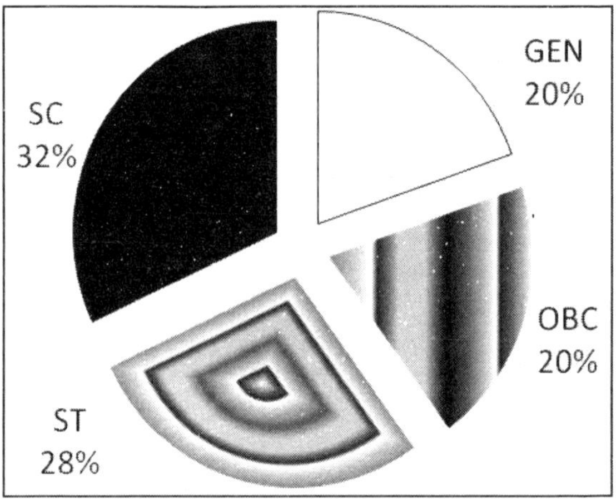

Fig. 4.1: Distribution of Sample Households by Castes.
Source: Field survey 2012-13.

Second, the numbers of household members vary from one to thirteen, though there are 51 per cent households having members four to five. The number of members is higher than seven in only nine per cent households. The average number of members of 600 sample households is 5. The distribution of sample households by number of members is presented in Figure 4.2.

Third, education level of the members of sample households was relatively low. All members of 7.2 per cent households were illiterate. The average years of education was seven or more for only 12 per cent households. There are 58.5 per cent households having average years of education (average years of schoolings of all members) less than 4 years. The share of households with average years of education six years or less was 81 per cent (Figure 4.3).

Fourth, the housing condition of the poor households is assessed by the nature of wall and roof and number of rooms (Table 4.7). As many as 85.7 per cent houses had mud wall. The bricks (pukka) walls have been

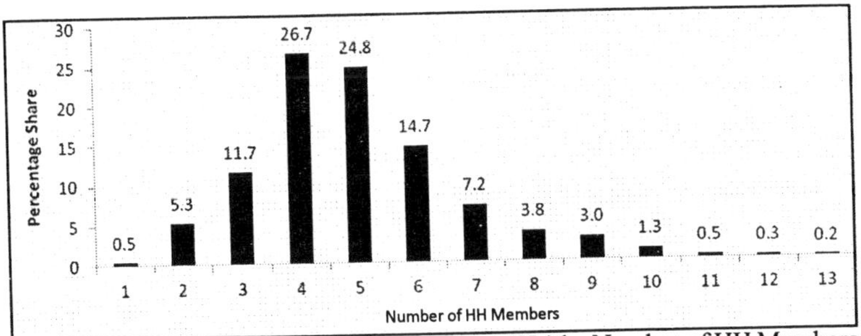

Fig. 4.2: Distribution of Sample Households (HHs) by Number of HH Members

Source: Field survey 2012-13.

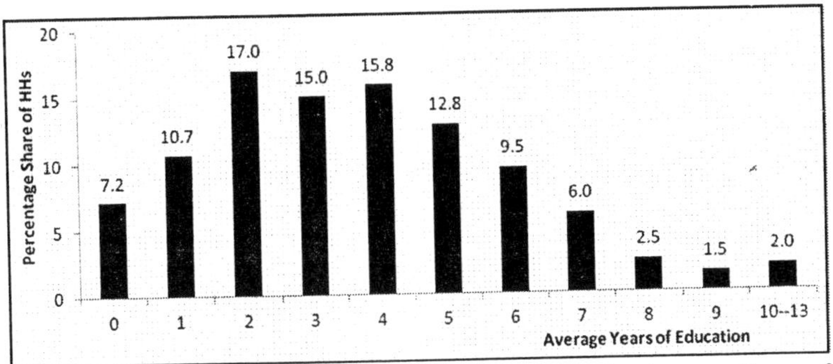

Fig. 4.3: Distribution of Sample Households (HHs) by Average Years of Education

Source: Field survey 2012-13.

found in only 6.2 per cent households. The roofs of 30.5 per cent houses were made of grass or straw, 26 per cent of Tiles and 25.2 per cent of asbestos. There were only 2.2 per cent households having concrete roof. Majority of the houses (75.5%) were small having one to two rooms. Most of the houses (94.3%) were one-floored. The households who enjoyed the benefit of Indira Awas Yojana (IYA) had better housing condition. But many more were eligible to obtain the benefit of IYA.

Fifth, in case of sanitation facility most of the households are still deprived. Only 22 per cent households had latrine (either open or close pit) facilities. Electricity did not reach every household even in 2013. There were 68.8 per cent houses electrified and in case of the rest of the houses either house-owner were not able to access the electricity or there was no facility of electricity.

Sixth, among 600 sample households, 82.2 per cent have bi-cycle, 61

Table 4.4: Housing Conditions of Sample Households

Room		*House Wall*		*HH Roof*	
Number of Rooms	*Percentage of HHs*	*Nature of House Wall*	*Percentage of HHs*	*Nature of Roof Top*	*Percentage of HHs*
1	28.7	Bamboo	4.2	Grass or Straw	30.5
2	46.8	Polyethene Sheet	1.0	Polyethene Sheet	1.3
3	17.0	Mud	85.7	Tails	26.0
4	6.7	Raw Bricks	3.0	Asbestos	25.2
5	0.8	Pukka Bricks	6.2	Tin	14.8
				Concrete	2.2

Source: Field survey 2012-13.

per cent had mobile, 9.3 per cent had TV and even 2.7 per cent had motor bike. But the other productive assets were hardly found. The pump set for irrigation has been found in only 2.2 per cent households and spray machine (used for spraying chemical pesticide in agriculture) in 0.8 per cent household. The rikshaw and cow cart were also used as the means of transport but only a few households had these assets (Fig. 4.4).

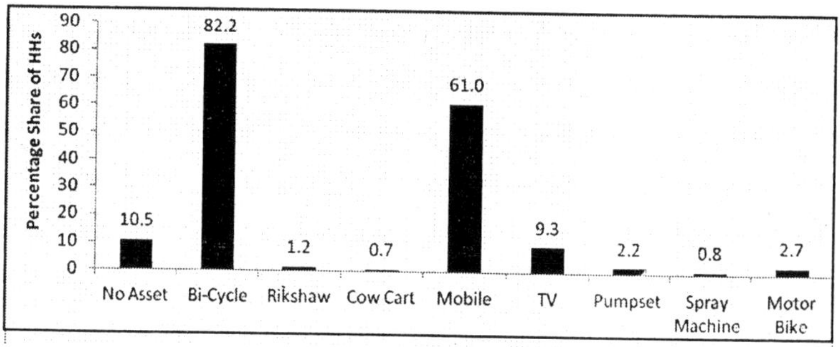

Fig. 4.4: Assets owned by the Sample Households

Source: Field survey 2012-13.

Seventh, in the field survey we have found that 34 per cent of sample households had taken loan. They had borrowed from formal as well as informal sources (Table 4.6). The amount of credit was relatively low (Table 4.5).

But the rates of interest widely vary from one source to another. It was relatively low in the formal sources like bank and self-help groups (SHG). It was least in case of bank loan with Kisan Credit Card (KCC). But only 5 per cent of the sample households had KCC and they were

Table 4.5: Distribution of the Households by Amount of Credit

Distribution of Credit	No. of HHs	Percentage (%)	Distribution of Credit	No. of HHs	Percentage (%)
0	421	70.17	10001-20000	28	4.67
1000 or less	11	1.83	20001-30000	14	2.33
1001-2000	25	4.17	Above 30000	7	1.17
2001-5000	51	8.50	**Total**	**600**	**100.00**
5001-10000	43	7.17			

Source: Field survey 2012-13.

getting the desired benefits. In the field survey we realize that most of the households were not aware about the KCC; some others had raised the question against the Bank. About 37 per cent of the borrowed households had taken loan form moneylender where rate of interest was abnormally high and varies from 40 to 60 per cent per annum. There was also the evidence of borrowing from their close relative without interest (Table 4.6).

Table 4.6: Sources of Credit and Corresponding Rate of Interest

Sources	No. of HHs	% of HHs	Yearly Interest (%)	Sources	No. of HHs	% of HHs	Yearly Interest %
Bank	35	22	12	Moneylender	75	37	40 to 60
Bank with KCC	9	5	7 to 8	Relative	32	21	0
SHG	28	15	10 to 24	Total	179	79	-

Source: Field survey 2012-13.

4.3 Scope, Extent and Level of SP Benefits of Sample Households

Wide varieties of social protection schemes have been introduced in India to protect the poor and vulnerable. The present section analyses the benefits of different social protection programmes (SPPs) that the households (or members) have enjoyed. The coverage of social protection programme is assessed by three components:

Scope, this is measured here by the range (number) and type of social protection branches (programmes) to which the household or the members of the households are eligible;

Extent, this usually refers to the percentage of persons covered within the whole population or the target group, by social protection measures in each specific branch; and

Level, this refers to the adequacy of coverage by a specific branch of social security: for example, it can be measured by the level of cash benefits provided. In social health protection it may measure the amount of health-care costs covered by existing financial protection mechanisms. The level of coverage can also be measured by the quality of services provided.

The coverage of the social protection programmes in respect of scope, extent and level for 600 sample households is shown in Table 4.7. The list of the social protection programmes are not exhaustive. Here we have listed programmes which carry benefit to at least one sample household. Accordingly, in our sample survey we observed 23 social protection programmes. For each programme we had estimated the eligible households (or persons), i.e., scope, who are benefited, i.e. extent and average amount of benefit per household (or per person) in Rupees or quality of the benefit.

4.3.1 Coverage and Benefits of TPDS

Among 600 sample households 82 per cent (and 60% sample population) had BPL ration cards and they were eligible for PDS facilities. Among the eligible households (persons) 93 per cent obtained the benefit. The estimated amount of benefit per year (during 2012-13) was Rs. 3929 per household and Rs. 1103 per person. For AAY 47 per cent households were eligible, and among eligible households only 37 per cent were benefited while the benefited amount was Rs. 1170 per household per annum. The coverage of AY was relatively poor, out of 133 eligible households only three per cent households obtained benefit and each household were benefited to the tune of Rs. 2000. Out of 600 BPL listed households, the status of the ration card of 6 per cent households was APL and they were excluded from the benefit of subsidized PDS (Table 4.7).

Table 4.8 describes the per capita benefits of households and their distribution in cash and kind. The left side of the Table shows the distribution of the sample households by per capita per month foodgrain received from PDS. Out of 600 households 7 per cent were not getting any benefit, whereas 78 per cent households were getting less than 8 kg foodgrains per capita per month, the amount was less than the statutory provision for the poor household. Only 15 per cent were getting more than 8 kg foodgrains per capita per month.

The right-hand part of the Table 4.8 shows distribution of households by the market price of the PDS benefits which include the value of Rice,

Table 4.7: Coverage of Social Protection Programmes for Sample Households

	Scope				*Extent*				*Level**	
	HHs		*Persons*		*HHs*		*Persons*		*(In Rupees)*	
	No.	*%*	*No.*	*%*	*No.*	*%*	*No.*	*%*	*HHs*	*Person*
Food										
(1a) PDS with BPL	492	82	1779	60	458	93	1659	93	3929	1103
(1b) PDS with APL	36	6	227	8	31	86	204	90	1433	218
(1c) PDS with AAY	283	47	1242	42	104	37	385	31	4331	1170
(1d) PDS with AY	133	22	152	5	4	3	4	3	2000	2000
Health										
(2) PHC	600	100	2989	100	511	85	2574	86	392	78
(3) JSY	212	35	290	10	96	45	126	43	500	500
(4) RSBY	600	100	2989	100	369	62	1847	62	5779	1156
Water and Sanitation										
(5) NRDWP	600	100	2989	100	520	87	2600	87	*	*
(6) TSC	600	100	2989	100	132	22	697	23	334	63
Education										
(7) ICDS	215	36	309	10	201	93	290	94	1256	871
(8) SSK	209	35	279	9	203	97	271	97	*	*
(9) MSK	172	29	238	8	158	92	221	93	*	*
(10) MDM	285	48	517	17	265	93	442	85	1353	811
(11) BBG	300	51	517	17	297	99	492	95	224	178
(12) OG	258	43	404	14	228	91	241	60	332	245
(13) EMC	7	1	11	0	6	86	6	55	*	*
Housing										
(14) IAY	218	36	1092	37	120	55	601	55	32283	6446
Income										
(15) MGNREGA	512	85	1265	87	464	91	1166	92	3049	1213
(16) SGSY and SHG	540	90	500	91	113	21	113	23	*	*
(17) NTFP	300	50	1476	50.9	140	46.7	689	46.7	1093.6	222.2
Social Security										
(18) NOAPS	144	24	144	5	41	28	41	28	4678	4678
(19) NWPS	76	13	76	3	32	42	33	43	4956	4806
(20) NDPS	12	2	12	0	3	25	3	25	10100	10100
(21) NFBS	3	1	3	0	0	0	0	0	0	0
(22) MSY	46	8	46	2	15	33	15	33	250	250
(23) BCTG	33	6	33	1	7	21	7	21	3000	3000

Note: * Household or her members not obtained any monetary benefit.
Source: Field Survey 2012-13.

Table 4.8: Distribution of Sample Households (HHs) by Benefit Received from PDS (in Market Price) and in the form of Food Grains (Per Capita Per month)

Food Grain (Kg)	*Number of HHs*	*Percentage Share of HHs*	*PDS Benefit in Market Price (Rs.)*	*Number of HHs*	*Percentage Share of HHs*
0	42	7	0	18	3
<1	12	2	1-20	56	9
1-2	64	11	21-40	132	22
2.1-3	103	17	41-60	118	20
3.1-4	91	15	61-80	78	13
4.1-5	57	10	81-100	58	10
5.1-6	53	9	101-120	55	9
6.1-7	40	7	121-140	45	8
7.1-8	50	8	141-160	26	4
8.1-9	19	3	161-180	4	1
9.1-10	25	4	181-200	6	1
10.1-11	29	5	>200	4	1
11.1-12	10	2			
>12	5	1			
Total HHs	600	100	Total HHs	600	100

Source: Field Survey 2012-13.

Wheat, Sugar and Kerosene. Three per cent households were not benefited from PDS, 55 per cent of households had obtained benefits between Rs. 20 and Rs. 80 per capita per month and only 1 per cent households were benefited above 200 rupees. It is to note that the estimated food security line was Rs. 527.68 per capita per month (2012-13). In the absence of other source of earning, the extent of PDS benefits was not adequate to overcome the problems of food insecurity of the sample households.

In comparison to other SPPs, the coverage of TPDS is significantly higher and the majority of the sample households (as they were belonging to BPL) obtain subsidized foodgrains. But in the field survey we observed that the ration cards were old documented and seven per cent households had no ration card at all. They were not aware of getting the ration card. It was also observed that some members like married woman, children had no ration card in some other households. The process of obtaining ration card is complicated. The newly issued ration cards are APL in nature. Exclusion and inclusion errors are other problems.

4.3.2 Health Benefits

In the field survey we have observed that people obtain benefits from health centres (sub-centre, PHC, etc.), Janani Suraksha Yojana (JSY) and Rashtriya Swasthya Bima Yojana (RSBY). The coverage and benefits of these programmes are discussed as follows:

Health Centres

All households and their members are eligible for health services in health centres. But 85 per cent of sample households obtained benefit from health centres during 2012-13. Their average level of benefit was Rs. 392 per household and Rs. 78 per person. The health benefit is estimated by considering the cost of medicine, doctor fee, cost of diagnostic test etc. The distribution of households by the level of health benefit is presented in Table 4.9. There were only 13 per cent households who obtained benefit of Rs. 500 and more. Seventy-four per cent households obtained benefits less than Rs. 400 per year and only 2 per cent benefited more than Rs. 1000. We observed that the people were compelled to do their health treatment from out of packet. In most of the sample villages we observed that the health centres were not widely covered. Health centres were located at very long distance from their village they live in. The problems they faced were: health centres were not regularly opened; there were insufficient health personalities; and medicines were also not available.

Table 4.9: Distribution of Sample Households by Health Facility (Rs. per year)

Rs. per year	*Number of HHs*	*Percentage of HHs*	*Rs. per year*	*Number of HHs*	*Percentage of HHs*
No facility	89	15	601-700	12	2
100 and less	44	7	701-800	17	3
101-200	93	16	801-900	2	0
201-300	128	21	901-1000	14	2
301-400	116	19	More than 1000	14	2
401-500	50	8	**Total**	**600**	**100**
501-600	21	4			

Source: Field Survey 2012-13.

Janani Suraksha Yojana (JSY)

For JSY 35 per cent of sample households and only 10 per cent of sample population were eligible for benefit. Only 45 per cent eligible households and 43 per cent eligible beneficiaries had obtained the benefit to the extent of Rs. 600 per capita per year (Table 4.7). It is one-time benefit for the pregnant and lactating mother.

Rashtriya Swasthya Bima Yojana (RSBY)

At present RSBY covers the health insurance coverage of both BPL and APL households. Therefore, all sample households are eligible for this programme. But up to 2012-13, 62 per cent sample households were enrolled in RSBY and only 5 per cent of them obtained benefits for medical (institutional) treatment. Their average amount of benefit was Rs. 5779 during the financial year 2012-13 (Table 4.7).

4.3.3 Drinking Water and Sanitation Facilities

National Rural Drinking Water programme (NRDWP) and Total Sanitation Campaign (TSC) promote the basic facilities of drinking water and sanitation for rural people. Generally, all rural households are eligible to get benefit for these programmes. Among 600 sample households 87 per cent had obtained the drinking water facilities under NRDWP. The remaining households were suffering the problem of non-availability of safe drinking water. We have noted that during recent years NRDWP have significantly performed and its achievement exceeded the target in the three backward districts of Purulia, Bankura and Paschim Medinipur. But some habitations are still not covered with the facilities of safe drinking water. The crisis of drinking water is noticed during summer in drought prone blocks of these districts. Households mitigate the problem of drinking water by carrying water from a long distance.

On the other hand, TSC programme which is more essential for every household has experienced very worst performance in the sample region. Among the 600 hundred sample households (who are all eligible under TSC) only 22 per cent got the benefits. The estimated amount of benefit was very low—Rs. 334 per household (Table 4.7). People of this region mainly use open sources which may cause serious threat on their health.

4.3.4 Educational Benefits

A number of programmes have been introduced for education facilities and support services. They are ICDS, MDM, SSK, MSK and Grants (different types). Integrated Child Development Scheme (ICDS) has the objective to cover nutritional and pre-primary educational benefits for children (0-6 years age). In the selected sample households, 36 per cent had children of age group below six years and they were eligible for ICDS facilities. The extent of coverage of this programme was relatively high. Among the eligible children 94 per cent were getting benefits. The estimated amount of benefits per year (during 2012-13) was Rs. 1256 per household and Rs. 871 per child (Table 4.7). There was the provision of at least 250 meals during a year. But only 4 per cent households obtained that benefit. Among all eligible children 6 per cent had not taken any meal, 61 per cent had taken 101 to 200 meals and 24 per cent had taken 201 to 250 meals (Table 4.10).

Table 4.10: ICDS Meal and Mid-Day Meal (for Class I to VIII) per Beneficiary among the Sample Households, 2012-13

ICDS Meal			*Mid-Day Meal*		
	No. HHs	*Percentage*		*No. HHs*	*Percentage*
No Meal Taken	14	6	No Meal Taken	20	7
20 to 100	11	5	50 to 100	45	16
101 to 200	131	61	101 to 200	180	63
201 to 250	51	24	201 to 250	40	14
251 to 263	8	4	250 to 275	10	
Total	**215**	**100**	**Total**	**285**	**100**
Average meal	189	--	Average	170	--

Source: Field Survey 2012-13.

SSK covers primary education and MDM benefits of children. Out of the sample households 35 per cent are eligible for this programme. Among the eligible households (Persons) 97 per cent got the benefits. MSK covers secondary education, precisely for class IX and X students. About 29 per cent of households were eligible for this programme and among them 92 per cent households obtained benefits from this program.

MDM programme provides nutritional food at primary and upper primary schools and encourages the attendance rate of the children. Among the sample households 48 per cent of sample houses were eligible for this programme and 93 per cent of them were benefited under this program. The estimated amounts of benefits during a year was Rs. 1353 per household and Rs. 811 per person. Among the beneficiaries seven per cent did not obtain any meal, whereas 63 per cent obtained 101 to 200 meals and 11 per cent obtained 201 to 250 meals during 2012-13. Only three per cent have obtained the statutory provision at least 250 meals during a year.

The primary and upper primary students were also benefited from free books. SC, ST and OBC students were also benefited with the book grants. Fifty-one per cent of sample households were eligible for getting benefits of free books and book grants and among them 99 per cent households were benefited. The estimated benefits were Rs. 224 per household per year which is not sufficient in the present scenario. In case of other grants (which are generally for dresses of poor children) 43 per cent of sample households are eligible for getting benefits and 91 per cent of them have benefited. The estimated amounts of benefits are Rs. 332 per household per year and Rs. 245 per beneficiary per year. There is also the provision of benefits for education for minority children and only 1 per cent of the sample households were eligible for these benefits. Among the eligible 86 per cent households and 55 per cent students were benefited from this programme.

On the whole, the education related programmes are enforced by RTE Acts and therefore most of the eligible households were benefited from these programmes. But the level of benefits is not adequate. Majority of the beneficiaries have not obtained the statutory provision of benefits in the backward region.

4.3.5 Income Generation

MGNREGA is one of the landmark programmes for employment generation, which is enforced by Employment Guarantee Act. It is a universal programme and covers all households for benefit. But the households having Job Cards are eligible for the benefit of employment under this programme. Among 600 sample households only 85 per cent were eligible for benefits and among the eligible households 91 per cent obtained the benefits (Table 4.7). The mandays of employment widely vary across households—22 per cent households did not obtaine any employment and another 43 per cent households had obtained employment less than 20 mandays. The average mandays of employment of 600 households during 2012-13 was 23 days. There is the provision of 100 days guaranteed employment per household every year. But among 600 sample households no one has received 100 days employment (Fig. 4.5).

Non-Timber Forest Produces (NTFP) is also one of the important programmes for poor people who live near the forest. Fifty per cent of sample households were eligible for benefits under NTFP and only 46.7 per cent of eligible households got benefits during 2012-13 (Table 4.7). The Households who failed to receive any government assistance under

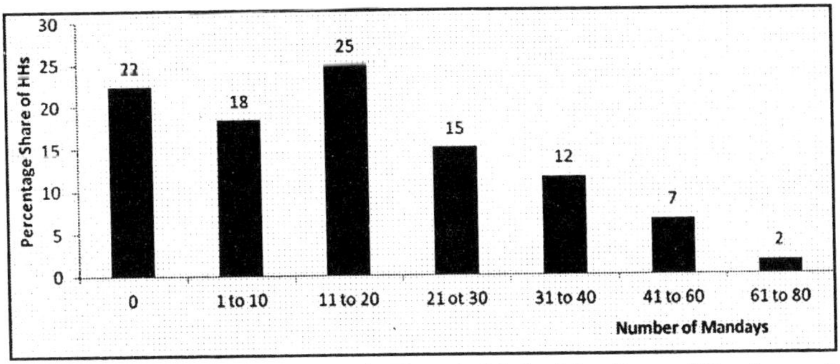

Fig. 4.5: Distributions of Sample Households by Man Days of Employment under MGNREGA

Source: Field Survey 2012-13.

this programme were benefited from forest resources. The amount of benefit widely varies across the households (as shown in Table 4.11). The average amount of benefits was Rs. 1093 per household and Rs. 222 per person during 2012-13.

Table 4.11: Per capita Benefits (Yearly) of the Sample Households under Non-Timber Forest Produces

Benefits (Rs.)	*No. HHs*	*Percentage*	*Benefits (Rs.)*	*No. HHs*	*Percentage*
No Benefit Received	460	76.7	801–1000	25	4.2
200 and less	6	1.0	1001–1500	17	2.8
201–400	19	3.2	1501–2000	17	2.8
401–600	21	3.5	>2000	11	1.8
601–800	24	4.0	**Total**	**600**	**100**

Source: Field Survey 2012-13.

4.3.6 Benefits from Social Security

Social security related programmes like IGNOAPS, IGNWPS and IGNDPS are for specific beneficiaries; therefore, their coverage is limited. For old age pension 24 per cent sample households and five per cent of sample population were eligible for benefit. Among eligible old age people only 28 per cent received the pension. The average amount of pension (per capita per year) was Rs. 4678. In case of widow pension scheme 13 per cent sample households and 3 per cent of sample population were eligible. About 43 per cent of eligible widows obtained pension to the extent of

Rs. 4606 per widow during 2012-13. For disabled pension only 2 per cent of sample households and 0.4 per cent of sample population were eligible for benefit. Only three disabled persons out of 12 got benefit to the extent of Rs. 10100 each.

Among the sample households no one were benefited under NFBS and under MSY only 15 per cent of eligible mothers were benefited at the extent of Rs. 250 each. In the Jangal Mahal area ST girl students are eligible for bicycle but only 21 per cent of them have received bicycles from government, whose estimated value is Rs. 3000.

The relative importance of different social protection programmes are realized from the distribution of the households by the share of benefits of particular programmes to total benefits (Table 4.12). Among SPPs, the relative importance of PDS benefits was highest, followed by NREGP, ICDS and MDM. These programmes are now legally enforced. That is, the legally enforced SPPs are better executed and they create more benefits to the households.

Table 4.12: Percentage distribution of Sample Households by the Percentage Share of SPB for different SPPs

Share of SPB	PDS	Health	ICDS	MDM	Free Books	Other Grants	NR EGP	IGNO APS	IGN WPS	IGN DPS	IG MSY
0.0	2	15	67	56	51	62	23	93	95	99	98
0.1–20	12	84	24	30	49	36	21	0	0	0	2
20.1–40	30	1	7	12	0	2	29	2	3	1	0
41.1–60	31	0	2	2	0	0	18	3	2	0	0
61.1–80	18	0	1	0	0	0	8	2	0	0	0
81.1–100	7	0	0	0	0	0	1	0	0	0	0
Total HHs	100	100	100	100	100	100	100	100	100	100	100

Source: Field Survey 2012-13.

4.3.7 Comparison of Benefits from PDS between Jangal Mahal and Non-Jangal Mahal Areas

In our sample study Jangal Mahal region is most backward relative to Non-Jangal Mahal and the people of Jangal Mahal are relatively more deprived. The State Government has extended the extra benefits by different SPPs for the people living in the Jangal Mahal area. This section makes an attempt to test whether the people of Jangal Mahal area obtained more SPP benefits or not in comparison with the people of Non-Jangal Mahal area. Table 4.13 presents the distribution of PDS benefits enjoyed by the sample households in Jangal Mahal area and Non-Jangal Mahal area. Distribution of PDS (per capita per month) of Jangal Mahal and Non-Jangal Mahal has been quite different. About 46 per cent sample households in Jangal Mahal area have obtained per capita per month PDS benefits worth more than Rs. 100, while only 7 per cent sample households of Non-Jangal Mahal area obtained this benefit. That is, Jangal Mahal people obtained more PDS benefits than Non-Jangal Mahal people. To analyze whether this difference was statistically significant or not we have conducted the test of mean difference by t-test. The result of t-test is summarized in Table 4.14. It is found that the per capita per month PDS benefit in the Jangal Mahal area was significantly higher than the Non-Jangal Mahal area.

Table 4.13: Distribution of Per Capita Per Month PDS Benefit (Rs.) of Sample Huseholds in the Jangal Mahal and Non-Jangal Mahal Areas

PDS Benefits (Rs. Per Capita Per Month)	*Jangal Mahal*		*Non-Jangal Mahal*	
	Number of HHs	*% of HHs*	*Number of HHs*	*% of HHs*
0	2	0.8	16	4.6
1–50	49	19.6	201	57.4
51–100	84	33.6	109	31.1
101–150	98	39.2	20	5.7
151–200	13	5.2	4	1.1
More than 200	4	1.6	0	0.0
Total Households (HHs)	250	100	350	100.0

Source: Field survey 2012-13.

The distribution of sample households by per capita per month SPP benefits in Jangal Mahal and Non-Jangal Mahal regions is shown in Table 4.15. To analyze whether the difference of benefits between Jangal Mahal and Non-Jangal Mahal regions is significant or not we conduct the test of mean difference of SPP benefits by t-test. The result of t-test is summarized in Table 4.16. The per capita per month social protection benefit in Jangal Mahal area is significantly higher than Non-Jangal Mahal area.

4.4 Excess Demand of SPPs

Most of the social protection programmes are deficient to fulfil their objectives. There is mismatch between supply side (actual outcome of the programme) and demand side (demand of the beneficiary as per

Table 4.14: Testing the Difference of Per Capita Per Month PDS Benefits of the Sample Households in the Jangal Mahal (X_1) and Non-Jangal Mahal Areas (X_2)

Indicators	*Values*	*F-Test*	*t-test*
		$H_0 : \sigma_1^2 = \sigma_2^2$ $(H_1 : \sigma_1^2 > \sigma_2^2)$	$H_0 : \mu_1 = \mu_2$ $(H_1 : \mu_1 > \mu_2)$
m_1	91.73	$F = (s_1^2 / s_2^2) / (\sigma_1^2 / \sigma_2^2)$ = 1.91	$t_{n1} + n_2 = \frac{m_1 - m_2}{\sqrt{\left(\frac{s_1^2}{n_1} + \frac{s_1^2}{n_2}\right)}}$ Has upper α-point approximately the same as (w_1 t α, n_1–1 + w_2 t α, n_2–1)/ (w_1 + w_2) = 12.80
m_2	47.99		
s_1^2	2110.1	Table Value of F = 1.21 (p value one tail is 0.000)	Table Value of t = 1.96 (p value one tail is 0.114)
s_2^2	1104.9		
N_1	250	Calculated value of F > Table Value of F, i.e., H_0 is rejected	Calculated value of t > Table Value of t, i.e., H_0 is rejected
N_2	350		
Df		249,349	427

Notes: X_1 denotes per capita per month PDS benefits of 250 sample households of Jangal Mahal and X_2 denotes per capita per month PDS benefit of 350 sample households of Non-Jangal Mahal. The corresponding means are m_1 and m_2 and variances are s_1^2 and s_2^2. N_1 and N_2 are sample observations and df is the degrees of freedom.

Source: Author's calculation.

statutory provision of the programme). The supply of social protection benefits is lagging behind the demand. We have estimated the excess demand of social protection benefits. For each SPP we have articulated the number of sample households (and their share in sample) who were not benefited at all. These households were treated as 'households not covered'. It is pre-supposed that SPPs cover at least the poor households and accordingly we have estimated the least possible excess demand for poor households who were not covered. The excess demand is estimated by considering the households which are not yet covered by SPP benefits. The rate of benefit per household is the average rate of existing benefit

Table 4.15: Distribution of Households by Per Capita Per Month Total Social Protection Benefits in the Jangal Mahal and Non-Jangal Mahal Areas

SPP Benefits (Rs. Per Capita Per Month)	*Jangal Mahal*		*Non-Jangal Mahal*	
	Number of HHs	*% of HHs*	*Number of HHs*	*% of HHs*
0	0	0.0	2	0.6
1–100	39	15.6	94	26.9
101–200	137	54.8	177	50.6
201–300	64	25.6	61	17.4
301–400	7	2.8	9	2.6
401–500	2	0.8	7	2.0
More than 500	1	0.4	0	0.0
Total Households (HHs)	250	100.0	350	100.0

Source: Field Survey 2012-13.

(as realized by the sample households) or statutory benefit (for some programmes). The number of poor households in three backward districts namely Purulia, Bankura and Paschim Medinipur are estimated from NSSO unit level data. Accordingly, the estimated number of poor households in these three districts were 620492 in 2011-12. The number of households which are not covered by SPP in these three districts are estimated on the basis of the proportion of not covered sample households. Finally, total expected benefits for not covered households is calculated by multiplying estimated number of not covered poor households with expected benefit per household per year. This total expected benefit for not covered poor households is treated as total excess demand for the specific SPP. For PDS and Rural Primary Health Care we have also considered the households which are partially covered.

In case of PDS among eligible households seven per cent households have not obtained any benefit and another 49.7 per cent households were partially benefited. The estimated number of eligible (for PDS) poor households in three districts for full benefit were 42879 and for partial benefit were 333259. The expected benefit per household per year for full benefit of PDS was Rs. 6181 (average of the benefits enjoyed by the sample households) and for partial benefit (difference between average benefit and actual benefit) of PDS was Rs. 2251. The total value of expected benefit, i.e., total demand for PDS benefit was Rs. 958 lakh. Similarly, for Rural Primary Health Care, the estimated amount of benefit was Rs. 914 lakh. In case of JSY, 19.3 per cent eligible households were

Table 4.16: Testing the difference of Per Capita Per Month Social Protection Benefits of Sample Households in Jangal Mahal (X_1) and Non-Jangal Mahal areas (X_2)

Indicators	*Values*	*F-Test*	*t-test*
		$H_2:\sigma_1^2=\sigma_2^2$ $(H_1:\sigma_1^2>\sigma_2^2)$	$H_0:\mu_1=\mu_2$ $(H_1:\mu_1>\mu_2)$
m_1	172.1	$F=(s_1^2/s_2^2)/(\sigma_1^2/\sigma_2^2)$ = 0.85	$t_{n1}+n_2=\frac{m_1-m_2}{\sqrt{\left(\frac{s_1^2}{n_1}+\frac{s_1^2}{n_2}\right)}}=3.40$ Has upper *a*-point approximately the same as (w_1 t α, n_1–1 + w_2 t α, n_2–1)/ (w_1 + w_2)
m_2	150.8		
s_1^2	5375.0	Table Value of F = 0.83 (p value one tail is 0.097	Table Value of t = 1.65 (p value one tail is 0.000)
s_2^2	6268.9		
N_1	350	Calculated value of F > Table Value of F, i.e., H_0 is rejected	Calculated value (absolute) of t > Table Value of t, i.e., H_0 is rejected
N_2	250		
Def		249. 349	560

Notes: X_1 denotes PCPM Social Protection income of 250 sample households of Jangal Mahal and X_2 denotes PCPM Social Protection income of 350 sample households of Non-Jangal Mahal. The Corresponding means are m_1 and m_2 and variances are s_1^2 and s_2^2. N_1 and N_2 are sample observations and df is the degrees of freedom.

Source: Author's calculation.

not covered and at the statutory rate of benefit Rs. 500 per household the total expected benefit was Rs. 23 lakh. The expected demands of other programmes are shown in Table 4.14. Total expected demand of all SPPs was Rs. 16815 lakh for all eligible households. It is roughly spoken that around Rs. 168.15 crore additional fund is required to extend the social protection benefits to all eligible households in three backward districts during a year. That is, the estimated additional cost is Rs. 27099 per household per year to fulfil the excess demand of all eligible households.

Table 4.17: Estimation of Demand of Social Protection Benefits for Poor Sample Households which are not yet Covered in the Backward Region

Name of the Social Protection Programme	*HHs Not Covered*		*Estimated Poor HHs#*	*Estimated No. of HHs not Covered*	*Expected Benefit per HH (in Rs.)*	*Total Demand (Rs. Lakh)*
	Number	*Per cent*				
1. PDS*	42	7	620492	42879	6181	959
	(298)	(49.7)		(333259)	(2251)	
2. Rural Primary Healtn Care*	90	15	620492	527418	1810	914
	(510)	(85.0)		(92039)	(1418)	
3. JSY	116	19.3	620492	45757	500	23
4. RSBY	231	38.4	620492	257795	30000	7734
5. TSC	468	78.0	620492	523374	1571	822
6. ICDS	14	2.3	620492	15656	871	14
7. Mid-Day Meal	34	5.7	620492	38119	811	31
8. Free Books	3	0.5	620492	3444	178	1
9. Book Grand & Other Grants	22	3.7	620492	24603	245	6
10. Education for Minority Children	1	0.2	620492	1118	4000	4
11. IAY	98	16.3	620492	109595	42452	4653
12. MGNREGA	48	8.0	620492	53679	11048	593
13. IGNOAPS	103	17.2	620492	115187	5393	621
14. NFBS	3	0.5	620492	3355	10000	34
15. IGNWPS	44	7.3	620492	49206	5360	264
16. IGNDPS	9	1.5	620492	10065	4710	47
17. IGMSY	31	5.2	620492	34668	250	9
18. Bi-Cycle for Tribal Girls	26	4.3	620492	29076	3000	87
					Total	16815
					Per HH	27093.16

Notes:
1. * For this programmes we have estimated partially not covered as well as fully not covered households.
2. Figures in parenthesis indicate partial not covered households or amount of benefits.
3. # Poor households are estimated from the NSSO unit level data. No. of Estimated Poor in 2011-12 are 620492 in three backward districts—Purulia, Bankura and Paschim Medinipur.
4. HHs = Households.

5
Entitlement of the Poor Households
Perspective from the Sample Survey in the Backward Region

5.1 Revisit of the Entitlement Approach of A.K. Sen

It is more than three decades since Amartya Sen published *Poverty and Famines*, a fact that some of us who have been writing about entitlements since 1980s might prefer to forget. For the reason that the entitlement approach has been around for such a long time, it may be assumed that a lengthy discursive exposition is unnecessary. Entitlements have been defined by Sen (1981) as "the set of alternative commodity bundles that a person can command in a society using the totality of rights and opportunities that he or she faces". In other words, a person's "entitlement set" is the full range of goods and services that he or she can acquire by converting his or her "endowments" (assets and resources, including labour power) through "exchange entitlement mappings". That is, the entitlement approach is based on three conceptual categories, namely, the Endowment Set; the Entitlement Set; and the Entitlement Mapping.

The *endowment set* is defined as the combination of all those legally owned resources by a person conforming the established norms and practices. The said resources include both tangible assets, such as land, equipment, animals and intangibles such as knowledge and skill, labour power, or membership of a particular community.

The entitlement approach of A.K. Sen. to starvation and famines concentrates the ability of people to command food through the legal means available in the society, including the use of production possibilities, trade opportunities, entitlement *vis-à-vis* the state, and other methods of acquiring food. In each society there are rules governing this right. The entitlement approach concentrates on each person's entitlement.

Entitlement relations accepted in a private ownership market economy typically includes the following among others (Sen. 1981):

> *Trade based entitlement:* one is entitled to own what one obtains by trading something one owns with a willing party (or multilaterally with a willing set of parties);
> *Production based entitlement:* one is entitled to own what one gets by arranging production using one's owned resources, or resources hired from willing parties meeting the agreed conditions of trade;
> *Own-labour entitlement:* one is entitled to one's own labour power, and thus to the trade-based and production-based entitlements related to one's labour power;
> *Inheritance and transfer entitlement*: one is entitled to own what is willingly given to one by another who legitimately owns it, possibly to take affect after the latter's death (if so specified by him).

The *entitlement set* is defined as the set of all possible combinations of goods and services (not just the one actually being enjoyed) that a person can legally obtain by using the resources of his endowment set. The entitlement approach aims comprehensively to describe all legal sources of food, which Sen (1981) categorises into four heads namely: "production-based entitlement" (growing food), "trade-based entitlement" (buying food), "own-labour entitlement" (working for food) and "inheritance and transfer entitlement" (being given food by others).

The set of all alternative bundles of commodities that a person can acquire in exchange for what he owns may be called the *exchange entitlement* of what he owns. The exchange entitlements depend not merely on market exchanges but also on those exchanges, if any, that the state provides as a part of social protection programme. These social protection provisions are essentially supplementations of the process of market exchange and production. These affect the commodity bundles over which a person can have command. Therefore, the social protection arrangements are particularly important in the context of food insecurity. The *entitlement mapping*, called E-mapping, is simply the relationship between endowment set and entitlement set. It is the rate at which the resources of the endowment set can be converted into goods and services included in the entitlement set. Figure 5.1 shows the relationship among these three basic concepts:

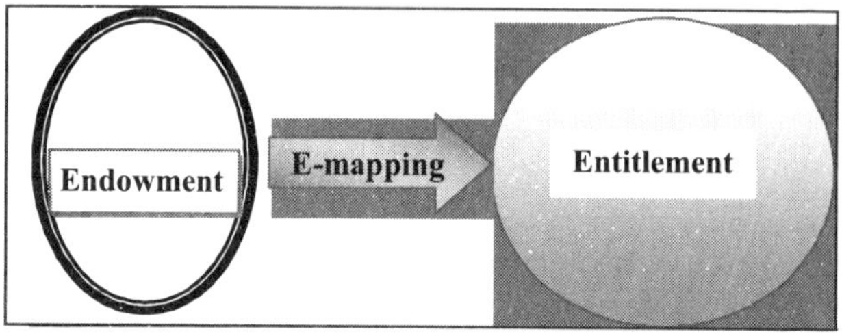

Fig. 5.1: Endowment and Entitlement Relationship

A person is said to suffer from the *failure of food entitlement* when his entitlement set does not contain enough food to enable him for avoiding food insecurity or starvation in the absence of non-entitlement transfers, such as charity (Sen, 1981).

A person's ability to avoid starvation/food insecurity will depend both upon his ownership and on the exchange entitlement mapping that he faces. A general decline in food supply may indeed cause him to be exposed to hunger through a rise in food prices with an unfavourable impact on his exchange entitlement. Even when his starvation is caused by food shortage in this way, his immediate reason for starvation will be the decline in his exchange entitlement.

5.2 Endowment Set and Exchange Entitlement of the Sample Households

Different households have different endowments that cause their different exchange entitlements. That is, the exchange entitlement is the function of endowment. Given the endowment set of the household, the exchange entitlement may vary due to the following reasons (Sen 1981):

(a) whether he can find employment, and if so for how long and at what wage rate;
(b) what he can earn by selling his non-labour assets;
(c) what he can produce with his own labour power and resources; and
(d) the social security benefits he is entitled to and the taxes, etc., he must pay.

A person's ability to avoid poverty or food insecurity depends both on endowment and on the exchange entitlement mapping that he faces.

In our study all the sample households belong to BPL category. They are deficient in assets endowment—both tangible and intangible. Here we have specified the assets owned by the households that have been witnessed in our field survey.

Cultivable Land

The cultivable land holding, the important asset endowment in the rural area, is relatively low for most of the sample households. The distribution of sample households by per capita gross cropped area (GCA) is depicted in Figure 5.2. Among 600 sample households in the three less developed districts (Paschim Medinipur, Bankura and Purulia), 36.2 per cent were landless and non-cultivating households. The households having per capita gross cropped area 10 decimals or less account for 25.4 per cent. Among the rest, most of the households were marginal landholding households which implies that the cultivable land, the main asset endowment of rural households was low. The land productivity is treated as the exchange entitlement of the asset 'land'. The exchange entitlement of land was also deficient due to low productivity.

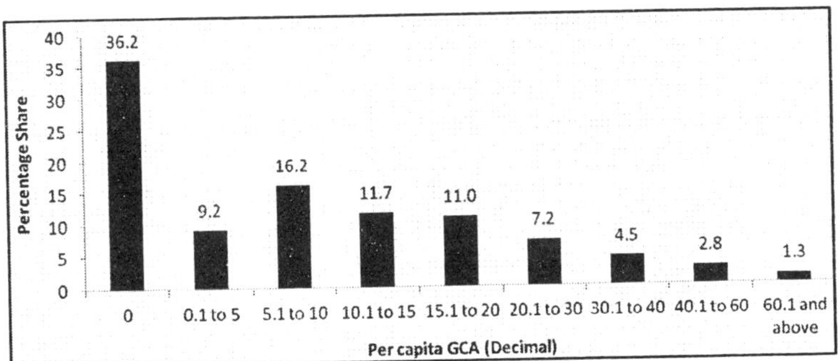

Fig. 5.2: Distribution of Sample Households by per capita Gross Cropped Area (GCA)

Source: Field survey 2012-13.

Figure 5.3 depicts the land productivity (value of production per decimal of GCA) of cultivating households. The land productivity of 86 per cent cultivating households is less than Rs. 100[1]. The main reason behind this low productivity is that a significant portion of these three districts are drought prone together with inadequate irrigation facilities. Now let us see the other means of productions of the households.

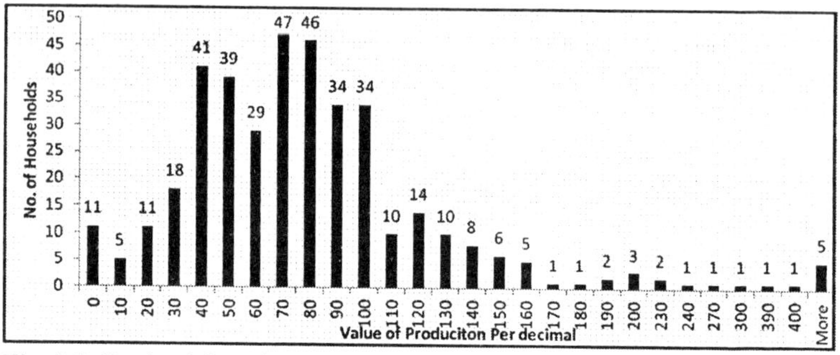

Fig. 5.3: Productivity of Land of the Sample Households

Source: Field survey 2012-13.

Equipment and other Productive Assets including Animals

Among 600 sample households, 82.2 per cent had bi-cycle, 61 per cent had mobile, 9.3 per cent had TV and only 2.7 per cent had motor bike. But the productive assets were hardly found. The pump set for irrigation was found in only 2.2 per cent households and spear machine (used for spearing chemical pesticide in agriculture) in 0.8 per cent household. The rickshaw and cow cart were also used as the means of transport but only a few households had these assets (Figure 5.4). Cattles (like cow, goat, sheep, buffalo etc.), agri-allied productive asset were also found in some households. But in most of the cases they served the household activities and in some cases they were sold by the households to cope with the adverse situation or shocks. We have estimated the value of equipments and productive assets including animals and their income (if

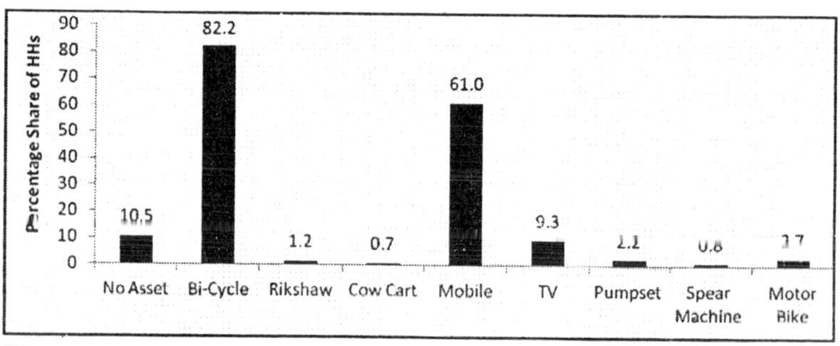

Fig. 5.4: Assets Owned by the Sample Households

Source: Field survey 2012-13.

any). Out of 600 sample households, 41 per cent households failed to occupy any assets.

Table 5.1 shows the distribution of income of the households by asset values. It is evident that the earning from assets of 40 per cent asset holders (140 out of 353 households) appeared to be zero (or even negative in some cases). For the failure of exchange entitlement mapping they failed to earn from their asset during 2012-13. The earnings of other households from assets were also low whereas for most of the households, it was less than Rs. 1000. Figure 5.5 depicts the income from assets across the asset values of the sample households. In horizontal axis, the households with asset values are arranged in ascending order and the vertical axis measures the asset income of the corresponding households. Their relationship is not stable. The ups and downs of asset income line indicate that the exchange entitlement mappings of different asset holders are highly volatile.

Table 5.1: Distribution of Income of the Households by Asset Values

Asset Value	*Income Distribution*	*No. of HHs*	*Asset Value*	*Income Distribution*	*No. of HHs*	*Asset Value*	*Income Distribution*	*No. of HHs*
1000 and Less	0	16	5001-8000	0	28	15001-20000	0	5
	1-300	8		1-1000	10		1000-3000	9
	301-600	3		1001-2000	12		4000-7000	6
	601-2500	5		2001-6000	9		9000-10000	3
1001-2000	0	18	8001-11000	0	15	20001-30000	0	5
	1-300	3		500-1500	9		600-3000	8
	301-1000	7		2000-4000	6		3001-5000	4
	1001-2400	4		4000-6000	5		10000-20000	4
2001-5000	0	53	11001-15000	0	16	30000 and More	0	5
	1-1000	11		200-1500	12		1000-4000	4
	1001-2000	15		2000-4000	9		7000-9000	2
	2001-7000	10		5000-15400	11		20000-35000	3
Total HHs		153			142			58

Source: Field Survey 2012-13.

Labour Power

The labour power is one of the most crucial endowments for the rural households. For the deficiency of land and other means of production, households depend on their labour power to survive. One's labour power is used either in trade-based and production-based entitlement or in sale other or in both but the majority of the labourers (52%) of sample

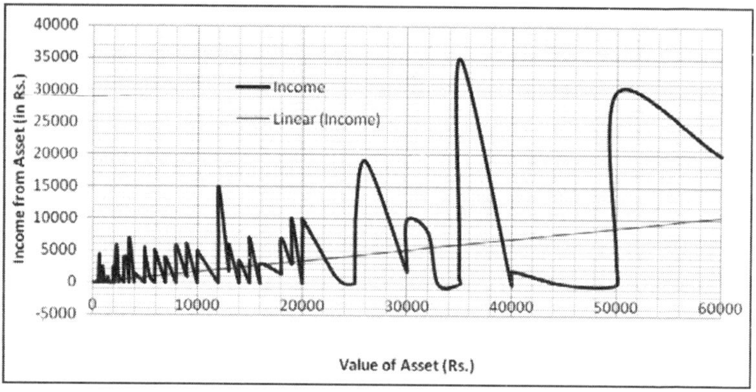

Fig. 5.5: Income from Other Productive Assets in relation to Asset Value.
Source: Field Survey 2012-13.

households were engaged in casual labour. Only 12 per cent of labourers were regularly employed (Figure 5.6a). The extent of sale of their labour power and earnings widely vary from one household to another, which also depends upon whether they can find employment, and if so for how long and at what wage rate. Figure 5.6b depicts the extent to which the

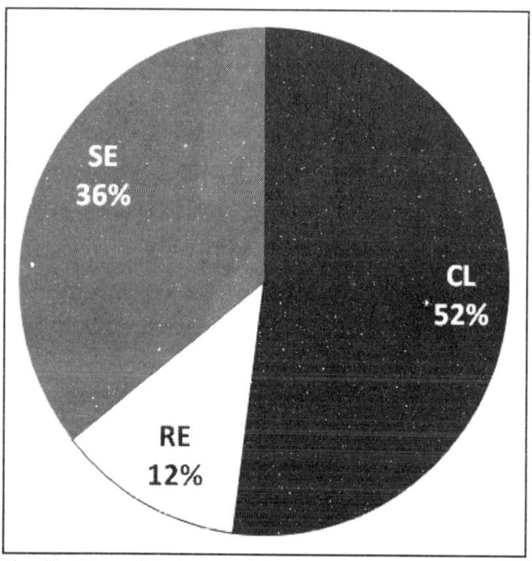

Fig. 5.6a: Distribution of Labour of Sample Households by the Status of Employment

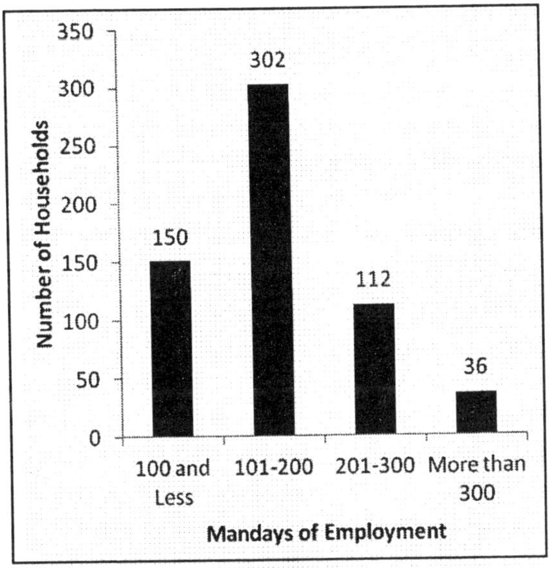

Fig. 5.6b: Average Mandays of Employment of Sample Households

Source: Field Survey 2012-13.

households were able to employ their labour power, i.e., mandays of employment. A manday is the engagement of a worker in any productive activity for eight hours and average mandays of a household is the ratio of total mandays during a year to total workers of that household. Among 600 sample households 150 households failed to use their labour power for more than 100 mandays during a year (2012-13). About 50 per cent households have used their labour power at the extent of 100 to 200 mandays. Only 36 households (6%) were able to employ their labour power for more than 300 mandays. Thus, it is evident that a number of households failed (partially) in respect of exchange entitlement of labour. The extent of failure is estimated in Figure 5.7. In this figure, the upward line is the 'labour exchange entitlement' line which shows how long the households have obtained employment and the dashed horizontal line indicates the standard[2] 300 average mandays of employment. The area between these two lines (i.e., ABC) is the extent of exchange entitlement failure of labour. The main reason behind the failure of this exchange entitlement is the deficiency of skill and education of workers as well as the availability of job.

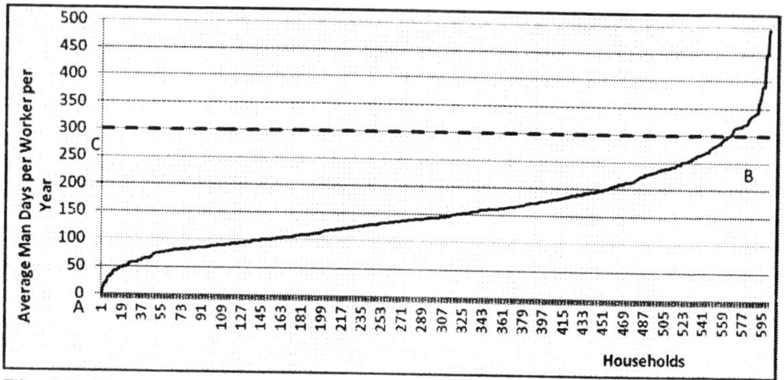

Fig. 5.7: Exchange Entitlement of Labour of Sample Households

Source: Field Survey 2012-13.

Knowledge and Skill of the Workers

The knowledge and skill of the workers are also non-tangible endowment of the households. This endowment directly affects the labour exchange entitlement and its deficiency is caused due to the failure of labour entitlement. The education level of the worker is considered a proxy measure of this endowment. Education level of the workers of the sample households was relatively low (Figure 5.8). All the members of 7.2 per cent households were illiterate. The average years of schooling were seven years or more for only 12 per cent households.

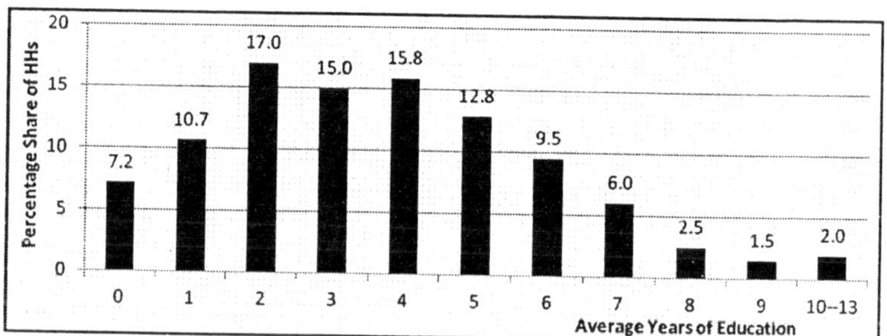

Fig. 5.8: Distribution of Sample Households (HHs) by Average Years of Education of Workers.

Source: Field survey 2012-13.

There were 58.5 per cent households having average years of schooling (of all members) less than 4 years. The share of households with average years of schooling six years or less was 81 per cent. Hardly any worker was found who had formal technical or professional education. However, in respect of skill some workers were expertise to do specific activity. Some of them acquire their skill by heredity.

Membership

Households having the membership of different social protection programmes or institutions provided them the opportunity to increase their entitlements. For the poor households, the membership creates the opportunity to receive the benefits of different public welfare measures. The details of the public welfare measures in the form of social protection programmes is analysed in Chapter 2. The membership of a household or her member in a particular programme depends on the eligibility criteria of that programme. Accordingly, in the Field Survey we have identified the membership of different programmes. Figure 5.9 shows the percentage share of household's membership of different social protection programmes. For example in case of BPL Public Distribution System (PDS) 82 per cent of the sample households had BPL ration card and therefore, they were the members of this programmes. All or some members of these 82 per cent households had BPL ration cards and therefore about 60 per cent of total sample persons were the members of this programme. But household's entitlement in respect of social protection programmes depends on whether the household (or her members) gets benefit or not and to what extent she is benefited, that is, the exchange entitlement mapping. The benefited households (and persons) and the extent of benefits was also analysed in Chapter 4.

5.3 Entitlements of the Households

The entitlement set confers the command over goods and services and it depends on endowment set as well as exchange entitlement mapping of the household. Here we assume that the earning of the household is used as the proxy of entitlement. Total annual income of a household is the sum of the earnings of different sources that are generated by exchanging her entire endowment during a year. Two households with different entitlements are compared as follows: If household A has higher annual income in comparison to household B then it is supposed that household A has higher entitlement to command on food than B and also have better opportunity to overcome poverty and food insecurity. For empirical

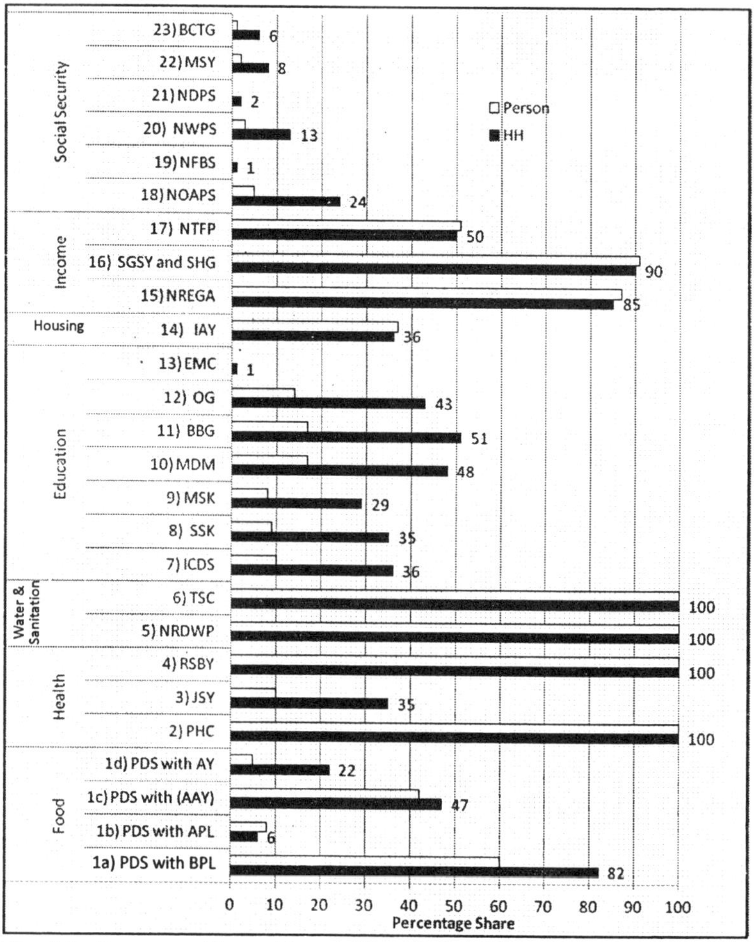

Fig. 5.9: Percentage Share of Sample Household and Person Membership across different Social Protection Measures

Source: Field Survey 2012-13.

justification we make this simplification to compare the households in respect of their entitlement. For a particular household, the relative importance of different entitlements (i.e., labour entitlement, production entitlement, trade entitlement and transfer entitlement) is analysed by earnings incurred from these sources.

Earnings of the households by means of different forms of entitlements are categorized as labour entitlement, production based entitlement (both agriculture and other than agriculture), and trade-based entitlement and transfer entitlement (from common property resources (CPR) and social protection schemes (SPS) are presented in Table 5.2. Among 600 sample households per capita per day earnings from labour entitlement was higher than Rs. 18 (i.e., income near to food security line Rs. 17.59) for only 17.3 per cent households. Only five per cent households were able to earn labour income more than Rs. 29 (equivalent poverty line income). The failure of labour entitlement was found for 10.7 per cent households. Earning from production is insufficient for majority of the households. The per capita per day income from agricultural production of 35.3 per cent non-cultivating households was zero and other 52.5 per cent households' earning was less than Rs. 5. As many as 56.8 per cent and 81.3 per cent households were not able to earn from other than agricultural production and trade respectively. CPR is another important source of earning. Most of the sample villages are located near forest. Forest resources are used by the villagers for their own purpose as well as for sale. Other households who were located near river were benefited from the river resources. By exchange entitlement mapping, CPRs are transformed into household's income through the process of either production or trade or both.

Exchange entitlements are also dependent on the benefits of SPS that the state provides. The SPSs affect the commodity bundle over which

Table 5.2: Distribution of Sample Households by Per Capita Per Day Income (Rs.) from different Sources (entitlements)

Per Capita Per Day Income (Rs.)	*Labour*		*Agriculture Production*		*Other than Agriculture Production*		*Trade*		*CPR*		*SPS*	
	No. of HHs	*% of HHs*	*No. of HHs*	*% of HHs*	*No. of HHs*	*% of HHs*	*No. of HHs*	*% of HHs*	*No. of HHs*	*% of HHs*	*No. of HHs*	*% of HHs*
0	64	10.7	212	35.3	341	56.8	488	81.3	165	27.5	2	0.3
0.1 to 5	112	18.7	315	52.5	180	30.0	41	6.8	386	64.3	303	50.5
5.1 to 10	156	26.0	46	7.7	43	7.2	24	4.0	36	6.0	270	45.0
10.1 to 18	164	27.3	21	3.5	26	4.3	30	5.0	10	1.7	24	4.0
18.1 to 29	73	12.2	6	1.0	9	1.5	8	1.3	2	0.3	1	0.2
29.1 to 40	17	2.8	–	–	1	0.2	5	0.8	1	0.2	–	–
Above 40	14	2.3	–	–	–	–	4	0.7	–	–	–	–
Total	600	100	600	100	600	100	600	100	600	100	600	100

Note: HHs = Households, CPR = Common Property Resources, SPS = Social Protection Schemes.

Source: Field Survey 2012-13.

a person can have command. The benefits of social protection programmes are also treated here as the earnings of the household. All households, as they fall under the BPL category, were benefited from SPS. There were 50.5 per cent of the households who were benefited with less than Rs. 5 and another 45 per cent households were benefited with Rs. 5 to Rs. 10 per capita per day from SPS.

The average income from different sources of earnings is presented in Figure 5.10. Among all entitlements the contribution of labour entitlement was highest followed by social protection. The per capita per day average income from labour was Rs. 11.4 and social protection was Rs. 5.3. Other sources of earnings like agricultural and non-agricultural production, trade and common property resources (CPR) were relatively less important for the sample BPL households.

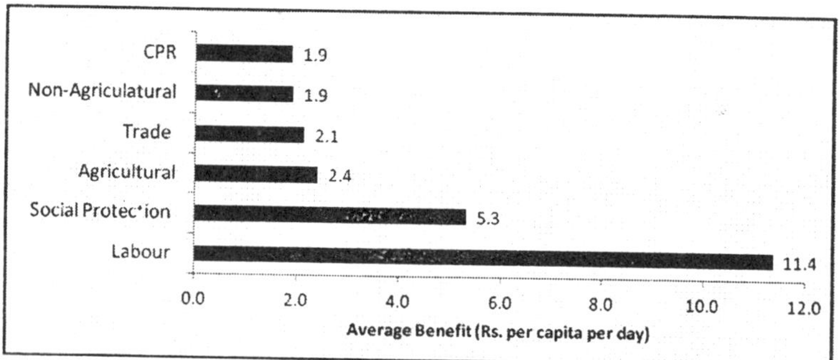

Fig. 5.10: Average Income (Rs. Per Capita Per Day) from different form of Entitlements of Sample Households

Source: Field Survey 2012-13.

The relative importance of different entitlements is also understood from the distribution of households by the share of income from different sources. Higher share of income is generated by the households from selling their labour power and from social protection benefits (Table 5.3).

5.4 Distribution of Income of the Households

Total income of the household is composed of the earnings from different entitlements. Distribution of the households by level of per capita per day income (PCPDI) is depicted in Figure 5.11. Among 600 sample households, the PCPDI of 0.8 per cent households was found to be very low (less than Rs. 10). The PCPDI of 27.3 per cent households lies between

Table 5.3: Distributions of Sample Households by Share of Income from different Entitlements

Share of Income	*Labour*	*Agriculture production*	*Production other than agriculture*	*Trade*	*Common Property Resource*	*Social Protection Benefits*
0	11	35	56	81	27	0
0.1 to 10	4	31	23	4	49	9
10.1 to 20	8	19	7	3	11	31
20.1 to 30	9	7	4	2	6	36
30.1 to 40	12	4	4	3	4	16
40.1 to 50	14	1	2	3	1	6
50.1 to 60	12	2	1	1	0	1
60.1 to 70	15	1	2	1	0	0
70.1 to 80	9	0	0	1	0	0
80.1 to 90	6	0	1	1	0	0
90.1 to 100	2	0	0	1	0	0
Total HHs	100	100	100	100	100	100

Source: Field Survey 2012-13.

Rs. 10.1 and Rs. 18 and of another 46.5 per cent households it lies between Rs. 18.1 and Rs. 29. Only 25 per cent households earned more than Rs. 29 per capita per day (Figure 5.11a). That is, there are 28.2 per cent sample households with PCPDI less than Rs. 18 (equivalent expenditure of food security line)[3] and nearly 75 per cent households with PCDI less than Rs. 29 (equivalent expenditure of poverty line)[4] (Figure 5.11b).

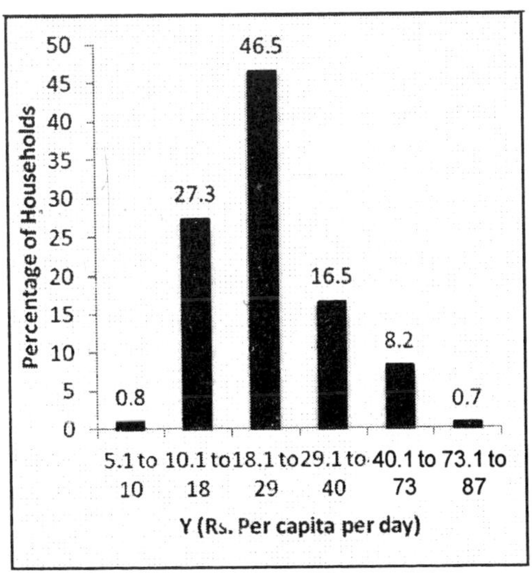

Fig. 5.11a: Distribution of HHs by Income Level (per capita per day)

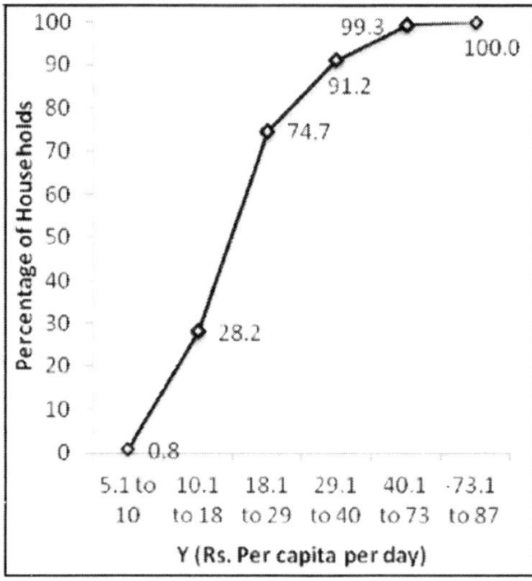

Fig. 5.11b: Cumulative Distribution of HHs by Income Level (per capita per day)

Source: Field survey 2012-13.

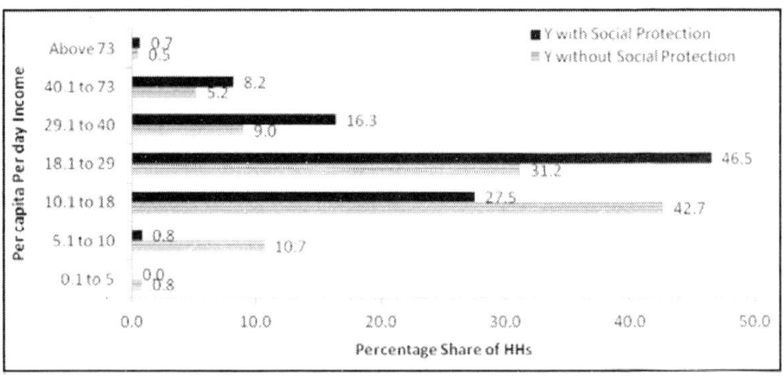

Fig. 5.12: Distribution of the Sample Households by per Capita Per Day Income with and without Social Protection Benefits

Source: Field Survey 2012-13.

The contribution of social protection benefits to the household's income is realized by comparing between the income without social protection benefits (SPBs) and income with social protection benefits. The average PCPDI of 600 sample households was estimated to be

Rs. 19.7 without SPBs and Rs. 25.0 with SPBs. That is, the SPBs increased the average PCPDI of these households to the extent of 21.2 per cent. When the SPBs are added with income, the PCPDI of the households with lower ranges Rs. 0.1 to 5, Rs. 5.1 to 10 and Rs. 10.1 to 18 have declined 0.8, 9.9 and 15.2 percentage points respectively. The SPBs uplift the households to the upper income groups (Figure 5.12). Hence, the percentage share of the households with upper income groups, e.g., Rs. 18.1 to 29, Rs. 29.1 to 40 and Rs. 40.1 to 73 have increased to the extent of 15.3 percentage points, 7.3 percentage points and 3 percentage points (Table 5.4).

Table 5.4: Distribution of Sample Households by PCPDI with SPBs and without SPBs

PCPDI (in Rs.)	*Income without SPBs*		*Income with SPBs*		*Change# of % of HH*
	Number of HHs	*% of HHs*	*Number of HHs*	*% of HH*	
0.1 to 5	5	0.8	0	0.0	-0.8
5.1 to 10	64	10.7	5	0.8	-9.9
10.1 to 18	256	42.7	165	27.5	-15.2
18.1 to 29	187	31.2	279	46.5	15.3
29.1 to 40	54	9.0	98	16.3	7.3
40.1 to 73	31	5.2	49	8.2	3
Above 73	3	0.5	4	0.7	0.2
Total	600	100	600	100	0

Note: # Change of % share of households (HHs) is calculated by subtracting % share of HHs without SPBs from % share of HHs with SPBs.

Source: Field Survey 2012-13.

The effect of SPBs on income level of the households is significant or not is tested statistically. The difference between the incomes of the households without SPBs and with SPBs is tested by applying *t*-test. The test results are summarized in Table 5.5. The result of *t*-test indicates that PCPDI with SPBs is significantly higher than the PCPDI without SPBs. That is, the SPBs significantly affect the income of the households and also corresponding entitlements of the households.

Table 5.5: Result of the Test of the difference between PCPDI without SPBs (X_1) and PCPDI with SPBs (X_2) of the Sample Households

Indicators	*Values*	*F-Test*	*t-test*
		$H_2 : \sigma_1^2 = \sigma_2^2$ $(H_1 : \sigma_1^2 \neq \sigma_2^2)$	$H_0 : \mu_1 = \mu_2$ $(H_1 : \mu_1 < \mu_2)$
m_1	19.69	$F = (s_1^2 / s_2^2) / (\sigma_1^2 / \sigma_2^2)$ = 0.93	$t_{n1} + n_2 = \frac{m_1 - m_2}{S\sqrt{\left(\frac{1}{n_1} + \frac{1}{n_2}\right)}} = -8.28$ Where, S = $\left[(n_1 - 1)s_1^2 + (n_2 - 1)s_2^2\right] / (n_1 - n_2 - 2)$
m_2	25.01		
s_1^2	119.23	Table Value of F = 0.874 (p value one tail is 0.193)	Table Value of t = 1.647 (p value one tail = 0.000)
s_2^2	127.98		
N_1	600	H_0 is not rejected	H_0 is rejected at 1% level
N_2	600		
df		599,599	1198

Notes: X_1 and X_2 denote PCPDI of 600 sample households without SPBs and with SPBs respectively. The Corresponding means are m_1 and m_2 and variances are s_1^2 and s_2^2.

Source: Author's calculation.

Notes

1. Food grains productivity in West Bengal as whole is 12 kg per decimal in 2012-13 whereas the average productivity of our sample cultivating households is 8 kg per decimal in 2012-13.
2. Here we assume 300 days of employment during a year to be the standard days of employment for a typical worker.
3. Estimated food security line for rural West Bengal is Rs. 17.59 in 2012-13.
4. Estimated poverty line for rural West Bengal is Rs. 28.81 in 2012-13.

6
Status of Food Security of the Poor Households
The Role of Social Protection Programmes

6.1 Introduction

What constitutes food security has gone through two phases of understanding and definition. In the 1970s, food security was understood as the 'availability at all times of adequate world food supply of basic foodstuffs.....' (UN, 1975). But the 1981 publication of Amartya Sen's '*Poverty and Famines: An Essay on Entitlement and Deprivation*' brought forward a new understanding of the problem of hunger or food security. Rather than just 'availability' of food, Sen emphasized 'access' to food through what he called 'entitlements'—a combination of what one can produce, exchange in the market plus state or other socially provided supplies. Sen postulated that availability or supply of food does not itself create entitlement for food. What an individual or household can consume or access depends on the individual's or household's entitlement. Entitlement draws attention to the conditions under which people access food, whether from direct production (or exchange with nature), market exchange (income from either goods produced or wage labour) and social security measures.

> Entitlements point to the fact that hunger is situated within poverty, rather associated with extreme poverty, as a result of which households and individuals do not have adequate entitlements to food. Thus, the elimination of hunger is the first landmark in reducing poverty (Sen, 1981).

Entitlements also draw attention to the rules that govern intra-household allocation, as a result of which women and girls may face hunger or deprivation even though they are part of households whose general entitlements are sufficient. Food, of course, is not an end in itself. Food is consumed for nutrition. Instead of focusing attention on commodity, one can look at the objective for which food is consumed, that is providing nutrition for the body. The purpose of nutrition is not just to survive, but to lead a healthy and meaningful life to be in a state one wants to be (well-being) and to do various things one wants to do.

All of the above changes in understanding and context meant that 20 years after the 1975 World Food Summit, there was a substantial shift in understanding the meaning of food security. From 1975 emphasizing on adequate food supply, the 1995 World Food Summit declared:

> '.....food security, at the individual, household, national, regional and global levels.....exists when all people at all times, have physical and economic access to sufficient, safe and nutritious food to meet their dietary needs and food preferences for an active and healthy life' (FAO, 1996).

Food security is a combination of access to food and its absorption by the body, which depends on a number of non-food factors such as sanitation, access to clean drinking water, access to health facilities, and so on. The outcome of food security can be taken to be the nutritional status of individual, with the understanding that food intake is the basic, though not the only factor that affects nutritional status.

In this brief background, the present chapter seeks to explore the status of food security of the households and examine the impact of entitlements on the status of food security.

Remaining of this chapter is organized as follows. Section 2 analyses the basic concept of food security and entitlement of the household. Section 3 presents the theoretical framework to examine the impact of social protection along with other entitlements on the status of food security of the households. Section 4 analyses the empirical findings regarding status of food security of the households. Section 5 examines the impact of entitlements on the status of food security of the poor households on the basis of an empirical model.

6.2 Household's Entitlement and Food Security: Basic Concepts

On the basis of the concept of poverty of A.K. Sen, the condition of food insecurity of the households is illustrated as follows: Let X be the set of all non-negative vectors of all commodities, representing the amounts of n commodities and P is the n-vector prices faced by the person. Y is the power set of X. By mapping from X to Y, we mean the correspondence *f* (.) which associates with each element of X is one and only one element of Y. The element of Y which corresponds to the element of x of X is called the value of mapping at x and denoted by *f*(x)

Let x be the vector of commodities (including labour power) that a household owns, i.e., the *endowment set* of the household and *E*(x) is the set of vectors any one of which the household can acquire by exchanging x, i.e., the *exchange entitlement set* of the households. And

$$E(x)=\{y:\in X \,\&\, py \leq px\}$$

The function *E* (.) from X to Y is the '*exchange entitlement mapping*' or E-mapping of the households.

Let, F is the set of commodity vectors that satisfy the specific minimum food requirements of the household and I is the set of commodity vector that do not satisfy the specific minimum food requirements, *i.e.*, food insecurity set. Where, $F \subseteq X$ and $I \subseteq F$ and $E(x) \cap F = I$

The food insecurity set I of ownership vectors consists of those vectors x in X such that exchange entitlement set *E*(*x*) contains the vector that do not satisfy the minimum food requirements. Obviously, I depends on F and E-mapping, *i.e.*,

$$I=\{x:x \in X \,\&\, E(x) \cap F = I\}$$

6.3 Utility Maximization Model for Food Security in Relation to Entitlement

A Houschold Utility Maximisation Model is called for to analyse the food security in relation to entitlement. It is based on a simple non-separable household model where market is imperfect (Singh *et al.* 1986; Sadoulet and de Janvry 1995).

Consider the utility function of a household (following Klein and Rubin, 1948)[1]

$$U=\alpha_F \log\left(C_F - F\right)+\alpha_{NF} \log\left(C_{NF} - Z\right) \qquad (1)$$

with the domain $C_F > F$, $C_{NF} > Z$.

Where, C_F = consumption of food items, C_{NF} = consumption of non-food items,

F and Z are interpreted as minimum subsistence quantities and are positive, α's are also positive. Apply the positive monotonic transformation $U' = U(\alpha_F + \alpha_{NF})$, obtain

$$U' = \beta_F log(C_F - F) + \beta_{NF} \log(C_{NF} - Z) \quad \text{... (2)}$$

The coefficients β_F and β_{NF} (where $\beta_F + \beta_{NF} = 1$) are called "share" parameters.

The household is assumed to maximize utility subject to constraints imposed by different types of entitlements—Production Entitlement, Labour Entitlement, Trade Entitlement, and Transfer Entitlement (i.e., Social Protection from Government).

(A) Production Constraints

The production of the household represents the constraint on the household's consumption possibilities. Farm output (Q_F) depends on the gross crop area (T_F) that includes household land (T^h) and lease in land (T^r), labour (L_F) and a vector of purchased input factors (X_F). The production function is assumed to be strictly concave. The Production constraint can be specified as (Sadoulet and de Janvry, 1995; Woldehanna, 2000):

Farm Production Function $Q_F = Q_F(T_F, L_F, X_F)$ ... (3)

Similarly,

Non-Farm Production Function $Q_{NF} = Q_{NF}(I_{NF}, L_{NF}, X_{NF})$ ... (4)

Where, Non-Farm output (Q_{NF}) depends on the investment in non-farm production (I_{NF}), labour (L_{NF}) and a vector of purchased input factors (X_{NF}).

(B) Labour Constraint

The household allocates its total labour endowment (L) in to two categories—household labours and wage labours. The household labours are used in the farm production (L_F) as well as non-farm production (L_{NF})

and trade activities (L_T). Wage labours sell to the other (Ls). Ls includes both casual labour as well as regular employment.

Hence, $L = L_F + L_{NF} + L_T + L_s$ ... (5)

(C) Trade Constraint

The income from trading of the household also represents the constraint on the household's consumption possibilities. Volume of the Trade (V) depends on the labours allocated for trade activities (L_T), investment in trade activities (I_T) and a vector of purchased input factors (X_T). *That is,*

$$V = V(L_T, I_T, X_T) \quad \text{... (6)}$$

(D) Social Protection

Benefits from social protection programmes are also constraints on the household's consumption possibilities. Benefits from social protection programmes (S) depend on the household's membership of the programmes and benefits enjoyed from these programmes. That is

$$S = \sum_{i=1}^{m} SPB_i \quad \text{... (7)}$$

Where, m is the numbers of programmes in which the household has membership and SPB is the social protection benefits of ith programme.

Consumption is constrained by household income, composed of exchange entitlement mapping relating to: (a) labour income, which is the sum of earnings of all household members by selling their labour power from both farm as well as non-farm activities; (b) income from production; (c) income from trade activities; (d) and actual benefits received from Social Protection Programmes.

The resulting budget constraint is:

$$\underbrace{\{P_F Q_F(T_F, L_F, X_F) - rT^r - P_{XF} X_F\}}_{\textit{Farm Profit } (\Pi_F)} + \underbrace{\{P_{NF} Q_{NF}(I_{NF}, L_{NF}, X_{NF}) - RI_{NF-} P_{NF} X_{NF}\}}_{\textit{Non-farm Profit } (\Pi_{NF})} +$$

$$\underbrace{\{V(L_T, X_T) - P_{XT} X_T\}}_{\textit{Trade Profit } (\Pi_T)} + wL_s + S = P_F C_F + P_{NF} C_{NF} \quad \text{... (8)}$$

Where, P_i are prices (i = F for farm and NF for non-farm); w is the wage.

That is,

$$Y = P_F C_F + P_{NF} C_{NF} \qquad ...(9)$$

The optimal solution is characterized by the Kuhn-Tucker conditions, which are the first-order conditions for maximizing the Lagrange function:

$$\xi = \beta_F log(C_F - F) + \beta_{NF} log(C_{NF} - Z) + \lambda [\{P_F Q_F(T_P, L_P, X_P) - rT - P_{XF} X_F\} + \{P_{NF} Q_{NF}(I_{NF}, L_{NF}, X_{NF}) - RI_{NF-} P_{NF} X_{NF}\} + \{V(L_T, X_T) - P_{XT} X_T\} + wL_s + S - P_F C_F - P_{NF} C_{NF}] \qquad ... (10)$$

$$\frac{\partial \xi}{\partial C_F} = \frac{\beta_F}{C_F - F} - \lambda P_F = 0 \qquad ... (11)$$

$$\frac{\partial \xi}{\partial C_{NF}} = \frac{\beta_{NF}}{C_{NF} - Z} - \lambda P_{NF} = 0 \qquad ... (12)$$

$$\frac{\partial \xi}{\partial \lambda} = Y - P_F Q_F - P_{NF} Q_{NF} = 0 \qquad ... (13)$$

Solving Equation (11) to (13) for optimal quantities gives the demand functions of C_F and C_{NF}

$$C_F = F + \frac{\beta_F}{P_F}(Y - P_F F - P_{NF} Z) \qquad ... (14)$$

$$C_{NF} = Z + \frac{\beta_{NF}}{P_{NF}}(Y - P_F F - P_{NF} Z) \qquad ... (15)$$

Multiplying the equation (14) by P_F and (15) by P_{NF} gives the expenditure functions

$$P_F C_F = P_F FZ + \beta_F (Y - P_F F - P_{NF} Z) \qquad ... (16)$$

$$P_{NF} C_{NF} = P_{NF} Z + \beta_{NF} (Y - P_F F - P_{NF} Z) \qquad ... (17)$$

which are linear in income and prices.

By rearranging the terms of equation (16) may be expressed as

$$P_F C_F = P_F F = fs = \beta_F (Y - P_F F - P_{NF} Z)$$

The household is food secured (as $fs > 0$) if $P_F C_F > P_F F$, otherwise, food insecure. Along with the prices of food (P_F) and non-food (P_{NF}) the food security of the household depends on the share parameter (β_F) and income of the household. And the income of the household is the outcome of the exchange entitlement mapping and the endowment set of the household.

6.4 Status of Food Security of the Sample Households

Estimation of Food Insecurity Line and the Measurement of Food Insecurity

In the present study the food insecurity line is estimated from the poverty line following the guideline of the Planning Commission of India (2009). They estimated the separate poverty lines in each state for rural and urban areas in 2011-12. For West Bengal, the estimated Rural Poverty Line was Rs. 783 in 2011-12 (Planning Commission of India 2013). To find out the food insecurity line, the rural state poverty line was updated first with Consumer Price Index for Rural (CPI-R)[2] West Bengal. The value became Rs. 864.35 in 2012-13. Poverty line was estimated upon a combination of several items like food, clothing, footwear, durables, education and institutional health expenditure, etc. The food insecurity line that corresponds to above poverty line has been estimated from NSSO (2011-12) budget share of food items around Poverty Line Class. The budget share was estimated to be 60.39 per cent in 2011-12 and its equivalent value Rs. 472.80 is considered as the food insecurity line. This value was updated with CPI for food expenditure for Rural West Bengal[3]. It was thus Rs. 527.68 in 2012-13. That is, if a person has spent at least Rs. 527.68 on food consumption he can secure his minimum food requirement. In that case on an average the household's per capita per day consumption expenditure on food should be Rs. 17.59.

The status of food insecurity is measured by using the methodology of Foster, Greer and Therbecke (1984):

$$FI_\alpha = \frac{1}{N}\sum_{i=1}^{q}\left(\frac{Z_F - F_i}{Z_F}\right)^\alpha ; \ \alpha=0,\ 1, \text{ and } 2$$

where, Z_F is the food security line (here Rs. 17.59), E_i is the per capita per day food expenditure of the *i-th* household, N is the total number of individuals in the population, q is the number of poor individuals having food expenditure less than Z_F and α is a measure of sensitivity.

If, $\alpha = 0$, FI_0 implies the Incidence of Food Insecurity (FI)
$\alpha = 1$, FI_1 (= Food Insecurity Gap (FIG)) implies the depth of food insecurity
and $\alpha = 2$, FI_2 (= Square Food Insecurity Gap (SFIG)) implies the severity of food insecurity

The measure of food insecurity (FF_α) can be decomposed into sub-groups as

$$FI_\alpha = \sum_{k=1}^{k} \left(\frac{N_k}{N}\right)^\alpha FI_{\alpha k}; \alpha = 0, 1, \text{and } 2$$

Where, N_k/N and FI_α are the *k-th* subgroups' population share and food insecurity measure respectively. A subgroup food insecurity risk (R) is the ratio of its share of food insecurity to its share of population (Pathak and Mishra, 2013):

$$R_K = \frac{N_k FI_{\alpha k} / NFI_\alpha}{N_k / N} = \frac{FI_{\alpha k}}{FI_\alpha}$$

Food Consumption

Actually in our sample, as we have noted earlier, all 600 sample households are BPL category households[4]. Among the 600 households, the estimated poor households on the basis of per capita monthly expenditure were 490. The distribution of per capita per day food expenditure of 600 sample households is shown in Figure 6.1. The average food expenditure (per capita per day) of the households was Rs. 16.57 which was substantially low as compared to the food security line of Rs. 17.59. Among 600 sample households, 390 households were food insecure and the rest 210 were food secure. The entitlement of 390 households was not sufficient to command the minimum requirement of food for food security.

The food consumption function of the households is estimated where per capita per day food consumption expenditure (C) is the function of per capita per day income (Y) (Figure 6.2). From the estimated consumption, it is revealed that the marginal propensity to food consume

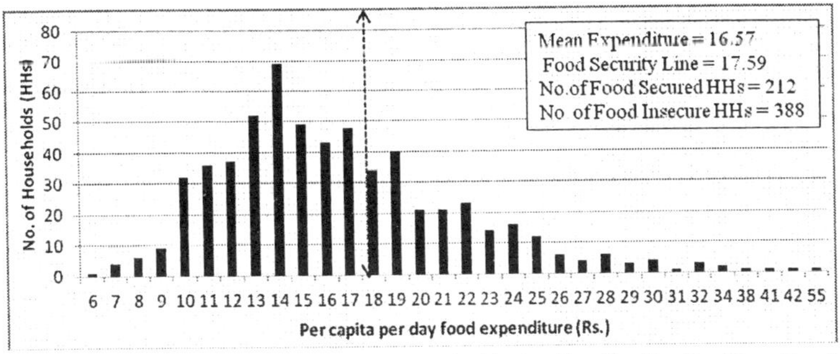

Fig. 6.1: Distributions of Sample Households by Per Capita Per Day Food Expenditure

Source: Field Survey 2012-13.

(MPC) is relatively low (0.25). That is, for 1 per cent increase of per capita per day income across households per capita per day food consumption is increased by 0.25 per cent only. This implies that income responsiveness on food consumption is relatively low for the poor households.

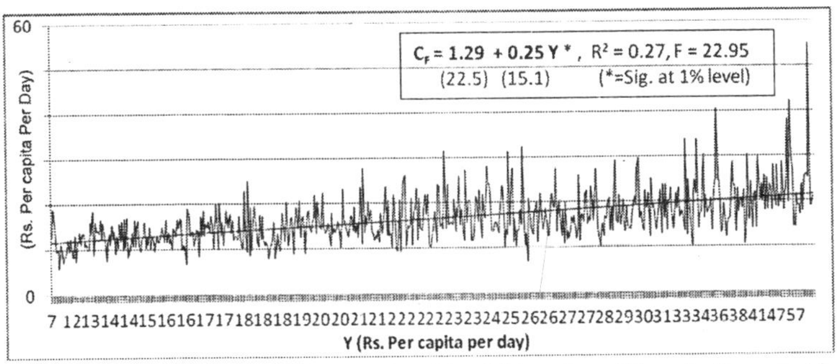

Fig. 6.2: Estimation of the Consumption (Food) Function of Sample Households

Source: Field Survey 2012-13.

Status of Food Insecurity of Sample Households by Caste

Number of food insecure households (FISH) widely varies across social castes (Figure 6.3). Food insecure households are relatively high for SCs (72.4% of total SC households). The status of food security of sample households is shown in Table 6.1. On the whole, 64.7 per cent households were food insecure. Incidence of food insecurity was also high for SCs, 80.2 per cent of the SC people were food insecure, followed by STs, OBC and GEN. For the entire sample households, the incidence of food insecurity was 71.8 per cent. Food insecurity gap (FIG) and squared food insecurity gap (SFIG) are also high for the SCs and STs (Figure 6.4). The population share for SCs and STs is 32.8 per cent and 27.3 per cent

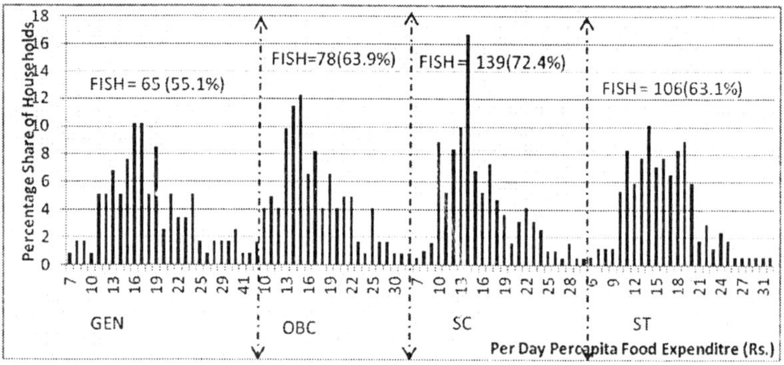

Fig. 6.3: Distributions of Sample Households by Per Capita Per Day Food Expenditure for GEN, OBCs, SCs and STs

Source: Field Survey 2012-13.

respectively whereas their share of food insecurity was 35.9 per cent and 28 per cent respectively (Figure 6.5). Poverty risk was the highest for SCs followed by STs, other backward castes (OBCs) and GEN.

Table 6.1: Status of Food Insecurity of Sample Households by Caste

	GEN	*OBC*	*SC*	*ST*	*Total*
Total Households	118	122	192	168	600
Food Insecure HHs (%)	55.1	63.9	72.4	63.1	64.7
Number of Population	557	636	980	814	2987
Incidence of Food Insecurity (%)	62.5	69.2	80.2	70.1	71.8
Food Insecurity Gap (%)	13.7	15.6	20.7	18.3	17.7
Squared Food Insecurity Gap (%)	4.4	4.7	6.7	6.3	5.7
Share of Population (%)	18.6	21.3	32.8	27.3	100
Share of Food Insecurity (%)	16.2	20.5	36.6	26.6	100
Decomposition of Food Insecurity	11.7	14.7	26.3	19.1	71.8

Source: Author's Estimation on the basis of Field Survey 2012-13.

Status of Food Insecurity in Jangal Mahal vis-à-vis Non-Jangal Mahal

Jangal Mahal region[5] of Paschim Medinipur, Bankura and Purulia districts of West Bengal are the most backward and historically deprived regions. The situation worsens during 2009 to 2011 and the livelihood of the

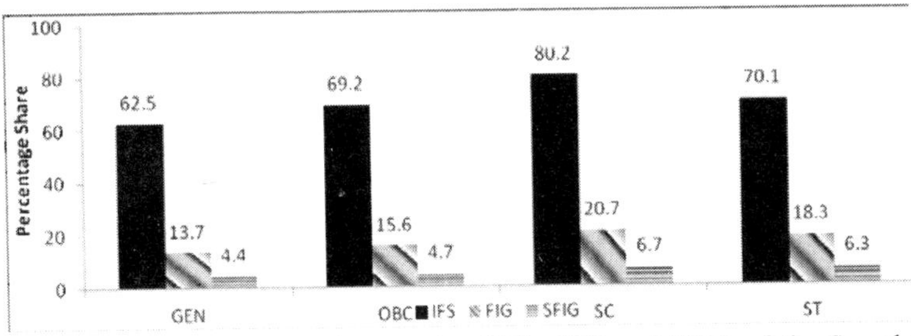

Fig. 6.4: Incidence of Food Insecurity (IFS), FIG and SFIG of the Sample Households Across Castes

Source: Author's Estimation on the basis of Field Survey 2012-13.

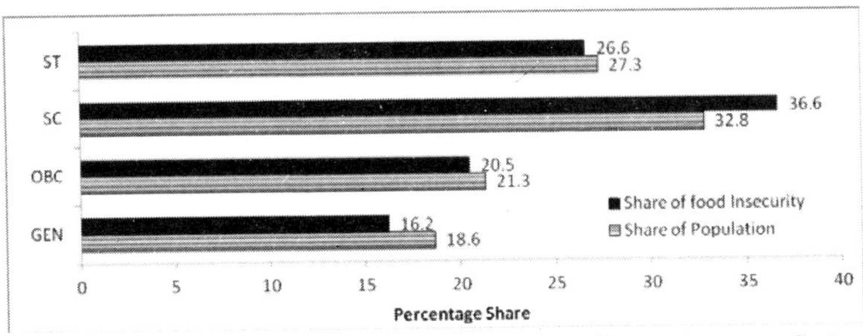

Fig. 6.5: Relative Share of Population and Share of Food Insecurity across Castes.

Source: Author's Estimation on the basis of Field Survey 2012-13.

people in Maoist affected area in the Jangal Mahal was deteriorating. That was witnessed from food security status of the people in this region in 2012-13. After 2011, to restore the livelihood of the rural poor, West Bengal State Government has extended a number of social protection programmes. But still now this region persists with very high level of food insecurity and poverty. The backward region, our study area, is classified into two sub regions—one is Jangal Mahal and another is Non-Jangal Mahal. Among 600 sample households—250 households are located in Jangal Mahal and the rest 350 households in Non-Jangal Mahal region. The average per capita per day food expenditure in Non-Jangal Mahal area was higher than that of Jangal Mahal area. To analyse whether this difference is significant or not, we have conducted the test of mean difference by *t*-test. The result of *t*-test is summarized in Table 6.2 and it was found that the per capita food expenditure in the Jangal Mahal region is significantly higher than that of Non-Jangal Mahal region. Most of the villages in the Jangal Mahal region are drought prone and more backward than Non-Jangal Mahal region; hence their income substantially differs from one region to other.

Table 6.2: Results of the Test of the difference of Per Capita Per Day Food Expenditure of the Sample Households in Non-Jangal Mahal (X_1) and Jangal Mahal Regions (X_2)

Indicators	*Values*	*F-Test*	*t-test*
		$H_0:\sigma_1^2=\sigma_2^2$ $\left(H_1:\sigma_1^2>\sigma_2^2\right)$	$H_0:\mu_1=\mu_2$ $\left(H_1:\mu_1>\mu_2\right)$
m_1	17.14	$F=\left(s_1^2/s_2^2\right)/\left(\sigma_1^2/\sigma_2^2\right)$ = 2.12	$n_1 = t_{n1}+n_2=\frac{m_1-m_2}{\sqrt{\left(\frac{s_1^2}{n_1}+\frac{s_1^2}{n_2}\right)}}$ Has upper α-point approximately the same as (w_1 t α, n_1–1 + w_2 t α, n_2–1)/ (w_1 + w_2) = 3.25
m_2	15.77		
s_1^2	37.08	Table Value of F = 1.21 (p value one tail is 0.000)	Table Value of t = 1.647 (p value one tail is 0.114)
s_2^2	17.47		
N_1	350	Calculated value of F > Table Value of F, i.e., H_0 is rejected	Calculated value of t > Table Value of t, i.e., H_0 is rejected
N_2	250		
df		249, 349	597

Notes: X_1 denotes PCPD Food Expenditure of 350 sample households of Non-Jangal Mahal and X_2 denotes PCPD Food Expenditure of 250 sample households of Jangal Mahal. The Corresponding means are m_1 and m_2 and variances are s_1^2 and s_2^2.

Source: Author's calculation.

The status of food security in these two regions is estimated on the basis of per capita food expenditure. The status of food insecurity in the Jangal Mahal region in comparison to the Non-Jangal Mahal region is shown in Table 6.3. The situation of food insecurity is significantly high in the Jangal Mahal region than that of Non-Jangal Mahal region. The percentage share of food insecure households and incidence of food insecurity (FIS) in Non-Jangal Mahal region were 60.0 and 67.6 respectively. Whereas in the Jangal Mahal region 71.2 per cent were food insecure households and the incidence of food insecurity was 77.6. Irrespective of all social castes the situation of food insecurity in Jangal Mahal was worse than the situation in Non-Jangal Mahal. The situation was worst for OBCs and SCs in Jangal Mahal. The FIS in Jangal Mahal for SCs and OBCs were 88.0 per cent and 77.5 per cent respectively in comparison to 76.3 per cent and 55.3 per cent in Non-Jangal Mahal. In entire Jangal Mahal region, the State Government has extended the quasi-universal access of subsidized foodgrains[6] through PDS. These benefits are found to be crucial for the people in Jangal Mahal region but not enough to overcome their food insecurity. Other SPBs were also extended in this region and their outcomes were also limited to overcome food insecurity.

Table 6.3: Status of Food Insecurity in Jangal Mahal and Non-Jangal Mahal Regions by Social Castes

	Jangal Mahal Region					*Non Jangal Mahal Region*				
	GEN	*OBC*	*SC*	*ST*	*Total*	*GEN*	*OBC*	*SC*	*ST*	*Total*
Total Households	38	73	63	76	250	81	48	129	92	350
FIS HHs (%)	63.2	72.6	81.0	65.8	71.2	51.9	50.0	68.2	60.9	60.0
FIS	69.5	77.5	88.0	72.4	77.6	59.5	55.3	76.3	68.3	67.6
FIG	14.1	16.8	23.7	17.5	18.4	13.8	13.3	19.2	19.0	17.1
SFIG	4.6	5.1	7.8	5.8	5.9	4.4	3.7	6.2	6.7	5.6

Source: Author's Estimation on the basis of Field Survey 2012-13.

Status of Food Insecurity in Presence and Absence of SPBs

The role of social protection programmes on food security is analyzed by comparing the status of food security in presence of PDS benefits (as given in Table 6.1) with the status of food security in absence of PDS benefits (as in Table 6.4). Figure 6.6 depicts the situation of food insecurity of the sample households with PDS benefits and in absence of PDS benefits. The state of food insecurity is worsening in absence of PDS benefits. The percentage share of food insecure households decreased from 76.7 per cent in absence of PDS benefits to 64.7 per cent in presence of PDS benefits and the incidence of food insecurity has decreased from 81.4 per cent to 71.8 per cent. FIG and SFIG of the sample households have also decreased. That is, the benefits from PDS have reduced food insecurity of 12 per cent sample households and 10 per cent sample people. The extent of the benefit of social protection floor in the backward region has only partially succeeded to overcome food insecurity of the BPL households.

Table 6.4: Status of Food Insecurity of Sample Households by Caste in the Absence of PDS Benefits

	GEN	*OBC*	*SC*	*ST*	*Total*
Total Households	118	122	192	168	600
Food Insecure HHs (%)	66.9	75.4	79.2	81.5	76.7
Number of Population	557	636	980	814	2987
Incidence of Food Insecurity (%)	72.7	78.9	84.9	85.1	81.4
Food Insecurity Gap (%)	18.7	23.9	26.8	26.1	24.5
Squared Food Insecurity Gap (%)	6.4	8.5	9.9	10.2	9.0
Share of Population (%)	18.6	21.3	32.8	27.3	100
Share of Food Insecurity (%)	16.7	20.6	34.2	28.5	100
Decomposition of Food Insecurity	0.14	0.17	0.28	0.23	0.81

Source: Author's Estimation on the basis of Field Survey 2012-13.

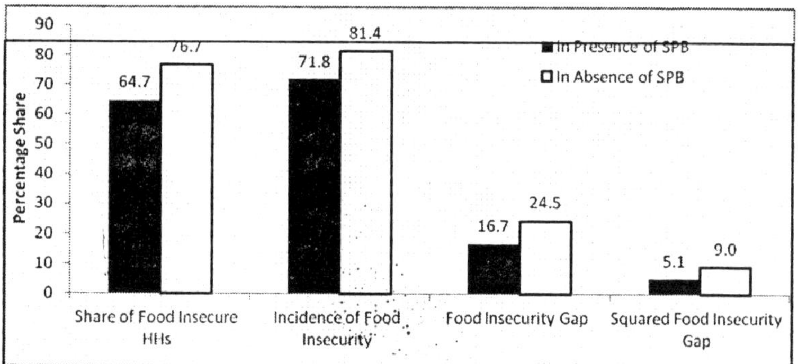

Fig. 6.6: Status of Food Insecurity among the Sample Households in Presence and Absence of PDS Benefits

Source: Author's Estimation on the basis of Field Survey 2012-13.

6.5 Econometric Model to Analyse Food Insecurity

The Framework of the Model

Heckman selection model (two-step) is used to analyze the effect of social protection benefits along with other entitlements of the households on the status of food insecurity of the households.

Consider a model with two variables d_i and y_i which linearly depend on observable independent variables x_i and z_i, respectively

$$d_i = z_i y + v_i$$
$$y_i = x_i \beta + \varepsilon_i$$

The error terms v_i and ε_i are independently (across observations) and jointly normally distributed with covariance $\rho\delta_{\varepsilon}$.

In the present case d_i indicates whether *i-th* household is food insecure or not and y_i indicates the food insecurity gap of the *i-th* household. We only observe an indicator d_i when the latent variable d_i* (food consumption expenditure) is less than the expenditure of food insecurity line (Rs. 17.59 per capita per day). Similarly, the value of the variable $y_i = y_i^*$ is only observed if the indicator is 1:

$$d_i = 1 \text{ if } d_i^* < \text{Rs. } 17.59$$
$$0 \text{ otherwise}$$
$$y_i = y_i^* \text{ if } d_i = 1$$
$$\text{n.a. otherwise}$$

Heckman's (1979) two-step procedure involves the estimation of a standard probit and linear regression model[7]. The two step procedure draws on the conditional ($d_i = 1$) mean

$$E(y_i/x_i, z_i) = E(y_i^*/d_i=1, x_i, z_i) = x_i\beta + \rho\delta_{\varepsilon}[\phi(z_i\gamma)/\psi(z_i\gamma)]$$
$$= x_i\beta + \rho\delta_{\varepsilon}\lambda(z_i\gamma)$$

of the fully observed y's.

Step 1 is the consistent estimation of γ *by ML using the full set of observation in the standard probit model*

$$d_i^* = z_i\gamma + v_i \qquad \textit{(First Equation)}$$
$$di = 1 \text{ if } i\text{-th household is food insecure, 0 otherwise}$$

We can use this and consistently estimate the Inverse Mills Ratio $\lambda_i = \phi(z_i\gamma)/\psi(z_i\gamma)$ for all observations.

Step 2 is the estimation of the regression equation with the Inverse Mills Ratio as an additional variable

$$y_i^* = x_i'\beta + \beta_{\lambda}\lambda_i + u_i \qquad \textit{(Second Equation)}$$

for the sub sample of full observations. Here y_i^* is the food insecurity gap (FIG) of the *i*-th household. The OLS regression yields β, β_{λ}, δ_{ε} and thus the correlation $\rho = \beta_{\lambda}/\delta_{\varepsilon}$.

There is often a practical problem of identification (almost multicolinearity) when the variables in both equations are the same, i.e. $x_i = z_i$ (Vella, 1998). The parameters β and β_λ are theoretically identified by the non-linearity of the Inverse Mills Ratio $\lambda(\cdot)$. It is therefore strongly advised that at least one independent variable of the first equation is not included in the second equation. Here x_i is the matrix of independent variables that includes the characteristics, entitlements and consumption pattern of the households and z_i is the subset of x_i.

The Specification of the Variables in the Model

The variables identified to capture these processes and their specifications are presented in Table 6.5.

To estimate the incidence of food insecurity (FIS) and food insecurity gap (FIG) of the households three sets of independent variables are included in the regression equations: those relating to the control variables measuring household's characteristics; household's entitlements including social protection benefits and those measuring consumption characteristic. Here we include control variables because the personal characteristics may influence the measures of food insecurity.

The household's characteristics are specified by caste of the households (CAST) and location of the households (JMAHAL). Caste variable (CAST) is defined as a dummy variable taking the value 0 if the head of the household belongs to scheduled caste or scheduled tribe, and 1 if otherwise. Upper caste households have better access to physical capital and dynamics of development which help them overcome food insecurity. JMAHAL is also a dummy variable taking the value 1 if the household is located in Jangalmahal region and 0 if it is not. The Jangalmahal region is most backward and the households located in this region are faced with the problems of food security.

The entitlements of the households are specified by average mandays (MDAY) of the households and earnings from agriculture (AGY), labour power (LABY), trade (TRADY), common property resources (CPRY). These entitlements create command over food and the household with higher entitlements is able to overcome food insecurity. The entitlement also includes transfer entitlement from the government in the form of social protection benefits. This entitlement is specified by the foodgrains received from public distribution system (PDSF) and the higher access of PDSF by the households is likely to reduce the food insecurity. The consumption pattern of the households as measured by the share of food expenditure to total expenditure (SFEX) is also relevant for food security. The food insecurity is likely to be reduced if the household increases SFEX.

Table 6.5: Notation, Specification and Descriptive Statistics of Variables Used in Regression Analysis at the household level

Notation	*Specification*	*Mean*	*SD*	*Max*	*Min*
Dependent Variables					
FIS	Whether the household is food insecure or not? Yes = 1, No = 0	0.65	0.48	1.00	0
FIG	Food insecurity gap of the household	0.06	0.31	0.66	-2
Independent Variables					
Households Characteristics					
CAST	Whether the Household belongs to SC or ST community or nor? Yes = 1, No = 0	0.60	0.49	1.00	0
JMAHAL	Is the Household located in the Jangal Mahal Region? Yes = 1, No = 0	0.42	0.49	1.00	0
Entitlement of the Households					
MDAY	Average Mandays (per month) per workers of the Household	13.33	6.94	41.83	0
AGY	Per capita per month income (Rs.) of the households from agricultural production	71.68	108.55	805.56	-104
LABY	Per capita per month income (Rs.) of the household by selling labour power	340.95	304.71	2333.33	0
TRDY	Per capita per month income (Rs.) of the households from trade	63.95	206.31	2222.22	0
CPRY	Per capita per month income (Rs.) of the households from common property resources	26.95	80.81	937.50	0
PDSF	Per capita per month availability of food (Kg.) from PDS	4.70	3.13	18.67	0
Consumption Characteristic					
SFEX	Percentage share of food expenditure to total expenditure of the household	72.50	11.38	98.66	31

In order to get a preliminary understanding of the nature of the relationship between the dependent and independent variables a correlation matrix of all the variables is presented in Table 6.6.

The Empirical Results: Estimation of Heckman Two-Step

The empirical analysis of the relationship between entitlements of the households including social protection benefits and the status of food security is made on the basis of household's utility maximization model as given in Section 6.3. Heckman two-step model helps us to determine the food insecurity and the depth of food insecurity. The two-step model

Table 6.6: Correlation Matrix of Dependent and Independent Variables

	FIS	*FIG*	*CAST*	*JMAHAL*	*MDAY*	*AGLY*	*LABY*	*TRDEY*	*CPRBFT*	*PDSF*	*SFEXP*
FIS	1										
FIG	.773**	1									
CAST	.084*	.160**	1								
JMAHAL	.116**	.124**	-.073	1							
MDAY	-.098*	-.163**	-.154**	.006	1						
AGY	-.232**	-.237**	-.016	-.061	-.022	1					
LABY	-.212**	-.174**	.020	-.139**	.107**	-.066	1				
TRDY	-.192**	-.316**	-.205**	.035	.094*	-.051	-.236**	1			
CPRY	.005	.002	.090*	-.068	.014	-.072	-.085*	-.074	1		
PDSF	-.169**	-.196**	-.010	.504**	.081*	.038	-.106**	.015	.008	1	
SFEXP	-.126**	-.217**	-.021	-.135**	-.064	-.044	-.359**	-.019	-.081*	.008	1

**. Correlation is significant at the 0.01 level (2-tailed).
*. Correlation is significant at the 0.05 level (2-tailed).

is also useful to test selectivity bias (if any). Heckman (1979) noted that the sample selection bias might arise in practice for two reasons. *First,* there may be self-selection by the individuals or data units being investigated. *Second,* sample selection decisions by analysts or data processors operate in much the same fashion as self-selection. There is no selectivity bias if the coefficient of ***Inverse Mills Ratio*** **(λ)** is statistically not significant. The software package ***STATA*** offers the possibility to use the Heckman two-step procedure. The empirical results of Heckman selection model—two-step estimates (regression model with sample selection) are presented in Table 6.7.

In Table 6.7, the lower panel presents the results of probit estimation of food insecurity (FIS) and the upper panel is the estimation of food insecurity gap (FIG) that examines how entitlements of the households impact on food insecurity and depth of food insecurity respectively. The ***Inverse Mills Ratio*** is not significant, that is there is no selectivity bias.

Results indicate that household's entitlements play a role in reducing food insecurity or food insecurity gap. We find statistically significant coefficient of LABY, AGY, TRDY, CPRBFT, PDSF and SFEX for food insecurity and LABY, TRDY, CPRBFT, PDSF and SFEX for food insecurity gap. These variables have the expected negative sign. CAST and JMAHAL are significant only for FIG and they have positive sign.

The result suggests that as the income from labour (LABY), trade (TRDY), common property resources (CPRY), food from public distribution system (PDSF) and share of food expenditure to total expenditure (SFEX) increase the probability of food insecurity (FIS) as

Table 6.7: Heckman Selection Model—Two-Step Estimates Based on STATA

Dependent Variable	*Independent Variables*	*Coef.*	*z*	*P>z*	
FIG(yi)	Constant	0.755	6.64	0.000	Number of
	CAST	0.036	2.74	0.006	Observations = 600
	JMAHAL	0.032	1.65	0.098	
	AGY	0.000	-1.63	0.102	
	LABY	0.000	-3.15	0.002	Censored
	TRDY	0.000	-3.03	0.002	Observations = 212
	CPRY	0.000	-2.75	0.006	
	PDSF	-0.022	-4.63	0.000	Uncensored
	SFEXP	-0.005	-3.87	0.000	Observations = 388
FIS(di)	Constant	6.069	9.09	0.000	Wald chi2(6) = 185.74
	CAST	0.081	0.63	0.531	
	JMAHAL	0.540	3.35	0.001	Prob> chi2 = 0.000
	MDAY	-0.009	-1.00	0.317	
	AGY	-0.005	-6.82	0.000	
	LABY	-0.003	-9.04	0.000	
	TRDY	-0.003	-7.08	0.000	
	CPRY	-0.002	-3.06	0.002	
	PDSF	-0.157	-6.11	0.000	
	SFEXP	-0.049	-7.00	0.000	
	Inverse Mills (λ)	0.027	0.41	0.685	
	rho (ρ)	0.224			
	sigma(δ_{ε})	0.119			

Notes: ** Significant at 1 per cent level, * Significant at 5 per cent level, # Significant at 10 per cent level.

well as depth of food insecurity (FIG) of the household decreases. Increased income from agriculture (AGY) also decreases the probability of food insecurity but not the depth of food insecurity. This implies that for the household with inadequate cultivable land and low productivity (due to drought), the agricultural production is not sufficient to overcome the depth of food insecurity. For insufficient productive assets endowment, labour entitlement is much more important than production entitlement. They are surviving by selling their labour power. But the labour entitlement is also not sufficient for the poor households to cope with the food insecurity. The households who managed to earn by participating in trading increases the overall income and are able to reduce the level of food insecurity. The common property assets also play an important role to overcome food insecurity. The majority of the sample households are located near forest and others are located near river and have accessed the common property resources (CPR). The CPR in the form of Non-timber Forest Products (NTFP) and resources from river (like fish, stone and sand) also play an important role (directly or indirectly) to overcome food insecurity. The benefits of social protection programmes, particularly public distribution system (PDS) has played crucial role for food security of the poor households—higher access of foodgrains from PDS significantly reduces the incidence and depth of food security. The increase of consumption of the sample households in favour of food consumption (SFES) also reduces the incidence as well as depth of food insecurity.

The result also indicates that the household's characteristics like CAST and location (JMAHAL) are significantly associated with food insecurity gap. That is, the depth of food insecurity is significantly high for the households who are belonging to SC and ST communities and located in Jangal Mahal region.

Notes

1. The function is known as the Klein-Rubin or Stone-Geary Utility function.
2. The Central Statistics Office (CSO), Ministry of Statistics and Programme Implementation, introduced a new series of Consumer Price Indices (CPI) on base 2010=100 for all-India and States/UTs separately for rural, urban and combined with effect from January, 2011. CPI for Rural West Bengal increased from 116.30 in 2011-12 to 128.38 in 2012-13.
3. On the basis of NSSO consumption basket we estimated the budget share of food items corresponding to poverty line class. CPI for food in Rural West Bengal increased from 114.34 in 2011-12 to 127.6 in 2012-13.
4. The status of the households whether they have BPL or not was judged by the status of Ration Card which were given to them on the basis of BPL Census 2002. There is some inclusion and exclusion error. The economic condition of the household improved over time as they might be non-poor. Our estimation of poverty on the basis of MPCE helps to identify who are poor and who are not poor.
5. Bankura, Purulia and part of Paschim Medinipur districts are landmarked as Jangal Mahal. More than forty per cent of this region is covered by forest.
6. Provision of getting per head rice for specially identified BPL in Jangalmahal area is 2 KG/week (@ Rs. 2 and for Wheat is 750 gm/week (@ Rs. 3.
7. Cameron and Trivedi (2010, 556–562) and Greene (2012, 873–880) provide good introductions to the Heckman selection model. Adkins and Hill (2008, 395–400) describe the two-step estimator with an application using Stata. Jones (2007, 35–40) illustrates Heckman estimation with an application to health economics.

7
Poverty and Deprivation of the Households in Relation to SPP
A Multidimensional Analysis

7.1 Introduction

Poverty, as a serious problem in most of the developing countries, has attracted a lot of attention among analysts in India too. However, most of the studies in India have tended to focus on poverty at a point of time and their methods of analyses have usually suffered from a uni-dimensional limitation (Filippone *et al.*, 2001), whereby they referred to only a unique proxy of poverty, namely equivalent income or consumption. They have also shared the traditional need to dichotomize the population into the poor and the non-poor by means of the so-called poverty line. Thus in view of Satterthwaite (2001) uni-dimensional poverty measures, at best, can lead only to partial understanding of poverty, and often to unfocused or ineffective poverty reduction programmes. They fail to capture many aspects of deprivation. These limitations of uni-dimensional poverty measures are also compounded by other technical difficulties of income measurement, especially in developing countries that reduce the value of such income-based uni-dimensional poverty results. All these give indications of serious limitations to measures of poverty based on a single monetary indicator of resources (Atkinson and Bourguignon 1982, Maasoumi 1998) and underscore the strong need for a multidimensional approach to poverty analysis that widens the concept of poverty to reflect, for instance, dimensions other than just the monetary one.

The past few years have seen a surge in mainstream multidimensional approaches to poverty and well-being in countries at variable levels of economic development as poverty reduction becomes a shared mandate across the world. In the academic literature, this trend can be seen, for example, in the two volumes on multidimensional poverty edited by Kakwani and Silber (2008) as well as in the proliferation of empirical papers on multidimensional poverty and inequality in traditional journals. In the policy environment, a mainstream interest in multidimensional approaches is exemplified by the Sarkozy Commission's sub-group on Quality of Life measures called the Commission on the Measurement of Economic Performance and Social Progress. At the level of international institutions, since 1997 the World Bank has viewed poverty as a multidimensional phenomenon. The United Nations Development Programme has begun consultations to inform its 2010 report *Re-thinking Human Development* that almost certainly includes a multidimensional measure to complement the Human Development Index (HDI).

The impetus to develop a multidimensional framework has a range of diverse sources, which gives it a distinctive strength and stability. Amartya Sen, Robert Fogel, and other leading social scientists have given a normative account of the need for broader approaches, while Inglehart, Kahnemann, Layard and others have documented the lack of satisfaction resulting from development based on income alone. At the same time, empirical research has clarified the reach and limitations of income-based measures as well as the flaws in foundational assumptions regarding human preferences and behaviours. In practical terms, relevant data sources have expanded greatly, and better computer infrastructure enables better multidimensional analyses. In terms of policy space, the Millennium Development Goals (MDGs) in the year 2000 and Sustainable Development Goal of 2015 drew attention to different interconnected aspects of human suffering and achievement which have formed the basis of campaigns that are ongoing in many countries. National and international interest in multidimensional measures of poverty and well-being is sharpened post-2009, as the economic down turn lends a political incentive to focus on dimensions of well-being that can grow even during economic recession (Alkire and Sarwar 2009).

Poverty in India has traditionally been measured in terms of consumption expenditure. The measurement of poverty remains centred on the ability to spend on goods and services rather than the capability to enjoy valuable beings and doings (Sen 1985) despite methodological revisions, debates (Planning Commission of India 2009; Deaton and Drèze 2002), acknowledgement of the multidimensional nature of poverty and of the need for inclusive growth (Ahluwalia 2011). Poverty is multifaceted and deprivation in per-capita expenditure is an important dimension of poverty. But, perhaps more surprisingly, income poverty docs not accurately proxy other deprivations. Such measures can be used to track national poverty levels; to monitor changes by region, caste, and dimension; and to inform the Below Poverty Line (BPL) targeting methodologies that are commonly non-monetary in nature (Alkire and Seth 2013a).

In the present study we exercise both uni-dimensional as well as multidimensional measure of poverty. The uni-dimensional measure of poverty is based on consumption expenditure. The main dimensions associated with the measurement of multidimensional poverty and deprivations are indentified in Oxford Poverty and Human Development Initiative (OPHI) and Multidimensional Poverty Assessment Tool (MPAT). The OPHI has developed a new international measure of poverty—the Multidimensional Poverty Index or MPI—for the 20th Anniversary edition of the UNDP's flagship Human Development Report.

7.2 Status of Poverty of the Sample Households

7.2.1 Consumption Expenditure

The distribution of per capita per day consumption expenditure (PCPDE) of 600 sample households is shown in Figure 7.1. In our sample, as we noted earlier, all 600 sample households are BPL category households[1]. But on the basis of PCPDE, the estimated poor households were 490 in 2012-13. The average PCPDE of the households was Rs. 23.30 which is substantially low as compare, to poverty line of Rs. 28.80. The entitlements of 490 households are not enough to command the minimum requirement of consumption.

The consumption function of the households is estimated, where per capita per day consumption expenditure (C) is the function of per capita per day income (Y) (Figure 7.2). The estimated consumption reveals that the marginal propensity to consume (MPC) was relatively low (0.56). That is, for 1 per cent increase of Y across households C is increased by 0.56 per cent. This implies that income responsiveness on consumption is not very high for the poor households. Consumption is categorized as food consumption and non-food consumption. The estimated MPC for food consumption was 0.25 (Figure 6.2, Chapter 6) which is lower than the estimated MPC for non-food consumption (Figure 7.3). This implies that the income responsiveness of food consumption is lower than the non-food consumption. The income level of the sample households are

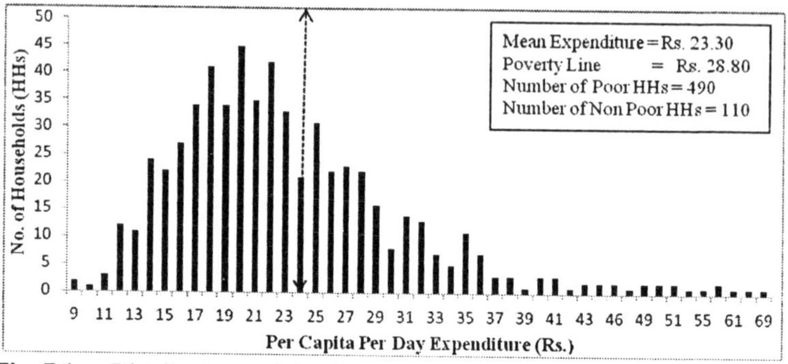

Fig. 7.1: Distributions of the Sample Households by Per Capita Per Day Expenditure

Source: Field Survey 2012-13.

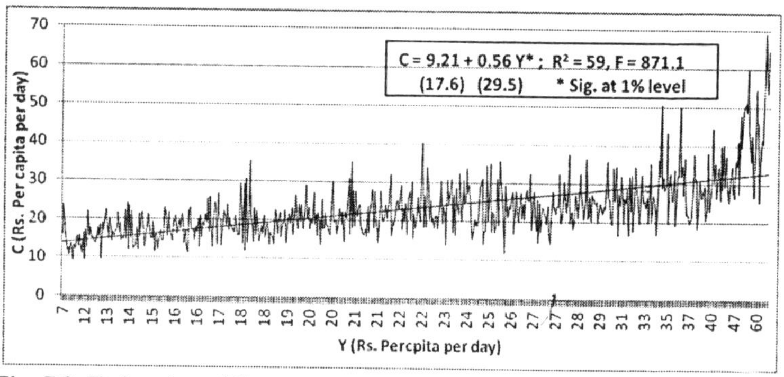

Fig. 7.2: Estimation of Consumption Function of the Sample Households

Source: Field Survey 2012-13.

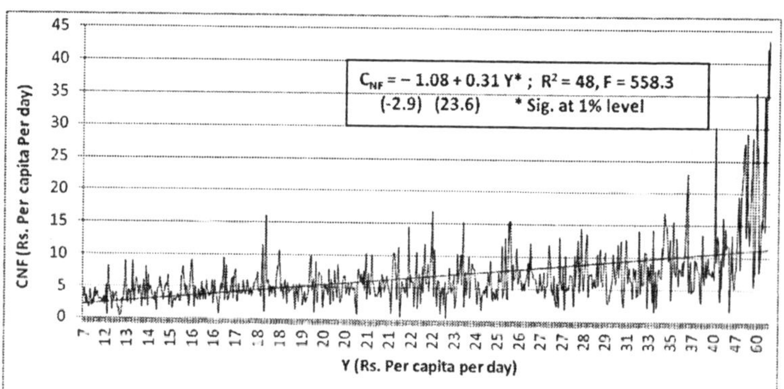

Fig. 7.3: Estimation of Non-Food Consumption Function of the Sample Households

Source: Field Survey 2012-13.

relatively low and a sizable portion (65%) of them are food insecure. Therefore, improvements in income do tend to improve food consumption at higher rate than non-food consumption. But in the present case, the cross section budget study shows the opposite result. The increased income across households increases the consumption, but the increased consumption is little lower for food than the non-food. That is, the outcome of increased income confirms that there has been worsening of nutritional intake in India even though increase in the overall incomes and expenditures were observed. This outcome has been a long-standing puzzle in the Indian context (Deaton and Dreze 2009; Patnaik 2010; Gaiha, Jha, and Kulkarni 2010; and Gaiha *et al.*, 2012). The possible explanation is that the social inequality is influencing individual's consumption and inducing greater consumption of the so-called status goods and in presence of social inequality a status-driven utility function reconciles the conflict (Marjit 2011 & 2013). The status driven utility function induces the households to spend more on non-food consumption than food consumption.

7.2.2 Status of Poverty of Sample Households by Caste

In our study 600 sample households are BPL listed households and that BPL list was prepared by Government of West Bengal on the basis of some socio-economic attributes. But the procedure of inclusion in BPL list raised questions along with political means of unfairness. The estimation of poverty on the basis of MPCE or PCPDE indicates that among 600 sample households 81.7 per cent are poor. That is, nearly 18 per cent are mismatching. During the Field Survey we have observed that there is exclusion (poor but not in the BPL list) and inclusion (non-poor in the BPL list) problems. The inclusion of the household in the BPL list is important because it is the basis of obtaining the benefits of majority of social protection programmes (SPPs).

The status of poverty of sample households is shown in Table 7.1. Poor households were relatively high in case of STs (87.5%), followed by SCs (82.8%) and little lower for OBCs (82.0) (Figure 7.4). The head count ratio (HCR) was also high for STs, SCs and OBCs— 90.4 per cent, 88.5 per cent and 85.2 per cent respectively. For GEN caste households the HCR was quite low (76%). Poverty gap (PGP) and squared poverty gap (SPGP) were also high for the SCs and STs. (Figure 7.5). Among the social castes, the shares of poverty of SCs and STs were higher than the shares of population, whereas for GEN and OBC the shares of population were higher than the shares of poverty (Figure 7.6). That is, the poverty risk was relatively higher for SC/ST than the others.

Table 7.1: Measurement of Poverty of Sample Households: Uni-Dimensional Measure

	GEN	*OBC*	*SC*	*ST*	*Total*
Total Households (HHs)	118	122	192	168	600
Share of Poor HHs	71.2	82.0	82.8	87.5	81.7
Number of Population	557	636	980	814	2987
Incidence of Poverty (HCR)	75.9	85.2	88.5	90.4	86.0
Poverty Gap (PGP)	22.5	24.4	30.4	29.1	27.3
Squared Poverty Gap (SPGP)	8.8	8.4	12.3	11.6	10.6
Share of Population	18.6	21.3	32.8	27.3	100
Share of Poverty	16.5	21.1	33.8	28.7	100
Decomposition of Poverty	14.2	18.1	29.0	24.6	86.0

Source: Author's Estimation on the basis of Field Survey 2012-13.

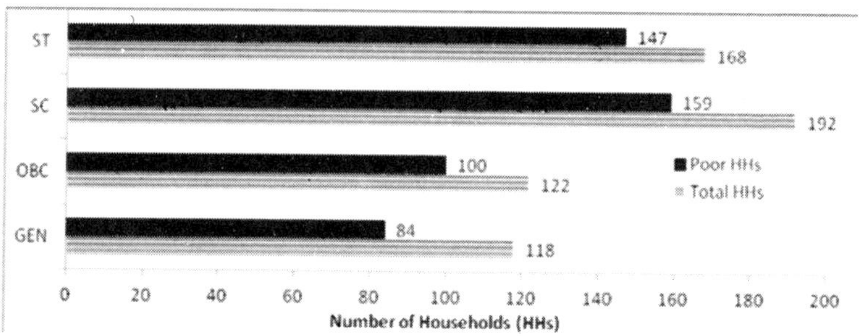

Fig. 7.4: Poor Households in Comparison to Total Sample Households by Castes
Source: Author's Estimation on the basis of Field Survey 2012-13.

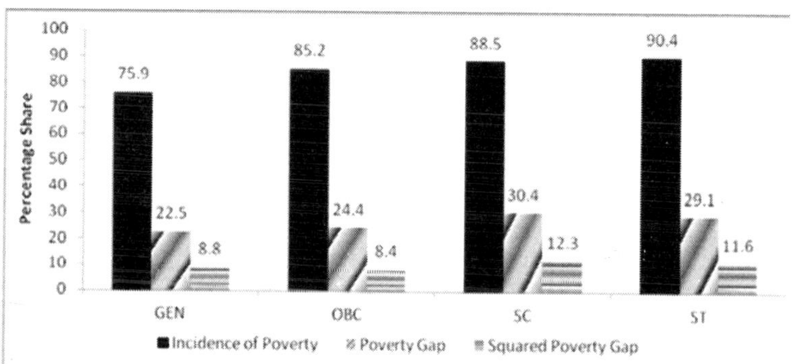

Fig. 7.5: Status of Poverty of Sample Households by Castes
Source: Author's Estimation on the basis of Field Survey 2012-13.

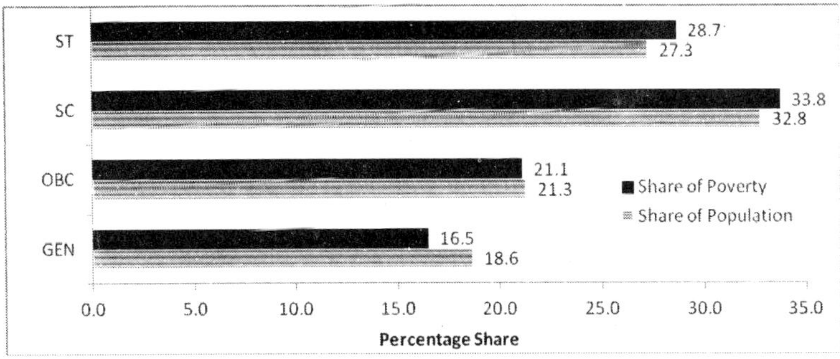

Fig. 7.6: Percentage Share of Poor in comparison to Percentage Share of Population of Sample Huseholds by Castes

Source: Author's Estimation on the basis of Field Survey 2012-13.

7.2.3 Status of Poverty in Jangal Mahal vis-à-vis Non-Jangal Mahal Region

Most of the villages in the Jangal Mahal region are drought prone and more backward than Non-Jangal Mahal region; hence the income level of the households differ from one region to other. The status of poverty in Jangal Mahal and Non-Jangal Mahal regions was estimated on the basis of per capita expenditure. The average per capita per day expenditure in Non-Jangal Mahal was higher than that of Jangal Mahal. To analyse whether this difference is significant or not we have conducted the test of mean difference by using the *t*-test. The result of *t*-test is summarized in Table 7.2 and it is found that the per capita expenditure in Non-Jangal Mahal Region is not significantly higher than that of Jangal Mahal Region.

The status of poverty of sample households in Jangal Mahal region in comparison to Non-Jangal Mahal region is shown in Table 7.3. The incidence of poverty was higher in Jangal Mahal than in Non-Jangal Mahal region. The percentage share of poor households and the head count ratio (HCR) in Non-Jangal Mahal region were 79.1 and 84.4 respectively, whereas, in Jangal Mahal the respective share was 85.2 and 88.6. Incidence of poverty in Jangal Mahal was also higher in case of all castes except STs. Most of the ST households in Jangal Mahal region are located in the vicinity of the forest area and have benefited by the profuse of forest resources (mainly Non-Timber Forest Products). The abundance of the forest resources helps them (ST) to overcome the poverty to some extent. The PGP and SPGP in Jangal Mahal were marginally lower than those of Non-Jangal Mahal. The insufficient asset endowment and the

Table 7.2: Testing of the difference of Per Capita Per Day Expenditure of the Sample Households in Non-Jangal Mahal (X_1) and Jangal Mahal region (X_2)

Indicators	*Values*	*F-Test*	*t-test*
		$H_0:\sigma_1^2=\sigma_2^2$ $\left(H_1:\sigma_1^2>\sigma_2^2\right)$	$H_0:\mu_1=\mu_2$ $\left(H_1:\mu_1>\mu_2\right)$
m_1	23.66	$F=\left(s_1^2/s_2^2\right)/\left(\sigma_1^2/\sigma_2^2\right)$ = 1.545	$t_{n1}+n_2=\frac{m_1-m_2}{\sqrt{\left(\frac{s_1^2}{n_1}+\frac{s_1^2}{n_2}\right)}}$ Has upper α-point approximately the same as (w_1 t α, n_1–1 + w_2 t α, n_2–1)/ (w_1 + w_2) = 1.205
m_2	22.86		
s_1^2	80.49	Table Value of F = 1.215 (p value one tail is 0.000)	Table Value of t = 1.647 (p value one tail is 0.114)
s_2^2	52.09		
N_1	350	Calculated value of F > Table Value of F, i.e., H_0 is rejected	Calculated value of t < Table Value of t, i.e., H_0 is not rejected
N_2	250		
df		249,349	590

Table 7.3: Status of Poverty of Sample Households in Jangal Mahal and Non-Jangal Mahal Regions

	Jangal Mahal					*Non-Jangal Mahal*				
	GEN	OBC	SC	ST	Total	GEN	OBC	SC	ST	Total
Total Households	38	73	63	76	250	81	48	129	92	350
Poor HHs (%)	76.3	87.7	84.1	88.2	85.2	69.1	72.9	82.2	87.0	79.1
HCR	77.5	89.7	90.5	89.6	88.1	75.5	77.9	87.5	91.1	84.4
PGP	21.1	23.7	34.1	26.9	26.9	23.1	24.9	28.6	30.9	27.5
SPG	7.7	7.8	14.2	10.1	10.1	9.3	9.3	11.4	12.8	11.0

Source: Author's Estimation on the basis of Field Survey 2012-13.

failure of exchange entitlements of the households were observed in most of the sample households in both Jangal Mahal and Non-Jangal Mahal regions. The social protection benefits (SPBs) were also extended in this region but their outcome were limited to overcome poverty. The next section finds out to what extent the SPBs helps in reducing poverty.

7.2.4 Status of Poverty in Presence and Absence of SPBs

The role of social protection programmes on poverty is analyzed by comparing the status of poverty in presence of SPBs (as given in Table 7.1) with the status of poverty in absence of SPBs (as in Table 7.4). Figure 7.7 also depicts the comparative picture of the status of poverty of the sample households with SPBs and without SPBs. The percentage share of poor households has decreased from 87 per cent in absence of SPBs to 81.7 per cent in presence of SPBs and the incidence of poverty has also decreased from 90 per cent to 86 per cent. The SPBs also reduced the level of FIG and SFIG of the sample households. The benefits from social protection programmes (SPPs) have reduced the incidence of poverty to

Table 7.4: Status of Poverty of Sample Households in the Absence of SPBs

	GEN	*OBC*	*SC*	*ST*	*Total*
Total Households (HHs)	118	122	192	168	600
Share of Poor HHs (%)	80.5	87.7	87.5	90.5	87.0
Number of Population	557	636	980	814	2987
Incidence of Poverty	83.3	89.9	91.4	92.4	89.9
Poverty Gap	27.9	32.0	36.8	37.1	34.2
Squared Poverty Gap	12.0	13.2	16.8	17.1	15.2
Share of Population	18.6	21.3	32.8	27.3	100
Share of Poverty	19.3	18.6	32.0	30.0	100
Decomposition of Poverty	0.17	0.17	0.29	0.27	0.90

Source: Author's Estimation on the basis of Field Survey 2012-13.

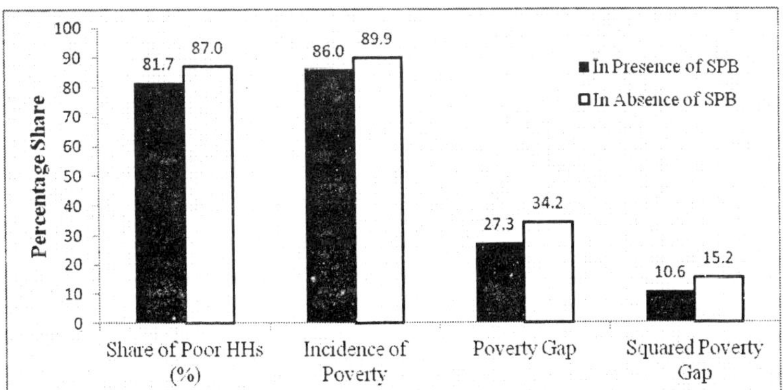

Fig. 7.7: Status of Poverty of the Sample Households in Presence and Absence of Social Protection Benefits (SPBs)

Source: Author's Estimation on the basis of Field Survey 2012-13.

the extent of 4 per cent. With the help of entire SPBs only 5.3 per cent poor households managed to overcome poverty. That raises question in regard to the effectiveness of SPPs on poor households. The leakages and inefficient delivery mechanisms are the main reasons for the insignificant effect on SPPs on poor households. The extent of the benefit of social protection floor in the backward region has only partially succeeded to overcome the poverty of the BPL households.

7.3 Econometric Model to Analyse the Status of Poverty

The Framework of the Regression Model

Heckman selection model (two-step) is used to analyze the effect of social protection benefits along with other entitlements on the status of poverty of the households.

Consider a model with two variables d_i and y_i which linearly depend on observable independent variables x_i and z_i respectively

$$d_i = z_i\gamma + v_i$$
$$y_i = x_i\beta + \varepsilon_i$$

The error terms v_i and ε_i are independently (across observations) and jointly normally distributed with covariance $\rho\delta_\varepsilon$.

In the present case d_i indicates whether i-th household is poor or not and y_i indicates the poverty gap of the i-th household. We only observe an indicator d_i when the latent variable d_i^* (consumption expenditure) is less than the expenditure of poverty line (Rs. 28.8 per capita per day). Similarly, the value of the variable $y_i = y_i^*$ is only observed if the indicator is 1:

$$d_i = 1 \text{ if } d_i^* < \text{Rs. } 28.8$$
$$\quad 0 \text{ otherwise}$$
$$y_i = y_i^* \text{ if } d_i = 1$$
$$\quad n.a. \text{ otherwise}$$

Heckman's (1979) two-step procedure involves the estimation of a standard probit and linear regression model. The two step procedure draws on the conditional ($d_i = 1$) mean

$$E(y_i/x_i, z_i) = E(y_i^*/d_i=1, x_i, z_i) = x_i\beta + \rho\delta_\varepsilon[\phi(z_i\gamma)/\psi(z_i\gamma)]$$
$$= x_i\beta + \rho\delta_\varepsilon\lambda(z_i\gamma)$$

of the fully observed y's.

Step 1 is the consistent estimation of γ by ML using the full set of observation in the standard probit model

$$d_i^* = z_i\gamma + v_i \qquad \textit{(First Equation)}$$
$$di = 1 \text{ if } i\text{-th household is poor, 0 otherwise}$$

We can use this and consistently estimate the Inverse Mills Ratio $\lambda_i = f(z_i\gamma)/\psi(z_i\gamma)$ for all observations.

Step 2 is the estimation of the regression equation with the Inverse Mills Ratio as an additional variable

$$y_i^* = x_i'\beta + \beta_\lambda\lambda_i + u_i \qquad \textit{(Second Equation)}$$

for the subsample of full observations. Here y_i^* is the poverty gap (FIG) of the i-th household. The OLS regression yields β, β_{ε}, δ_ε and thus the correlation $\rho = \beta_\lambda/\delta_\varepsilon$.

There is often a practical problem of identification (almost multicolinearity) when the variables in both equations are the same, i.e. $x_i = z_i$ (Vella, 1998). The parameters β and β_γ are theoretically identified by the non-linearity of the Inverse Mills Ratio $\lambda(\cdot)$. It is therefore strongly advised that at least one independent variable of the first equation should not be included in the second equation. Here the household's characteristics and exchange entitlements of i-th household are denoted by x_i and z_i is the subset of x_i.

The Specification of the Variables in the Model

The variables identified to capture these processes and their specifications are presented in Table 7.5. To analyse the variation of incidence of poverty (POVT) and poverty gap (POVTG) across households two sets of independent variables are included in the regression equations: those relating to the control variables measuring household's characteristics and household's entitlements including social protection benefits. Here we include control variables because the personal characteristics may influence poverty.

Table 7.5: Notation, Specification and Descriptive Statistics of Variables Used in Regression Analysis at the Household Level

Notation	*Specification*	*Mean*	*SD*	*Max*	*Min*
	Dependent Variables				
POVT	Whether the household is poor or not? Yes = 1, No = 0	0.82	0.39	1.00	0
POVTG	Poverty gap of the household	0.19	0.29	0.68	-1
	Independent Variables				
Households Characteristics					
EDHOD	Education level (Years of Schooling) of the head of the household	3.11	3.58	16	0
CAST	Whether the Household belongs to SC or ST community or nor? Yes = 1, No = 0	0.60	0.49	1.00	0
JMAHAL	Is the Household located in the Jangal Mahal Region? Yes = 1, No = 0	0.42	0.49	1.00	0
Entitlement of the Households					
MDAY	Average Mandays (per month) per worker of the Household	13.33	6.94	41.83	0
AGY	Per capita per month income (Rs.) of the households from agricultural production	71.68	108.55	805.56	-104
NAPY	Per capita per month income (Rs.) of the households from non-agricultural production	19.44	62.97	1041.67	0
LABY	Per capita per month income (Rs.) of the household by selling labour power	340.95	304.71	2333.33	0
TRDY	Per capita per month income (Rs.) of the households from trade	63.95	206.31	2222.22	0
CPRY	Per capita per month income (Rs.) of the households from common property resources	26.95	80.81	937.50	0
PDSF	Per capita per month availability of food (Kg.) from PDS	4.70	3.13	18.67	0
SPB	Per capita per month social protection benefits (Rs.)	159.51	76.94	611.33	0

The household's characteristics are specified by the education level of the head of the households (EDHOD), caste of the households (CAST) and location of the households (JMAHAL). The level of education of the head of the household (EDHOD) is computed as the total years of schooling completed by that member of the household. The higher education level of the head of the household gives the opportunity to access higher wage or salaried jobs that help the households to overcome poverty. Caste variable (CAST) is defined as a dummy variable taking the value 0 if the head of the household belongs to Scheduled Caste or Scheduled Tribes, and 1 if otherwise. Upper caste households have better access to physical capital and dynamics of development which help them to overcome poverty. JMAHAL is also a dummy variable taking the value 1 if the household is located in Jangal Mahal region and 0 if it is not. The Jangal Mahal region is most backward and therefore, the depth of poverty was found to be higher in Jangal Mahal region than in Non-Jangal Mahal region.

The entitlement of the households are specified by average mandays (MDAY) of the households and earnings from agriculture (AGY), non-agricultural production (NAPY), selling the labour power (LABY), trade (TRADY), common property resources (CPRY). These entitlements create command over food as well as non-food items and the household with higher entitlements is less likely to be poor. The entitlement also includes transfer entitlement from the government in the form of social protection benefits. For the BPL category households this entitlement plays an important role to overcome the incidence and depth of poverty. The social protection entitlement is specified by the overall benefits (SPB) that the households received from SPPs. Among other means of social protection benefits, the benefits of public distribution system (PDSF) in the form of foodgrains is also considered to be independent variables to explain the status of poverty across households because it automatically increases size of consumption baskets. The higher access of PDSF by the household is likely to reduce the poverty.

In order to get a preliminary understanding of the nature of the relationship between the dependent and independent variables a correlation matrix of all the variables is presented in Table 7.6.

The Empirical Results: Estimation of Heckman Two-Step

The empirical analysis of the relationship between entitlements of the households including social protection benefits and the status of poverty

Table 7.6: Correlation Matrix of Dependent and Independent Variables

	POVT	POVTG	EDHOD	CAST	JMAHAL	MDAY	AGLY	LABY	TRDY	CPRY	PDSF	SPB
POVT	1											
POVTG	.764**	1										
EDHOD	-.125**	-.168**	1									
CAST	.104*	.133**	-.155**	1								
JMAHAL	0.077	0.047	-0.022	-0.073	1							
MDAY	-.139**	-.204**	.093*	-.154**	0.006	1						
AGY	-.184**	-.231**	.142**	-0.016	-0.061	-0.022	1					
LABY	-.302**	-.449**	0.013	0.020	-.139**	.107**	-0.066	1				
NAPY	-.134**	-.219**	0.023	.084*	-0.077	-0.060	.193**	0.054				
TRDY	-.201**	-.284**	.113**	-.205**	0.035	.094*	-0.051	-.236**	1			
CPRY	-0.029	-0.054	-.100*	.090*	-0.068	0.014	-0.072	-.085*	-0.074	1		
PDSF	-.087*	-.178**	0.049	-0.010	.504**	.081*	0.038	-.106**	0.015	0.008	1	
SPB	-.128**	-.201**	0.023	0.076	.140**	-0.032	.096*	-0.015	-0.068	.116**	.548**	1

** Correlation is significant at the 0.01 level (2-tailed).

* Correlation is significant at the 0.05 level (2-tailed).

is made on the basis of Heckman two-step model as specified above. Heckman two-step model helps us to determine the incidence of poverty and the depth of poverty simultaneously. The two-step model is also useful to test selectivity bias (if any). The sample selection bias might arise in practice for two reasons. *First*, there may be self-selection by the individuals or data units being investigated. *Second*, sample selection decisions by analysts or data processors operate in much the same fashion as self-selection. There is no selectivity bias if the coefficient of ***Inverse Mills Ratio*** ***(λ)*** is statistically not significant. The software package ***STATA*** offers the possibility to use the Heckman two-step procedure. The empirical results of Heckman selection model—two-step estimates (regression model with sample selection) are presented in Table 7.7.

In Table 7.7, the lower panel presents the results of probit estimation of incidence of poverty (POVT) and the upper panel presents the estimation of poverty gap (POVTG). The ***Inverse Mills Ratio*** is not significant, that is there is no selectivity bias. To avoid the problem of identification two independent variables namely EDHOD and NAPY are excluded in the upper panel, that is, in estimation of poverty gap.

The estimated results indicate that household's entitlements play a role in reducing poverty or poverty gap. The characteristics of the households are also important determinants of poverty. We find statistically significant coefficients of CAST, JMAHAL, AGY, NAPY,

LABY TRDY, CPRY and PDSF for incidence of poverty and CAST, JMAHAL, AGY, LABY, TRDY, CPRY, PDSF and SPB for poverty gap. All these variables other than CAST and JMAHAL have the expected negative signs. CAST and JMAHAL are positively related with POVT and POVTG.

Table 7.7: Heckman Selection Model—Two-Step Estimates Based on STATA

Dependent Variable	*Independent Variables*	*Coef.*	*z*	*P>z*	
POVTG(y_i)	Constant	0.5152	22.13	0.000	Number of
	CAST	0.0367	2.84	0.005	Observations = 600
	JMAHAL	0.0254	1.65	0.098	
	AGY	-0.0004	-4.59	0.000	
	LABY	-0.0003	-5.82	0.000	Censored
	TRDY	-0.0003	-4.13	0.000	Observations = 110
	CPRY	-0.0003	-3.52	0.000	
	PDSF	-0.0157	-5.00	0.000	
	SPB	-0.0003	-2.89	0.004	Uncensored
					Observations = 490
POVT(d_i)	Constant	2.5377	10.51	0.000	
	EDHOD	-0.0302	-1.60	0.109	
	CAST	0.2707	1.87	0.062	Wald chi2(6) = 169.58
	JMAHAL	0.3113	1.84	0.066	Prob> chi2 = 0.000
	AGY	-0.0025	-4.36	0.000	
	NAPY	-0.0025	-1.80	0.072	
	LABY	-0.0020	-7.96	0.000	
	TRDY	-0.0021	-6.33	0.000	
	CPRY	-0.0018	-2.42	0.016	
	PDSF	-0.0693	-2.46	0.014	
	SPB	-0.0013	-1.37	0.172	
	Lambda (λ)	0.0380	0.59	0.554	
	Rho (ρ)	0.3017			
	Sigma (δ)	0.1260			

The result suggests that as the income from agriculture (AGY), non-agricultural production (NAPY), labour (LABY), trade (TRDY), common property resources (CPRY) and food from public distribution system (PDSF) increases, the probability of poverty (POVT) as well as depth of poverty (POVTG) of the household decreases. Increased income from non-agricultural production also decreases the incidence of poverty but not depth of poverty. This implies that for the sample households non-agricultural production is not sufficient to overcome the depth of poverty. The higher level of different forms of entitlement of the households can cause reduction of poverty. The empirical result confirms that the failure of entitlements is the cause of poverty. The common property assets also play an important role to overcome poverty. The majority of the sample households are located near the forest and others are located near river and have accessed the common property resources (CPR). The CPR in the form of Non-timber Forest Products (NTFP) and resources from river (like fish, stone and sand) also play important roles in their livelihood. The benefits from public distribution system (PDSF) have played crucial role for reduction of poverty—higher access of foodgrains from PDS reduces the incidence and depth of poverty. The overall social protection benefits (SPB) significantly reduced the depth of poverty but not the incidence of poverty but the relationship is not statistically significant. It is significantly explaining the variation of depth of poverty across households.

The result also indicates that the household's characteristics like CAST and location (JMAHAL) are significantly associated with POVT and POVTG. That is, the incidence and depth of poverty are significantly high for the households who belong to SCs and STs Communities and located in Jangal Mahal region.

7.4 Measurement of Poverty: A Multidimensional Approach

The Oxford Poverty and Human Development Initiative (OPHI) have developed a new international measure of poverty—the Multidimensional Poverty Index (MPI)—for the 20th Anniversary edition of the United Nations Development Programme's flagship Human Development Report. The International Multidimensional Poverty Index (MPI), which was developed by Alkire and Santos (2010, 2013) in collaboration with the UNDP and first appeared in the *Human Development Report 2010*, is one particular adaptation of the adjusted headcount ratio (M_0) as proposed in Alkire and Foster (2011).

The Multidimensional Poverty Index (MPI) identifies multiple deprivations at the individual level in education, health and standard of living. It uses micro data from household surveys, and—unlike the Inequality-adjusted Human Development Index—all the indicators needed to construct the measure must come from the same survey (more details can be found in Alkire and Santos 2010).The international MPI is an adaptation of a particular choice of indicators, deprivation cut-offs and relative weights, and a poverty cut-off. The international MPI is based on ten indicators grouped into three dimensions reported in Table 7.8. The first column reports three dimensions: health, education and standard of living. The second column reports ten indicators. Each dimension is equally weighted and indicators within each dimension are also equally weighted. The third column reports the deprivation cut-off of each of the ten indicators. It is to note that except electricity and flooring other eight indicators were specified in MDG. The measurement of MPI as designed by Alkire and Foster is given in the Box 8.1.

Table 7.8: Dimensions, Indicators, Deprivation Cut-offs and Weights to Measure the Multidimensional Poverty

Dimension (Weight)	*Indicator (Weight)*	*Deprivation Cut-off*
Education (1/3)	Schooling (1/6)	No household member has completed five years of schooling
	Attendance (1/6)	Any school-aged child in the household is not attending school up to class VIII[2]
Health (1/3)	Nutrition (1/6)	One household member who is malnourished[3]
	Mortality (1/6)	Any child has passed away in the household
Standard of Living (1/3)	Electricity (1/18)	The household has no electricity
	Water (1/18	The household does not have access to safe drinking water or safe water is more than a 30-minute walk (round trip)
	Sanitation (1/18)	The household's sanitation facility is not improved or it is shared with other households
	Flooring (1/18)	The household has a dirt, sand or dung floor
	Cooking fuel (1/18)	The household cooks with dung, wood or charcoal
	Assets (1/18)	The household does not own more than one asset (e.g. radio, telephone, TV, bike, motorbike or refrigerator; and does not own a car or truck)

Source: Alkire, Roche, Santos, and Seth (2011).

The formation of MPI (as measured by OPHI) involves the following steps:

Box 7.1: Measurement of MPI

Scoring

- Each person is assigned a deprivation score according to his or her household's deprivations in each of the 10 component indicators.
- The maximum score is 100%, with each dimension equally weighted; thus the maximum score in each dimension is 33.3%.
- The education and health dimensions have two indicators each, so each component is worth 33/2, or 16.7%.
- The Standard of living dimension has six indicators, so each component is worth 33.6/6, or 5.6%.

Cut-off for Poverty, Vulnerability and Severity

- To identify the multidimensionally poor, the deprivation scores for each household are summed to obtain the household deprivation, c.
- A cut-off of 33.3%, which is the equivalent of one-third of the weighted indicators, is used to distinguish between the poor and non poor.
- Households with a deprivation score (c) greater than or equal to 20% but less than 33.3% are vulnerable to or at risk of becoming multidimensionally poor.
- If c is 33.3% or greater, that household (and everyone in it) is multidimensionally poor.
- Households with a deprivation score of 50% or higher are severely multidimensionally poor.

The MPI

- *Multidimensional Headcount Ratio* (H) is the proportion of the population who are multidimensionally poor and $H = \frac{q}{n}$, where q is the number of persons who are multidimensionally poor and n is the total population.
- *Multidimensional Intensity of Poverty* (A) reflects the proportion of the weighted component indicators in which, on average, poor people are deprived. For poor households only (c greater than or equal to 33.3%), the deprivation scores are summed and divided by the total number of poor persons. That is $A = \frac{1}{q}\sum_{i=1}^{q} c_i$, where c is the deprivation score that the poor experience.
- The MPI can be expressed as the product of H and A, i.e., $MPI = A \times H$.

The Contribution of Dimension j

The deprivation score c of a poor person can be expressed as the sum of deprivations in each dimension j (j = 1, 2, 3), $c = c_1 + c_2 + c_3$. The contribution of dimension j to multidimensional poverty can be expressed as $Contrib\ j = \left(\left(\sum_i^q c_j\right)/n\right)/MPI$

Source: HDR 2013, UNDP.

Achievement Matrix

Let X is $n \times d$ dimension achievement matrix, where x_{ij} is the achievement of person i in dimension j.

Deprivation Cut-off

A threshold z_j is defined as the minimum required in order to be non-deprived. If $x_{ij} < z_j$ the person is said to be deprived in that dimension.

Deprivation Matrix

We obtained a deprivation matrix g^0 such that

$$g_{ij}^{0} = 1 \text{ when } x_{ij} < z_j$$
$$= 0 \text{ otherwise, } \forall\ z = 1, \ldots\ldots, d \text{ and } \forall\ i = 1, \ldots\ldots, n.$$

Weights and Deprivation Score

A vector $(w_1, \ldots.., w_d)$ of weights is used to indicate the relative importance of deprivation in each dimension.

The deprivation value attached to dimension j is denoted by $w_j > 0$. The deprivation score is given by

$$c_j = \sum_{j=1}^{d} w_j g_{ij}^{0}$$

c_j increases as the number of deprivations a person experience increases and *vice-versa*.

Poverty Cut-off

The poverty cut-off, ***k***, is used to identify the multidimensional poor. ***K*** is implemented using an identification function P_k.

Notionally $\rho_k(x_i; z) = 1$ *if* $c_i \geq k$, the person is poor

$= 0$ otherwise, the person is not poor

By $\cup$ approach the person i is identified as multidimensionally poor if she is deprived in least one dimension $(c_i > 0)$.

By $\cap$ approach the person *i* is identified as multidimensionally poor if she is deprived in all dimension ($c_i = 0$).

Multidimensional Poverty Index (MPI)

MPI is the mean of the censored deprivation score vector

$$MPI = \mu(c(k)) = \frac{1}{n}\sum_{i=1}^{n} c_i(k) = \frac{1}{n}\sum_{i=1}^{n}\sum_{j=1}^{d} w_j g_{ij}^0$$

$$= \frac{q}{n} \times \frac{1}{q}\sum_{i=1}^{n} c_i(k)$$

$$= H \times A$$

7.5 The Impact of Social Protection on Poverty and Deprivations of Sample Households

7.5.1 Scoring in Presence and Absence of SPBs

The present section makes an endeavour to analyse the multidimensional deprivation of the sample households and examines to what extent social protection benefits (SPBs) trim down the deprivations.

The application of MPI is limited in India because of the non-availability of information in respect of the indicators. We have made an attempt to measure the MPI on the basis of field survey data of 600 sample households. From each household we collected the response in respect of ten specified indicators of MPI under two separate circumstances—one is in presence of social protection benefits (SPBs) and the other in absence of SPB. Table 7.9 represents the descriptive statistics of the ten indicators of multidimensional poverty of the households in presence of social protection benefits as well as in the absence of the same. The average (of 600 sample households) deprivation scores for all ten indicators are higher in absence of SPBs than that in presence of SPBs.

7.5.2 Deprivations in Presence and Absence of SPBs

According to the MPI measurement a household is deprived or poor in respect of a particular indicator if the deprivation score exceeds 33.3 per cent. Percentage share of deprived (poor) households across different indicators of MPI in presence and in absence of SPB is shown in

Table 7.9: Descriptive Statistics of Indicators in Presence and Absence of SPBs

Indicators of Multidimensional Poverty	*Presence of SPBs*				*Absence of SPBs*			
	Max	*Min*	*Mean*	*S.D.*	*Max*	*Min*	*Mean*	*S.D.*
1. No one has completed five years of schooling	16.7	0	6.25	8.02	16.7	0	11	3.31
2. Non-attendance in School by Children	16.7	0	2.31	5.58	16.7	0	5.6	2.36
3. One household member who is malnourished	16.7	0	7.33	8.22	16.7	0	12.3	3.51
4. Having had one or more children's death	16.7	0	0.42	2.60	16.7	0	2.1	1.44
5. No electricity	5.6	0	1.73	2.58	5.6	0	3.6	1.89
6. No access to clean drinking water	5.6	0	1.09	2.21	5.6	0	2.9	1.70
7. No access to adequate sanitation	5.6	0	4.32	2.31	5.6	0	4.7	2.18
8. House has dirty floor	5.6	0	4.25	2.36	5.6	0	4.6	2.15
9. Household Cooking Materials	5.6	0	2.9	1.70	5.6	0	5.18	1.40
10. Absence of Household Assets	5.6	0	2.58	2.77	5.6	0	2.7	1.64

Source: Author's Estimation on the basis of Field Survey 2012-13.

Figure 7.8. It has decreased for all indicators in presence of SPBs. In presence of SPBs the percentage share of deprived households has decreased significantly for the indicators namely Electricity, Drinking Water, Malnourished and Schooling. The social protection programmes like NRDWP for safe drinking water, provision of meals by ICDS and MDM for reduction of malnutrition, and SSK and MSK for schooling are playing important role for reduction of deprivation of the household. There is also the provision of free connection of electricity for BPL households in the villages. Other programmes like Rural Primary Health Care, JSY and RSBY are helpful to reduce the Infant Mortality, TSC for Sanitation facilities, and IAY for Housing facilities to the poor played an important role in reducing deprivation of the households. Most of the sample households in the village have used natural products for their cooking; therefore SPPs have insignificant effect on the indicator Cooking Fuel. As far as asset is concerned the SPP like Bicycle for Tribal Girls provides bicycle to the school going tribal girls, and for our sample households there is no evidence of receiving other assets from SPPs. Therefore, the share of deprived households in respect of asset has marginally differed.

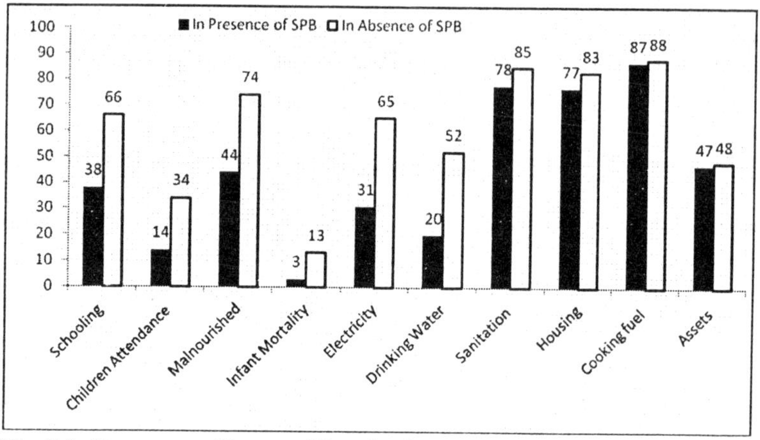

Fig. 7.8: Percentage Shares of Deprived Households across Indicators in Presence and Absence of SPBs

Source: Author's Estimation on the basis of Field Survey 2012-13.

The study represents a comparative picture of the status of household's deprivation. According to UNDP, to identify the multidimensionally poor, the deprivation scores for each household are summed to obtain the household deprivation, c. A cut-off of 33.3 per cent, which is the equivalent of one-third of the weighted indicators, is used to distinguish between the poor and the non poor. If c is 33.3 per cent or greater the household (and everyone in it) is multidimensionally poor. Households with a deprivation score greater than or equal to 20 per cent but less than 33.3 per cent are vulnerable to or at risk of becoming multidimensionally poor. Households with a deprivation score of 50 per cent or higher are severely multidimensional poor. In absence of SPBs, the distribution of households is skewed towards high degree of deprivations. The percentage of households being severely multidimensionally poor is very high (42.33) in absence of SPBs in comparison with that in the presence of SPBs (Table 7.10).

7.5.3 Status of Muli-dimensional Poverty in Presence and Absence of SPBs

Table 7.11 presents the results of multidimensional poverty in presence and absence of SPBs. In presence of SPBs (in comparison to the presence of SPBs) the percentage share of the vulnerable to poor households, multidimensionally deprived households and severely poor households

Table 7.10: Distribution of Sample Households by Deprivations in Presence and Absence of SPBs

Deprivation	*Presence of SPBs*		*Absence of SPBs*	
	No. of HHs	*Percentage*	*No. of HHs*	*Percentage*
0.00-19.99	87	14.50	31	5.17
20.00-33.33	191	31.83	125	20.83
33.34-50.00	202	33.67	190	31.67
>50.00	120	20.00	254	42.33
Total	600	100.00	600	100.00

Source: Author's Estimation on the basis of Field Survey 2012-13.

Table 7.11: Measurement of Multidimensional Poverty of the Sample Households (HHs)

	Presence of SPBs	*Absence of SPBs*
Vulnerable to Poor HHs (20-33.33)	20.8	31.8
Multidimensionally Deprived HHs (>33.33)	53.7	74.0
Severely poor HHs (>50)	31.5	54.2
MPI	0.30	0.36
Multidimensional Head Count Ratio	58.2	77.1
Monetary Measure of HCR	86.0	89.9

Source: Author's Estimation on the basis of Field Survey 2012-13.

decreased to the extent of 11, 21.3 and 12.7 percentage points respectively. The values of these indicators were substantially high for SCs and STs (Table 7.12). In the presence and absence of social protection benefits MPI scores are 0.30 and 0.36 and headcount ratios are 58.2 per cent, and 77.1 per cent respectively. But the monetary poverty (that measured on the basis of per capita consumption expenditure) is quite high—the HCR was 86.0 per cent in presence of SPBs and 89.9 per cent in absence of SPBs. That is, monetary measurement of poverty is substantially higher than multidimensional poverty.

Table 7.12: MPI Indicators of the Sample Households

	Presence of SPBs				*Absence of SPBs*			
	Gen	*OBC*	*SC*	*ST*	*Gen*	*OBC*	*SC*	*ST*
Vulnerable to Poor HHs (20-33.33)	29.7	23.8	15.6	18.5	39.8	36.1	25.5	30.4
Multidimensionally Deprived HHs (>33.33)	39.8	50.0	60.4	58.3	63.6	71.3	78.7	78.0
Population in Severely Poor HHs (>50)	17.0	26.2	39.1	36.9	44.1	50.8	54.7	63.1
MPI	0.2	0.3	0.4	0.3	0.4	0.4	0.5	0.5

Source: Field Survey 2012-13.

7.6 Status Match between Monetary Poverty and Multidimensional Poverty

The estimations of the poor and the non-poor on the basis of monetary measurement of poverty side by side multidimensional measurement of poverty (MP) is presented in Table 7.13. For the sample households in absence of SPBs the percentage shares of the multidimensionally poor and the monetary/consumption poor were 69.17 per cent which decreased to 50.17 per cent in presence of SPBs. But percentage share of the non-poor in respect of both measures increases from 8.33 per cent to 14.67 per cent.

Table 7.13: Cross Classifications of Monetary Poverty and Multidimensional Poverty

		Monetary Poverty *(measured by Consumption Expenditure)*			
		Presence of Social Protection		*Absence of Social Protection*	
		Poor	*Non Poor*	*Poor*	*Non Poor*
Multidimensional Poverty	Poor	50.17	3.5	69.17	4.83
	Non Poor	31.67	14.67	17.67	8.33
Poverty Status Match*		64.84		77.50	

Note: * Status match is the percentage of households with similar status in both measures.

Source: Author's Estimation on the basis of Field Survey 2012-13.

The percentage share of multidimensional poor households also declined across consumption quintile (Table 7.14). For bottom 20 per cent households in consumption quintile (i.e., very poor) 86.67 per cent were multidmensional poor in the presence of social protection which was 92.5 per cent in the absence of social protection. Whereas for top 20 per cent households (very good) in consumption quintile, 20.8 per cent were multidimensional poor in presence of social protection and were 42.5 per cent in absence of social protection.

Empirical studies have shown that significant percentages of those who are multidimensionally deprived are not income poor and *vice versa*. There is a need to supplement India's long and august tradition of monetary poverty measurement with multidimensional poverty measures that capture the joint distribution of deprivations across the population.

Table 7.14: Comparison of the Status of Poverty of the Sample Households between Consumption Quintile and Multidimensional Poor

Consumption Quintile	*Multidmensional Poor (% of HHs)*	
	Presence of SPBs	*Absence of SPBs*
Very Poor	86.67	92.50
Poor	76.67	90.00
Satisfactory	50.83	77.50
Good	33.33	67.50
Very Good	20.83	42.50

Note: The consumption quintiles are classified by the level of household's consumption expenditure.

Source: Author's Estimation on the basis of Field Survey 2012-13.

Notes

1. BPL Survey 2005, Government of West Bengal.
2. If a household has no school-aged children, the household is treated as non-deprived.
3. Houesehold's member is malnourished if his/her calorie intake is less than 2400 kcal.

8
Summary and Conclusions

8.1 Summary

The high growth rate in India in recent decades has gone hand in hand with a decline in poverty and infant mortality rate, and improvements in indicators like life expectancy and educational attainments. However, these promising achievements still continue to co-exist with persistently high levels of poverty and food insecurity; low levels of education, skills and productivity, low nutritional status among socially disadvantaged groups. There is also the evidence of rising inter-group and inter-class inequalities. Within Asia, India is home to the largest number of malnourished persons in the world. The food insecurity and poverty co-exist because of poverty-nutrition traps in India. The improvement in income in India was accompanied by a decline of 210 calories intake per capita per day during 1993-94 to 2009-10.

For food security and reduction of poverty entitlements to food are very important. People gain entitlements to food by: producing their own food; by exchanging money (that they have earned through labour) for food; or through transfers from kin, community or state. The public policy instruments to strengthen food security support these entitlements in terms of incentives, relationships and assets. Comprehensive social protection programmes address the problems of food insecurity in particular and poverty in general. The State helps the poor in times of insecurity and ensures minimum levels of provision to those unable to gain from the growth process.

Perception of Social Protection

Social Protection comprises those measures which aim at preventing, reducing and eliminating economic and social vulnerabilities to poverty and deprivation. Social Protection is defined by the ILO as a set of public measures that a society provides for its members to protect them against economic and social distress caused by the absence or a substantial reduction of income from work as a result of various contingencies (sickness, maternity, employment injury, unemployment, invalidity, old age or death of the bread earner), the provision of healthcare and the provision of benefits for families with children. *In the present study, we view social protection as a set of public measures evolved by the Central or State Government that create direct benefits to the households or members of households to eliminate poverty and deprivations.*

Although social protection floor (SPF) is an integrated set of social policies designed to guarantee income security and access to social services for all, paying particular attention to vulnerable groups, and protecting and empowering people across the life cycle, it includes guarantees of: (a) *basic income security* in the form of various social transfers, such as pensions for the elderly and persons with disabilities, child benefits, income support benefits and/or employment guarantees and services for the unemployed and working poor; and (b) *universal access to essential affordable social services* in the areas of health, water and sanitation, education, food security, housing, and others defined according to national priorities (UNCEB, 2009a; ILO–WHO, 2009).

Social protection directly reduces poverty and helps make growth more pro-poor. It stimulates the involvement of the poor in economic growth, protects the poorest and most vulnerable in a downturn and contributes to social cohesion and stability. It helps build human capital, promote investment and entrepreneurship, improve participation in labour markets and manage risks.

Social Protection has acquired greater relevance in the context of shocks and systemic risks which are being faced by the working poor in the context of globalization and regional imbalance. Spatial disparities in India align with other cleavages which threaten national unity and peace, whether it is the extreme of the 'Maoist Corridor' that matches the corridor of deprivation. The south-west part of West Bengal state in India, one of the backward regions, was also affected by extreme Maoist movement during 2009 and 2011. That generated shocks and risk on livelihood. Pro-backward area policies and programmes play significant role for reduction of shocks and risk of livelihood.

Social Protection Programmes in India

After liberalization, social protection measures were neglected in the initial phase, but this began to change from the mid-1990s when there was an expansion in the budget for rural employment generation and social assistance programmes. While the ambit of social protection schemes relating to workers and being statutory in nature has also grown in the last few years a major expansion has occurred in the expenditure on sectors where the Courts or the Constitution have created specific entitlements through legislative changes or legal oversight. The total expenditure by the Government of India on six of the major social protection related sectors (elementary education, health and family welfare, labour and labour welfare, social security and welfare and rural development) increased from 1.06 per cent of GDP in 1995-96 to 1.35 per cent of GDP in 2005-06 and further to 1.75 per cent of GDP in 2010-11.

In India, there is the evidence of protective, promotional and preventive social protection programmes. In the present study, we have listed only those social protection programmes that directly enhance the entitlement of the households, which, *inter alia*, include food, health, education, housing, employment & income, and social assistance related programmes. The SPF, as envisaged by UNCEB, in India is formed by these programmes. The SPF in rural India includes the guarantees of (a) ***basic income security*** in the form of *income support benefits and/or employment guarantees* by Mahatma Gandhi National Rural Employment Guarantee Act (NREGA), Swarna Jayanti Gram Swarozgar Yojana (SGSY) and Procurement of Non-timber Forest Produces (NTFP), along with *pensions for the elderly and persons with disabilities* by National Old Age Pension Scheme (NOAPS), National Family Benefit Scheme (NFBS), National Widow Pension Scheme (NWPS), National Disability Pension Scheme (NDPS) and Indira Gandhi Matritva Sahayog Yojana (IGMSY); and (b) ***universal access to essential affordable social services*** in the areas of *food security* by Targeted Public Distribution System (TPDS), *health* by rural primary health care, Rashtriya Swasthya Bima Yojana (RSBY) and Janani Suraksha Yojana (JSY), *water & sanitation* by National Rural Drinking Water Programme (NRDWP) and Total Sanitation Campaign (TSC), *education* by Integrated Child Development Services (ICDS), Sishu Siksha Karmasuchi (SSK), Madhyamik Siksha Karmasuchi (MSK), Mid Day Meal (MDM), etc., and *housing* by Indira Awas Yojana (IAY).

Most of these programmes are centrally sponsored but implemented by the States which generally contribute 25 per cent to their cost. A number of programmes are now legally enforced—TPDS by National Food Security Bill (2013), education related programmes by Right to Education Act (2009), employment by National Rural Employment Guarantee Act (2005) and collection of forest resources (NTFP) by Forest Rights Act (2006). In addition, some State governments have their own poverty-reduction schemes. In West Bengal State Government has also implemented a number of programmes among which quasi-universal PDS in specially disadvantaged region (Jangal Mahal, Draught Prone, Hill etc.), *Kanyashree* for empowerment of girls child, scholarships/grants for students of SC/ST/minority and bi-cycle for school going children are important. There has been multiplicity of programmes on the grounds of multidimensionality of poverty, heterogeneity of the poor and inter-state variations in the efficacy of the delivery system.

Social Protection Benefits in the Backward Region of West Bengal

Three consecutive districts of West Bengal, namely Purulia, Bankura and Paschim Medinipur which are treated as one of the backward regions in West Bengal are purposively chosen in the present study. A major part of this region is marked as Jangal Mahal and drought prone which were badly affected by Maoist Movement during 2009 to 2011. During 2009-10 to 2011-12 the head count ratio in this backward region stood near about 32 per cent, while in West Bengal as a whole the head count ratio fell from 28.8 per cent to 22.5 per cent. The situation of tribal people was worst in the backward region in the aftermath of Maoist movement. The head count ratio of Scheduled Tribes in this region was as high as 53 per cent in 2011-12 in comparison to just 19 per cent of general caste people. In 2011-12, 10.8 per cent households were food insecure in this region. The incidence of food insecurity was substantially high for SCs and STs.

The State Government has provided the quasi-universal PDS in the Jangal Mahal region by the means of Jangal Mahal BPL and drought prone BPL ration since 2011. Before 2011 nearly 15 per cent people of these three districts were not covered by any kind of ration card for PDS benefits. Now most of the people have got the benefits of PDS. The provision of getting per head rice for specially identified BPL in the Jangal Mahal area is 2 Kg/week and for wheat it is 0.750 Kg/week. Per capita allotment of food grains in these three districts is higher than that in West Bengal as a whole.

Three backward districts are widely covered with rural hospitals, block primary health centres, primary health centres and sub-centres. Number of rural population served per bed in three backward districts is lower than the state average, i.e., the backward region is better covered by health centres. But the quality of health service and the access of health service are not satisfactory. Recently, the Government of West Bengal has opened fair price medicine shop through government hospital and medical centre to save the out of pocket expenditure of the poor people by means of 48 to 72.6 per cent subsidized price. But these shops are concentrated in cities and district head quarters. JSY promotes institutional delivery. The percentage share of institutional delivery to total JSY beneficiaries in these three districts gradually increased from 60 per cent in 2010-11 to 72 per cent in 2011-12 and further to 80 per cent in 2012-13, the target of full institutional delivery is, however, not achieved. In these three districts about 61 per cent of targeted families are enrolled under RSBY. Private and public hospitals are empanelled to get health facilities under RSBY. But actual benefits are significantly low—only 2.90 per cent enrolled families had obtained the benefits of hospitalization.

NRDWP provides drinking water facilities to the rural people by piped water supply system, hand pump, bore wells etc. The sanctioned amount was not fully utilized. On the whole nearly 78 per cent of sanctioned fund is utilized in these three districts during 2011 to 2014. The scenario of population coverage in respect of drinking water facilities is quite satisfactory; the facilities provided crossed the targeted coverage of population. But the relatively low percentage of populations was covered by quality drinking water facility. The physical achievement of TSC for sanitation is also limited. Paschim Medinipur district managed to fulfil the target of individual household latrine (IHHL) for BPL households. In Purulia and Bankura districts only 52 per cent of targeted BPL households had IHHL. The percentage share of households having IHHL to total (both BPL and APL) targeted households was 41 per cent in Purulia and 68 per cent in Bankura, which was much lower than the share of West Bengal as a whole (81%). The backward region is lagging behind not only in household sanitation but also in sanitation in schools, *Anganwadi* centres and sanitation complexes.

ICDS aims to improve nutritional status of pregnant and lactating women, thereby impacting on the nutritional outcomes among children having broken intergenerational cycle of undernutrition. ICDS Projects are operating through *Anganwadi* Centres (AWCs) and most of the Projects and Centres are operating in the three backward districts. But in respect of supplementary nutritional programme (SNP), the programme under ICDS where AWC provides nutritional meals to the children and pregnant & lactating mother, the three backward districts remain far lagging behind the target. We observe that the percentage share of targeted AWCs providing SNP for 21+ days in a month is perceptibly low in Purulia (77.7%) and Bankura (83.1%) in comparison to West Bengal as a whole (92.8%). These three districts have witnessed substantial number of malnutrition children. The children with severe malnutrition are also relatively high in these three districts—3.1 per cent in Bankura, 2.8 per cent in Purulia and 1.6 per cent in Paschim Medinipur. MDM programme was also introduced to provide nutritional benefit to the school going children and to reduce drop-out from school (primary and upper primary level).

Primary Schools and Shisu Shiksha Kendras extended the education services at fundamental level. In West Bengal about 1557 number of habitations still have neither any primary nor SSK within 1 km. A substantial number of these types of habitation are in the three backward districts (nearly 40%). In Purulia there are 141 habitations with no primary schools. These numbers are quiet high in Paschim Medinipur (289) and Bankura (225) districts. The State Government provides hostel grants for SC/ST students. The hostels are attached to the Junior High or Secondary Schools. This scheme provides opportunity to SC/ST students to grow up in an academic environment free from the hazards of undertaking long journeys for attending their schools. Number of hostels and benefited SC/ST students in three backward districts—Purulia, Bankura and Paschim Medinipur are higher than that of other districts of West Bengal. Fifty one per cent of total running hostels of the states are located in these three districts and 46 per cent of total SC benefited students and 73 per cent of total ST benefited students belong to these three districts. A number of stipend and scholarship schemes have also been introduced for the development of SC/ST, minority and other backward caste students. During the recent years, the State Government has introduced a unique scholarship programme *Kanyashree* for the empowerment of girl child. Most of the eligible school going girl students has been benefited from these schemes. The State Government is implementing a scheme of distribution of bi-cycles to the tribal girl students from Class IX to XII in Jangal Mahal blocks of Paschim Medinipur, Bankura and Purulia districts. In 2013-14, funds for 34265 bicycles have been provided to girl students of Class IX to XII in this region.

In the region with high unemployment and underemployment it is expected that MGNREG plays an important role by creating sufficient man days. But the performance of MGNREGA is not satisfactory and shows the hopelessness of rural aspirants. During 2013-14, in the backward region, MGNREGA has provided, on average, 37 person days of employment per household and only 5 per cent households obtained 100 days employment. The self-employment generating programme, SGSY and its component self-help group's programme promotes the formation of organization of the poor at the grassroots level through a process of social mobilization of women for poverty reduction. The formation of SHGs is relatively low in Purulia and Paschim Medinipur districts and very few groups have started economic activities.

The number of beneficiaries and the amount of cash benefits under social assistance programmes like IGNOAPS, IGNWPS and IGNDPS have, however, gradually increased during recent years.

Social Protection Benefits for Poor Households in the Backward Region of West Bengal

In the field survey we have found the evidence of 24 social protection programmes in respect of benefits obtained by households (at least one). The coverage of the social protection programmes is analysed in respect of scope (the benefited households/persons), extent (average amount of benefit per household/per person) and level (the amount of benefit) on the basis of the information from 600 sample households during 2012-13.

Among 600 sample households 82 per cent (and 60 per cent sample population) have BPL ration cards and they are eligible for BPL facilities. Among the eligible households (persons) 93 per cent obtained benefit. The estimated amount of benefit during 2012-13 was Rs. 3929 per household and Rs. 1103 per person. For Antyodaya Anna Yojana (AAY) 47 per cent households were eligible, and 37 per cent among them have been benefited where the benefited amount was Rs. 1170 per household per annum. The coverage of Annapurna Yojana (AY) was relatively poor, out of 22 per cent eligible households only three per cent have obtained benefit and each household has been benefited to the extent of Rs. 2000. The status of the ration card of 6 per cent households was APL in nature and they are excluded from subsidized PDS. The PDS benefits also widely vary across households. Seven per cent households did not get any benefits, while 78 per cent households were getting less than 8 kg food grains per capita per month; the amount is less than the statutory provision for the poor household. Only 15 per cent are getting more than 8 kg food grains per capita per month.

Nearly 85 per cent of sample households have obtained benefit from public health centres during 2012-13. Their average level of benefit was Rs. 392 per household (and Rs. 78 per person). We, however, observe that the families are compelled to do their health treatment out of pocket. Public health centres are located at very long distance from their villages they live in. The problems that we observe are: health centres are not regularly opened; there are insufficient health personalities; and medicines are also not available. In case of JSY there is the provision of one time benefit for the pregnant and lactating mother and only 43 per cent eligible beneficiaries have obtained benefit and their average amount of benefit is Rs. 600 per capita per year. At present RSBY covers the health insurance coverage of both BPL and APL households. Up to 2012-13, 62 per cent sample households are enrolled in RSBY and only 5 per cent of them obtain benefits for medical (institutional) treatment. Their average amount of benefit was Rs. 5779 during the financial year 2012-13.

Among 600 sample households 87 per cent have obtained the drinking water facilities under NRDWP. The crisis of drinking water is severe during summer in drought prone blocks of the three backward districts. In respect of sanitation facility most of the households were deprived. Only 22 per cent households had latrine (either open or close pit) facilities. TSC programme which is very essential for every household had experienced the worst performance in the sample region.

Among the sample households, 36 per cent had children of age group below six years and they were eligible for ICDS facilities. Among the eligible children, 94 per cent were getting the benefits. That is, the extent of coverage of this programme was relatively high. There is the provision of at least 250 meals during a year. But only 4 per cent households had obtained that benefit. Among all eligible children, 6 per cent had not taken any meal and 66 per cent had taken meals less than 200. Forty eight per cent of sample households were eligible for MDM programme and 93 per cent of them were benefited. Among the beneficiaries 7 per cent did not obtain any meal whereas 74 per cent obtained meals less than 200 during 2012-13. Only three per cent got the facility of the statutory provision of at least 250 meals during a year.

MGNREGP is a universal programme but the households having Job Cards were eligible for the benefit of employment. Accordingly, among 600 sample households only 85 per cent were eligible for benefits and among them only 91 per cent obtained benefits. The average man days of employment of 600 households during 2012-13 were 23 days and none of them received 100 days employment. NTFP is another income generating programme, especially for poor people who live near the forest. Fifty per cent of sample households are eligible for benefits under NTFP and only 46.7 per cent of them got the benefits during 2012-13. The average amount of benefits was Rs. 1093 per household.

Social security related programmes like IGNOAPS, IGNWPS and IGNDPS are for specific beneficiaries; therefore, their coverage was limited. Among eligible old age persons only 28 per cent received the pension and the average amount of pension (per capita per year) was Rs. 4678. In case of widow pension scheme 43 per cent of eligible widows have obtained pension to the extent of Rs. 4606 per widow during 2012-13. In case of disabled pension only three disabled persons out of 12 got the benefit to the extent of Rs. 10100 each.

Among SPPs the relative importance of PDS benefits is highest followed by NREGP, ICDS and MDM. These programmes are now legally enforced. That is, the legally enforced SPPs are better executed and they create more benefits to the households.

In our sample study region Jangal Mahal is backward relative to Non-Jangal Mahal area and the people of Jangal Mahal are also much more deprived. The State Government has extended the extra benefits by different SPPs for the people living in the Jangal Mahal area. It is found that the per capita per month PDS benefit as well as overall social protection benefit in Jangal Mahal area is significantly higher than that in Non-Jangal Mahal area.

Most of the social protection programmes are deficient in fulfilling their objectives. The supply of social protection benefits is lagging behind the demand. It is estimated that around Rs. 168.15 crore additional funds is required to cover the social protection benefits to all eligible households in the three backward districts during a year. That is, additional Rs. 27099 per household per year is required to fulfil the statutory provision of social protection benefits.

Entitlement of the Sample Households in Relation to SPPs

The entitlement approach of A.K. Sen is based on three conceptual categories, namely the Endowment Set; the Entitlement Set; and the Entitlement Mapping. The *endowment set* includes both tangible (such as land, equipment, animals) and intangible (such as knowledge and skill, labour power, or membership of a particular community) assets of the households. The *entitlement set* is the set of all possible combinations of goods and services (not just the one actually being enjoyed) that a person can legally obtain by using the resources of his endowment set. It includes "production-based entitlement" (growing food), "trade-based cntitlement" (buying food), "own-labour entitlement" (working for food) and "inheritancc and transfer entitlement" (being given food by others). The *entitlement mapping* is the rate at which the resources of the endowment set can be converted into goods and services included in the entitlement set. The exchange entitlements depend not merely on market exchanges but also on those exchanges, if any, that the state provides as a part of social protection programme.

The cultivable landholding, the important asset endowment in the rural area, is relatively low for most of the sample households. The households were either landless (36%) or belonged to marginal land-holding. The exchange entitlement of land was also deficient due to low productivity. The agri-allied productive assets were also found in some households. But in most of the cases they serve the household activity and in some cases they were sold by the households to cope with the adverse situation or shocks. The bitter truth is that the earning from assets of 40 per cent sample households was zero. The earning of other households from assets was also low and for most of them it was less than Rs. 1000. The labour power is another most crucial endowment for the rural households. But only 12 per cent of labourers were regularly employed. The majority of the labourers (52%) of sample households were casual labour. Households also failed (partially) in respect of exchange entitlement of labour. Among 600 sample households, 25 per cent households were unable to use their labour power for more than 100 man days and 50 per cent households used their labour power to the extent of 100 to 200 man days during the year. The main reason of this entitlement failure was the deficiency of skill and education of workers. The membership of different social protection programmes or institutions also gives opportunity to them to increase entitlement of the household. It creates the opportunity to receive the benefits of different public welfare measures. An access to common property resources (CPRs) also increases the entitlement of the households.

Total income of the household is composed of the earnings from different entitlements. In terms of income generation the contribution of labour entitlement was highest followed by social protection. The average per capita per day income (PCPDI) from labour was Rs. 11.4 and from social protection it was Rs. 5.3. Other sources of earnings like agricultural and non-agricultural production, trade and CPR was relatively low for sample households. There were 28.2 per sample households with PCPDI less than Rs. 18 (equivalent expenditure of food security line) and nearly 75 per cent households with PCPDI less than Rs. 29 (equivalent expenditure of poverty line). The social protection benefit significantly affected the income of the households and also their entitlements. It has increased the average per capita income of 600 sample households to the extent of 21.2 per cent.

Status of Food Security of the Sample Households and the Role of SPPs

Food security depends not merely on 'availability' of food but most importantly on the 'access' to food through 'entitlements'—a combination of what one can produce, exchange in the market plus state or other socially provided supplies. The average food expenditure (per capita per day) of 600 sample households was Rs. 16.57 which was substantially low as compared to the food security line of Rs. 17.59. Among 600 sample households only 35 per cent were food secure. The entitlements of the rest of 65 per cent households were not sufficient to command the minimum requirement of food. For the entire sample households, the incidence of food insecurity (FIS) was 71.8 per cent, food insecurity gap (FIG) was 17.7 per cent and square food insecurity gap (SFIG) was 5.7 per cent. FIS, FIG and SFIG were relatively high for socially disadvantaged classes (SCs and STs). The situation of food insecurity was significantly higher in Jangal Mahal region than that in Non-Jangal Mahal region. The percentage share of food insecure households and incidence of food insecurity in Jangal Mahal area were 71.2 per cent and 77.6 per cent in comparison to 60.0 and 67.6 in Non-Jangal Mahal region.

The PDS benefits played an important role in food security. The percentage share of food insecure households had decreased from 76.7 per cent in absence of PDS benefits to 64.7 per cent in presence of PDS benefits and the incidence of food insecurity has decreased from 81.4 per cent to 71.8 per cent. That is, the benefits from PDS have reduced food insecurity of 12 per cent sample households and 10 per cent sample person.

The empirical analysis of the relationship between entitlements of the households including social protection benefits and the status of food security is made on the basis of household's utility maximization model. The estimated probit regression results suggest that as the income from labour, trade, common property resources, food from public distribution system and share of food expenditure to total expenditure increases, the probability of food insecurity (FIS) as well as depth of food insecurity (FIG) of the household decreases. Increased income from agriculture also reduces the probability of food insecurity but not depth of food insecurity. The common property assets also play important role to overcome food insecurity. The benefits of social protection programmes, particularly PDS played a crucial role in insuring food security of the poor households—higher access of food grains from PDS reduces the incidence and depth of food security. The increase of consumption of the sample households in favour of food consumption also reduces the incidence as well as depth of food insecurity. The depth of food insecurity is significantly high for the households who belong to SC and ST communities and are located in Jangal Mahal region.

Poverty and Deprivation of the Sample Households in Relation to SPPs

Poverty in India was traditionally measured in terms of consumption expenditure. But income poverty does not accurately proxy other deprivations. Therefore, we have taken up both uni-dimensional and multidimensional measures of poverty. The average per capita per day expenditure (PCPDE) of the sample households was Rs. 23.30 which was substantially low as compared to the poverty line of Rs. 28.80. The estimated marginal propensity to consume (MPC) of sample households was 0.56; for food consumption it was 0.25 and for non-food consumption it was 0.31. That is, the increased income across households increases the consumption, but the increased consumption was little lower for food than that for non-food. The social inequality influences individual's consumption and induces greater consumption of the so-called status goods. The status driven utility function induces the households to spend more on non-food consumption than food consumption.

On the basis of PCPDE, 82 per cent of sample households were estimated to be poor. The entitlements of these households were not enough to command the minimum requirement of consumption. The estimated head count ratio (HCR) was 81.7 per cent, poverty gap (PGP) was 27.3 per cent and squared poverty gap (SPGP) was 10.6 per cent. Not only the HCR, PGP and SPGP but also the poverty risk was substantially high for STs and SCs relative to that of others.

The percentage share of poor households had decreased from 87 per cent in absence of SPBs to 81.7 per cent in presence of SPBs and the incidence of poverty had decreased from 90 per cent to 86 per cent. That is, the benefits from SPPs had reduced the incidence of poverty to the extent of 4 per cent. With the help of entire SPBs only 5.3 per cent poor households managed to overcome poverty. That raises the question as regards to the effectiveness of SPPs on poor households. The leakages and inefficient delivery mechanisms are the main reasons for the insignificant effect of SPPs on poor households. The extent of the benefit of social protection floor in the backward region has only partially succeeded to overcome poverty of the BPL households.

The empirical analysis of the relationship between entitlements of the households including social protection benefits and the status of poverty is made on the basis of Heckman two-step model. The result suggests that as the income from agriculture, non-agricultural production, labour, trade, common property resources and food from public distribution system increases, the probability of poverty as well as depth of poverty of the household decreases. Increased income from non-agricultural production also reduces the incidence of poverty but not depth of poverty. The majority of the sample households are located near the forest and others are located near river and their access to the common property resources significantly reduces the poverty. The benefits from PDS played a crucial role for reduction of poverty—higher access of food grains from PDS reduces the incidence and depth of poverty. The overall social protection benefits significantly affect the depth of poverty but not the incidence of poverty. The empirical results confirm that the failure of entitlements is the cause of poverty. The incidence and depth of poverty were significantly high for the households who belong to SC and ST communities and are located in Jangal Mahal region.

In presence of SPB, the percentage share of deprived households had significantly decreased in respect of the indicators like Electricity, Drinking Water, Malnourishment and Schooling. The social protection programmes like NRDWP for safe drinking water, provision of meals by ICDS and MDM for reduction of malnutrition, and SSK and MSK for schooling are playing important role for reduction of deprivation of the household. There is also the provision of free connection of electricity for BPL households in the villages. Other programmes like Rural Primary Health Care, JSY and RSBY were helpful in reducing Infant Mortality, TSC for Sanitation facilities and IAY for Housing facilities to the poor played important role in the reduction of deprivation of the households. Most of the sample households in the sample villages used forest products for cooking purpose; therefore SPPs have insignificant effect on the indicator namely Cooking Fuel.

The percentage share of the vulnerable to poor households,

multidimensionally deprived households and severely poor households decreased to the extent of 11, 21.3 and 12.7 percentage points respectively in the presence of SPB in comparison to the absence of SPB. The values of these indicators were also substantially high for SCs and STs in comparison to those for other castes. In the presence and absence of social protection benefits, the overall MPI scores were 0.30 and 0.36 respectively and head count ratios were 58.2 per cent and 77.1 per cent respectively.

8.2 Conclusions

The SPF in rural India includes *food security* by TPDS, *health* by rural primary health care, RSBY and JSY, *water & sanitation* by NRDWP and TSC, *education* by ICDS, SSK, MSK, MDM, etc., *housing* by IAY, *income support benefits and/or employment guarantees* by NREGP, SGSY and NTFP, along with *pensions* by NOAPS, NFBS, NWPS, NDPS and IGMSY. A number of programmes like TPDS, MGNREGS, SSA and NTFP are now legally enforced. In the last few years, a major expansion has occurred in the expenditure on these programmes where the Courts or the Constitution have created specific entitlements through legislative changes or legal oversight. Along with these central programmes, some State Governments in India have their own poverty-reduction schemes. In West Bengal State Government has also implemented a number of programmes among which quasi-universal PDS in specially disadvantaged region (Jangal Mahal, Drought Prone, Hill etc.), *Kanyashri* for empowerment of girls child, scholarships/grants for students of SC/ST/minority, bi-cycle for tribal school going girls and fair price medicine shop are important. There is the provision of transfer of benefits of SPPs in cash and kind. The benefits of SPPs relating to food, health (except RSBY and JSY), education and water & sanitation are in kind and those of the rest of the programmes are in the form of cash.

The quasi-universal PDS in the backward region of West Bengal overcomes the exclusion and inclusion errors and helps to extend TPDS benefits to most of the households. The PDS benefits played an important role in food security. The extent of the benefit of PDS in the backward region partially succeeded to overcome food insecurity of the BPL households. The people of most backward area were benefited more than those in other areas. The failure of other entitlements caused food insecurity and poverty of the households. On account of insufficient productive assets endowment, labour entitlement is much more important than production entitlement. They survive by selling their labour power.

But the labour entitlement is also not sufficient for the poor households to cope with the food insecurity. The benefits from other social protection programmes lead to increase the overall income of the poor households and also consumption. But the increased consumption was little lower for food than for non-food and the households were not able to overcome the food insecurity.

The social protection benefits significantly help in the reduction of incidence and depth of food insecurity as well as poverty. It also significantly reduces the deprivations of the households relating to malnourishment, schooling, drinking water, sanitation, housing and electricity. But the benefits of social protection programmes are limited in respect of overcoming the problems of food insecurity and poverty. Most of the social protection programmes are deficient in fulfilling their objectives with respect to statutory provisions. The supply of social protection benefits is also lagging behind the demand. That raises the question as regards to the effectiveness of SPPs on improving the status of poor households. The leakages and inefficient delivery mechanisms are the main reasons for the insignificant effect of SPPs on poor households. The provision of direct cash transfer is not the solution because the importance of PDS benefits is higher than the conditional cash transfer under MGNREGS.

8.3 Policy Recommendations

From the above discussion the following policy recommendations may be made.

First, since the ration cards are old documented and some of the households or the members have no ration cards on account of exclusion and inclusion errors, there is the urgent need for the issue of new ration card. Since the Government of India is implementing the National Food Security Bill-2013 for benefits of 75 per cent targeted rural people, the identification of the poor or stakeholders by appropriate statistical method at frequent time intervals is important. In this context, the Socio Economic Caste Census 2011 played a crucial role.

Second, since PDS benefit in kind certainly increases the food consumption baskets while cash benefits from other programmes diversify the consumption of the poor households in favour of luxury items, the study strongly recommends for PDS benefits in kind to overcome food insecurity and poverty.

Third, to bridge the gap between demand and supply in most of the sectors where social protection programmes are implemented, management and supervision has been decentralized to the local level and steps are taken to strengthen the capacity of local governments, rules have to be enforced for the creation of stakeholder committees at the local institutional level.

Fourth, digitization of the records of the functioning of SPPs by Information Technology-enabled service is important for transparency and to minimize corruption.

Fifth, for effective execution of social protection programmes such rules for quality of services for each programme are essential.

Sixth, since the household's income from labour is supportive to overcome the incidence of food insecurity and poverty and since the education level and the skill formation of workers are relatively poor, in order to strengthen the labour entitlement spread of education is needed. Besides basic education, vocational training and technical skills are useful in gaining access to non-agricultural jobs or self-employment. Effective micro-entrepreneurship development programme is helpful for promotion of non-farm activities.

Seventh, since as per our finding production entitlement, specifically agricultural production is important for food security and to overcome poverty and the greater part of the backward region is deficient in respect of irrigation, for the sake of multiple cropping which helps the households to increase production on one hand and increase labour demand on the other, spread of irrigation for production of compatible crops in the dry region is indispensable for production-led food security.

Eighth, while access to income from common property resources significantly reduces the incidence of food insecurity and poverty, for the sake of improvement existing rights to use the forest resources by villagers is strongly recommended.

Ninth, while in the short run the social protective measures are important for the poor and vulnerable and the excessive dependence on social protection has raised the question of sustainability of livelihood in the long run therefore the study strongly recommends measures to enhance the own entitlement of the households to cope with poverty and deprivations.

Tenth, given the limitations of the SPPs for poverty alleviation the accent should be placed on the overall development of rural areas because the backward region is predominantly rural. For rural transformation of this region the rapid development of infrastructure like road and power is must. Rural development programmes are to be so designed and directed such that they gradually make the poor and vulnerable rely on their own selves based on infrastructure.

Lastly, the resources of this regions being limited, great emphasis should be placed on decentralized planning and participating development of this area, which would ensure the efficient utilization of the available resources to accelerate economic development of the region along with social justice. This is essential to make development of this region broad-based, effective and sustainable.

Appendix

Table A1: Selected Development Indicators 2011

Districts	*FPG*	*NFGA*	*CI*	*UPOP*	*LTR*	*RDEN*	*PCID*	*GEP*	*UNEP*	*PSPI*	*SMF*	*RPOV*	*Rank#*
Paschim Medinipur	2687	19.4	161	12.2	76.9	2922	34788	1.53	56.5	47308	85.8	30.8	12
Bankura	2963	14.1	134	8.3	68.9	1664	33458	0.07	58.8	35611	68.2	28.5	17
Purulia	2595	1.9	100	12.7	62.7	1089	28142	0.72	55.8	36626	79.1	40.7	18
24-Parganas (N)	2633	33.7	156	57.3	77.4	2132	436442	1.34	63.6	8072	89.6	8.7	1
24-Parganas (S)	2255	6.7	123	25.6	75.7	3352	35754	1.63	63.7	77000	87.5	6.4	7
Birbhum	2816	12.5	153	12.8	69.1	2676	30289	1.19	61.7	40726	72.5	14.2	11
Burdwan	2939	14.6	155	39.9	72.7	1695	46456	1.08	59.7	44610	71.9	20.7	8
Cooch Behar	2275	32.5	175	10.3	73.2	2748	32465	1.47	59.5	52205	75.5	25.5	10
Darjeeling	2037	45.7	83	39.4	74.3	1299	50933	0.63	61.7	33579	83.6	11.8	13
Dakshin Dinajpur	2601	22	131	14.1	70.1	2386	31595	1.15	57.4	55876	76.1	8.8	14
Hooghly	2908	25.6	177	38.6	78.5	3534	42944	0.61	59.5	58096	86.1	28.6	4
Howrah	2090	17.7	159	63.4	80.0	4048	40582	-0.53	62.3	62180	92.9	13.9	2
Jalpiguri	2116	39.7	129	27.4	69.7	1346	36842	0.15	60.1	60513	80.5	31.0	16
Malda	2808	16.1	146	13.6	59.4	2195	30550	0.55	61.3	71229	83.4	31.7	15
Murshidabad	2617	26.4	169	19.7	65.3	1992	31329	1.68	64.8	63427	81.5	33.9	9
Nadia	2659	41.2	202	27.8	70.9	1812	37207	0.24	65.4	48751	79.8	23.9	6
Purba Medinipur	2506	8.3	154	11.6	86.8	3563	52570	1.53	61.9	62912	93.5	21.1	3
Uttar Dinajpur	2929	26.7	151	12.1	56	2512	25152	1.35	63.9	93973	77.3	34.2	5

Notes: FGP = Foodgrain productivity (Q /hect), NFGA = Percentage share of non-foodgrain area to total area.(%), CI = Cropping Intensity, UPOP = Percentage share of urban population to total population, LTR = Rural literacy rate, RDEN = Road density (per '000 sq. km), PCDI = per capita district domestic product, GEP = Annual compound growth rate of employment (Rural), UNEP = Rural unemployment rate, PSPI = Population served per Government medical institute, SMF = Share of marginal farmer to total farmer, RPOV = Rural poverty ratio.

\# Ranking is made on the basis of the value of group dimension index (GDI) of the districts. GDI is sum total (standardized) of these 12 indicators.

Table A 2: Sample Frame

1st Stage	*2nd Stage*		*3rd Stage*	*4th Stage*
Districts (3)	Blocks (12)		Village (24)	Households (600)
Paschim Medinipur	Jangal Mahal Block	Jamboni	Belia	25 BPL Households from each Village
			Murakati	
		Sankrail	Jarasol	
			Phulbani	
	Non-Jangal Mahahal Block	Dantan-I	Dakshin Amria	
			Kotpada	
		Keshiary	Lenga Mara	
			Murakata	
Bankura	Jangal Mahal Block	Ranibundh	Nachna	
			Mitha-Am	
	Non-Jangal Mahahal Block	Vishnupur	Kulupukur	
			Baramara	
		Taldangra	Panchmura	
			Saldaha	
		Khatra	Chandania	
			Bantilla	
Purulia	Jangal Mahal Block	Jaipur	Nutandi	
			Mukundpur	
		Jhalda-II	Dimu	
			Chekya (CT)	
	Non-Jangal Mahahal Block	Hura	Khairipihira	
			Dholkata	
		Kashipur	Rudra	
			Shampur	

REVIEW OF EXISTING LITERATURE

Unni and Rani (2002) reported that nearly half of the informal workers (of sample SEWA members) felt that the nature of their work had an adverse effect on their health. The vulnerability of the poor informal workers increases when they have to pay fully for their medical care with no subsidy or support. The study found that about 79 per cent of the workers paid for the entire cost of medical care without any support. Further, less than 5 per cent of the workers had some form of medical insurance.

Schwarzer and Querino (2002) observed that despite labour market informality Brazil achieved remarkable benefit coverage among the elderly over the last decades. The two elements of this success are the Rural Social Security programme and the Social Assistance Pensions.

Sinha (2003) pointed out that among the poor women facing the additional burden of economic activity in the informal sector where the conditions of work were strenuous, the chances of maternal mortality would be higher, particularly if these women have no access to proper health facilities. Another concern expressed by the poor informal women workers is the loss of income during the advanced period of maternity and immediately after childbirth, when they are not able to work for some time. It is obvious that the distinct problems of women workers are crucial. But the study did not endeavour the effectiveness of rural health mission in this respect.

Baulch *et al.,* (2005) developed a social protection index for six countries in Asia to be used as a policy instrument by the Asian Development Bank's work on social protection. A key innovation in this work is the attempt to connect overall social protection expenditure to poverty reduction. The index combines measures of expenditure, coverage, poverty targeting, and impact on the poverty gap. A comparison of the index with the Human Development Index (HDI) rankings for the six countries shows a high correlation, as the authors conclude, this "is not unexpected as, by and large as GDP per capita (one of the HDI components) increases, the amount of spent on social protection will increase" (Baulch *et al.,* 2005:15). (Source: Social Protection and Poverty Article)

Rajasekhar *et al.*, (2005), in a study in Karnataka, used a participatory method to derive the perceived social security needs of unorganised sector workers. They noted that among the workers surveyed, 92.3 per cent felt that benefits towards old age, unemployment, death, sickness and employment injury were relevant for them. Women in the reproductive age groups also felt that maternity benefits were important. Agricultural labourers and construction workers reported the fear of not being able to work during the old age. The study was more descriptive than analytical. It explored the needs of the social security but not examined the coverage, if any, of social security for unorganized workers.

Sakthivel and Joddar (2006) estimated that India's workforce comprised nearly 92 per cent in the unorganized segment, with entire farm sector falling under informal category, while only one-fifth of the non-farm workers are found in the organized segment. Their estimates suggested that in the non-farm sectors, as we move up the income ladder, the share of the informal sector gradually declines. However, as far as the agricultural sector is concerned, irrespective of economic class, the share of the unorganized workforce remains flat. They noticed that the non-farm unorganized sector workers virtually been left out of social security arrangements.

National Commission for Enterprises in the Unorganized Sector (NCEUS) (2006) estimated the unorganized informal workers as about 86 per cent of the workforce in the Indian economy in 2004-05, informal employment both in the unorganized and organized sector as 93 per cent. One of the major significance of this representative is the existence and qualification of the unorganised or informal workers defined, as those who do not have employment, work security and social security. The workers are mostly self-employed or wage workers, sometimes located in their homes but mostly outsides. Some are lucky to have some kind of regular work but majority of workers are employed on casual basis. Most of the wages are too low to enable them to come out of their poverty. Discrimination is the norm when it comes to women, children, bonded or migrant workers. Such positions of disadvantage are often reinforced by one's social identity rural location and low education. The situation calls for immediate steps to ensure minimum condition of work for the unorganized workers as well as measures of lively hood promotion. The commission has therefore proposed two comprehensive Bills for the unorganized agricultural and non-agricultural workers to ensure minimum level of condition as well as minimum level of social security. It has further proposed a number of measures to improve the livelihood of the unorganized sector workers. So Commission has recommended for creating the foundations of decent-work, and for the target-oriented public intervention is also necessary, the Public Distribution System though limited in coverage, the Mid Day Meal for the school children, pension for the destitute and all other schemes especially for those belonging to SCs and STs can be cited as good example. There is some positive commitment of the state in the field of elementary education (Sarva Shiksha Abhiyan) and basic health (Rural Health Mission) and right based manual employment, guarantee for rural households (national rural guarantee programme). The other livelihood promoting measures are: (a) Promotional policies for non-agricultural unorganized sector, (b) availability of institutional credit, (c) micro credit and SHGs, (d) raw material, (e) marketing, (f) cluster Development and growth poles, (g) National fund for unorganized sector, and (h) policy initiatives, programmes and scheme for agricultural workers, promotional measures of expansion of employment such as schemes like self-employment programme like Prime Minister Yojana, Rural Employment Guarantee Programe (REGP), Swarnajayanti Gram Swarojgar Yojana (SGSY), formation of Self Help Group approach and enterprise development. The National Rural Employment Guarantee Act, 2005 is a major step in the direction of providing assurance and security of employment to rural workers and providing at least 100 days of guaranteed wage employment in every year to every household.

Unni and Lu (2007) observed that the informalisation process of India and China was very similar in respect of increasing proportion of the population in private enterprises with flexible contracts and minimum social security coverage. However, while most of the Indian workforce was informal since the early years, the phenomenon is as recent as 1996 in China. They also noticed that about a quarter of the workforce in China is now in private enterprises, though much of this is supported by the government or by foreign firms and another 7 per cent are self-employed. The Chinese workers still have the advantage of basic literacy and numeracy and capacity to follow basic written instructions. They compared only the informalisation process in two countries.

ILO (2008) pointed out that despite the widespread lack of coverage, a number of middle-income countries have successfully expanded coverage of their social security systems in recent years. For example, Costa Rica has achieved full health coverage through a combination of health insurance and free access to public health services. India's National Old-Age Pension Scheme, financed by central and state resources, reaches one-fourth of all the elderly: about half of pensioners who live in poverty. A newly introduced social security scheme helped in the Republic of Korea to adjust more smoothly to the Asian financial crisis of the late 1990s. In particular, a newly introduced unemployment insurance programme helped the country cope with a quadrupling of the jobless rate. But how the social security systems help the people to cross the poverty line was not explored in the study.

According to Kannan (2007), the major and recent initiating for providing social security to the workers in the informal economy is a legally guarantee drive. It emerges as a development policy of the country and two major approaches are the National Rural Employment Guarantee (NREG) and the second relates to social security for unorganized social workers. The NREG has already been enacted and the second one is in initial stage of enactment.

Barrientos (2010) pointed out two main aims: to provide an overview of social protection, and to provide an assessment of its potential contribution to addressing poverty and vulnerability in developing countries. He argued that social protection as a policy framework against a context of poverty and vulnerability trends in the 1980s and 1990s in Latin America. It pays particular attention to the growing influence of multidimensionality in poverty analysis. He examines different approaches to social protection and traces them to underlying development perspectives. There are different versions of social protection, emphasizing either risk, rights or needs as the organizing concept. The likely impact on poverty and vulnerability of the extension of social protection under way in developing countries is not in doubt. Investment in social protection and social assistance can be extremely effective in reducing current poverty and vulnerability, as well as poverty persistence across time and generations.

According to Rabi Srivastava (2011) there are six dimensions of social protection they are: (1) children's education, nutritional and health care facilities, (2) Employment and livelihood securities, (3) Social pension, (4) Social health care protection, (5) food security, (6) Housing security. The social protection programme of Central Government of India are: (A) Education, Nutritional & Health support programmes like (i) Sarva Siksha Abhiyan, (ii) Integrated Child Development Scheme, (iii) National Programme for Mid-day Meal, (iv) National Rural Health Mission, (v) Rashtriya Sasthya Bima Yojana, (vi) Total Sanitation Campaign, and (vii) National Rural Drinking Water Programme; (B) Employment & Livelihood for rural and urban poor like (i) MGNERGS, (ii) Swarna Jayanti Gram Sa-rojgar Yoyana, (iii) Prime Ministers Employment Guarantee Programme; (C) Pension schemes like (i) National Old Age Pension, (ii) Indira Gandhi National Widow Pension, (iii) Indira Gandhi National Disability Pension; and (D) Housing for the poor like (i) Indira Abash Yojana, and (ii) Am Admi Bima Yojana. But question arises how far the poor informal workers are benefited through these policies and programme.

According to Srivastava (2012) in the recent past, the Indian state has connected some space to right based social protection measures. This has led to an increased financial allocation by the Central Government to access to social protection which come within the ambit of rights. But on the minimum conditions of work, there has been little programme in recent years. While examining the major social security programmes, including social programmes emerging out of the NCEUS proposals, the study finds an increase in recent years, particularly the programmes for employment creation and food security. However, the total expenditure on protective social security remains small.

Bibliography

Adams, R.H. and J. Page. 2003. 'International Migration, Remittances and Poverty in Developing Countries'. *World Bank Policy Research Working Paper 3179*, December, Washington, D.C., World Bank.

Afridi, F. 2008. 'Can Community Monitoring Improve the Accountability of Public Officials?'. *Economic and Political Weekly*, Vol. 43(42), October 18, 2008, pp. 35-40.

Agnihotri, B. Satish 1999. 'Eliminating Severe Malnutrition in Orissa: Profile of a Campaign'. *Economic and Political Weekly*, Vol. 34(51): 3616-3621.

Ahluwalia, M.S. 2011. 'Prospects and Policy Challenges in the Twelfth Plan'. *Economic and Political Weekly* 46(21): 88-105.

Alam, Moneer 2004, 'Ageing, Old Age Income Security and Reforms: An Exploration of Indian Situation', *Economic and Political Weekly*, Vol. 39(33): 3732.

Alkire, S. and Sarwar. 2009. 'Measures of Poverty & Well-being'. *Report Working Paper*. Oxford Poverty & Human Development Initiative (OPHI), Oxford Dept. of International Development, University of Oxford, January 2009, http://www.ophi.org.uk/publications/ophi-working-papers, accessed on 19 March 2014.

Alkire, S. and Santos M.E. 2010. 'Acute Multidimensional Poverty: A New Index for Developing Countries', *OPHI Working Paper 38*, http://www.ophi.org.uk/publications/ophi-working-papers.accessed on 19 March 2014.

Alkire, S. and Yalonetzky. 2011. 'Why Multidimensional Poverty Measures?'. *OPHI-HDCA Summer School Delft*. Oxford Department of International Development, University of Oxford, http://www.ophi.org.uk, accessed on 19 March 2014.

Alkire, S., Roche, J.M., Santos, M.E., and Seth, S. (2011). 'Multidimensional Poverty Index 2011: Brief Methodological Note' University of Oxford. www.ophi.org.uk/multidimensional-poverty-index/, accessed on 19 March 2014

Alkire, S. and J. Foster. 2011. 'Counting and multidimensional poverty measurement', *Journal of Public Economics*, Vol. 95: 476–487.

Alkire, S. and S. Seth. 2013a. 'Multidimensional Poverty Reduction in India between 1999 and 2006: Where and How?' *OPHI Working Paper No. 60*. Oxford Dept. of International Development, University of Oxford, March 2013.http://www.ophi.org.uk, accessed on 19 March 2014.

Alkire, S. and Santos M.E. 2013b.'Measuring Acute Poverty in the Developing World: Robustness and Scope of the Multidimensional Poverty Index', *OPHI Working Paper 59*, http://www.ophi.org.uk/publications/ophi-working-papers, accessed on 11 March 2014.

Ambasta, Pramathesh, Shankar, P.S. Vijay and Mihir, S. 2008. 'Two Years of NREGA: The Road Ahead', *Economic & Political Weekly*, Vol.-XLIII No. 08, February 23, pp. 41-50.

Anand, S. and Sen, A.K. 1997. *Concepts of Human Development and Poverty: A Multidimensional Perspective.* New York, UNDP.

ASER (Annual Status of Education Report). *Annual Status of Education Reports 2012*. Facilitated by PRATHAM.http://img.asercentre.org/docs/Publications/ASER%20Reports/ASER%202014/National%20PPTs/aser2014indiaenglish.pdf, accessed on 09 December 2014.

ASER (Annual Status of Education Report). 2013. *Annual Status of Education Reports 2013*. Facilitated by PRATHAM.http://img.asercentre.org/docs/Publications/ASER%20Reports/ASER%202014/National%20PPTs/aser2014indiaenglish.pdf, accessed on 09December 2014

Atkinson, A. and F. Bourguignon (1982). "The Comparison of Multidimensional Distribution of Economic Status", *Review of Economic Studies*, Vol. 49: 183-201.

Atkinson, A.B. (1987), "On the Measurement of Poverty", *Econometrica*, Vol. 55(4): 749–64.

Atkinson A.B. Cantillon, E. Marlier and B. Nolan (2002). *Social Indicators: The EU and Social Inclusion*, Oxford University Press, Oxford.

Bachelet, Michelle 2011.'Social Protection Floor for a Fair and Inclusive Globalization' Geneva: *ILO*.http://www.ilo.org/public/english/protection/spfag/download/background/bachrep_en.pdf, accessed on 07 December 2013

Bagchi, Kanak Kanti. 2011. *Regional Disparities in India's Socio-economic Development*. New Century Publications, http://www.researchandmarkets.com/reports/1719102/ regional_disparities in indias_socioeconomic accessed on December 4, 2013.

Bajpai, Nirupam and Ravindra H. Dholakia. 2011. 'Improving the Performance of Accredited Social Health Activists in India'. Working Paper Series, No. 1. Mumbai: Columbia Global Centres.

Banerjcc, A.B. Chakrabarty, M. Thakur, R. Chattopadhyay and S. Chaudhuri. 2011.'Restructuring of School Education System in West Bengal', *Indian Institute of Management*, Calcutta.

Banerjee, A. and A. Newman (1994), "Poverty, Incentives and Development", *American Economic Review, Papers and Proceedings*, 84-2: 211-215.

Barbara, Caracciolo, 2014.'Social Protection: An Instrument for Poverty Reduction and Social Cohesion', Available at: http://www.socialwatch.eu/

wcm/instrument_for poverty_reduction_ and_social_cohesion.html accessed on 28 September 2014.

Benerjee, K. and P. Saha. 2010. 'The NREGA, the Maoists and the Developmental Woes of the Indian State', *EPW*, July 10, Vol. XLV No. 28: 47.

Berg, E., S. Bhattacharyya, R. Durgam and, M. Ramachandra. 2012. 'Can Rural Public Works Affect Agricultural Wages: Evidence from India', CASE *Working Paper WPS/2012-05*, www.csae.ox.ac.uk/workingpapers/pdfs/csae-wps-2012-05.pdf, accessed on 19 April 2014.

Bhatty, K. 2006. 'Employment Guarantee and Child Rights', *EPW*, Vol. 41(20). May, 20, pp. 1965-7.

Bisiaux, R.2013. 'Understanding the Mismatch among the Three Definitions of Poverty: New Micro-Level Evidence from Delhi Slums'. *Economic and Political Weekly*, Vol-XLVIII No. 01, January 05.

Booth, C.1892. *Life and Labour of the People of London*, Vol. 1, Macmillan, London.

Bourguignon, F.2002. 'Multi-dimensional Poverty Orderings'. *Working Paper 2002/22,* World Bank.

Bourguignon, F. and S.R.Chakravarty. 2003.'The Measurement of Multidimensional Poverty'. *Journal of Economic Inequality,* 1, 25-49.

CAG (Comptroller and Auditor General of India). 2013. *Report of the Comptroller and Auditor General of India on Performance Audit of Integrated Child Development Services (ICDS) Scheme.* http://saiindia.gov.in/english/home/Our_Products/Audit_Report/Government_Wise/union_audit/recent_reports/ union_performance/ 2012_2013/Civil/Report_22/Report_22.html, accessed on 7 August 2013.

CHSJ (Centre for Health & Social Justice). 2010.'National Alliance on Maternal Health and Human Rights' *EPW* pp. 94-104, January 20, http://www.chsj.org/namhhr.htm.

Cerioli, A. and S. Zani.1990. 'A Fuzzy Approach to the Measurement of Poverty', *Income and Wealth Distribution, Inequality and Poverty*, (eds.) C. Dagum & M. Zenga Studies in Contemporary Economics, Springer Verlag, Berlin.

Chakravarty, S.R., D. Mukherjee, R.R. Ranade.1998. 'On the Family of Subgroup and Factor Decomposable Measures of Multidimensional Poverty'. *Research on Economic Inequality 8*, 175-194.

Chakraborty, P. 2007. 'Implementation of Employment Guarantee: A Preliminary Appraisal', *Economic and Political Weekly*, Vol. 42(7), February 17, 2007, pp. 548-551.

Cheli B. and A. Lemmi.1995. "A 'Totally' Fuzzy and Relative Approach to the Multidimensional Analysis of Poverty", *Economic Notes*, Vol. 24: 115-134.

Chakraborty, A. and S. Mukherjee. 2011. 'Implementation of SSA in four districts of West Bengal', Interim report in *Institute of Development Studies (IDSK)*, Kolkata.

Cichon, M. 2006. 'Social security for all: Investing in global social and economic development'. Labour Education.

CMS. 2011. 'Assessment Study of Impact and Sustainability of Nirmal Gram Puraskar' Study for Department of Drinking Water and Sanitation. Delhi: *Ministry of Rural Development*, Government of India.

Cohen, A. 2010. 'The Multidimensional Poverty Assessment Tool: A new framework for measuring rural poverty'. *Development in Practice*, Volume 20, Issue 7.

Costa, M. 2003. 'A Comparison Between Unidimensional and Multidimensional Approaches to the Measurement of Poverty: An Integrated Research Infrastructure in the Socio-Economic Sciences'. *IRISS Working Paper Series No. 2003-02*.

Dagum, C. and Costa, M. 2004. 'Analysis and Measurement of Poverty Univariate and Multivariate Approaches and their Policy Implications: A case study of Italy'. In Dagum C and Ferrari G. (eds.), Household Behaviour, Equivalence Scales, Welfare and Poverty, Springer Verlag, Germany, 221-271.

Das, Pinaki 2010. *Rural Non-Farm Employment in India: Pattern of Growth and Determinants*, Firma KLM Pvt. Ltd., Kolkata.

Das, Pinaki (2012). 'Growth Trajectory and its Implications for Employment in India'. *The Indian Economic Journal,* Special Issue, December 2012.

Das, Pinaki. 2013. 'Social Protection for Food Security of the Poor: A Micro Level Analysis'. *The paper presented in the UGC Sponsored National Seminar*, Vidyasagar University, West Bengal.

Das, S. and Y. Mishra. 2006. 'Gender Budgeting Statement: Misleading and Patriarchal Assumptions'. *Economic and Political Weekly*, Vol. 41(30) (Jul. 29-Aug. 4), pp. 3285-3288.

Das, Vidhya and Promod Pradhan. 2007. 'Illusions of Change'. *EPW*, Vol. 42(32): 3283-3287.

Deaton, Angus and Jean Dreze. 2009. 'Food and Nutration in India: Facts and Interpretations'. *Economic and Political Weekly* 44(7): 42-65.

Deaton, A. and J. Drèze 2002. 'Poverty and Inequality in India: A Re-Examination', *Economic and Political Weekly*, 37 (7): 42-65.

Deaton, A. 1997. 'The Analysis of Household Surveys: A Micro-econometric Approach to Development Policy', Washington DC: World Bank.

Deaton, Angus and Jean Dreze. 2009. 'Food and Nutrition in India: Facts and Interpretations'. *Economic and Political Weekly* 44 (7): 42-65.

Desai, Vasant. 2012. *Rural Development in India.* Himalaya Publishing House, Delhi, http://india.unfpa.org/drive/JSYConcurrentAssessment.pdf, accessed on July 24, 2014.

De, Anuradha, R. Khera, M. Samson, and A.K. Shiva Kumar. 2011. *PROBE Revisited: A Report on Elementary Education.* Delhi: Oxford University Press.

Dey, Subhasish and Arjun S. Bedi. 2010. 'The National Rural Employment Guarantee Scheme in Birbhum'. *Economic & Political Weekly*, October 9, 2010 vol xlv No. 41, http://www.indiaenvironmentportal.org.in/files/NREGA%20in%20Birbhum.pdf, accessed on September 14, 2014.

Dev, S. Mahendra. 1991. 'Is PDS Urban Biased and Pro-Rich?: An Evaluation', *Economic and Political Weekly*, Vol. 26(41): 2357-2359+2361-2366.

Dev, S. Mahendra and Alakh N. Sharma. 2010. 'Food Security in India: Performance, Challenges and Policies'. *Oxfam India Working Papers Series* 7, September.

Dev, S. Mahendra. 2011. 'NREGS and Child Being'. *IGIDR,* Mumbai, publication/ WP-2011-004. Available at www.igidr.ac.in/pdf/publication/WP-2011-004 accessed on 04/06/2012.

Dhar, A.2012. Left Out of Benefits, *The Hindu*, September 20.

Dongre, A. and A. Kapur. 2011. 'How is Janani Suraksha Yojana Performing in Backward Districts of India? Accountability Initiative'. http:// www.accountabilityindia.in/accountabilityblog/2590-howjanani-suraksha-yojana-performing-backward-districtsindia-part-2, accessed on 7 September 2013.

Dror, David M. and S. Vellakkal. 2012.'Is RSBY India's platform to implementing universal hospital insurance?'. *Indian J. Med. Res.* 135, January, pp. 56-63.

Dreze, J. 2007.'Dismantling the Contract Raj'. *The Hindu*, 20 November.

Drèze, J. and A.K. Sen. 2011.'Putting Growth in Its Place'. *Outlook*, November 2011.

Dreze, Jean and A. Sen.1989. *Hunger and Public Action.* Clarendon Press, Oxford.

Dreze, Jean and A. Sen. 2002. *India: Development and Participation.* Oxford University Press, New Delhi and Oxford.

Dubey, A. and A. Hann. 2005.'Poverty, Disparities, or the Development of Underdevelopment in Orissa'. *Economic and Political Weekly*, Vol.–XL No. 22-23, May 28.

Duclos, Jean-Yves & David E. Sahn & Stephen D. Younger. 2006.'Robust Multidimensional Poverty Comparisons'. Economic Journal, *Royal Economic Society*, vol. 116(514), 943-968, October.

Duetsch, J. and Silber. 2005.'Measuring Multidimensional Poverty: An Empirical Comparison of Various Approache'. *Review of Income and Wealth,* 51 (1): 145-174.

FAO. 1996. *Report of the World Food Summit*, ROME, www.fao.org.

Filippone, A.F.; B. Cheli, A. D'Agostino. 2001.'Addressing the Interpretation and the Aggregation Problems in Totally Fuzzy and Relative Poverty Measures'. *Working Papers of the Institute for Social and Economic Research, paper 2001-22,* Colchester, University of Essex.

Foster, J., J. Greer, and E. Thorbecke.1984. 'A Class of Decomposable Poverty Measures'.Econometrica, 52 (3).

Gaiha, R., R. Jha, and V. Kulkarni. 2010.'Prices, Expenditure and Nutrition in India'. *ASARC Working Paper* 2010/15, Australian National University.

Gaiha, R., N. Kaicker, K. Imai, and G. Thapa. 2012. 'Demand for Nutrients in India: An Analysis Based on the 50th, 61st, and 66th Round of NSS'. *ASARC Working Paper* 2012/08, Australian National University.

Gajwani, Kiran, Ravi Kanbur and Xiaobo Zhang. 2007. 'Comparing the

Evolution of Spatial Inequality in China and India: A Fifty-Year Perspective'. Annual World Bank Conference on Development Economics, pp. 155-177, 2007.

Gangopadhyay, K. and K. Sing. 2013. 'Extent of Poverty in India: A Different Dimension'. *Economic and Political Weekly,* Vol.-XLVIII No. 06, February 09.

Garcia, A.; Bonilla; Gruat J. 2003. *Social Protection.* Geneva, ILO.

Garg, M. and K. Sankar Mandal. 2013. 'Mid-Day Meal for the Poor, Privatised Education for the Non-Poor'. *Economic & Political Weekly*, VOL. XLVIII, July.

George, Benny. 2009. 'Sanitation Programmes: A Glass Half-Full'. *Economic and Political Weekly*, Vol. 44(8) (Feb. 21-27, 2009), pp. 65-67.

Ghosh, B. 2002.'Panchayats and Elementary Education'. *Economic and Political Weekly*, Vol. 37(19) (May 11-17), pp. 1850-1851.

Gopal, K.S. 2009. 'NREGA Social Audit: Myths and Reality'. *EPW*, Vol. 44, January 17, pp. 70-71.

Gopalan, S. 1996. 'The State and the Child: Who is Responsible?'. India International Centre Quarterly, Vol. 23, No. ¾, Second Nature Women and the Family (Winter 1996), pp. 156-176.

GoI (Government of India). National Health Policy 2002. www.*mohfw.nic.in/NRHM/Documents/National_Health_policy_2002.pdf. 2002*, accessed on October 12, 2010.

GoI (Government of India). 2008. 'Rashtriya Swasthya Bima Yojana (RSBY)', Available at www.rsby.gov.in, accessed on April 10, 2011.

GoI (Government of India). 2009. *Report of The Expert Group to Review The Methodology for Estimation of Poverty*, Planning Commission, November.

GoI (Government of India). 2009. 'Report of the Expert Group to Review the Methodology for Estimation of Poverty', New Delhi: Planning Commission.

GoI (Government of India). 2010. 'Indira Gandhi Matritva Sahyog Yojana: A Conditional Maternity Benefit Scheme', No.9-5/2010-IGMSY.

GoI (Government of India). 2010. *Annual Report 2009-10.* http://www.anagrasarkalyan. gov.in/htm/bi-cycle-schm.html accessed on 25 September 2014.

GoI (Government of India). 2012. 'Press Note on Poverty Estimates, 2009-10'. New Delhi: Planning Commission, March 19.

GoI (Government of India). 2012. *Annual Report 2011-12.*http://www.anagrasarkalyan. gov.in/htm/bi-cycle-schm.html accessed on 25 September 2014.

GoI (Government of India). 2013. *Annual Report 2012-13.*http://www.anagrasarkalyan. gov.in/htm/bi-cycle-schm.html accessed on 25 September 2014.

GoI (Government of India). 2013. *Annual Report 2009-10, 2011-12, 2012-13*, Bharat Nirman, Government of India.

GoI (Government of India). 2013, *Press Note on Poverty Estimates, 2011-12*, Planning Commission, July.

GoI (Government of India). 2013. *IAY Briefing Book*, August, 2013. http://iay.nic.in/netiay/Original Briefing Book/sept.pdf. accessed on September 12, 2014.

GoI (Government of India). 2014. Ministry of Consumer Affairs, Department of Food and Public Distribution, http://dfpd.nic.in/?q=node/101 accessed on September 12, 2014.

GoI (Government of India). 2014. Total Sanitation Campaign (TSC), Reporting month: Upto July, 2010, Department of Drinking Water and Sanitation, http://rural.nic.in/sites/downloads/our-schemes-glance/SalientFeaturesTSC.pdf accessed on September 12, 2014.

GoWB (Government of West Bengal). 2007. 'Proposal for MSK 2006-07'.http://wb.ssa.nic.inaccessed on August 03, 2014, accessed on March 4, 2013.

GoWB (Government of West Bengal). 2008. *Annual Report 2007-2008*.Department of School Education.www.wbsed.gov.in/wbsed/.../AnnualReportSchoolEducation_07-08.pdf accessed on 25 December 2014.

GoWB (Government of West Bengal). 2011. *Annual Administrative Report 2010-11*. Health and Family Wealthfare Department.

GoWB (Government of West Bengal). 2013. *Economic Review 2012-13*.

GoWB (Government of West Bengal). 2014. *Annual State Plan 2013-14*.http://wbplan.gov.in/htm/ ImportantLinks.htm, accessed on 28 September 2014.

GoWB (Government of West Bengal). 2013. *Health on the March 2012-13*, State Bureau of Health Intelligence, Directorate of Health Services

GoWB (Government of West Bengal). 2014. *Annual State Plan 2013-14*.http://wbplan.gov.in/htm/ Important Links.htm accessed on 25 September 2014.

GoWB (Government of West Bengal). 2014. *Economic Review 2013-14*.

GoWB (Government of West Bengal). 2014. *Annual State Plan 2013-14*.http://wbplan.gov.in /htm /ImportantLinks.htm.accessed on 12 May 2014

GoWB (Government of West Bengal). 2014. *Budget 2013-14*.

Greene, W.H. 2012. *Econometric Analysis*. 7th ed. Upper Saddle River, NJ: Prentice Hall.

Gupta, V. and M. Pal. 2008.'Community Sanitation Campaign: A Study in Haryana'. *Economic and Political Weekly*, Vol. 43(33) (Aug. 16-22, 2008), pp. 20-23.

Hagen-Zanker, J., McCord, A. and Holmes, R. 2011. Systematic Review of the Impact of Employment Guarantee Schemes and Cash Transfers on the Poor. London: ODI, http://www.odi.org/sites/odi.org.uk/files/odi-assets/publications-opinion-files/7161.pdf. accessed on 12 September 2014.

Heckman, J. 1979. 'Sample selection bias as a specification error'. *Econometrica* 47: pp. 153–161.

Himanshu and Abhijit Sen. 2011.'Why not a Universal Food Security Legislation?' *Economic and Political Weekly* 46(12): 38-47.

Himanshu. 2008.'What Are These New Poverty Estimates and What Do They Imply?'. *Economic and Political Weekly*, Vol-XLIII No. 43, October 25.

Himanshu. 2013.'Poverty and Food Security in India'. ADB Economics Working

Paper Series No. 369, http://adb.org/sites/default/files/pub/2013/cwp-369.pdf, accessed on 10 March 2014.

Hirway, Indira; Saluja, M.R. and B. Yadav. 2008. 'The Impact of Public Employment Guarantee Strategies on Gender Equality and Pro-Poor Economic Development'. *LEVY INSTITUTE, Project No. 34.*www.levyinstitute.org/pubs/rpr_01_08_IN.pdf, accessed on 10 April 2014.

Hirway, I.; Saluja, M.R. and B. Yadav. 2010. 'Employment Guarantee Programme and Pro-Poor Economic Growth: The Study of a Village in Gujarat'. *Academic Foundation,* New Delhi.

Hutton, Guy and Jamie Bartram. 2008. *Regional and Global Costs of Attaining the Water Supply and Sanitation Target (Target 10) of the Millennium Development Goals.* Public Health and the Environment, World Health Organization, Geneva.

CIFOR (Centre for International Forest Research, http://www.cifor.org/publications/corporate/factSheet/NTFP.htm, accessed on 10 April 2014.

IAMR (Institute of Applied Manpower Research) 2009. 'All-India Report on Evaluation of NREGA Survey of Twenty Districts'. http://planningcommission.gov.in/reports/genrep/rep_NREGA_03-08-2009.pdf, accessed on 14 July 2014

IIM-(Lucknow).2009. 'Quick Appraisal of Five Districts of Uttar Pradesh'. Report submitted to the Ministry of Rural Development/UNDP, Lucknow: Indian Institute of Management, 2009.

International Labour Office (ILO). 2001. *Social Security: A new consensus,* Geneva.

ILO. 2004.'Social protection matters' in *The Social Protection Newsletter*, No. 4, June, (Geneva).

ILO. 2009a. *Social Protection Floor*. Geneva. 2009b. *Recovering from the crisis: A Global Jobs Pact* (Geneva).

ILO. 2010. *Social Protection Floor Initiative,* Geneva.

ILO. 2011.'Social security for social justice and a fair globalization: Recurrent discussion on social protection (social security)' under the ILO Declaration on Social Justice for a Fair Globalization Report VI, *International Labour Conference,* 100th Session, Geneva, 2011.

ILO. 2012. *Social Protection Floors for Social Justice and a fair Globalization* Report IV (1), International Labour Conference, 101st Session, Geneva.

Imbert, Clement; and John Papp (2011), 'Government Hiring and Labour Market Equilibrium: Evidence from India's Employment Guarantee', *J Econ Inequal.* www.isid.ac.in/~pu/conference/dec_11_conf/.../ClementImbert.pdf.

IRDR (India Rural Development Report).2013. 'India Rural Development Report 2012-13'. IDFC, Rural Development Netework, Orientblackswan, New Delhi.

Iqbal, Sultan.2014. 'Expansion of 'Red Corridor' in Jangal Mahal: A Demand for Ethical Justice'. IOSR Journal of Humanities and Social Science (IOSR JHSS) Vol. 19, Issue 4, Ver. VII. pp. 59-65

Iyengar, Sharad D.; Kirti Iyengar and V. Gupta. 2009. 'Maternal Health: A Case

Study of Rajasthan' *Journal of Health, Population and Nutrition*, Vol. 27, No. 2, pp. 271-292.

Jacob, A. and R. Varghese. 2006. 'Reasonable Beginning in Plakkad, Kerala'. *EPW*, Dec.2, Vol. 41(48): 4943-4945.

Jacob, Naomi.2008. 'The Impact of NREGA on Rural-Urban Migration: Field survey of Villupuram District, Tamil Nadu', available at, http://knowledge.nrega.net/653/1/NREGA-Paper-202.pdf. accessed on 10 April 2014.

Jalan, J. and J. Panda. 2010. 'Low Mean & High Variance: Quality of Primary Education in Rural West Bengal'. *Centre for Studies in Social Sciences*, Calcutta.

Jayaraman, Rajshri, Dora Simroth and Francis de Vericourt. 2010. 'The Impact of School Lunches on Primary School Enrollment: Evidence from India's Midday Meal Scheme'. Presented at CESifo Conference Centre, Munich. Sep. 3–4. http://www.cesifo-group.de/portal/page/portal/CFP_CONF/CFP_CONF_2010/Conf-ee10-Hanushek/Papers/ ee10_Jayaraman.pdf, accessed on September 3, 2013.

Jayaraj, D. and S. Subramanian. 2010. 'A Chakravarty-D'Ambrosio View of Multidimensional Deprivation: Some Estimates for India'. *Economic and Political Weekly*, Vol-XLV No. 06, February 06.

James, Gracious. 2013.'Fighting Classroom Hunger-Achievements of Mid-Day Meal Scheme'. http://yojana.gov.in/mid-day-meal-scheme.asp

Jehan, K., Sidney, K., Smith, H., & D'costa, A.2012.'Improving access to maternity services: an overview of cash transfer and voucher schemes in South Asia'.

Johnson, D. 2009. 'Can Workfare Serve as a Substitute for Weather Insurance? The Case of NREGA in Andhra Pradesh'. Working Paper 32, Chennai: Institute of Financial Management and Research (IFMC).

Jones, A. 2007.'Applied Econometrics for Health Economists: A Practical Guide' 2nd (eds) Abingdon, UK: Radcliffe.

Joint Review Mission on Mid Day Meal, West Bengal, *Mission Dates: 19th November to 28th November 20.*

Kakwani, N.and J. Silber. 2008a. *The Many Dimensions of Poverty*, Palgrave MacMillan.

Kakwani, N. and J. Silber. 2008b. *Quantitative Approaches to Multidimensional Poverty Measurement,* Palgrave Macmillan.

Kanan, K.P. 2004. 'Social Security, Poverty Reduction and Development: Arguments for Enlarging the Concept of Social Security in Globalising World'. ILO, Extension of Social Security Papers, 21, Geneva.

Kanbur, Ravi and Anthony J. Venables. 2007. 'Spatial Disparities and Economic Development' in D. Held and A. Kaya (eds.). Global Inequality, Polity Press, pp. 204-215, 2007.

Kapur, Devesh, Partha Mukhopadhyay and Arvind Subramanian. 2008. 'More on Direct Cash Transfers'. *Economic and Political Weekly*, Vol. 43(47), Nov. 22-28, pp. 85-87.

Kavi Kumar, K.S. and A. Abraham. 2008.'Multidimensional Poverty and Vulnerability' *Economic and Political Weekly,* Vol.-XLIII No. 20, May 17.

Kelkar, Govind. 2009. 'Gender and productive Assets: implications of national rural employment Guarantee for Women's Agency and Productivity' *JIFAD, ILO.* www.fao-ilo.org/fileadmin/user_upload/...ilo/.../Kelkar_Final_NewV.pdf, accessed on October 3 2014.

Khera, R. 2008. 'Access to the Targeted Public Distribution System: A Case Study in Rajasthan'. EPW, Vol. 43(44): 51-56.

Khera, R. 2011a. 'Trends in Diversion of Grain from Public Distribution System'. *Economic and Political Weekly* 46 (21): 106–114.

Khera, R. 2011b. 'Revival of the Public Distribution System: Evidence and Explanations'. *Economic and Political Weekly* 46 (44 & 45): 36-50.

Khullar, V. 1998. 'Integrated Child Development Services: A Critique of Evaluation Techniques', *Economic and Political Weekly*, Vol. 33(10) (Mar. 7-13), pp. 537-545.

Khera, R.2008. 'Empowerment Guarantee Act', *EPW*, XLII (35), August 30, pp. 8-10.

Khera, R. and Nandini Nayak. 2009. 'Women Worker and Perceptions of the National Rural Employment Guarantee Act', *EPW*, October 24, Vol. XLIV No. 43: 49-57.

Khosla, R.2011. 'Caste, Politics and Public Good Distribution in India: Evidence from NREGS in Andhra Pradesh'. *EPW*, March 19, Vol. XLVI No.12: 63-69.

Khera, R. 2013. 'Mid-Day Meals: Looking Ahead', *Economic & Political Weekly.*

Klein, R.N. and H. Rubin.1948.'A Constant-Utility Index of the Cost of Living'. *Review of Economics Studies*, Vol. 15.

Kolm, S.C.1977. 'Multidimensional Egalitarianism', *Quarterly Journal of Economics*, Vol. 91: 1-13.

Kumar, R. Samantak Das, Amrita Sengupta and Abdur Rafique. 2003.'State of Primary Education in West Bengal', *Economic and Political Weekly*, Vol. 38, No. 22 (May 31-Jun. 6), pp. 2159-2164, Vol.-XLVIII (August, 10). State: West Bengal, PAB-MDM 2012-13.

Lelli, S. 2001. 'Factor analysis Vs. Fuzzy sets Theories Assessing the Influence of Different technique on Sen's Functioning Approch'. Centre for economic studies, Katholieke Universiteit Leuven, discussion paper 01.21.

Lim, Stephen S., Lalit Dandona, Joseph A. Hoisington, Spencer L. James, Margaret C. Hogan, and Emmanuela Gakidou. 2010. 'India's Janani Suraksha Yojana, a Conditional Cash Transfer Programme to Increase Births in Health Facilities: An Impact Evaluation'. *The Lancet* 375(9730): 2009–2023.

Lingam, L., & Yelamanchili, M. 2011.*Reproductive Rights and Exclusionary Wrongs: Maternity Benefits*, October 22.

Maasoumi, E. 1998.'Multidimensional Approaches to Welfare Analysis'. Department of Economics, SMU, Dallas, TX 75275-0496, (http://

faculty.smu.edu/maasoumi/ Pdf%20Files/ Multidimension.pdf), accessed on October 13, 2014.

Mack, J. and S. Lansley.1985. *Poor Britain*, Allen & Unwin, London.

Maggio, G. 2004. 'Multidimensional Analysis of Poverty Dynamics in Great Britain'. Institute for Social and Economic Research (ISER) Working Paper.

Mathur, Lalit. 2007.'Employment Guarantee: Progress So Far', *EPW*, Vol. 42(52) (December), pp. 17-20.

Marjit, S.2011. 'Conflicting measures of poverty and inadequate savings by the poor: The role of status driven utility function' DP 424. School of Economics, University of Queenstand.

Marjit, S. 2013. 'Measures of Poverty and Relative Social Status'. *Arthabisleshon* 1(1).

Mazumdar, Sumit, A.J. Mills, and Timothy Powell-Jackson. 2011. 'Financial Incentives in Health: New Evidence from India's Janani Suraksha Yojana', Available at http://www.herc.ox.ac.uk/people/tpowelljackson/ financial%20incentives%20 in%20health, accessed on 30 April 2013.

MDM-PAB meeting to consider and approve AWP&B 2013-14 Govt. of India, Ministry of Human Resource Development, Dept. of School Education and Literacy, Mid Day Meal Division.

M. Dinesh Kumar, Nitin Bassi; M.V. Sivamohan and V. Niranjan. 2011.'Employment Guarantee and Its Impact: Are the Claims Valid?', *EPW*, Vol.-XLVI, No. 34 (August, 20).

Mehrotra, Nilika and S.M. Patnaik 2008.' Culture versus Coercion: Other Side of Nirmal Gram Yojana', *Economic and Political Weekly*, Vol. 43(43) (Oct. 25-31, 2008), pp. 25-27.

Mehta, A.K., R. Panigrahi, and S. Sivramkrishna. 2002. 'Operationalizing Multidimensional Concept of Chronic Poverty: An Exploratory Spatial Analysis', Paper presented at the Research Design Workshop for Exploring Appropriate Solutions to Chronic Poverty Held at IIPA on 15th and 16th May, 2002.

Mehrotra, N. and S.M. Patanaik. 2008. Cultural versus correction: Other sides of Nirmal Gram Yojana'. *EPW*, October 25, http://www.academia.edu/183174/ Culture_versus_Coercion_ Other_Side_of_Nirmal_Gram_Yojana, accessed on December 20, 2014.

Michele, Gragenolati; Meera, Shekar; Monica, Das Gupta; Caryn, Bredenkamp and Yi-kyoung Lee. 2005.'India's Undernourished Children: A Call for Reform and Action', *HNP* Discussion Paper. Available at http:// siteresources.worldbank.org/ SOUTHASIAEXT/ Resources /223546-1147272668285/IndiaUndernourished Children Final.pdf.

MODE, G.K. 2009. Concurrent Assessment of JSY Scheme in Selected States of India, Development and Research Services (P) Ltd, New Delhi, May, 2009.

MoDWS (Ministry of Drinking Water & Sanitation). 2014. 'Annual Report. 2013-14'. Government of India, Available at www.mdws.gov.in accessed on 22 July 2014.

MoDWS (Ministry of Drinking Water and Sanitation). 2013. 'National Rural Drinking Water Programme'. Govt. of India, http://mdws.gov.in/sites/ upload_files/ddws/files/ pdf/NRDWP_Guidelines_2013.pdf, accessed on October 20 2014.

MoHFW. 2006.'Janani SurakshaYojana: Features & Frequently Asked Question and Answer'.http://mohfw.nic.in/dofw%20website/JSY_features_FAQ_ Nov_2006. htm. accessed on October 16, 2014.

MoHFW (Ministry of Health and Family Welfare). 2007. 'District Level Household and Facility Survey 2006–07' (DLHS-2). Mumbai: International Institute for Population Sciences, Government of India.

MoHFW (Ministry of Health and Family Welfare). 2008. 'District Level Household and Facility Survey 2007–08' (DLHS-3). Mumbai: International Institute for Population Sciences, Government of India.

MoHFW and WHO. 2009. 'Reproductive and Sexual Health of Young People in India', Secondary analysis of data from National Family Health Surveys of India-1, 2, 3 (1992-2006) for the age group 15-24 years, Government of India, July 2009.

MoHFW (Ministry of Health & Family Welfare).2012.'Rural Health Statistics in India 2012' Statistical Division, Government of India.

MoHFW 2014, 'Janani Suraksha Yojana: Guidelines for implementation', Ministry of Health & Family Welfare, Government of India available at http:/ /hphealth.nic.in/pdf/GUIDELINES-%20JSY.pdf accessed on July 2, 2014.

MoHRD (Ministry of Human Resource Development). 2001. 'Approach Paper to the Tenth Five Year Plan (2002-2007)' Planning Commission, Government of India, New Delhi (1st September, 2001), http://mhrd.gov.in/sites/ upload_files/mhrd/files/document-reports/appdraft_1.pdf, accessed on July 2, 2014.

MoHRD (Ministry of Human Resource Development). 2011. Sarva Shiksha Abhiyan: Framework for Implementation based on the Right of Children to Free and Compulsory Education Act, 2009, (Department of Education and Literacy, New Delhi) Mar. 2011.

MoRD (Ministry of Rural Development). 2009. *Govt. Order No. J-11012/1/ 2009-NSAP*, Government of India.

MoRD, 2009. Report of the Committee on, Credit Related Issues Under SGSY, Department of Rural Development, Government of India, http://rural.nic.in/ sites/downloads/programmes-schemes/Credit_Report_2304.pdf, accessed on October 10, 2014.

MoRD. (Ministry of Rural Development). 2009. 'Report of the Committee on Credit Related Issues Under SGSY', Department of Rural Development, Government of India.

MoRD (Ministry of Rural Development). 2010. Credit Mobilised Under SGSY During 2009-10, Available at http://rural.nic.in/sites/downloads/ programmes-schemes/Credit_Mobilisation_09-10.pdf, accessed on October 17, 2014

MoRD (Ministry of Rural Development). 2012. *G.O. No. J-11015/1/2012-NSAP.* Government of India.

MoRD (Ministry of Rural Development). 2013. 'National Level Monitoring of Rural Development Programmes'. Regular monitoring by NLMs 2012-13,13 Phase-II, http:// www.ruralmonitor.in/nlmreport/RM_12-13_Phase-II_All%20India.pdf, accessed on August 10, 2014.

MoRD (Ministry of Rural Development). 2014. 'Best Practices in Indira Awaas Yojana (IAY)—A Study in 12 States': Report of the National Institute of Public Co-operation and Child New Delhi: Executive Summary, http:// iay.nic.in/netiay/ research highlights_IAY_MoRD.pdf, accessed on July 10, 2014.

MoRD (Ministry of Rural Development). 2012. 'Movement towards Ensuring People's Drinking Water Security in Rural India'. Rajiv Gandhi National Drinking Water Mission: National Rural Drinking Water Programme'. Government of India.http://indiawater.gov.in/. accessed on October 03, 2014.

MoRD (Ministry of Rural Development). 2013. Annual Report 2012-13, Government of India, www.rural.nic.in, accessed on October 17, 2014.

MoRD (Ministry of Rural Development) (IAY). 2014. 'Guidelines of Indira Awaas Yojana' Government of India, *Department of Rural Development*, Available at http://iay.nic, accessed on June 05, 2014.

MoRD (Ministry of Rural Development). 2014. 'Revised Guidelines Special Projects for Placement Linked Skill Development of Rural Youths under Aajeevika'. http://rural.nic.in/ sites/downloads/programmesschemes/ SGSY_SpecialProjectsGuidelines.pdf, accessed on June 05, 2014.

Mondal, D. 2014. 'Trend and Patterns of Economic Inequality in Major States of India in the Liberalize Era: A Critical View'. *Arthabeekshan*, Vol. 22, No. 4.

M.S. Swaminathan Research Foundation (MSSRF). 2008.'Report on the State of Food Insecurity in Rural India'. Chennai: Nagraj and Company.

MoWCD (Ministry of Women and Child Development). 2011. Indira Gandhi Matritva Sahyog Yojana—A Conditional Maternity Benefit Scheme, Government of India, New Delhi, April.http://wcd.nic.in/SchemeIgmsy/ IGMSYImpGuidelines Apr11.pdf, accessed on April 30, 2013.

Mohanty, S. 2012. 'Mahatma Gandhi National Rural Employment Guarantee Act (MGNREGA) and Tribal Livelihoods: A Case Study in Sundargarh District of Odisha'. *Department of Humanities and Social Sciences*, National Institute of Technology, Odisha, India.

Mukherjee, Diganta and Uday Bhanu Sinha. 2011. 'Understanding NREGA: A Simple Theory and Some Facts'. *CDE, Department of Economics, Delhi School of Economics, Working Paper No. 196.* www.researchgate.net/ ...Understanding_NREGA_A_Simple_Theory_accessed on 15/04/2012.

Mukherjee, A.C., Upendranadh, B. Jones and M. Roncarti. 2010. 'Social Access and Social Protection for Food Security in Asia Pacific'. *CAPSA Occasional Paper*, July 2010.

Muralidharan, Karthik. 2012. 'Priorities for Primary Education Policy in India's 12th Five Year Plan'. Paper presented at the India Policy Forum 2012. Delhi: National Council of Applied Economic Research (NCAER)-Brookings Institution, 17–18 July.

Narayanan Devadasan, Maya Annie Elias, Denny John, Shishir Grahacharya, & Lalnuntlangi Ralte. 2008. 'A conditional cash assistance programme for promoting institutional deliveries among the poor in India: process evaluation results'. Studies in HSO&P, 24.

National Health Systems Resource Centre. Programme evaluation of the Janani Suraksha Yojana: A comparative case study of the programme in the eight high focus states. National Health Systems Resource Centre, New Delhi.

Narayanan, Sudha. 2008. 'Employment Guarantee, Women's Work and Childcare', *EPW*, Vol. 43(9); 1-7 March, pp. 10-13.

Nayak, Shibananda. 2012. 'What motivates to participate in an employment guarantee programme in India? A logit model analysis', *Economic Bulletin*, Vol. 32, Issue 3, pp. 2113-2127. Available at http://www.accessecon.com/Pubs/EB/2012/Volume32/EB-12-V32-I3-P204.pdf (accessed on 25/02/2013).

NCEUS (National Commission for Enterprises in the Unorganised Sector). 2006. 'Report on Social Security for Unorganised Workers'. Government of India.

NHSRC.National Health Systems Resource Centre. 2011. 'Programme Evaluation of the Janani SurakshaYojana'. Delhi: Ministry of Health and Family Welfare, Government of India.

NHSRC (National Health Systems Resource Centre). 2012. *Annual Work Report 2011-12,* NIHFW Campus, Baba Gangnath Road Munirka, New Delhi, http://nhsrcindia.org/ annual_report/NHSRC%20Annual%20Work%20Report%20 2011-12.pdf, accessed on December 20, 2014.

NIPCCD. 1992. The National Evaluation of Integrated Child Development Services.

NRHM. 2012. *National Rural Health Mission (2005-2012)*, Mission Document, Government of India.www.nrhm.nic.in accessed on 20th September, 2014.

N.G Hegde, 'Development of Non-Timber Forest Product Species for providing Sustainable Livelihood in India'. http://www.baif.org.in/doc/Agri_Horti_Forestry/ Non% 20 Timber%20Forest %20Products%20Morocco.doc. accessed on December 24, 2014.

OECD. 2009. *Promoting pro-poor growth: Social protection*, Paris: Organization for Economic Co-operation and Development.

OFDC (Orissa Forest Development Corporation).2014. http://www.odishafdc.com/about_ofdc.php, accessed on November 24, 2014.

Palanichamy, A.P. 2011. 'A study on MGNREGP in Thuinjapuram block Thiruvannamalai district in Tamilnadu', *International Multidisciplinary*, Available at http://irjs.info/index.php /irjs/article /view/ 9140/4635 accessed on October 09, 2014.

Pathak, Durgesh C., and Srijit Mishra 2013. 'Poverty in India and Its Decompositions: A Critical Appraisal of the New Method', *India Development Report 2012-13*, Oxford University Press, New Delhi.

Patnaik, U. 2010. 'A Critical Look at Some Propositions on Consumption and Poverty', *Economic and Political Weekly*. 45 (6): 74-80.

PEO (Programme Evaluation Organisation). 2010b. 'Evaluation Report on Sarva

Shiksha Abhiyan'. Report No. 203. Planning Commission, Delhi: Government of India.

Piachaud, D.1987. 'Problems in the Definition and Measurement of Poverty', *Journal of Social Policy*, Vol. 16(2): 147-164.

Pillai, S. 2011. 'The Social Protection Floor in India'. Available at: www.icsw.org/doc/2011-Social-Protection-Floor-in-India.doc, accessed on 4 Mar. 2013.

Planning Commission.1981. Report on General Issues Relating to Backward Areas Development, National Committee on the Development of Backward Area. Government of India.

Planning Commission.2003.'Identification of Districts for wage and self Employment Programmes'. Report of the Task force, Government of India.

Planning Commission. 2005. *Performance Evaluation of Targeted Public Distribution System (TPDS)*. Delhi: Programme Evaluation Organisation, Government of India.

Planning Commission. 2009. *Report of The Expert Group to Review The Methodology for Estimation of Poverty*, Government of India, November.

Planning Commission. 2009. Evaluation Report On National Old Age Pension Scheme (NOAPS), Government of India

Planning Commission. 2011. 'High Level Expert Group Report on Universal Health Coverage for India'. Delhi, Government of India.

Planning Commission. 2013. 'Twelfth Five Year Plan 2012–17'. Delhi: Government of India.

Planning Commission. 2011. Report of the Sub-Group-II on NTFP and Their Sustainable Management in the12th 5-Year Plan, 2011, New Delhi, September.

Pratichi Education Report II.2009.'Primary Education in West Bengal: Changes and Challenges' *Pratichi Trust*, West Bengal.

Pratichi Education Report II. 2009. 'Primary Education in West Bengal Changes and Challenges'. with an Introduction by Amartya Sen.

Programme Evaluation Organisation (PEO). 2011b. 'Evaluation Report on Integrated Child Development Services'. Delhi: Planning Commission, Government of India. http://planningcommission.nic.in/reports/peoreport/peo/peo_icds_vol1.pdf, accessed on 18 September, 2013.

Qizilbash, M. 2001. 'Vague Language and Precise Measurement: The Case of Poverty'. *Working Paper, 2001-5,* School of Economic and Social Studies, University of East Anglia, Norwich.

Raabe, K., Regina, Birner; Madhushree Sekher, K.G. Gayathridevi, Shilp, Amrita., Eva, Schiffer. 2010. 'How to Overcome the Governance Challenges of Implementing NREGA', *International Food Policy Research Institute*, Discussion Paper 00963 (April), Available at http://knowledge.nrega.net/760/1/Implementation-_Bihar.pdf accessed on July 10, 2014.

Radhakrishna, R. and K. Subbarao with S. Indrakant and C. Ravi 1997. 'India's PDS: A National and International Perspective', *World Bank Discussion Paper* No. 380, Washington DC: World Bank.

Rao, C., D.K. Srivastava, P. Chakraborty, and S.K. Sanyal. 2007. 'Rural Poverty in Madhya Pradesh'. *Economic and Political Weekly*, Vol-XLII, No. 05, February 03, 2007.

Rathi, Prateek, Arnab Mukherji and Gita Sen. 2012. 'Rashtriya Swasthya Bima Yojana: Evaluating Utilisation, Roll-out and Perceptions in Amaravati District, Maharashtra'. *Economic and Political Weekly* 47 (39): 57-64.

Ray, Sandip Kumar, S. Basu and Amal Kumar Basu. 2011. 'An Assessment of Rural Health Care Delivery System in Some Areas of West Bengal—An Over View'. IJPH, 55(2). http://www.ijph.inaccessed on October 09, 2014.

Ravallion, Martin.1996. 'Issues in measuring and modeling poverty'. *Policy Research Working Paper Series 1615*, The World Bank.

Ravallion, M. 2008. 'A Global Perspective on Poverty in India'. *Economic and Political Weekly*, Vol.-XLIII No. 43, October 25.

Ravi, C. and S. Mahendra Dev. 2008. 'Revising Estimates of Poverty'. *Economic and Political Weekly*, Vol.-XLIII No. 10, March 08, 2008.

Reddy, D. Narasimha, Tankha, Rukmini and C. Upendranadh and Alakh N. Sharma. 2010. 'National Reproductive Health Matters'. Joint Secretary to the GOI, V.J. pp. 142-154.

Rosenzweig, M. and H. Binswanger. 1993. 'Wealth, Weather Risk and the Composition and Profitability of Agricultural Investments', *Economic Journal*, Vol. 103 (January), 56-78.

Rowntree, B.S. 1901. *Poverty: A Study of Town Life.* Macmillan, London.

Roy, Bijoya and Siddhrth Gupta. 2011.'Public-private Partnership and User Fees in Health Care: Evidence from West Bengal'. *Economic and Political Weekly*, Vol. XVLI, September 17, 2011.

Sadoulet, E., and A. de Janvry.1995. 'Quantitative Development Policy Analysis'. The John Hopkins University Press, Baltimore and London.

Saisana, M. and A. Saltelli 2010. 'The Multidimensional Poverty Assessment Tool (MPAT): Robustness issues and Critical assessment'. *Joint Research Centre*, European Commission.

Saksena, Priyanka, KeXu and Varatharajan Durairaj. 2010. 'The Drivers of Catastrophic Expenditure: Outpatient Services, Hospitalisation or Medicines?' Background Paper No. 21. World Health Report 2010, http://www.who.int/healthsystems/topics/financing/healthreport/21whr-bp.pdf, accessed on 19 July, 2013.

Sankaran, Kamala. 2011. 'NREGA Wages: Ensuring Decent Work', *EPW*, February 12, Vol. XLVI, No. 7: 2325.

Satterthwaite, D. 2001. 'Rural and Urban Poverty: Understanding the Differences'. In: *Economic Perspectives, An Electronic Journal of the U.S. Department of State*, Vol. 6, No. 3, http://usinfo.state.gov/ journals/ites/0901/ijee/satterthwaite.htm, accessed on October 10, 2014.

Sau, Sachinandan 2014. 'Globalisation and Elementary School Education in West Bengal'; *International Journal of English Language, Literature and Humanities*, Volume II, Issue II, June, http://www.ijellh.com, accessed on August 10, 2014.

Sau, S.N. 2012. Paschim Banga Sarva Shiksha Mission (PBSSM) Report.

Saxena, N.C., Srivastava N. 2009. *Integrated Child Development Services: Policy, Design, and Delivery Issues*, IDS Sussex, Special Bull, Discussion Paper on Lifting the Curse: Overcoming Persistent Undernutrition in India, Volume 40, No 4, July (Launched in India on Sept 16, 2009 and in London on Oct. 20, 2009).

Sen, A.K. 1976. 'Famines as Failures of Exchange Entitlements'. *Economic and Political Weekly*, Special Number, August.

Sen, A.K 1977. 'Starvation and Exchange Entitlements: A General Approach and its Application to the Great Bengal Famine', *Cambridge Journal of Economics*, Vol. 1, pp. 33-53.

Sen, A.K.1981. '*Poverty and Famines: An Essay on Entitlement and Deprivation*', Clarendon Press, Oxford.

Sen, A.K. 1985. *Commodities and Capabilities*, North-Holland, Amsterdam.

Sen, A.K. 1991. 'Food Economics, and Entitlements' in Dreze, Jean and A. Sen (Eds), *The Political Economy of Hunger: Volume 1: Entitlement and Well-being*. Oxford University Press, New Delhi and Oxford.

Sen, A.K. 1993. 'Capability and Well-being', in M.C. Nussbaum and A.K. Sen (Eds), *The Quality of Life*, Clarendon Press, New Delhi and Oxford.

Shariff, A. 2009. 'Assesment of Outreach and Benefits of National Rural Employment Guarantee Scheme of India'. *The Indian Journal of Labour Economics*, Vol. 52, No. 2, pp. 243-268.

Silber, J. and M. Sorin, 2006. 'Poverty in Israel: Taking a Multidimensional Approach'. Chapter 9 in Petmesidou M. & Papatheodorou C. (eds), *Poverty and Social Deprivation in the Mediterranean Area: Trends, Policies and Welfare Prospects in the New Millennium*, London: Zed Books/CROP Series.

Shah, Mihir.2007. 'Employment Guarantee, Civil Society and Indian Democracy', *EPW*, November 17, pp. 43-50.

Shah, Mihir. 2008. 'Direct Cash Transfers: No Magic Bullet', *EPW*, 23 August, pp. 77-79

Shah, Mihir. 2008. 'Structures of Power in Indian Society: A Response', *EPW*, Vol. 43, No. 46, November 15, pp. 78-83.

Shah, Mihir. 2008. 'Radicalism of NREGA' *EPW*, June 7, Vol. 43, No. 23, pp. 4, 74

Shahrawat, Renu, and Krishna D. Rao. 2012. 'Insured yet Vulnerable: Out-of-pocket Payments and India's Poor'. *Health Policy and Planning* 27 (3): 1-9.

Shariff, Abusaleh. 2009. 'Assessment of Outreach and Benefits of National Rural Employment Guarantee Scheme of India'. *The Indian Journal of Labour Economics*, Vol. 52, No. 2, 2009, http://www.crddp.com/documents/publications/Assessment_of_Outreach_and_Benefits_of_National_Rural_Employment_Guarantee_Scheme_of_India_.pdf, accessed on August 10 2014.

Singh, I., L. Squire and John Strauss. 1986. '*Agricultural Household Models: Extensions, Applications, and Policy*' Baltimore: Johns Hopkins University Press.

Siddhartha and Anish Vanik. 2008. 'CAG Report on NREGA Fact and Fiction', *EPW*, Vol. 43(25), June 21, pp. 39-45.

Snehalatha, M., V. Anitha. 2011. 'Total Sanitation Campaign—Progress and Issues Situational Analysis of Andhra Pradesh with reference to Total Sanitation Campaign Wash Cost' *CESS* Working Paper No. 99, May, 2011.

Spears, Dean. 2012. 'Policy Lessons from Implementing India's Total Sanitation Campaign'. Paper presented at India Policy Forum, 17 and 18 July, 2012, at India International Centre, New Delhi.

Srivastava, R. 2012. 'Social Protection for Workers in India: Struggling for Basic Rights under Increasing Labour Market Flexibility'. *Indian Journal of Labour Economics,* Vol. 55, Number-3, July-September.

Srivastava, Ravi. 2013. 'A Social Protection Floor for India' *International Labour Office (ILO)*, DWT for South Asia and ILO Country Office for India—New Delhi.

Srivastava, N., Bhaskar, A. 2011. 'The Challenge of Persisting Undernutrition'. In The International Journal of Arts and Sciences, Vol. 4(13), Nov.

Standing, Guy. 2007. 'Social Protection'. *Development in Practice*, Vol. 17(4-5), August, pp. 511–522.

Sudarshan, M. Ratna; Rina Bhattercherya and Grace Fernandez. 2011.'Women's Participation in the NREGA: Some Observation from Fieldwork in Himachal Pradesh, Kerala and Rajasthan'. *IDS Bulletin*, Vol. 41(July, 4).

Swaminathan, M. 2008. 'Programmes to Protect the Hungry: Lessons from India'. *DESA* Working Paper No. 70.

Swaminathan, M. 2000. *Weakening Welfare: The Public Distribution of Food in India.* New Delhi: LeftWord Books.

Swarnjayanti Gram Swarozgar Yojana (SGSY)-Quick Study on Gap Between Sanction and Disbursement of Loans Under SGSY, Reserve Bank of India, July 2003, http://rbi.org.in/scripts/NotificationUser.aspx?Id=1261&Mode=0 accessed on September 09 2014

Townsend, P. 1979.'Poverty in the United Kingdom'. Penguin Books, Middlesex.

Townsend, P. 1993. *The International Analysis of Poverty,* Harvester Wheatsheaf, London, UK.

Tsui, Kai-yuen 2002.'Multidimensional poverty indices,' Social Choice and Welfare, *Springer*, Vol. 19(1): 69-93.

UNFPA.2009. 'Concurrent Assessment of Janani Surakhsha Yojana (JSY) Scheme in Selected State in India'. Development and Research Services (P) Ltd., New Delhi.

UNICEF, 2012.'Integrated Social Protection Systems. Enhancing Equity for Children' *UNICEF* Social Protection Strategic Framework (New York).

UNDP. 2009. 'Conditional Cash Transfer Programmes for Alleviating Human Poverty: Relevance for India', (pp. 1-29).

UNDP. 2013. Human Development Report 2013'http://hdr.undp.org/sites/default/files/reports/14/hdr2013_en_complete.pdf.

UNICEF. 1993, Towards a Comprehensive Strategy for the Development of the

Young Child: An Inter Agency Policy Review. Education Cluster/Publication Division. New York.

UNICEF. 2008. 'Community Approaches to Total Sanitation: Based on case studies from India, Nepal, Sierra Leone, Zambia'. http://www.unicef.org/wash/files/CATS_Field_Note_-_Final_Mar_10_2010_print.pdf, accessed on December 09, 2014.

UN (United Nations). 1975. *Report of the World Food Conference*, Rome 5-16 November, New York.

UN (United Nations). 2008. 'The Millennium Development Goals Report 2008'. New York. http://www.un.org/millenniumgoals/2008highlevel/pdf/newsroom/mdg%20reports/MDG_Report_2008_ENGLISH.pdf, accessed on December 09, 2014.

UNSCO. 2011. Colombo Declaration on Forum of Ministers in Charge of Social Development from South Asia, 20-22 February 2011 Colombo, Sri Lanka.http://unesdoc.unesco.org/images/0019/001914/191402e.pdf, accessed on January 02, 2015.

Vanaik, Anish. 2008. 'NREGA and the Death of Tapas Soren'. *EPW*, Vol XLIII, No. 29 July 26, pp. 8-10.

Vanaik, Anish and Siddhartha. 2008. 'Bank Payments: End of Corruption in NREGA?', *EPW*, Vol.-XLIII No. 17, April 26, pp. 33-39.

Vaidyanathan, A. 2013.'Use and Abuse of the Poverty Line'. *Economic and Political Weekly*, Vol.-XLVIII No. 44, November 02.

Vella, F. 1998. 'Estimating Models with Sample Selection Bias: A Survey', *Journal of Human Resources*, 33, 127-169.

Vij, Nidhi. 2011. 'Building Capacities for Empowerment: the Missing Link between Social Protection and Social Justice', *Centre for Social Protection*, April (13-15).

Vikram, K., A.K. Sharma & A.T. Kannan. 2013. 'Beneficiary level factors influencing Janani Suraksha Yojana utilization in urban slum population of trans-Yamuna area of Delhi'. Department of Community Medicine, University College of Medical Sciences & Guru Teg Bahadur Hospital, Delhi, India, *Indian J. Med. Res.* 138, September 2013, pp. 340-346.

Viswanathan, Brinda.2006. 'Access to Nutritious Meal Programmes: Evidence from 1999-2000 NSS Data', *Economic and Political Weekly*, Vol. 41(6) (Feb. 11-17).

WEF. 2012. *The Case for an Integrated Model of Growth, Employment and Social Protection*, World Economic Forum, Available at http://www3.weforum.org/docs/WEF_GAC_Case Integrated Model Growth Employment Social Protection_Report_2012.pdf accessed on 28 September, 2014.

WHO, 2010. World Health Statistics, Geneva.

WHO/UNICEF. 2004. 'Meeting the MDG drinking-water and sanitation target-A mid-term assessment of progress'. Joint Monitoring Programme on Water Supply and Sanitation.http://www.who.int/water_sanitation_health/monitoring/jmp2004/en/. accessed on May 25, 2014.

Woldehanna, T. 2000. 'Economic Analysis and Policy Implications of Farm and Off-farm Employment: A Case Study in the Tigray Region of Northern Ethiopia.' *Ph.D. Thesis*, Wageningen University.

World Bank. 1990. 'World Development Report 1990'. Oxford University Press, Oxford.

World Bank. 1996. 'India's Public Distribution System: A National and International Perspective'. *Poverty and Social Policy Department*, November (Reprinted as Radhakrishna, R. and Subbarao, K. 1997. World Bank Discussion Paper No. 380).

World Bank. 2011. 'Social Protection for a Changing India, Volume II. *The International Bank for Reconstruction and Development,* Washington DC.

Yamada, Yumiko. 2013. 'Potable Water Problems in West Bengal Analysis towards the creation of a non-profit social enterprise', *Master in International Business*, The Fletcher School, Tuft University.

Index